BRITISH CONSERVATIVE LEADERS

BRITISH CONSERVATIVE LEADERS

EDITED BY

Charles Clarke, Toby S. James, Tim Bale & Patrick Diamond

First published in Great Britain in 2015 by
Biteback Publishing Ltd
Westminster Tower
3 Albert Embankment
London SE1 7SP

ISBN 978-1-84954-921-9

10 9 8 7 6 5 4 3 2 1

A CIP catalogue record for this book is available from the British Library.

Set in Bulmer MT Std

Printed and bound in Great Britain by
CPI Group (UK) Ltd, Croydon CR0 4YY

CONTENTS

Preface ... vii

List of tables and figures ... ix

Author biographies ... xi

PART I: FRAMEWORKS FOR ASSESSING LEADERS

Chapter 1 Introduction: purpose and scope of the book – *Tim Bale, Patrick Diamond and Alan Wager* ... 3

Chapter 2 Statecraft: a framework for assessing Conservative Party leaders – *Toby S. James and Jim Buller* ... 11

Chapter 3 Measuring the success or failure of Conservative leaders: the general election test – *Charles Clarke* ... 31

PART II: ASSESSMENTS OF CONSERVATIVE LEADERS

Chapter 4 Sir Robert Peel – *Richard A. Gaunt* ... 59

Chapter 5 Lord Derby – *Angus Hawkins* ... 75

Chapter 6 Benjamin Disraeli – *Robert Saunders* ... 93

Chapter 7 Lord Salisbury – *T. G. Otte* ... 111

Chapter 8 Arthur Balfour – *Nigel Keohane* ... 133

Chapter 9 Andrew Bonar Law – *Andrew Taylor* ... 155

Chapter 10 Austen Chamberlain – *David Dutton* ... 177

Chapter 11 Stanley Baldwin – *Anne Perkins* 195

Chapter 12 Neville Chamberlain – *Stuart Ball* 211

Chapter 13 Winston Churchill – *John Charmley* 237

Chapter 14 Anthony Eden – *David Dutton* 251

Chapter 15 Harold Macmillan – *D. R. Thorpe* 267

Chapter 16 Alec Douglas-Home – *Andrew Holt* 281

Chapter 17 Edward Heath – *Mark Garnett* 301

Chapter 18 Margaret Thatcher – *John Campbell* 319

Chapter 19 John Major – *Anthony Seldon and Mark Davies* 333

Chapter 20 William Hague – *Jo-Anne Nadler* 347

Chapter 21 Iain Duncan Smith – *Timothy Heppell* 363

Chapter 22 Michael Howard – *Tim Bale* 381

Chapter 23 David Cameron – *Matthew d'Ancona* 397

PART III: LEADERSHIP PERSPECTIVES

Chapter 24 Michael Howard on leadership, the Conservative Party and statecraft theory – *Michael Howard, Toby S. James and Charles Clarke* 413

Chapter 25 William Hague on leadership, the Conservative Party and statecraft theory – *William Hague, Toby S. James and Charles Clarke* 427

Bibliography 449

Index 467

PREFACE

This book arises from a collaboration between the University of East Anglia and Queen Mary University of London, designed to focus upon issues in political leadership. The project has been supported by the political leadership sub-group of the Political Studies Association.

It began with a seminar at UEA on 17 January 2014, entitled 'Political Leadership and Statecraft in Challenging Times'. This was then followed by a seminar on Labour leaders, from Keir Hardie to Gordon Brown, on 28 June 2014 at UEA London, and then by a symposium on Conservative leaders, from Stanley Baldwin to David Cameron, on 5 December 2014 at Queen Mary's east London campus.

The purpose of all these was to think about how we can assess party leaders and what it takes to be a successful leader, and then to evaluate who has been more, or less, successful. The seminars were an essential part of the background to this book and we are grateful to Hussein Kassim, Lee Marsden, Nansata Yakubu, Catrina Laskey and Natalie Mitchell for helping to make them a success. The assistance of Marlon Gomes and Mark Byrne at Queen Mary is greatly appreciated, along with all who came along and contributed to what was a stimulating event on Conservative leadership in December. Alan Wager acted as the principal researcher on the project, demonstrating diligence and commitment throughout. His contribution to the book has simply been enormous.

We would particularly like to thank the biographers and chroniclers of the political leaders, who contributed to the seminars and who have written the chapters in this book. Their commitment has made the whole project possible and the standard of their contribution has been outstanding. Equally, the thoughts, reflections and time of William Hague and Lord Howard were greatly appreciated. Bringing the transcripts of their interviews together would not have been possible without the help of Josh Gray and Sophie Moxon.

This book, *British Conservative Leaders*, has a companion, *British Labour Leaders*, which has been edited by Charles Clarke and Toby James. Duncan Brack and colleagues from the Liberal History Group have edited a further volume, *British Liberal Leaders*, with contributions from Charles and Toby that set out a similar path towards understanding statecraft. We believe that the three books together make an important contribution to the study of political leadership in Britain.

We would like to thank Iain Dale and Olivia Beattie at Biteback, who have been a pleasure to work with as we have brought this book towards publication.

Charles Clarke, Toby S. James, Tim Bale and Patrick Diamond
London and Norwich, June 2015

LIST OF TABLES AND FIGURES

Figure 2.1: The Conservative Party's vote share and seat share in the House of Commons at general elections, 1832–2015.

Table 2.1: Contextual factors to be considered when assessing leaders.

Table 3.1: Conservative performances in each of the forty-five general elections, 1835–2015.

Table 3.2: Conservative performances in each of the forty-five general elections, 1835–2015, ranked by seats gained or lost.

Table 3.3: Conservative performances in each of the forty-five general elections, 1835–2015, ranked by share of vote gained or lost.

Table 3.4: Overall cumulative Conservative leaders' performances in the forty-five general elections, 1835–2015, ranked by seats.

Table 3.5: Overall cumulative Conservative leaders' performances in the forty-five general elections, 1835–2015, ranked by share of vote gained or lost.

Table 3.6: Leaders' 'league table', ranked by seats.

Table 3.7: Conservative performances in votes gained or lost in the forty-five general elections, 1835–2015.

Table 3.8: Overall cumulative Conservative leaders' performances in the forty-five general elections, 1835–2015, ranked by votes gained or lost.

Table 3.9: Conservative leaders in previous rankings of British prime ministers.

AUTHOR BIOGRAPHIES

MATTHEW D'ANCONA is an award-winning journalist and influential political commentator. Formerly editor of *The Spectator* and deputy editor of the *Sunday Telegraph*, he is a columnist for *The Guardian*, the *Evening Standard*, the *International New York Times* and *GQ*. His recent book *In It Together: The Inside Story of Coalition Government* described the politics of the coalition government, with unrivalled access to many of the key players. He is a visiting research fellow at Queen Mary University of London, chair of Bright Blue (the independent think tank that promotes liberal conservatism), and a trustee of the Science Museum.

TIM BALE graduated from Gonville & Caius College, Cambridge, completed a Master's at Northwestern University and earned his PhD from Sheffield. He specialises in political parties and elections in the UK and Europe. Tim's media work includes writing for the *Financial Times*, *The Guardian*, the *Telegraph* and *The Observer*. He has also appeared on various radio and television programmes to talk about politics. In 2011, he received the Political Studies Association's W. J. M. Mackenzie Book Prize for *The Conservative Party from Thatcher to Cameron*. He has since published *The Conservatives Since 1945: The Drivers of Party Change*, the third edition of *European Politics: A Comparative Introduction*, and *Five-Year Mission: The Labour Party Under Ed Miliband*.

STUART BALL is professor of modern British history at the University of Leicester. He has published extensively on the history of the Conservative Party in the twentieth century, and his most recent books are *Dole Queues and Demons: British Election Posters from the Conservative Party Archive*, *Portrait of a Party: The Conservative Party in Britain 1918–1945*, and *Conservative*

Politics in National and Imperial Crisis: Letters from Britain to the Viceroy of India 1926–1931. He has also edited, with Anthony Seldon, *Conservative Century: The Conservative Party since 1900* and *Recovering Power: The Conservatives in Opposition since 1867*.

JIM BULLER is a senior lecturer in politics at the University of York. He has a PhD from the University of Sheffield and has previously worked in the department of political science and international studies at the University of Birmingham. He has written widely on the subject of British politics and public policy, including recent articles in the *New Political Economy*, *British Journal of Politics and International Relations*, *West European Politics*, *Contemporary European Politics* and *British Politics*. He has recently co-edited a special issue of *Parliamentary Affairs* on 'Assessing Political Leadership in Context – British Party Leadership During Austerity'. He is also chair of the PSA Anti-Politics and Depoliticisation Specialist Group.

JOHN CAMPBELL is a British political writer and biographer. He is a graduate of the University of Edinburgh. His works include biographies of F. E. Smith, Aneurin Bevan, Edward Heath and Margaret Thatcher – the last consisting of two volumes, *The Grocer's Daughter* and *The Iron Lady*. He was awarded the NCR Book Award for his biography of Heath in 1994. He has also written *If Love Were All … The Story of Frances Stevenson & David Lloyd George* and *Pistols At Dawn: Two Hundred Years of Political Rivalry from Pitt & Fox to Blair & Brown*. His most recent book is the official biography *Roy Jenkins: A Well-Rounded Life*, which won Political Biography of the Year at the Political Book Awards, and was shortlisted for the 2014 Samuel Johnson Prize.

JOHN CHARMLEY is professor of history at the University of East Anglia, where he is head of the Interdisciplinary Institute for the Humanities. He is the author of nine books, including *Churchill: The End of Glory* and *A History of Conservative Politics since 1832*.

CHARLES CLARKE was Member of Parliament for Norwich South from 1997 to 2010. He served as Education Minister from 1998 and then in the Home Office from 1999 to 2001, before joining the Cabinet as Minister without Portfolio and Labour Party chair. From 2002 to 2004, he was Secretary of State for Education and Skills, and then Home Secretary until 2006. Charles was previously chief of staff to Leader of the Opposition Neil Kinnock. He now holds visiting professorships at the University of East Anglia, Lancaster University and King's College London, and works with educational organisations internationally. He edited *The 'Too Difficult' Box* and co-edited *British Labour Leaders*.

MARK DAVIES holds a Master's degree in history from Cambridge University, and a Master's degree in law from University College London.

PATRICK DIAMOND is a public policy lecturer at Queen Mary University of London, a visiting fellow at Kellogg College, Oxford, and an associate member of Nuffield College. He is also a local councillor in the London Borough of Southwark, and vice-chair of the think tank Policy Network. He is the former head of policy planning at 10 Downing Street. His recent books include *After the Third Way* and *Governing Britain: Power, Politics and the Prime Minister*.

DAVID DUTTON spent his entire teaching career at the University of Liverpool, from where he retired in 2009 as professor of modern history. His research interests focused on British political history in the twentieth century, with particular reference to the Conservative and Liberal parties. He has also written biographies of, among others, Austen Chamberlain, John Simon and Anthony Eden. While now enjoying his garden and playing squash, he continues to write in his retirement, but, without the constraints of the Research Excellence Framework, can explore pastures new. His most recent book, *Tales From the Baseline: A History of Dumfries Lawn Tennis Club*, was published in 2014.

DR MARK GARNETT is a senior lecturer in politics and international relations at Lancaster University. He is the sole or joint author of numerous books and articles on UK politics, focusing mainly on the post-war Conservative Party. Among his jointly authored books are *Whatever Happened to the Tories?* (with Ian Gilmour), *Keith Joseph: A Life* (with Andrew Denham), and *Splendid! Splendid! The Authorised Biography of Willie Whitelaw* (with Ian Aitken). His most recent book is *British General Elections since 1964* (with David Denver). He also assisted Sir Edward Heath in the production of his memoir *The Course of My Life*.

RICHARD A. GAUNT is associate professor in modern British history at the University of Nottingham, where he has taught since 2000. A fellow of the Royal Historical Society and the Higher Education Academy, Dr Gaunt's principal research interests are late eighteenth- and early nineteenth-century British political and electoral history. Dr Gaunt's study *Sir Robert Peel: The Life and Legacy* was published in 2010; his latest book *Peel in Caricature: The 'Political Sketches' of John Doyle ('HB')* reproduces 150 contemporary caricatures featuring Peel. He is currently working on a study of Conservative politics in the age of reform (1780–1850). Dr Gaunt is joint editor of the journal *Parliamentary History*.

WILLIAM HAGUE was Member of Parliament for Richmond, Yorkshire, from 1989 to 2015. He served as Leader of the Opposition and Conservative leader between 1997 and 2001. He was Secretary of State for Foreign and Commonwealth Affairs from 2010 to 2014, before becoming Leader of the House of Commons from 2014, until his retirement from front-line politics at the 2015 general election. William was previously Secretary of State for Wales between 1995 and 1997, under John Major's premiership, and also held the Foreign Affairs brief throughout David Cameron's period as Leader of the Opposition.

ANGUS HAWKINS is professor of modern British history at Oxford University and a fellow of Keble College. He is a fellow of the Royal Historical

Society and was awarded the Gladstone Memorial Prize for research on the party politics of the 1850s. He has published widely on Victorian politics, some of his recent publications including *The Forgotten Prime Minister: The 14th Earl of Derby* (two volumes) and *Victorian Political Culture: 'Habits of Heart and Mind'*.

TIMOTHY HEPPELL is an associate professor of British politics at the University of Leeds, and is the treasurer of the PSA Political Leadership Specialist Group. He has written *The Tories from Winston Churchill to David Cameron*, and edited *Leaders of the Opposition: From Churchill to Cameron* and *Cameron and the Conservatives: The Transition to Coalition Government*. He is currently working on research projects on political rhetoric and manipulation, and books entitled *Justifying Thatcherism: The Political Persona, Rhetoric and Oratory of Margaret Thatcher* and *Theorising Cameron*.

ANDREW HOLT is a contemporary records specialist at The National Archives. He holds a PhD from the University of Nottingham and has previously worked at the University of Exeter and King's College London. He has also been an archives by-fellow at Churchill College, Cambridge. He is the author of *The Foreign Policy of the Douglas-Home Government: Britain, the United States and the End of Empire*.

MICHAEL HOWARD is a politician and peer who served as Leader of the Opposition and Conservative leader between November 2003 and December 2005. He was Member of Parliament for Folkestone & Hythe from 1983 to 2010. During John Major's time as Prime Minister, he served as Secretary of State for Employment and as Home Secretary, and held the posts of shadow Foreign Secretary and shadow Chancellor of the Exchequer during the Conservatives' period in opposition after 1997.

TOBY S. JAMES is senior lecturer in British and comparative politics at the University of East Anglia. He has a PhD from the University of York and has previously worked at Swansea University and the Library of Congress, Washington, DC. He is the co-convenor of the PSA's Political Leadership Group and has published on statecraft theory and political leadership in journals such as the *British Journal of Politics and International Relations*, *Electoral Studies* and *Government and Opposition*, including co-editing a special issue of *Parliamentary Affairs* on 'Assessing Political Leadership in Context – British Party Leadership During Austerity'. He is the author of *Elite Statecraft and Election Administration* and co-edited *British Labour Leaders*.

NIGEL KEOHANE is the research director at the Social Market Foundation – an independent public policy think tank based in Westminster. His publications there include studies on welfare, public service reform and the history of housing policy. He has also written widely on the history of the Conservative Party, including work on the leadership of the party in the late nineteenth century, and his book *The Party of Patriotism: The Conservative Party and the First World War*. He studied for his BA and MA at the University of Exeter and for his PhD at Queen Mary University of London, where he also taught on the First World War.

JO-ANNE NADLER is a political writer and commentator with particular expertise in the Conservative Party. She was a spin doctor, alongside David Cameron, during the Major government, and has been a BBC political reporter and freelance author. She has published two commended books about the party – a biography of William Hague as leader, and the memoir *Too Nice to be a Tory*, which became a must-read among a generation of Conservatives concerned to revive their party. She has written for many newspapers and magazines and is a regular commentator across the BBC and on Sky News.

T. G. OTTE is a professor of diplomatic history at the University of East Anglia. Among his latest books is *July Crisis: The World's Descent into War, Summer 1914*.

ANNE PERKINS is a journalist on *The Guardian*. She has written the authorised life of Barbara Castle (*Red Queen*), an account of the general strike 1926 (*A Very British Strike*), and a short life of Stanley Baldwin for the series 'The 20 Prime Ministers of the 20th Century'.

ROBERT SAUNDERS is a lecturer in modern British history at Queen Mary University of London. He is the author of *Democracy and the Vote in British Politics, 1848–1867: The Making of the Second Reform Act*, and the co-editor, with Ben Jackson, of *Making Thatcher's Britain*. He is currently writing a history of the 1975 Britain and Europe referendum.

ANTHONY SELDON is a political historian and commentator on British political leadership, as well as on education and contemporary Britain. He is also vice-chancellor of the University of Buckingham, and was co-founder and first director of the Institute of Contemporary British History. He is author or editor of some twenty-five books, including *The Coalition Effect*, *Cameron at 10*, *The Major Effect* and *The Powers Behind the Prime Minister: The Hidden Influence of Number Ten.*

ANDREW TAYLOR is professor of politics at the University of Sheffield. He has written on British trade unionism, state theory, political oratory, and the EU and south-eastern Europe, as well as on the Conservative Party. He is currently working on blue-collar conservatism in the United States and the United Kingdom.

D. R. THORPE is a senior member of Brasenose College, Oxford, and an acclaimed historian and biographer who has written biographies of three British prime ministers of the mid-twentieth century: Sir Anthony Eden, Sir Alec Douglas-Home and Harold Macmillan. After completing *Eden*, Thorpe published *Supermac: The Life of Harold Macmillan* in 2010. The book was one of the six shortlisted books for the Orwell Prize for political writing in 2010, and was awarded the Biennial English-Speaking Union Marsh Biography Award.

ALAN WAGER is a postgraduate researcher at Queen Mary University of London, where he teaches politics. He is writing a PhD on coalitions and inter-party negotiations in the British context.

PART I

FRAMEWORKS FOR ASSESSING LEADERS

CHAPTER 1

INTRODUCTION: PURPOSE AND SCOPE OF THE BOOK

TIM BALE, PATRICK DIAMOND AND ALAN WAGER

The exact formula for leadership success in British politics is inherently elusive. Even if it could be bottled, it is far from certain the leaders of political parties would, or could, follow the rational path to glory, rather than any number of other choices. Party leaders are among those who most desire immediate electoral reward and a high ranking in the league tables of effective leadership that shape perceptions of their historical legacy. Yet it is these same politicians, with most at stake, who often find it difficult, if not impossible, to stick to a rational strategy in the light of changing circumstances and unanticipated events. These have the potential to throw a government or party off course if effective political leadership is absent.

For those who take an active interest in probing the performance of political leaders in Britain, there is some agreement about what constitutes the most effective path to elected office and how to stay there. Pragmatic appeasement of your own party tribe must be matched by electoral dynamism that transcends conventional partisan alignment and excites popular appeal. This book examines the question of both what defines leadership success, and what attributes are required to achieve it. What separates leaders who battle and succumb to the political elements from those who harness and adapt them to their advantage to successfully 'make the weather' in British politics? And which leaders of the Conservative Party have a strong record of achievement when it comes to dragging the party to electability, and keeping it there?

For much of the twentieth century, the story of the Conservative Party was one of extraordinary success. The span of this volume encompasses almost 100 years in which the Conservative Party held elected office. The book begins in 1834, with the leadership of Robert Peel and the birth of the modern Conservative Party. It concludes with the five years of coalition government headed by David Cameron.

During that long period, the party has reacted with surprising dexterity to political challenges as diverse as mass enfranchisement and the rise of universal suffrage, alongside the demands of negotiating coalition government. The Conservatives have been dominant in a parliamentary system that has evolved from one largely sheltered from the electoral judgements of the population, through periods of fracture and fragmentation, to the situation in 2015 where one-party government at Westminster has been reasserted through a show of the party's electoral strength that defied almost all predictions.

Nonetheless, anyone with a passing interest in the history of the Conservative Party will know that it has been far from plain sailing. Notably in the recent past, but also during periods in the nineteenth and the start of the twentieth century, the Conservative Party has often seemed uninterested, or profoundly incapable of, positioning itself as a prospective party of government. This is because what motivates parties is not only winning elections. A leader's job is to channel and harness the myriad factors that determine political success, shaping an over-arching strategy that enables the party to hold on to the levers of governmental office for as long as possible. These factors can be as distinct as: the personal ambition and appetite for power of leaders and their contemporaries; the ownership of governing competence and the appeasement of ideological factions over issues such as Europe; and the political institutions and constitutional rules of the game, which dictate, at least partially, the route to power.

STRUCTURE OF THE BOOK

The assessment of political leadership in this volume is based on the distinctive criteria of electoral success, strategic skill and governing competence. Of course, political figures can operate successfully outside the arena of electoral and party politics and still be historically significant. The broad consensus about each leader discussed in this book is often attached to a wider historical debate in British politics – one that can be traced to success or failure during periods of national crisis or warfare. But whether a leader is capable of garnering and sustaining support and enhancing their party's cause is certainly an important and valuable test of political vision, skill and communication. It is on these grounds that Toby James and Jim Buller, in Chapter 2, set out the framework for assessing leadership and statecraft in the Conservative Party. In Chapter 3, Charles Clarke undertakes an historical assessment of Conservative leaders, applying one of the most important criteria – their relative performances in general elections.

However, Charles Clarke, along with admirers of Conservative leaders past and present, is right to acknowledge that balanced judgement requires an analysis of the strategic context in which leaders operate. According to the historian Peter Clarke, 'If leadership is partly a question of vision about the direction in which policy ought to be developed, it is also a matter of projecting electoral appeal and putting together a winning coalition of effective support.' Each leader is inevitably faced with a different set of electoral, political and economic circumstances. Each has a personal story and a political personality that help explain their potential flaws as well as the unique characteristics that led them to secure the leadership of their party. Some figures have led the Conservatives for a generation; others never faced the electorate as leader. At times, leadership strategies were built, above all else, on the pursuit of consensus and a conciliatory approach to party management. Other leaders were unable to take fellow Conservatives with them, or lost them along the way. Certain leaders of the party have been more doctrinaire, having defined significant economic and political developments and creeds such as Thatcherism. Other politicians who appeared to display little direction or over-arching purpose have also led the Conservative Party at regular intervals. By drawing together the foremost experts on Conservative leadership – biographers, academics, journalists and practitioners – we aim to assess which Tory leaders have been most successful, and which leaders have failed to live up to the expectations of their supporters and parliamentary colleagues.

THE PARTY LEADERS — A BRIEF OVERVIEW

1832–1902

The burning questions for Conservative leaders of the nineteenth century were economic and constitutional – principally, whether to pursue protectionism over trade and how to manage the steady movement towards mass democracy. The re-christening of the Tory Party as the 'Conservatives' occurred almost simultaneously with the Great Reform Act of 1832. Robert Peel's response, outlined in Richard Gaunt's chapter, straddled the demands of the 'ultras', who resisted all attempts at democratic reform, and the 'radicals', who were impatient for more reform. Ultimately, divisions in the party over the repeal of the Corn Laws led to Peel's downfall. This, along with the repeal of the laws themselves, largely set the tone for the cautious piecemeal change pursued by Lord Derby – a period of leadership Angus Hawkins paints as conservative in strategy and outlook, but one that, despite a weak electoral record, consolidated a divided party and brought about gradual change that made for a united front.

Benjamin Disraeli, who Robert Saunders describes as a skilful parliamentary operator, succeeded Derby as leader, and heralded the arrival of, for many, the modern Conservatism of the twentieth century. Disraeli was able, following electoral defeat and a spell out of office, to divide the opposition and rebrand the Conservatives as a popular and natural party of government. Thomas Otte examines Lord Salisbury's tenure as the longest-serving Tory Party leader at the turn of the century, and concludes that his period as leader was underpinned by electoral and tactical flexibility, combined with a long-held belief in much of the essential tenets of conservatism – a railing against reform and a distrust of democracy – and the successful use of Irish home rule as a dividing line against Gladstone's Liberals.

1902–40

Salisbury's successor, his nephew Arthur Balfour, was symptomatic of the challenges of reorientation and transition the Conservatives faced in the new century. Nigel Keohane points to a detached, aloof style that damaged party relations and led to three successive defeats to a rejuvenated Liberal Party (and a fractious, frustrating spell in opposition). Bonar Law was a more astute manager of his party, and Andrew Taylor's chapter describes his role in the movement towards class-based, anti-socialist politics, later pursued to considerable effect. Bonar Law's junior position in electoral alliance with Lloyd George in 1918 (and the 1922 election, which he fought independently), saw the Conservative Party comfortably returned to government. But, in truth, Bonar Law was little more than a safe pair of hands. In contrast, Austen Chamberlain, who took over from Bonar Law for a brief, tumultuous period as leader, was, in the view of David Dutton, a disaster in terms of party management, and is now largely – perhaps best – forgotten.

Anne Perkins's portrait of the dominance of Stanley Baldwin during the inter-war period tells us he was a particularly effective Conservative leader: Baldwin drove a change in direction towards moderately reforming and interventionist governments, with an explicitly cross-class appeal. This meant Baldwin was able to create a united front between protectionists and tariff-reformers, alongside a new alliance between working-class and middle-class supporters. Neville Chamberlain's period as leader looked set to be similarly fruitful, before he lost the support of a significant section of his parliamentary party. Stuart Ball argues that our assessment of Neville Chamberlain ought to be revised: his strengths as a party leader have been too easily lost given his infamously disastrous pursuit of appeasement preceding the Second World War.

1940–65

The same cannot be said of Winston Churchill, one of the most conventionally successful Conservative leaders. John Charmley believes that Churchill's period as party leader was not altogether convincing – electorally or organisationally. A 'light-touch' approach to party management directly impacted on Churchill's far-from-convincing electoral record, with his final (narrow) success in 1951 being the result of external forces, over which he had little control – notably, the exhaustion of the ageing Attlee government. Indeed, one of the key figures credited with revitalising the post-war Tory Party image was Anthony Eden, whose long, tortuous wait to take over the reins, David Dutton argues, directly impeded his leadership performance – notably, but not exclusively, during the lead-up to the Suez Crisis. Another key figure in reversing Labour's 1945 landslide was Harold Macmillan, who took over the leadership at a time of deep crisis for the party. His electoral success was seen, in large part, as a personal triumph, and D. R. Thorpe portrays Macmillan's time as leader as one of electoral dominance buoyed by economic prosperity. While Macmillan's leadership is acknowledged as among the most significant and impressive in modern political history, Alec Douglas-Home's period as leader is rarely considered to be of much historical importance. Andrew Holt shows why this broadly remains the case, with some caveats: the political winds Douglas-Home faced were highly constraining; organisationally, at least, he left the party in better shape than it was when he arrived; and, after all, Douglas-Home was only narrowly defeated by Harold Wilson in 1964.

1965–97

While attempting to overcome Wilson's ascendency in the 1960s, Edward Heath was the first Tory leader to be elected by a secret ballot of his parliamentary contemporaries. Previously, leaders had 'emerged' through a patrician system, which was successfully abolished by Douglas-Home, whose own leadership had been damaged by a perception of impenetrable elitism reinforced by his path to the job. Heath's securing of the backing of his MPs indicated he had a keen eye for forging internal alliances within the party, as a former Chief Whip. Mark Garnett infers that, although Heath lost touch with his parliamentary party, it was his failure to shape a winning electoral strategy that ultimately undermined his leadership during a period of economic and political crisis. Of this, Margaret Thatcher could hardly be accused. She epitomised the newly dominant creed of market liberalism and limited government. But Thatcher's translation of this ideological commitment into winning political strategy meant her leadership rapidly became iconic. As is so often the case, however, the strengths that carry leaders to the top can work against them. John Campbell demonstrates that, as Thatcher's leadership evolved, her momentum and political antennae weakened, leaving her vulnerable to being deposed once electoral success could no longer be guaranteed.

The party and country Thatcher bequeathed to her successor John Major were both characterised by stark divisions, which meant his subsequent victory in the 1992 election was a significant achievement. Major's period as leader ought to be seen in this context. Anthony Seldon and Mark Davies argue that any assessment of Major's leadership must account for the fact that, ultimately, the Conservative Party had become impossible to lead, and it would have been an extraordinary feat to remain in power in the face of the confident and assertive New Labour opposition under Tony Blair.

1997–2015

While the scale of Blair's landslide in 1997 meant the process of recuperation in opposition would always be arduous, the quality of party leadership in this period partly explains why electoral success remained so elusive. The first to make the attempt was William Hague, and, while he was never likely to overturn the dominance of New Labour in one term, his leadership was evidently a failure on its own conditions. Jo-Anne Nadler's chapter describes a worthy effort that ultimately failed due to an inability to enforce long-term, strategic thinking, alongside a lack of successful attempts to re-brand the Conservative Party's 'toxic' image and electoral appeal. These same failures, somewhat remarkably, were also endemic to Iain Duncan Smith's leadership of the Conservative Party. Tim Heppell describes an approach that showed Duncan Smith as unwilling, or unable, to substantially reform the party, while losing support from his parliamentary colleagues – twin failures that ultimately made his removal inevitable. That the Conservative Party had learned at least some lessons from those previous six years was clear when Michael Howard was chosen as leader, given the unanimous nature of his selection. Yet, as Tim Bale shows, it did not transpire to be the cathartic renewal required, and was instead a period that underlined the importance and limitations of managing your party and shoring up core support. That this must be supplemented by winning the political argument and broadening electoral support was something David Cameron understood, and he ran on that ticket as prospective leader. Cameron's objective was to enhance the electoral appeal of the party, while retaining the support of party members and parliamentarians. However, the process of appeasement coupled with modernisation was an uneasy marriage. It ultimately meant that the renewal of the party was a job half-finished – a theme Matthew d'Ancona addresses in the final biographical chapter.

• • •

The book concludes with interviews undertaken with former Conservative leaders, namely William Hague and Michael Howard. The maverick former Conservative politician Enoch Powell's infamous maxim was: 'All political lives, unless they are cut off in midstream at a happy juncture, end in failure, because that is the nature of politics and of human affairs.' However, any measured assessment of Conservative leaders past and present should not take Powell's judgement for granted. To be sure, some leaders never managed to build momentum, and quickly lost legitimacy and support. Others combined early success with subsequent failure. It must be said that few leaders ended their careers on an upward trajectory. Nonetheless, we need to understand political leadership in the round, as this book seeks to do, in order to appreciate what makes for successful leaders in British politics.

CHAPTER 2

STATECRAFT: A FRAMEWORK FOR ASSESSING CONSERVATIVE PARTY LEADERS

TOBY S. JAMES AND JIM BULLER

Assessing party leaders is not an easy task. In this chapter, Toby S. James and Jim Buller discuss the challenges that we face in trying to do so, and suggest a framework that can be used. Leaders can be assessed in terms of how well they practise statecraft – the art of winning elections and demonstrating a semblance of governing competence to the electorate. Practising statecraft involves delivering on five core tasks. They need to: devise a winning electoral strategy; establish a reputation for governing competence; govern their party effectively; win the battle of ideas over key policy issues; and manage the constitution so that their electoral prospects remain intact. This chapter outlines what these tasks involve and considers some of the contextual factors that might make them more or less difficult to achieve.

• • •

The British Conservative Party has seen many electoral highs and lows during its long history.

The landslide general election victory in 1931, based on the pure electoral mathematics, may stand out as one of its greatest moments. Nearly 44 per cent of the registered electorate voted Conservative, which won the party nearly 85 per cent of the seats in the House of Commons under the leadership of Stanley Baldwin.[1] *The Times* described it as an 'unprecedented verdict' that gave an 'enormous and astounding majority for the National Government', headed by Ramsay MacDonald.[2] MacDonald, who had left the Labour Party, flew from his constituency in Seaham, County Durham, to be met by a crowd celebrating outside Downing Street, as many of his former Labour ministerial colleagues (including William Adamson, William Wedgwood Benn, William Graham and Christopher Addison) had lost their seats entirely.[3] Stanley Baldwin, it was announced the following week, would become Lord President of the Council in a new Cabinet that included four Labour, eleven Unionist and five Liberal members in total. This was a major switch in the composition of power from the previous government, which had only four Unionist Cabinet members.[4] Baldwin later became Prime Minister in June 1935 as MacDonald's health failed, and he won another general election in the autumn of that year.

And the worst moment? William Hague attracted the lowest number of Conservative voters in modern times in 2001, with less than 19 per cent of registered citizens voting blue.[5] The Tories would make up only a quarter of the House of Commons. True, Hague brought about an increase in the number of MPs. But this increase of just one was widely seen as a poor result, given 1997 was often described as a failure for the Conservatives. The party actually lost more than a million voters compared with the 1997 general election. The final defeat was no surprise. In 1997, Hague, elected as leader at the relatively young age of thirty-six, staged a publicity stunt on a visit to an amusement park, where he wore a baseball cap emblazoned with his name across it. Rather than looking like prime ministerial material, Simon Heffer described the Tory leader

1 Colin Rallings and Michael Thrasher, *British Electoral Facts*, London, Total Politics, 2009. The registered electorate is given pp. 85–92; the votes cast for the Conservatives pp. 61–2.

2 'The Victory Complete', *The Times*, 29 October 1931, p. 12.

3 'The National Government Victory: Notable Gains and Losses', *The Times*, 29 October 1931, p. 16.

4 'The Cabinet', *The Times*, 6 November 1931, p. 14.

5 Lord Derby actually received the lowest vote share in a general election 1832–2015 – the period covered by this book – when 15.2 per cent of registered voters cast their ballot for him.

as looking 'like a child molester on a day-release scheme'.[6] By February 2001, 66 per cent of the public agreed that he came across as being 'a bit of a wally'.[7] More substantively, Hague made strategic campaign errors. As one political scientist noted, the Conservatives 'banged on about the euro, asylum seekers, tax cuts and crime in a dialogue of the deaf, while the public remained more concerned about schools and hospitals'.[8] Hague resigned on the morning of New Labour's second electoral landslide.

As Figure 2.1 shows, there have been many other moments of euphoria and despair; peaks and troughs; victories and defeats. It shows a gradual decline in the Conservative vote since 1931, with a sharper drop after 1992, but a slight reversal of the trend towards the end of the New Labour governments, when David Cameron became leader.

FIGURE 2.1: THE CONSERVATIVE PARTY'S VOTE SHARE AND SEAT SHARE IN THE HOUSE OF COMMONS AT GENERAL ELECTIONS, 1832–2015.

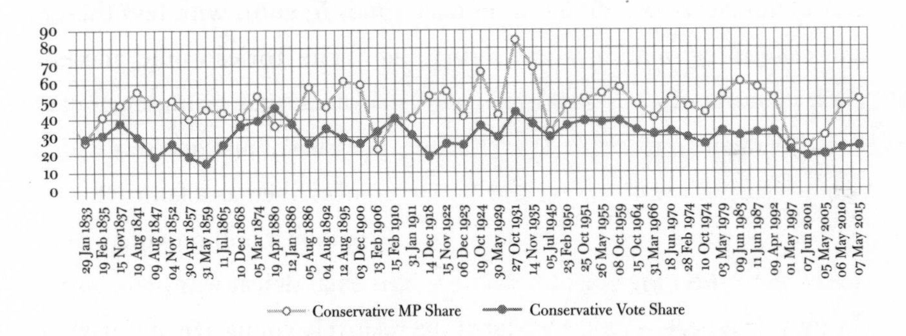

This shows the Conservative Party's vote share (votes cast for the party as a proportion of registered voters) and seat share in the House of Commons at general elections 1832–2015. Data is author's calculation based on information in Rallings and Thrasher, *British Electoral Facts*, London, Total Politics, 2009, Conservative vote (pp. 61–2), electorate (pp. .85–92), Conservative MPs (p. 59), total MPs (p. 3–58). Information for the 2010 and 2015 general elections is calculated from data provided by the BBC: http://news.bbc.co.uk/1/shared/election2010/results/ and http://www.bbc.co.uk/news/election/2015/results. Includes Liberal Conservatives, 1847-59; Liberal Unionists, 1886-1910(D); National, National Liberal and National Labour 1931-45.

6 'First 100 Days: William Hague', BBC News, last updated 16 March 2006, accessed 10 March 2015 (http://news.bbc.co.uk/1/hi/uk_politics/4745016.stm).

7 David Cowling, 'Poll Monitor: Labour looks hard to beat', BBC News, last updated 9 February 2001, date accessed 3 December 2014 (http://news.bbc.co.uk/1/hi/uk_politics/talking_politics/1162569.stm).

8 Pippa Norris, 'The Apathetic Landslide: The 2001 British General Election', *Parliamentary Affairs,* October 2001, 54(4), p. 573.

PARTY LEADERS MATTER

It is natural for observers to blame or credit the party leader of the time for changing fortunes. Britain has a parliamentary system of government in which citizens vote for a local parliamentary candidate to represent their constituency in the House of Commons. They do not directly vote for a president. Knowing little about their local candidates, however, voters commonly use the party leaders as cues for whom to vote for. Moreover, as time has passed, the powers of party leaders have grown. Whether as Prime Minister or Leader of the Opposition, party leaders have played an increasing role in shaping the direction of the party. They have become more important in shaping policy, making appointments within the party and articulating the party's key message.

Assessing party leaders is therefore important. A party leader without the communication skills necessary to present their vision could mean vital public policies are never implemented. A leader who fails to end party divisions could leave their party out of power for a generation. A leader who makes key strategic errors could see national interest hindered or damaged.

THE DIFFICULTIES OF ASSESSING POLITICAL LEADERS

Assessing political leaders, however, is not easy. There are at least three problems that must be faced.

Firstly, it is just a subjective process, in which we will all have our favourites. Can even the most detached observer really claim to make objective, scientific judgements about who was 'best', or will our own political views and values prevent us making a fair assessment? For example, could a left-leaning observer ever recognise Margaret Thatcher's leadership qualities, or a right-leaning one acknowledge the achievements of Clement Attlee?

The benchmarks for success and failure are not clear unless we nail down some criteria; ideological disagreement will always get in the way.

Secondly, who is the Conservative leader in question anyway? Thinking about leaders implies that the focus should be on assessing one single person. British party leaders rarely make substantive decisions on their own, even if they don't consult their entire Cabinet/shadow Cabinet team on every matter. They will seek out and receive crucial guidance from their advisors, and the contribution of the latter needs to be taken into account when evaluating political leadership. So, who should be the focus of our analysis?'

Thirdly, aren't leaders' fortunes influenced by whether they have to govern in difficult or favourable times? The political scientist James MacGregor Burns claimed that some US presidents were capable of transformative leadership: a great President could redesign perceptions, values and aspirations within American politics.[9] But is this always possible during times of economic crisis, party division or war? Do leaders really steer events or are they casualties of them? Are they like ships being crashed around on the waves during a storm? Or is the test of a leader their ability to successfully navigate through such waters? No two leaders are in power at the same time, so direct comparison is impossible. Context is important, however.

Certainly, closer analysis of the circumstances of the 1931 general election victory requires us to re-assess Stanley Baldwin, at least a little. The general election followed shortly after the collapse of the second Labour government. In August 1931, Ramsay MacDonald resigned and became leader of the all-party National Government, which included the Conservative leader Baldwin and the acting Liberal leader Sir Herbert Samuel. This was a response to the economic crisis that emerged following the Wall Street Crash and Great Depression. The aim was to balance the budget and restore confidence in the economy. Labour, however, fought against the National Government and expelled MacDonald from the party. When the 1931 election approached, which it was agreed would be fought on party

9 James MacGregor Burns, *Leadership*, New York, Harper & Row, 1978.

lines, Labour crumbled. The Conservatives have been popularly portrayed by historians as being the beneficiaries of these circumstances.[10]

Closer analysis of the circumstances of Hague's 2001 general election defeat requires us to re-assess him as well. Hague did not lose because of the theme park stunt with the hat. Arguably, more important was the fact that the Conservatives had long lost their reputation for competence on the economy, while Labour had established an image of credibility on this issue during the first Blair administration. The perceptions citizens had of the expertise of the parties for improving economic conditions in Britain was a key influence on party support in the 1997 parliament, and played a vitally important role in shaping the 2001 election defeat for Hague.[11] Hague's focus on other issues was therefore understandable. And while he could have challenged Blair on the issue of the economy, such a strategy would have probably had the effect simply of drawing attention to Labour's strong record in this area. There was evidence that the electorate had swung to the left by 2001, compared with the Thatcherite ethos of the late 1970s and '80s, and although Hague's party may have misread that, it now needs to be carefully read and responded to.[12] Hague faced a highly skilled public communicator in Tony Blair. Despite this, Hague was often praised for landing punches across the despatch box: his heavyweight criticisms of policy were famously laced with wisecracks. For example, of the Deputy Prime Minister John Prescott, who had been mocked in the press for owning two Jaguars, Hague quipped: 'Motorists don't want to be told they cannot drive their car by a Deputy Prime Minister, whose idea of a park-and-ride scheme is to park one Jaguar so that he can ride away with the other.'[13]

---

10 Stuart Ball, 'The Conservative Party and the Formation of the National Government: August 1931', *Historical Journal*, March 1986, 29(1), pp. 159–82.

11 David Sanders, Harold Clarke, Marianne Stewart and Paul Whiteley, 'The Economy and Voting', *Parliamentary Affairs,* October 2001, 54(4), pp. 789–802.

12 Norris, op. cit., pp. 565–89.

13 Andrew Grice, 'How a political joke is now having the last laugh', *The Independent*, last updated 20 November 1999, accessed 13 May 2015 (http://www.independent.co.uk/news/how-a-political-joke-is-now-having-the-last-laugh-1127343.html).

A STATECRAFT APPROACH

A clear framework is necessary to assess leaders. One way of providing an assessment is to evaluate Conservative leaders on whether or not they were successful in achieving statecraft, which is the art of winning elections and maintaining power.[14]

No doubt, many leaders will want to achieve more than this. They may be concerned about their legacy – how they are viewed by future generations – or driven by a desire to implement policies that they think will improve the good of their party and people. However, none of the latter is possible without first having office. Without office, they may not remain as party leader for long, due to the cut-throat nature of politics. General election defeats inevitably come with leadership challenges and expectations of resignation.

So how can we assess Conservative leaders' success in winning office? The simplest approach would be to count the number of elections that they fought, the number they won and the number they lost. This is indicative, but only takes us so far. A more detailed approach involves looking at what things political leaders need to achieve in order to accomplish the goal, and then evaluating them by each of these functions. The statecraft approach argues that leaders need to achieve five tasks; each of them is outlined below.

Yet, as has already been alluded to, some leaders are gifted more fortunate circumstances than others when trying to win elections for their party. We have argued elsewhere that the context in which leaders find themselves must be factored into our assessments of them. This is not an easy task either, however. Can we realistically say, for example, that Thatcher's circumstances were easier than Lord Derby's? Or Hague's twice as hard as Baldwin's? Given that leaders operate in different historical moments, *qualitatively* different in kind, quantitative measurement is

---

14 Jim Buller and Toby S. James, 'Statecraft and the Assessment of National Political Leaders: The Case of New Labour and Tony Blair', *The British Journal of Politics & International Relations*, 14(4), 2012, pp. 534–55.

difficult. The circumstances that leaders face are also different for each individual. In-depth historical studies are therefore needed to understand the circumstances under which leaders lead their office, and that is why this volume rightly invites individual biographers to provide detailed studies of each leader.[15] Nonetheless, some form of comparison is possible. To aid discussion, Table 2.1 lists some of the contextual factors that might be important and these will be unpacked under each statecraft task considered next.

TABLE 2.1: CONTEXTUAL FACTORS TO BE CONSIDERED WHEN ASSESSING LEADERS.

Statecraft task	Contextual factors
Winning electoral strategy	Party resources and campaign infrastructure Unfavourable electoral laws (constituencies, election administration, electoral system, party finance) Partisan alignment of the press Ability to call election when polls are favourable
Governing competence	Party reputation Conditions for successful economic growth Foreign policy disputes Time in office
Party management	Presence of credible rival leaders Rules for dethroning Levels of party unity Available mechanisms for party discipline Time in office
Political argument hegemony	Ideological developments at the international level Alignment of the press Available off-the-shelf strategies in the 'garbage can' Developments in the party system Time in office
Bending the rules of the game	Presence of policy triggers or favourable conditions to enact (or prevent) change

15 For an extended discussion, see Jim Buller and Toby S. James, 'Integrating Structural Context into the Assessment of Political Leadership: Realism, Gordon Brown and the Great Financial Crisis', *Parliamentary Affairs,* 68(1), January 2015, pp. 77–96.

WINNING ELECTORAL STRATEGY

Firstly, leaders need to develop a winning electoral strategy by crafting an image and policy package that will help the party achieve the crucial impetus in the lead-up to the polls. Opinion polls, and, to some extent, local/European election results, give a very good indication of how a party is faring in the development of a winning strategy, and allow a party leader's fortunes to be charted over time – although this information is not always as readily available for the earlier Conservative leaders, when polling was more infrequent or did not take place at all.

In developing a winning strategy, the leader will need to pay close attention to the interests of key segments of the population, whose votes might be important in gaining a majority. Leaders may need to respond to transformations in the electoral franchise, demography or class structure of society, and build new constituencies of support when necessary. These changes can often disadvantage a leader. The extensions of the franchise in the Great Reform Acts, for example, fundamentally altered the structure of the electorate. This had the potential to turn electoral politics upside down against the Conservative Party, in favour of the Liberal and emergent Labour Party. From 1832 onwards, Britain experienced a growth in the urban working class, from which trade unions emerged. The founding of organisations like the Fabians developed the intellectual basis of social democracy in Britain, while the Labour Party gave parliamentary representation to the movement. Many of the nineteenth-century parties in European parliaments were therefore forced to respond to the development of mass parties such as the British Labour Party by broadening their appeal.[16] As the twentieth century progressed, it is often argued that working-class identity subsided, leaving party leaders needing to review their electoral strategy once again.

It is not just a matter of getting more votes than the opposition, however,

---

16 Richard S. Katz and Peter Mair, 'Changing Models of Party Organisation and Party Democracy', *Party Politics*, 1(1), 1995, p. 5–28.

because the distribution of votes is just as important. The February 1974 general election saw Edward Heath win more votes than his opponent, but fewer seats, and he therefore lost office. Conversely, Winston Churchill's single electoral victory came in 1951 – an election in which Labour won nearly a quarter of a million more votes. A winning electoral strategy therefore takes this into consideration.

This point highlights how electoral laws can make it easier or more difficult for leaders to win power. The first-past-the-post electoral system has often advantaged the Conservative Party. It has reduced the chances of new parties entering the political system and has given the Tories a disproportionately high share of seats in the House of Commons for their proportion of the popular vote, as Figure 2.1 illustrated. The way in which the constituency boundaries are drawn has periodically conferred a systematic advantage on the party, but not always. In modern times, the system benefited the Conservatives from 1950 to 1966, had a net bias close to zero from then until 1987, and favoured the Labour Party until 2015.[17]

The laws on party funding and electoral administration will also directly affect a leader's chances of winning an election. Having money to spend does not guarantee success, but it helps. To some extent, leaders can build electoral resources by developing electoral momentum and credibility, and courting appropriate prospective funders. However, party resources and electoral war chests will also depend on other factors, such as the unions, and the historical relationships between the party and business. Electoral administration can matter, too. The procedures used to compile the electoral register and the process by which citizens vote can also disadvantage some parties and candidates.[18]

During the long life of the Conservative Party, the media has become

17 Charles Pattie and Ron Johnson, 'Electoral bias in the UK after the 2015 general election', LSE Politics and Policy blog, 18 June 2015, accessed 23 June 2015 (http://blogs.lse.ac.uk/politicsandpolicy/electoral-bias-in-the-uk-after-the-2015-general-election).

18 Toby S. James, 'Electoral Administration and Voter Turnout: Towards an International Public Policy Continuum', *Representation*, 45(4), 2010, pp. 369–89.

increasingly important, with the rising circulation of newspapers, radio and TV. The media, however, is rarely neutral. Although broadcast television has remained relatively neutral in Britain, newspapers are typically openly hostile towards leaders. Some broadcasters will be particularly influential and this will benefit some leaders and disadvantage others.[19] In more recent times, the press has often been argued to have had a pro-Conservative bias. But the emergence of the printing press in the nineteenth century was originally thought to be a voice for liberal politics, and therefore posed challenges to Tory leaders. In addition, the longer a government is in office, the harder it might be to achieve a winning electoral strategy. Criticisms may accumulate and governments that appeal to the electorate on platforms of 'renewal' or 'modernisation', for example, may see the efficacy of their appeal wane over time. Parties in government become increasingly tired, worn down by the daily grind of public administration. The option of escaping responsibility by blaming a previous party in government will become, as a strategy, more tenuous and increasingly difficult to work.

When the incumbent leader can decide the time of an election, in the absence of fixed parliamentary terms, (s)he may have some advantage. Leaders do not always get this right, though. Harold Wilson's Labour Party overtook the Conservative opposition in the opinion polls for the first time in three years in May 1970 and he called a snap election. However, support for Labour quickly collapsed again and the Conservatives won the election.[20] The act of timing an election has therefore been called 'the most important single decision taken by a British Prime Minister'.[21] The Fixed-Term Parliaments Act 2011 has also made this strategic option more complicated for future leaders. It does show, however, that leaders will never try to achieve a winning electoral strategy on a level playing field. Candidates enter with unevenly distributed constraints and opportunities.

---

19 John Street, *Mass Media Politics and Democracy*, Basingstoke, Palgrave, 2001.

20 Alastair Smith, 'Election Timing in Majoritarian Parliaments', *British Journal of Political Science*, 33(3), July 2003, p. 399.

21 Kenneth Newton, 'Caring and Competence: The Long, Long Campaign', in Anthony King ed., *Britain at the Polls 1992*, Chatham NJ, Chatham House, 1993.

GOVERNING COMPETENCE

Secondly, a leader must cultivate a reputation for governing competence, especially in the area of economic policy. Many have argued that leaders can be 'too far to the left' or 'too far to the right' and that this might adversely affect their chances of being re-elected. Many psephologists think, however, that what matters more is whether a leader is perceived to be competent on a problem that the public consider to be pressing.[22] The problem that is usually most pressing is, in the words of Bill Clinton's campaign strategist, the 'economy, stupid'. Or, as Harold Wilson put it: 'All political history shows that the standing of the government and its ability to hold the confidence of the electorate at the general election depends on the success of its economic policy.' Being seen as the party that will bring jobs and prosperity is a vote winner. On issues like the economy, there is less disagreement about what a voter wants: jobs, economic growth and prosperity. The paramount question for them is which leader and which party will deliver that.

Understood in this way, the fortunes of many leaders may be the result of their ability to generate a perception of them as competent in managing the economy. It is perception rather than reality that is important, however. John Major was initially successful in statecraft terms, in so far as he won the 1992 general election when the economy had suffered from the greatest recession since the 1930s. Yet, paradoxically, Major lost in 1997 when economic growth was strong and unemployment and inflation were falling. The Conservatives' long-term lead over the Labour Party on economic management was lost following 'Black Wednesday' on 16 September 1992, when sterling suffered a serious crisis, interest rates soured and Britain exited the European Exchange Rate Mechanism (ERM). An economic

22 Harold D. Clarke, David Sanders, Marianne C. Stewart and Paul Whiteley, *Political Choice in Britain*, Oxford and New York, Oxford University Press, 2004; *Performance Politics and the British Voter*, Cambridge, Cambridge University Press, 2009.

recovery followed, but there was no similar recovery of confidence among the electorate in the Conservatives' ability to manage the economy.[23]

A leader's ability to achieve governing competence is hindered or helped by a number of factors. Political leaders take office with a number of historical legacies. Their parties might be associated as being 'strong' or 'weak' on the economy. Once in office, the ability of a leader to develop a reputation for competence is strongly influenced by the state of the economy. They may inherit an economy with a balance-of-payments deficit, sluggish growth and a high public debt. Responsibility for slow growth can sometimes be shifted to predecessors or other factors. However, as already suggested, this strategy becomes increasingly implausible the longer the party is in office. Sometimes, politically difficult decisions are required, such as making Budget cuts or raising taxes, in order to invest in new industries or infrastructure and establish new growth.

In the domain of foreign policy, some leaders may inherit pressing international crises such as an ongoing war or a diplomatic conflict with a potential aggressor. The international political system is also increasingly interlinked, with the divide between 'domestic' and 'foreign' policy disappearing, especially for members of the European Union (EU). This integration of the internal and external realms may, in itself, present opportunities and constraints. There may even be times when political leaders utilise international institutions to help them manage or solve national problems, or use them as scapegoats for their own mistakes.

PARTY MANAGEMENT

Thirdly, leaders need to successfully manage their party. Party leaders do not always fall from office at election time. Most famously,

23 Neil T. Gavin and David Sanders, 'The Economy and Voting', *Parliamentary Affairs*, 50(4), 1997, pp. 631–40.

Margaret Thatcher was ejected by members of her own Cabinet. As Robert Saunders notes in this volume, during the mid-nineteenth century, governments won and lost power more through their management of the floor of the House of Commons than through the ballot box.[24] Leaders therefore have to ensure that the (shadow) Cabinet, parliamentary party, party management and grass-roots members are content enough with their performance to allow them to continue. This does not mean that the relationship between leaders and their party need always be harmonious. Leaders might deliberately harbour an antagonistic relationship in order to prove to the wider public that they are different. They will, however, need to fend off any potential leadership challenges and ensure sufficient coalescence so as not to threaten their credibility for being able to deliver legislation and competence in office.

Party management will also be more difficult for some leaders than others. Some leaders will face credible rivals equipped with the political skill and courage to challenge them; some will not. Rules for dethroning a leader – if they are bureaucratic or place a burden on challengers to gather significant support before challenging their leader – will make managing the party easier for the leader. It is in no one's interest to undertake a long and protracted internal leadership battle, because that may affect the party's chances of election. A failed attempt to oust a leader can also have negative consequences for the careers of the instigators. If a rival needs the backing of a significant amount of the parliamentary party to trigger a contest, many will be deterred.[25]

Party dissent can undermine the authority of a leader and result in such leadership challenges. The ability of leaders to resolve dissent can be influenced by: the sanctions they have available to discipline errant party members; the degree to which there is greater homogeneity of preferences within the party; whether there are strong traditions of party loyalty; and

24 See: Robert Saunders, 'Benjamin Disraeli', Chapter 6 in this volume.

25 Tim Heppell, *Choosing the Tory Leader*, London, I. B. Tauris, 2007; Thomas Quinn, *Electing and Ejecting Party Leaders in Britain*, Basingstoke, Palgrave, 2012.

whether there are specialist committee systems and established spokesmen on particular issues.

Although the degree of party discipline among the main political parties today is often overstated, the Conservative Party is typical of many other long-standing European parties in that they centralised their control over the parliamentary party from a time in the nineteenth century, when the party was a looser collection of men with shared interests.

The emergence of new issues can threaten to split a party. For example: the Corn Laws divided the Tories in the nineteenth century, after Robert Peel's 1846 repeal; tariff reform split the Conservatives at the start of the twentieth century; and Europe has been a continual source of friction and tension ever since Britain's entry in 1973. These divisions offer challenges but also opportunities. They can provide the opportunity for new leaders to emerge or they can split the opposition, as home rule did for the Liberals at the end of the nineteenth century, opening up an opportunity for Conservative hegemony in party politics.

It is also worth noting that the longer a government is in office, the greater opportunity there is for restlessness among backbenchers to occur and leadership challengers to arise. A honeymoon period of party discipline may appear and disappear.

POLITICAL ARGUMENT HEGEMONY

Fourthly, leaders will need to win 'the battle of ideas' so that the party's arguments about policy solutions and the general stance of government become generally accepted among the elite, and perhaps even the general public. In more grand terms, this has been coined 'political argument hegemony'. A party leader who is successful in these terms might find that political opponents adopt their policies as manifesto commitments in the run-up to an election, or their ideas become the hallmark of government policy in future years.

Winning the 'battle of ideas' might involve victories over particular policy issues, such as health care, nuclear disarmament, home rule or immigration. It might also, however, involve victories over more deep-rooted questions, such as the role of government in society. It is often thought, for example, that Margaret Thatcher was successful in generating a new discourse during the 1980s that moved the electorate towards the right and helped her win three consecutive elections. There is some evidence to suggest that Thatcher was less successful in achieving political argument hegemony among the public than was widely thought,[26] but subsequent Labour Party politicians certainly came to accept many of her Conservative government's policies during the 1990s, suggesting some success at the elite level.[27]

Some factors may make winning the battle of ideas more or less difficult for leaders. There have been major ideological changes across all western democracies since the formation of the Conservative Party. For example, industrial societies have undergone a 'cultural shift' since the 1970s, as new post-material issues like the environment and human rights have arisen, and old left/right politics are often thought to be no longer applicable.[28] The rise of these issues and the changing nature of British society – of course, in part – owes much to the actions of past leaders themselves. They also have profound implications for a party seeking to develop a winning electoral strategy.

Leaders will be better able to win the battle for political argument hegemony if they are given a credible set of policies. A leader may be reliant on think tanks or their party to develop a new narrative to win over political support. Time in office, events and the partisan bias of the media are all important for this statecraft task too.

---

26 Ivor Crewe, 'Has the Electorate Become Thatcherite?' in Robert Skidelsky ed., *Thatcherism*, Oxford, Blackwell, 1988, pp. 25–49.

27 Buller and James, op. cit., 2012.

28 Ronald Inglehart, *Culture Shift in Advanced Industrial Society*, Princeton NJ, Princeton University Press, 1990.

BENDING THE RULES OF THE GAME

Lastly, leaders may need to maintain or change the constitutional rules of the game to make winning elections easier to achieve.[29] As noted above, the electoral laws can benefit or disadvantage a party. Defending the first-past-the-post system from reform, whatever the democratic merits, has been good statecraft strategy for the Conservative Party in terms of the seats they got from the popular vote. A similar point can be made about their attitude to other electoral laws. Plural voting, for example, was important in Balfour's day, as Nigel Keohane argues in Chapter 8, as it was thought to have won the Conservatives thirty seats and 500,000 votes. It is not just electoral laws that might matter, however, as other aspects of the constitution can be important, too. For example, a House of Lords that is packed with Conservative peers has, historically, made it difficult for a Labour government to pass legislation. This legislation might be essential for developing winning electoral strategy or achieving governing competence. Maintaining any constitutional rules that advantage the party, and reforming those that do not, therefore equates to good statecraft.

Leaders might want to adopt other strategies to the constitution, however. They might want to back reforms that are popular with the public to win over voters. They might also promise reforms to other parties, in order to entice them into forming coalitions over legislation or government formation. David Cameron's promise to Nick Clegg to hold a referendum on electoral system reform was probably good, albeit risky, statecraft. Even though a reformed electoral system might have disadvantaged the Conservatives at future elections, refusing it would have been a 'deal-breaker' in forming the coalition and bringing Cameron to power. The 1832 Great Reform Act inspired a political narrative that the Whigs and Liberals were the progressive parties and the Tories were opposed to popular politics. Disraeli's pursuit of a Conservative

---

29 Toby S. James, *Elite Statecraft and Election Administration: Bending the Rules of the Game*, Basingstoke, Palgrave, 2012.

reform bill could therefore be understood as an attempt to recast his party as 'the friends of the people', but it also divided the opposition.[30]

Changing the rules of the game will be easier to achieve when there are few checks on executive power, as there traditionally have been in Britain's Westminster system. It is also easier when there are high levels of public support for change. Since universal suffrage was established, these moments have tended to be uncommon, as constitutional reform rarely features highly on the public's radar. An incident or scandal can, however, quickly put constitutional reform on the agenda. Pressures for electoral reform, for example, often follow unusual election results – when the party with the most votes did not win – or a scandal, like the parliamentary expenses incident of 2009. Exploiting these opportunities is important. For leaders seeking to maintain the status quo, the public's indifference is an advantage.

In other aspects of the constitution, the public have been highly animated, however. The most obvious exception to public indifference has been the Union. The issue of home rule dominated politics at the end of the nineteenth century and the early twentieth century. Welsh, but more notably Scottish, nationalism re-emerged in the 1960s, accelerated in the 1990s, and brought forward demands for devolution and independence that continue with new force. Consecutive waves of devolution left 'the English question' behind for subsequent leaders to contemplate. The approach leaders take to this issue will have significant consequences for their electoral strategy and party management.

The constitutional relationship between Europe and the United Kingdom has also had profound implications on the statecraft strategies of British party leaders. The emergence of the European Economic Community (EEC) and EU has left leaders of the main two parties with party management problems. UKIP – initially little more than a lobby group to promote Euroscepticism among Conservative MPs – became an electoral force in Britain after 2010,

30 Robert Saunders, 'Benjamin Disraeli', this volume; Robert Saunders, *Democracy and the Vote in British Politics*, London, Ashgate, 2011. See: James, 2012, for a further discussion.

as opposition to EU membership increased.[31] Europe has also been, as Jim Buller argues elsewhere, a key strategic tool for party leaders to shift blame to other tiers of government.[32]

Constitutional management is, therefore, a statecraft task all party leaders must confront. Even those leaders who only serve in opposition, knowingly or otherwise, will be developing policy positions that might help to consolidate the status quo in their party's (dis)advantage, and woo potential coalition partners and voters. It will have important consequences for their prospects of achieving a winning electoral strategy, party management and even governing competence. This is probably the most overlooked dimension of statecraft.

CONCLUSION

Assessing political leaders is difficult. The statecraft framework, however, offers one way in which we can assess party leaders. It suggests that we ask:

- Did they move their party towards the goal of winning and maintaining office, or not?
- How did they fare in achieving the five tasks needed for statecraft?
- What challenges did they face in trying to achieve statecraft?

We should 'reward', in our assessment, those who do well in realising the statecraft functions, and criticise those who do not. But we should also bear in mind that achieving these tasks is much easier for some than for others. This

31 Rob Ford and Matthew Goodwin, *Revolt on the Right*, London, Routledge, 2014.

32 Jim Buller, *National Statecraft and European Integration*, London, Cassell, 2000.

means that we should also 'reward' those leaders who did well in difficult circumstances, and 'punish' those who did less well in more favourable times.

The statecraft approach does not produce unambiguous answers. Assessing each of the leaders by the five statecraft functions described above requires the analyst to exercise some individual interpretation and judgement. No one context will be the same for all leaders, and there be might be disagreement on whether, for example, a leader has won the battle of ideas (political argument hegemony), or not. However, the statecraft approach does provide a clear framework for structuring the comparison of leaders, and hopefully furthers rather than hinders discussion.

CHAPTER 3

MEASURING THE SUCCESS OR FAILURE OF CONSERVATIVE LEADERS: THE GENERAL ELECTION TEST

CHARLES CLARKE

In this chapter, Charles Clarke examines whether or not the success or failure of leaders can be measured, particularly by their general election results. He provides tables that show the increase or decrease in the number of seats in Parliament, and the increase or decrease in the Conservative share of the vote. On this basis, he develops a 'league table' of Conservative leaders since 1834, and demonstrates that, as far as Conservative prime ministers are concerned, there is a reasonable correlation with the more subjective assessments that have been made, but also some surprising results. From this, he draws some conclusions about the reasons for their relative successes and failures.

• • •

The premise of this book is that the quality of political leadership is important. History is not driven only by inevitable forces, important though they are. The decisions and actions of political leaders make a difference and can change outcomes, with big consequences for people's lives.

That said, the mechanism of leadership is difficult to describe and even more difficult to measure. This chapter offers one means of measuring the success or failure of Conservative leaders over time.

It is important to begin with an understanding of the history of the role of 'Conservative leader'. Robert Peel, with his 'Tamworth Manifesto' at the 1835 general election, is generally regarded as the first Conservative Party leader, though, until 1922, there was no formal 'leader of the Conservative Party'. The leaders in each House of Parliament were regarded as equal, unless one of them was the Prime Minister or a former Prime Minister, or if a particular crisis had resulted in one clearly asserting authority over the other.

From 1922, the party's leader was elected by a joint meeting of MPs and peers. Between then and 1965, the leadership did not fall vacant at any time when the party was in opposition, and the meeting actually became a formality to rubber-stamp the individual who had already been asked by the monarch to form a government – usually on the recommendation of the outgoing Prime Minister, and sometimes following a rather cloudy consultation process. After 1963 when, having renounced his peerage, Alec Douglas-Home was appointed via such a process – one that contrasted poorly with the relatively open democracy of a vote by Labour MPs, and attracted bitter criticism from a number of prominent Tories, enraged that the party had turned to the Lords rather than to the Commons for its leader – leadership ballots were introduced. The precise rules for these varied over time through different contests.

Of the twenty Conservative leaders since 1834, only three (Austen Chamberlain, Neville Chamberlain and Duncan Smith) failed to lead their party into a general election, although one of them (Neville Chamberlain) nevertheless became Prime Minister. In almost all cases, it is thus difficult to disentangle their role as Conservative Party leader from that of Prime Minister. Leadership of political parties is not the same as leadership of countries or governments, though both are held to account at a general election.

Those twenty became leaders under very different circumstances, all of which are difficult to compare as political and social environments have shifted over the 180-year period. Of the seventeen Tory leaders who did contest general elections, all but two became Prime Minister. In contrast only six of Labour's fifteen leaders went on to become Prime Minister.

Only five of the Conservatives (Salisbury, Bonar Law, Heath, Thatcher and Cameron) became leader while in opposition and then won a general election to become Prime Minister. Two (Hague and Howard) led the opposition, but failed to win a general election. One (Austen Chamberlain) led the Conservatives within a coalition government, and another (Duncan Smith) led the opposition, but both were dismissed before polling day.

Ten (Peel, Derby, Disraeli, Balfour, Baldwin, Churchill,[33] Eden, Macmillan, Douglas-Home and Major) succeeded to the leadership of their party and the premiership – in very varied circumstances – and then contested a subsequent general election. One (Neville Chamberlain) also succeeded to the leadership and the premiership, but he was thrown out before polling day.[34]

In passing, it is interesting to note that few, if any, Conservative leaders have left that office at a moment of their own choosing – the biggest factor in that being the erosion of confidence and support in the parliamentary party. Indeed, this factor led directly to the departures of Peel, Austen Chamberlain, Neville Chamberlain, Heath, Thatcher and Duncan Smith, and indirectly to those of Balfour and Douglas-Home. It also contributed very significantly to the resignations of Eden and Macmillan, even if ill health was presented as the main reason in both cases. In more recent times, it has become customary for a leader to resign directly after a general election defeat, which happened with Major, Hague and Howard. Age and illness accounted for the remaining leaders – Disraeli, Salisbury, Bonar Law, Baldwin and Churchill. Derby left office voluntarily, but died soon after.

---

33 Churchill became Prime Minister in May 1940 but did not become leader of the Conservative Party until October that year.

34 Chamberlain remained leader of the Conservative Party until 4 October 1940, although he was succeeded as Prime Minister by Winston Churchill on 10 May 1940, and resigned from the government on 30 September 1940.

Despite the undoubted fact that the contexts and circumstances of these twenty leaders were all very different, it is worth considering how well each performed given the hands which they were dealt. It is certainly the case that the personality, style and leadership quality of each individual contributed – whether positively or negatively – to the fortunes of the Conservative Party and the success, or otherwise, of its governments.

It is more than just a parlour game to wonder how Conservative fortunes would have differed had Lord Curzon emerged as leader instead of Stanley Baldwin (1923); Rab Butler instead of either Anthony Eden (1955) or Alec Douglas-Home (1963); Michael Heseltine instead of John Major (1990); Ken Clarke instead of William Hague (1997); Clarke again or Michael Portillo instead of Iain Duncan Smith in 2001; or David Davis instead of David Cameron in 2005.

There are a number of possible numerical measures of success in leadership. These include: changes in the number of party members; opinion-poll ratings; and performances in other votes, for example, in local government or European Parliament elections. A number of more subjective assessments of performance (KPIs in modern management jargon) could be developed. Occasional comparisons of prime ministers have been generated in this way, though so far not of party leaders.

However, in a parliamentary democracy, the most authoritative measure must surely be performance in general elections. This is, in truth, what drives both political parties and their leaders. It is not always the absolutely definitive determinant of behaviour – political leaders, particularly in government, will sometimes take actions that they believe to be in the national interest, even if such actions don't favour their party support – however, no political leader will ever forget their party interest. They will always take into account the impact of their actions upon their party's performance at the forthcoming general election. Many quite genuinely believe that the interests of their party are the same as the interests of the nation.

So, this chapter consists principally of a simple statistical measurement of the general election performances of leaders since Robert Peel, in the form of an overall 'league table' of those leaders who have contested general elections.

For these, there are reasonably objective measures of success: the number of parliamentary seats won or lost in a general election, and the increase or decrease in the share of the vote. The latter is a rather more useful and consistent indicator than the change in the number of votes gained, though that is of some interest, too.

Other general election performance measures – such as the change in the proportion of the electorate, or the swings between the Conservatives and other main parties – could also have been chosen, but the simplest measures seem most appropriate.

This measure does mean, however, that three Conservative leaders – Austen Chamberlain, his younger half-brother Neville, and Iain Duncan Smith – do not appear, since they didn't lead in general elections.

Austen Chamberlain might well have succeeded Balfour in November 1911, but withdrew to permit a compromise candidate (Bonar Law) to become leader. Chamberlain was a senior figure in the coalition governments of the First World War and its immediate aftermath. When Bonar Law retired in March 1921, Chamberlain took over and lasted until October 1922, when his Conservative parliamentary colleagues forced him to stand down as they believed he was too committed to the Lloyd George-led coalition rather than the purely Conservative interest.

Neville Chamberlain's premiership was cut short because he seemed simply inadequate to meet the momentous challenge of war with Germany and the Axis powers. Following the famous parliamentary vote of 8 May 1940 – in which he lost the support of some of his Conservative colleagues – Chamberlain felt he could not continue without the backing of the Labour opposition. That was not forthcoming and so he resigned as Prime Minister. He continued as Conservative Party leader until October, though increasingly suffered from ill health until he died of bowel cancer on 9 November 1940, aged seventy-one.

Iain Duncan Smith – the second of three successive Conservative leaders who failed to beat Tony Blair, and themselves the only Conservative leaders never to become Prime Minister – was elected, inexplicably to some, because of his vitriolic anti-EU views (which supported those of the 'bastards',[35] whose disloyalty to John Major had fatally weakened the Conservative Party). It is less surprising that his colleagues came to the decision he had to be removed than that he was ever elected in the first place. He went on to serve in the Cameron governments.

Despite these absences, and some weaknesses in this form of measurement, general election performance does provide an interesting basis of comparison.

The overall results for the Conservatives are shown in the following tables. Tables 3.1 to 3.6 relate to the changes in parliamentary seats and vote shares from election to election, and rank the leaders accordingly. I have also included Tables 3.7 and 3.8, which show the change in number of votes cast, first for each election and then aggregated for each leader.

35 Paul Routledge and Simon Hoggart, 'Major hits out at Cabinet', *The Observer*, 25 July 1993 (http://www.theguardian.com/politics/1993/jul/25/politicalnews.uk).

TABLE 3.1: CONSERVATIVE PERFORMANCES IN EACH OF THE FORTY-FIVE GENERAL ELECTIONS, 1835–2015.[36]

Year	Leader	Seats change	Vote percentage change	Leader's cumulative seat change	Leader's cumulative vote percentage change	Term of office
2015	Cameron	+25	+0.8	+133	+4.5	9yr,5m
2010	Cameron	+108	+3.7			
2005	Howard	+32	+0.7	+32	+0.7	2yr,1m
2001	Hague	+1	+1.0	+1	+1.0	4y,3m
1997	Major	-171	-11.2	-211	-11.6	6y,9m
1992	Major	-40	-0.4			
1987	Thatcher	-21	-0.1	+99	+6.5	15y,10m
1983	Thatcher	+58	-1.5			
1979	Thatcher	+62	+8.1			
1974 Oct	Heath	-20	-2.1	-27	-7.6	9yr,7m
1974 Feb	Heath	-33	-8.5			
1970	Heath	+77	+4.5			
1966	Heath	-51	-1.5			
1964	Douglas-Home	-61	-6.0	-61	-6.0	1yr,9m
1959	Macmillan	+20	-0.3	+20	-0.3	6yr,9m
1955	Eden	+24	+1.7	+24	+1.7	1yr,9m
1951	Churchill	+23	+4.6	-108	-5.3	14yr,6m
1950	Churchill	+88	+3.8			
1945	Churchill	-219	-13.7			
1935	Baldwin	-93	-7.4	+75	+15.8	15yr,0m
1931	Baldwin	+252	+22.6			
1929	Baldwin	-152	-8.7			
1924	Baldwin	+154	+8.8			

36 Colin Rallings and Michael Thrasher, *British Electoral Facts 1832–2012*, London, Biteback, 2012, Tables 2.01 and 2.03. Note that the time served as leader is not always unambiguous. For example, for just over four years after the death of Disraeli in April 1881, Salisbury was leader of the Conservatives in the Lords, while Stafford Northcote was leader in the Commons. Some include that period in calculating Salisbury's term of office.

Year	Leader	Seats change	Vote percentage change	Leader's cumulative seat change	Leader's cumulative vote percentage change	Term of office
1923	Baldwin	-86	+0.5			
1922	Bonar Law	-38	-0.2	+73	-8.1	10yr,0m
1918	Bonar Law	+111	-7.9			
1910 Dec	Balfour	-1	-0.2	-131	-3.7	9yr,4m
1910 Feb	Balfour	+116	+3.4			
1906	Balfour	-246	-6.9			
1900	Salisbury	-9	+1.2	+165	+8.3	17yr,1m
1895	Salisbury	+98	+2.1			
1892	Salisbury	-80	-4.4			
1886	Salisbury	+144	+7.9			
1885	Salisbury	+12	+1.5			
1880	Disraeli	-113	-1.9	-52	+2.2	13yr,2m
1874	Disraeli	+79	+5.5			
1868	Disraeli	-18	-1.4			
1865	Derby	-9	+5.5	-78	-11.1	21yr,8m
1859	Derby	+34	+1.2			
1857	Derby	-66	-8.3			
1852	Derby	+5	-0.8			
1847	Derby	-42	-8.7			
1841	Peel	+53	+2.6	+192	+21.5	11yr,6m
1837	Peel	+41	+5.7			
1835	Peel	+98	+13.2			
1832	Wellington	-				

TABLE 3.2: CONSERVATIVE PERFORMANCES IN EACH OF THE FORTY-FIVE GENERAL ELECTIONS, 1835–2015, RANKED BY SEATS GAINED OR LOST.

Year	Leader	Seats change	Vote percentage change
1931	Baldwin	+252	+22.6
1924	Baldwin	+154	+8.8
1886	Salisbury	+144	+7.9
1910 Feb	Balfour	+116	+3.4
1918	Bonar Law	+111	-7.9
2010	Cameron	+108	+3.7
1835	Peel	+98	+13.2
1895	Salisbury	+98	+2.1
1950	Churchill	+88	+3.8
1874	Disraeli	+79	+5.5
1970	Heath	+77	+4.5
1979	Thatcher	+62	+8.1
1983	Thatcher	+58	-1.5
1841	Peel	+53	+2.6
1837	Peel	+41	+5.7
1859	Derby	+34	+1.2
2005	Howard	+32	+0.7
2015	Cameron	+25	+0.8
1955	Eden	+24	+1.7
1951	Churchill	+23	+4.6
1959	Macmillan	+20	-0.3
1885	Salisbury	+12	+1.5
1852	Derby	+5	-0.8
2001	Hague	+1	+1.0
1910 Dec	Balfour	-1	-0.2
1865	Derby	-9	+5.5
1900	Salisbury	-9	+1.2
1868	Disraeli	-18	-1.4

Year	Leader	Seats change	Vote percentage change
1974 Oct	Heath	-20	-2.1
1987	Thatcher	-21	-0.1
1974 Feb	Heath	-33	-8.5
1922	Bonar Law	-38	-0.2
1992	Major	-40	-0.4
1847	Derby	-42	-8.7
1966	Heath	-51	-1.5
1964	Douglas-Home	-61	-6.0
1857	Derby	-66	-8.3
1892	Salisbury	-80	-4.4
1923	Baldwin	-86	+0.5
1935	Baldwin	-93	-7.4
1880	Disraeli	-113	-1.9
1929	Baldwin	-152	-8.7
1997	Major	-171	-11.2
1945	Churchill	-219	-13.7
1906	Balfour	-246	-6.9

TABLE 3.3: CONSERVATIVE PERFORMANCES IN EACH OF THE FORTY-FIVE GENERAL ELECTIONS, 1835–2015, RANKED BY SHARE OF VOTE GAINED OR LOST.

Year	Leader	Seats change	Vote percentage change
1931	Baldwin	+252	+22.6
1835	Peel	+98	+13.2
1924	Baldwin	+154	+8.8
1979	Thatcher	+62	+8.1
1886	Salisbury	+144	+7.9
1837	Peel	+41	+5.7
1874	Disraeli	+79	+5.5
1865	Derby	-9	+5.5
1951	Churchill	+23	+4.6
1970	Heath	+77	+4.5
1950	Churchill	+88	+3.8
2010	Cameron	+108	+3.7
1910 Feb	Balfour	+116	+3.4
1841	Peel	+53	+2.6
1895	Salisbury	+98	+2.1
1955	Eden	+24	+1.7
1885	Salisbury	+12	+1.5
1859	Derby	+34	+1.2
1900	Salisbury	-9	+1.2
2001	Hague	+1	+1.0
2015	Cameron	+25	+0.8
2005	Howard	+32	+0.7
1923	Baldwin	-86	+0.5
1987	Thatcher	-21	-0.1
1910 Dec	Balfour	-1	-0.2
1922	Bonar Law	-38	-0.2
1959	Macmillan	+20	-0.3
1992	Major	-40	-0.4

Year	Leader	Seats change	Vote percentage change
1852	Derby	+5	-0.8
1868	Disraeli	-18	-1.4
1983	Thatcher	+58	-1.5
1966	Heath	-51	-1.5
1880	Disraeli	-113	-1.9
1974 Oct	Heath	-20	-2.1
1892	Salisbury	-80	-4.4
1964	Douglas-Home	-61	-6.0
1906	Balfour	-246	-6.9
1935	Baldwin	-93	-7.4
1918	Bonar Law	+111	-7.9
1857	Derby	-66	-8.3
1974 Feb	Heath	-33	-8.5
1847	Derby	-42	-8.7
1929	Baldwin	-152	-8.7
1997	Major	-171	-11.2
1945	Churchill	-219	-13.7

TABLE 3.4: OVERALL CUMULATIVE CONSERVATIVE LEADERS' PERFORMANCES IN THE FORTY-FIVE GENERAL ELECTIONS, 1835–2015, RANKED BY SEATS.

No. elections	General elections for this leader	Leader	Leader's cumulative seats change	Leader's cumulative vote percentage change	Term of office as leader
3	1835, 1837, 1841	Peel	+192	+21.5	11yr, 6m
5	1885, 1886, 1892, 1895, 1900	Salisbury	+165	+8.3	17yr, 1m
2	2010, 2015	Cameron	+133	+4.5	9yr, 5m
3	1979, 1983, 1987	Thatcher	+99	+6.5	15yr, 10m
5	1923, 1924, 1929, 1931, 1935	Baldwin	+75	+15.8	15yr, 0m
2	1918, 1922	Bonar Law	+73	-8.1	10yr, 0m
1	2005	Howard	+32	+0.7	2yr, 1m
1	1955	Eden	+24	+1.7	1yr, 9m
1	1959	Macmillan	+20	-0.3	6yr, 9m
1	2001	Hague	+1	+1.0	4yr, 3m
4	1966, 1970, 1974 Feb, 1974 Oct	Heath	-27	-7.6	9yr, 7m
3	1868, 1874, 1880	Disraeli	-52	+2.2	13r, 2m
1	1964	Douglas-Home	-61	-6.0	1yr, 9m
5	1847, 1852, 1857, 1859, 1865	Derby	-78	-11.1	21yr, 8m
3	1945, 1950, 1951	Churchill	-108	-5.3	14yr, 6m
3	1906, 1910 Feb, 1910 Dec	Balfour	-131	-3.7	9yr, 4m
2	1992, 1997	Major	-211	-11.6	6yr, 9m

Table 3.4 shows the cumulative performance of each Conservative leader over the total number of general elections for which they were leader (left-hand column). These are then ordered by total number of seats gained or lost over their period of leadership.

TABLE 3.5: OVERALL CUMULATIVE CONSERVATIVE LEADERS' PERFORMANCES IN THE FORTY-FIVE GENERAL ELECTIONS, 1835–2015, RANKED BY SHARE OF VOTE GAINED OR LOST.

No. elections	General elections for this leader	Leader	Leader's cumulative seats change	Leader's cumulative vote percentage change	Term of office as leader
3	1835, 1837, 1841	Peel	+192	+21.5	11yr, 6m
5	1923, 1924, 1929, 1931, 1935	Baldwin	+75	+15.8	15yr, 0m
5	1885, 1886, 1892, 1895, 1900	Salisbury	+165	+8.3	17yr, 1m
3	1979, 1983, 1987	Thatcher	+99	+6.5	15yr, 10m
2	2010, 2015	Cameron	+133	+4.5	9yr, 5m
3	1868, 1874, 1880	Disraeli	-52	+2.2	13r, 2m
1	1955	Eden	+24	+1.7	1yr, 9m
1	2001	Hague	+1	+1.0	4yr, 3m
1	2005	Howard	+32	+0.7	2yr, 1m
1	1959	Macmillan	+20	-0.3	6yr, 9m
3	1906, 1910 Feb, 1910 Dec	Balfour	-131	-3.7	9yr, 4m
3	1945, 1950, 1951	Churchill	-108	-5.3	14yr, 6m
1	1964	Douglas-Home	-61	-6.0	1yr, 9m
4	1966, 1970, 1974 Feb, 1974 Oct	Heath	-27	-7.6	9yr, 7m
2	1918, 1922	Bonar Law	+73	-8.1	10yr, 0m
5	1847, 1852, 1857, 1859, 1865	Derby	-78	-11.1	21yr, 8m
2	1992, 1997	Major	-211	-11.6	6yr, 9m

TABLE 3.6: LEADERS' 'LEAGUE TABLE', RANKED BY SEATS.

Ranking by seats	Leader	Ranking by share of vote	Prime Minister
1	Peel	1	Yes
2	Salisbury	3	Yes
3	Cameron	5	Yes
4	Thatcher	4	Yes
5	Baldwin	2	Yes
6	Bonar Law	15	Yes
7	Howard	9	No
8	Eden	7	Yes
9	Macmillan	10	Yes
10	Hague	8	No
11	Heath	14	Yes
12	Disraeli	6	Yes
13	Douglas-Home	13	Yes
14	Derby	16	Yes
15	Churchill	12	Yes
16	Balfour	11	Yes
17	Major	17	Yes

Table 3.6 is a reworking of Table 3.4 as a summary 'league table'. It orders the leaders by the number of seats won or lost. The figure in the third column is their position in the 'share of vote' league table. The final column indicates which leaders became Prime Minister.

TABLE 3.7: CONSERVATIVE PERFORMANCES IN VOTES GAINED OR LOST IN THE FORTY-FIVE GENERAL ELECTIONS, 1835–2015.[37]

Year	Leader	Votes change	Leader's cumulative vote change
2015	Cameron	+630,922	+2,549,661
2010	Cameron	+1,918,739	
2005	Howard	+427,300	+427,300
2001	Hague	-1,243,328	-1,243,328
1997	Major	-4,492,064	-4,159,640
1992	Major	+332,424	
1987	Thatcher	+748,267	+3,298,018
1983	Thatcher	-685,607	
1979	Thatcher	+3,235,358	
1974 Oct	Heath	-1,409,615	-1,540,077
1974 Feb	Heath	-1,272,943	
1970	Heath	+1,726,668	
1966	Heath	-584,187	
1964	Douglas-Home	-1,748,233	-1,748,233
1959	Macmillan	+439,984	+439,984
1955	Eden	-407,308	-407,308
1951	Churchill	+1,225,795	+1,962,545
1950	Churchill	+2,520,394	
1945	Churchill	-1,783,644	
1935	Baldwin	-1,401,136	+6,253,356
1931	Baldwin	+4,500,565	

37 A detailed account of the changes in the electorate can be found in the House of Commons research paper 13/14, 1 March 2013: 'The History of the Parliamentary Franchise' (http://www.parliament.uk/briefing-papers/RP13-14/the-history-of-the-parliamentary-franchise). The franchise changed very considerably over the period from 1835 to the present day, and so the numbers voting are not strictly comparable year by year. After 1832, the Reform Acts of 1867/68 and 1884 increased the electorate significantly, so that 1,478,395 more people voted in 1868 than in 1865, and in 1885, 1,278,819 more people voted than in 1880. In both 1918 and 1929, the franchise increased substantially – mainly because women voted for the first time. In 1918, 5,551,580 more votes were cast than in 1910. In 1929, 6,008,096 more votes were cast than in 1924 – an increase of more than a third.

1929	Baldwin	+801,702	
1924	Baldwin	+2,339,982	
1923	Baldwin	+12,243	
1922	Bonar Law	+1,358,106	+3,082,129
1918	Bonar Law	+1,724,023	
1910 Dec	Balfour	-684,238	+652,211
1910 Feb	Balfour	+682,336	
1906	Balfour	+654,113	
1900	Salisbury	-126,814	+341,607
1895	Salisbury	-264,378	
1892	Salisbury	+638,264	
1886	Salisbury	-500,041	
1885	Salisbury	+594,576	
1880	Disraeli	+334,729	+1,080,316
1874	Disraeli	+187,914	
1868	Disraeli	+557,673	
1865	Derby	+152,803	+39,721
1859	Derby	-46,480	
1857	Derby	-71,769	
1852	Derby	+106,000	
1847	Derby	-100,833	
1841	Peel	-73,380	+65,030
1837	Peel	+118,425	
1835	Peel	+19,985	

TABLE 3.8: OVERALL CUMULATIVE CONSERVATIVE LEADERS' PERFORMANCES IN THE FORTY-FIVE GENERAL ELECTIONS, 1835–2015, RANKED BY VOTES GAINED OR LOST.

Leader	Leader's cumulative vote change
Baldwin	+6,253,356
Thatcher	+3,298,018
Bonar Law	+3,082,129
Cameron	+2,549,661
Churchill	+1,962,545
Disraeli	+1,080,316
Balfour	+652,211
Macmillan	+439,984
Howard	+427,300
Salisbury	+341,607
Peel	+65,030
Derby	+39,721
Eden	-407,308
Hague	-1,243,328
Heath	-1,540,077
Douglas-Home	-1,748,233
Major	-4,159,640

A number of observations can be made about these tables, particularly 3.4 and 3.5:

- First, they do demonstrate the importance of major contextual issues. Peel undoubtedly scores so well because of his brilliance in understanding, after the Great Reform Act of 1832, the need to re-establish the concept of Conservatism in the light of the new, more democratic franchise. Salisbury was a beneficiary of the conflicts and divisions around Irish nationalism; Bonar Law's good result in terms of seats gained owes a good deal to the circumstances of the wartime coalition. Churchill's – in many ways, shocking and surprising – poor performance is almost entirely due to the massive worldwide leftward shift at the end of the Second World War, and cannot really be seen as a comment on his war leadership (though it is a comment on his purely party leadership). Cameron benefited strongly from the sense of national economic emergency following the 2008 financial crisis.

- Second, the performances of Arthur Balfour, Alec Douglas-Home, John Major and, to an extent, Anthony Eden, following, as they did, successful predecessors, show the difficulties of succeeding to political leadership late in the term of a governing political party. Similarly, Callaghan and Brown fared badly following Wilson and Blair, respectively. The tables judge Major a little unfairly, since he did well enough in 1992 to win an unexpected victory, but he then reaped the whirlwind in 1997 – as shown by the massive number of votes he lost overall – more than eliminating the votes gained by Margaret Thatcher. Derby's relatively unimpressive performance, despite a lengthy period of leadership, suffers by comparison with Peel's.

- Third, it helps if your opposition is weak. For example, Salisbury had to fight a disunited Liberal opposition, divided by Ireland. Baldwin was dominant at the time when Labour was gradually taking over from the weakening Liberals as the Conservatives' main opposition, but was then hopelessly divided itself by its response to the stock market crash. Thatcher in 1983 faced a Labour Party led by Michael Foot, and divided by the defection of the Social Democratic Party. Cameron faced very weak opposition in Gordon Brown, at the end of thirteen years of Labour government, and then Ed Miliband. That said, the successful leader still has to make the most of weak opposition and ideally to foment it.

- Fourth, these tables serve to suggest that those who did better were more successful at a particular one of Toby James and Jim Buller's criteria: 'devising a winning electoral strategy'.[38] Peel, Salisbury, Macmillan, Thatcher, Baldwin, Disraeli and Cameron (certainly in 2015) were all significantly more effective at doing this than the other leaders.

- Fifth, another of Toby James and Jim Buller's criteria – 'party management' – was better handled by Disraeli, Salisbury, Baldwin, Churchill (after 1945) and Cameron, and they performed better as a result.

- Sixth, James and Buller's 'government competence' criterion, which is particularly relevant for Conservative leaders who have been Prime Minister, notably benefits Peel, Disraeli, Salisbury, Baldwin, Macmillan and Thatcher. Possibly, in 1945, Attlee and Labour, rather than Churchill, were the beneficiaries of perceived 'government competence', as, before 1945, they were seen within the government coalition to have taken responsibility for many aspects of the Home Front.

- Seventh, there are some striking divergences between the change in share of vote and the change in the number of seats. For example, the Conservative results in the general elections of 1918 (Bonar Law), 1959 (Macmillan) and 1983 (Thatcher) showed significant increases in the number of Conservative parliamentary seats, despite decreases in their share of the vote. And, in both 1847 (Derby) and February 1974 (Heath), the Conservative share of the vote decreased substantially, but the reduction in parliamentary seats was much smaller. In contrast,

38 See Chapter 2.

> in 1865 (Derby) and 1923 (Baldwin), the Conservatives lost seats despite an increased share of the vote, and, in 1880 (Disraeli) and 1906 (Balfour), the loss of Conservative seats was much greater than might have been expected from the relatively low reduction in share of the vote. In the same way, the cumulative results for Disraeli and Bonar Law show a significant divergence between their performances in winning seats and in increasing vote share. Disraeli did significantly worse on seats than vote share, while Bonar Law was much more successful at winning seats than increasing the Conservative share of the vote – mainly as a result of the 'coupon' understanding at the 1918 election. The main reason for these divergences is, of course, either the performance of third parties, or the existence of inner-party divisions. The impact of either of these is exaggerated by the vagaries of the British voting system.

On this basis, five Conservative leaders do better than all of the others in relation to both vote share and increases in parliamentary seats. These are: Peel and Salisbury in the nineteenth century; and then Cameron, Thatcher and Baldwin in more modern times. The most surprising member of this elite group is David Cameron. He was widely criticised within his own party for his failure to win an overall majority in 2010, and, in his first term, he did not have a good reputation as a high-quality leader. But, whatever the reason, the number of seats gained in 2010 was the best Conservative result at any individual general election since 1931. His unexpected success in securing further gains in 2015 puts him firmly at the top level of Conservative leaders, at least in terms of electoral performance. The two twentieth-century Conservative success stories were Margaret Thatcher and Stanley Baldwin. Both benefited greatly from divisions in their opposition, and – perhaps it is no coincidence – both defeated miners' strikes that divided and distracted Labour. These two contested eight general elections between them, six successfully.

It may surprise that the two Victorian-era leaders, Peel and Salisbury, top the table of seats gained. Following the Great Reform Act, Peel clearly set a sense of direction for his party, which was reflected in the strong electoral outcomes, while Salisbury was able to benefit from continued Liberal divisions, notably in relation to Irish home rule. It is also worth noting that, like Peel and Salisbury (though not to the same extent as either), Disraeli was successful in building Conservative support and increasing the share of the vote as the democratic franchise widened – although the number of Conservative seats in Parliament did not match that change.

Of the rest, the most unexpected outcome for most people, including many historians and other commentators, is Winston Churchill's result. Fifteenth in seats gained or lost, and twelfth in increase or decrease in share of vote is surprising. This is obviously the consequence of the 1945 election result, which mainly resulted from a worldwide shift to the left. If this 1945 vote were excluded, and only the results of 1950 and 1951 are considered, Churchill is the most successful twentieth-century Conservative leader in terms of seats gained, and the second most successful (after Baldwin) in terms of share of the vote increase. His case is perhaps the starkest example of the distinction between the national political leader (of a coalition), which Churchill patently was, and the leader of a political party, which, in a sense, Churchill did not become until after he had lost in 1945 – if then.

In mid-table, Eden and Macmillan – successors of Churchill – were moderately successful in electoral terms, whatever their different strengths and weaknesses as Prime Minister. It may surprise that Eden did a little better than Macmillan in increasing both seats and vote share. Heath became Prime Minister in 1970 against most expectations, and principally as a result of Labour's political and economic failures. He was eventually unseated by his party through the then new democratic procedures – used for the first time to that end.

Both Hague and Howard failed to encourage their party to get the measure of New Labour and Tony Blair. As a result, they were unsuccessful in offering an effective challenge. Across the middle of the nineteenth century,

Derby, despite being the longest serving of all Conservative leaders, similarly failed to effectively contest a long period of Liberal dominance – though he did become Prime Minister for brief periods, leading minority governments three times (ten months, sixteen months and twenty months). These leaders demonstrate the difficulty in opposition of evolving a genuine winning strategy, while, at the same time, minimising party disunity.

Bonar Law (though he had only been Prime Minister for seven months after the Conservatives broke away from the Lloyd George coalition and won the 1922 election) benefits in these tables from the 1918 'coupon election', with its good result for the coalition Conservatives following their participation in the wartime coalition. This helps to explain the big divergence between the party's success in increasing seats and its decline in vote share.

At the bottom end, the performances of Balfour, Douglas-Home and Major reflect the difficulty of coming in at the end of a fairly lengthy period of Conservative dominance, though Douglas-Home did better than expected, and Major won in 1992 when many thought he would lose. After his massive defeat in 1906, Balfour simply demonstrated his continued inability to address the consequent challenges facing the Conservatives.

Some general corroboration of the rankings in this Conservative leaders' league table based on general election results comes from the various subjective assessments of prime ministers done in recent years.

A number of exercises have been carried out. Kevin Theakston and Mark Gill from Leeds University have written fairly full and substantial analyses of these, published in 2005[39] and in 2011 in *Political Quarterly*.[40]

There have been the following league-table exercises (listed chronologically in Table 3.9 with their ranked order of Conservative prime ministers).

39 Kevin Theakston and Mark Gill, 'Ranking Twentieth-Century British Prime Ministers', *British Journal of Politics and International Relations*, Vol. 8, 2006, pp. 193–213.

40 Kevin Theakston and Mark Gill, 'The Post-War Premiership League', *Political Quarterly*, 82(1), January to March 2011, pp. 67–80.

TABLE 3.9: CONSERVATIVE LEADERS IN PREVIOUS RANKINGS OF BRITISH PRIME MINISTERS.

Date	Survey organiser	Ranking
1999	BBC Radio 4, based on twenty historians	Churchill, Thatcher, Macmillan, Salisbury, Baldwin, Heath, Bonar Law, Douglas-Home, Balfour, Major, Chamberlain, Eden
2000	BBC Politics Group, from twenty-two academics[41]	Churchill, Thatcher, Macmillan, Salisbury, Baldwin, Heath, Bonar Law, Douglas-Home, Balfour, Major, Chamberlain, Eden
2004	Leeds University/MORI, 139 academics[42]	Churchill, Thatcher, Macmillan, Baldwin, Salisbury, Heath, Major, Bonar Law, Chamberlain, Balfour, Douglas-Home, Eden
2006	*BBC History Magazine*, by Francis Beckett[43]	Thatcher, Heath, Churchill, Macmillan, Salisbury, Baldwin, Balfour, Bonar Law, Douglas-Home, Major, Eden, Chamberlain
2008	BBC *Newsnight*, poll 27,000 respondents[44]	Churchill, Thatcher, Macmillan, Heath, Major, Douglas-Home, Eden
2010	Leeds University, 106 academics[45]	Thatcher, Macmillan, Churchill, Major, Heath, Douglas-Home, Eden
2010	*The Times*, from Phil Collins, Ben Macintyre, Matthew Parris, William Rees-Mogg, Peter Riddell and Phil Webster[46]	Churchill, Thatcher, Peel, Disraeli, Salisbury, Baldwin, Macmillan, Derby, Heath, Major, Balfour, Bonar Law, Chamberlain, Douglas-Home, Eden
2015	*The Times*, from Danny Finkelstein, Lucy Fisher, Oliver Kamm, Patrick Kidd, Damian McBride, Tim Montgomerie, Jenni Russell, Rachel Sylvester, Phil Webster and Giles Whittell[47]	Churchill, Thatcher, Macmillan, Baldwin, Salisbury, Cameron, Major, Bonar Law, Heath, Balfour, Douglas-Home, Chamberlain, Eden
2015	Royal Holloway Group PR3710 *MPs' assessment of Prime Ministers*[48]	Thatcher, Churchill, Macmillan, Major, Heath, Home, Eden

41 'Churchill "greatest PM of twentieth century"', BBC News, last updated 4 January 2000, accessed 19 February 2015 (http://news.bbc.co.uk/1/hi/uk_politics/575219.stm).

42 Theakston and Gill, op. cit., 2006, pp. 193–213.

43 'Thatcher and Attlee top PM list', BBC News, last updated 29 August 2006, accessed 19 February 2015 (http://news.bbc.co.uk/1/hi/uk_politics/5294024.stm).

44 'Churchill tops PM choice', BBC Newsnight, last updated 1 October 2008, accessed 19 February 2015 (http://news.bbc.co.uk/1/hi/programmes/newsnight/7647383.stm).

45 Theakston and Gill, op. cit., 2011, pp. 67–80.

46 '*The Times*'s Top 50 Prime Ministers', *The Times*, last updated 5 May 2010, accessed 19 February 2015 (http://www.timesonline.co.uk/tol/news/politics/article7116855.ece).

47 http://www.thetimes.co.uk/redbox/topic/2015-election-campaign/interactive-who-is-britains-greatest modern-day-prime-minister

48 The Royal Holloway Group PR3710, 'British MPs on British PMs: Parliamentary Evaluations of Prime Ministerial Success', Politics, 35(2), June 2015, pp. 111–127.

In 2010, Stephen Bray, for Iain Dale's Diary,[49] produced an amalgamation of most of these judgements, which suggested that the ranking of Conservative prime ministers was: Churchill, Peel, Disraeli, Thatcher, Macmillan, Baldwin, Derby, Salisbury, Heath, Major, Balfour, Bonar Law, Douglas-Home, Eden and Chamberlain.

Clearly the criteria for these assessments vary: they are about prime ministerial and governmental leadership rather than party leadership; they use different measures and timescales for the assessments; and they involve different techniques to come to the judgement.

Nevertheless, what is striking about these assessments, subjective though they are, is that they all[50] grade Churchill, Thatcher, Macmillan, Salisbury and Baldwin as the best five Conservative leaders since 1900, usually in that order. The 2015 *Times* assessment adds Cameron at sixth, and he might well have done better if the assessment had been made a week after, rather than a week before, the general election. In the surveys that included nineteenth-century Conservative leaders, Peel was featured in the top-five group.

The league table (Table 3.6, above) places Peel, Salisbury, Cameron, Thatcher and Baldwin in the top five places, whether measured by gain or loss of parliamentary seats, or by share of the vote. The subjective judgements of historians, MPs and others depart from this in two significant ways:[51] they rate the performances of Churchill and Macmillan significantly higher than the general election result methodology of this chapter would seem to justify.

The reasons for the generally high rating of Churchill in assessments that focus on national prime ministerial performance are obvious, and I address some of them above. It is interesting that Macmillan is so relatively well rated – generally ahead of Baldwin and Salisbury, for example – despite his relatively poor statistical performance. I have no good explanation for this,

---

49 Stephen Bray, 'Guest Post: The Greatest Prime Ministers of All Time', Iain Dale's Diary, last updated 5 August 2010, accessed 19 February 2015 (http://iaindale.blogspot.co.uk/2010/08/guest-post-greatest-prime-ministers-of.html).

50 Other than one survey that has Heath in the top five instead of Baldwin.

51 Other than the fact that Cameron wasn't included in any of the subjective assessments mentioned, since he hadn't become Prime Minister when they were conducted.

except, possibly, that he was a leader in a new media era – in which he excelled – when many of the historians canvassed were forming their own political views. He was also the last, great 'one-nation' Tory, and so offers an appeal to a wider group.

Similarly, there appears to be some consensus about the subjective judgements at the bottom of the league. Douglas-Home, Balfour, Bonar Law, Chamberlain, Eden and Major are consistently judged to be the bottom six. Of these, Chamberlain does not feature in my tables since he didn't contest a general election. Three (Douglas-Home, Balfour and Major) are indeed in the bottom six in terms of seats won or lost, and one (Bonar Law) is in the bottom six in terms of vote share. Eden's rather average general election rating preceded Suez, which destroyed his reputation for leadership. Moreover, despite the fact that Derby performed statistically poorly, he is not so poorly rated on the subjective assessments.

This correlation between subjective assessments and this chapter's general election result methodology should not be overstated, and, as indicated at the beginning of the chapter, any system for measuring the quality of leadership cannot be at all precise, given circumstances vary so greatly.

Nevertheless, it does imply that a rating based upon election performance does have some value, and, from the point of view of party leadership, can be extended to leaders who did not become Prime Minister. This is more important for Conservatives in the modern era than it was before the middle of the last century. At the very minimum, general election performances should be considered as a contributory criterion when assessing how Conservative leaders have done, not least because there are some modern leaders, such as Howard and Cameron, who deserve a rather more positive historical assessment than they sometimes receive.

PART II

ASSESSMENTS OF CONSERVATIVE LEADERS

CHAPTER 4

SIR ROBERT PEEL

RICHARD A. GAUNT

Sir Robert Peel's political career as de facto and official leader of the Conservative Party encompasses the period during, and following, the debate and enactment of the Great Reform Act – an inherently limited, but extremely significant movement towards democracy in Britain. As Richard A. Gaunt notes, Peel's leadership of the newly christened Conservative Party was defined, in large part, by his pragmatic opposition to, and subsequent acceptance of, the act. The Conservative Party reaped the parliamentary and organisational benefits of his electoral popularity, gaining significant swings in each election he fought – ninety-eight seats in 1835, forty-one in 1837, and a further fifty-three in 1841. However, ultimately, Richard A. Gaunt argues that Peel's high-handed, executive-facing approach was ill suited to a style of leadership that required appeasement and coercion of a national and parliamentary party. His inability to create a new 'Peelite' social and economic consensus within the Conservative Party – epitomised by his repeal of the Corn Laws – led to a mixed, if significant, record as a successful leader of the party.

• • •

Sir Robert Peel is generally acknowledged as the first leader of the Conservative Party in British history.[52] He assumed the role on becoming Prime Minister for the first time in December 1834,

52 The Duke of Wellington is listed as the first Conservative Party leader in N. J. Crowson, *The Longman Companion to the Conservative Party since 1830*, Harlow, Pearson Education, 2001, p. 5.

and relinquished it eleven and a half years later, on resigning the premiership for the second and, as it turned out, final time. The circumstances under which Peel gained and lost the Conservative leadership reflect the central tension running through his incumbency of the role. Peel's adult political career – from his first election to Parliament in 1809 – had been forged largely in ministerial office and service to the executive, rather than through leading and conciliating a sectional interest or party. This inbred bias towards a ministerial ethic was to remain with him for ever – to the detriment, as later Conservative leaders regarded it, of the party's interests.[53]

Peel had risen successively through the ranks of government during the premierships of the 2nd Earl of Liverpool and the 1st Duke of Wellington. He served as under-secretary of state for war and the colonies (1810–12), Chief Secretary to the Lord Lieutenant of Ireland (1812–18), and chairman of the finance committee that returned Britain to the gold standard (1819), before completing two periods as Home Secretary (1822–27 and 1828–30). By the time the long period of Tory rule came to an end in November 1830, Peel had established himself as the official – as well as the acknowledged – Leader of the House of Commons, whose close attention to detail, capacity in debate, and unrelenting work ethic marked him out as the almost inevitable choice to lead the opposition thereafter.[54]

However, Peel's marked and continuing reluctance to shoulder the burdens of opposition raised dissatisfaction among his backbenchers. In the end, it would take William IV's unexpected dismissal of his Whig ministers in November 1834, and Wellington's advice to recall Peel from his holiday in Italy, to force the issue, making Peel, in the process, both Prime Minister and leader of the Conservative Party.[55]

---

53 Richard A. Gaunt, *Sir Robert Peel. The Life and Legacy*, London and New York, I. B. Tauris, 2010, pp. 143–60.

54 See Norman Gash, '1812–1830', in Anthony Seldon ed., *How Tory Governments Fall: The Tory Party in Power since 1783*, London, Fontana Press, 1996, pp. 59–104.

55 Gaunt, op. cit., 2010, pp. 81–102.

PEEL AND THE GREAT REFORM ACT DEBATE, 1830–33

That Peel did not seize the initiative by leading the Conservatives during the Reform Bill debates of 1830–32 remained a source of irritation to his prospective followers in the House of Commons. The protracted campaign to secure the government's measure did not find Peel at his best. Though his continued parliamentary declarations were against the bill's sweeping nature, the experience of leading opposition to the King's government was unusual and uncongenial to him. Vocal anti-reform speeches were delivered by a number of 'hard-line' Conservative backbenchers, such as Sir Charles Wetherell, while crucial modifications to the bill's particulars were made by the likes of the Marquess of Chandos (heir to the Duke of Buckingham), whose famous amendment to the measure had the deliberate effect of enfranchising a body of rural society (the £50 'tenants at will') that was susceptible to landlord influence. Peel's most decisive action was resolutely refusing to cooperate with Wellington's eleventh-hour attempt to form a government that was committed to passing a measure of reform in May 1832. The circumstances were unfavourable politically and raised a firestorm of public hostility, which was immortalised in Francis Place's rallying cry: 'Stop the Duke; go for gold.' However, Peel was also motivated by the knowledge that – having helped Wellington pass the Roman Catholic Relief Act in 1829, after reneging on twenty years of public opposition to Catholic emancipation – he could not survive another such reversal. In a situation where reform was going to pass without need of his assistance, Peel took a shrewd and pragmatic course that secured his future political capital.[56]

Peel quickly took control of the reformed Parliament of 1833, taking the lead against ministers who had soon squandered their credit as the authors of the 'Great Reform Act'. In his first substantive statement to the Commons, on 7 February 1833, Peel accepted the Reform Act as passed, and ruled out any attempt to repeal it. In doing so, he indicated his future line of conduct,

---

56 The best account is still Michael Brock, *The Great Reform Act*, London, Hutchinson, 1973.

and distanced himself from the connotations of outright resistance – which the pre-1832 designation Tory had implied.[57]

The new term 'Conservative' was now adopted self-consciously by the opposition. It had gained currency after an influential article in the *Quarterly Review* in 1830, and subsumed the distinctions of 'anti-reformer' that had emerged during the debates over parliamentary reform. In 1831, the former MP Sir Robert Wilmot-Horton delivered a significant prophecy on the political realignment that would follow the Reform Act:

> From that period, we shall hear no more of Whigs and Tories, of radicals and ultras, of reformers and anti-reformers. An entirely new fusion will take place, and that House of Commons will, ultimately, resolve itself into two parties, who may be called, from the tenor of their opinions, Conservatives and Levellers. It will be the principle of the latter class that, to secure the happiness of the people, it is necessary to carry into effect some destruction of institutions, and some confiscation of property. It will be the principle of the Conservators that neither destruction of institutions, nor confiscation of property is necessary.[58]

PEEL'S ACTIVE OPPOSITION, 1835–41

Most of Peel's period as Leader of the Opposition (1835–41) was predicated on the basis of what he began to practise in 1833–34, and what he proclaimed to his Staffordshire constituents in the Tamworth Manifesto of December 1834. Although this document has been invested with more significance than is strictly justified, Peel's declaration – delivered as an incoming

57 *Speeches Delivered in the House of Commons by the Late Rt Hon. Sir Robert Peel, Vol. 2 [1853]*, New York, Kraus Publishers, 1972, pp. 604–13.

58 James J. Sack, 'The *Quarterly Review* and the Baptism of the "Conservative Party": A Conundrum Resolved', *Victorian Periodicals Review*, 24(4), 1991, pp. 170–72; Sir Robert Wilmot-Horton, *Reform in 1839 and Reform in 1831*, London, John Murray, 1839, p. 35 (I am indebted to my PhD student Stephen Lamont for this reference).

Prime Minister, rather than as a party leader – quickly gained the status of official Conservative policy. It committed the ministry to the review of institutions 'civil and ecclesiastical', and the reform of 'proven abuses'. This distinguished Peel's new Conservatism from the entrenched certainties of old Toryism, but it was capacious enough to accommodate a wide spectrum of political views. Many ultras were content to mute their lingering doubts about Peel's conduct on Catholic emancipation and reform, and committed their support during the 'Hundred Days' of his government (December 1834 to April 1835).[59]

Peel, relishing his role as chief executive, delivered a virtuoso performance as leader of a minority administration called into service at the behest of the crown. Though the party made commendable advances on its post-Reform Act nadir, rising from 175 to 273 seats in the general election of 1835, it did not secure anything like the numbers required to govern successfully.[60] Peel was forced back upon his meagre parliamentary resources, supplemented by such alliances as he could mediate, although he had high hopes of attracting moderate opinion from the Derby Dilly (led by the Earl of Derby's heir, Lord Stanley, together with the former Tories the Duke of Richmond, Sir James Graham and Lord Ripon). The Dilly – so-named, derisively, by the Irish MP Daniel O'Connell – had resigned from Grey's government in the summer of 1834 over the Whig Party's commitment to appropriate the surplus revenues of the Anglican Church and apply them to secular purposes. The same issue subsequently persuaded William IV to dismiss his ministers and call upon Peel. This raised the old Tory cry of 'the Church in danger', and was to prove an important part of the Conservatives' election success in 1841. Though Peel did not secure the Dilly immediately, its component parts gradually crossed the floor until, by 1838, Stanley and Graham had become two of Peel's leading lieutenants.[61]

---

59 The manifesto is republished in Lord Mahon and Edward Cardwell eds, *Memoirs of Sir Robert Peel, Vol. 2 [1856–67]*, New York, Kraus Publishers, 1969, pp. 58–67.

60 Crowson, op. cit., p. 37.

61 Angus Hawkins, *The Forgotten Prime Minister, The 14th Earl of Derby: Ascent, 1799–1851*, Oxford, Oxford University Press, 2007, pp. 144–78.

The reputation of the Conservatives – and of Peel, in particular – was immeasurably benefited by its brief experience of government. The later 1830s were to see the party capitalise on these gains not only in parliamentary terms, but, equally significantly, in its electoral organisation in the constituencies. Not the least of the unintended consequences of the Reform Act was its role in stimulating the party's local electoral organisation across the country. The Conservatives, by virtue of the fact that they had more to gain, as well as their perspicacity in seizing opportunities, took a leading role in establishing Conservative operative associations. These were particularly strong in the industrial Midlands, Yorkshire and the north-west, although they were turned to advocating a species of Tory paternalism that differed materially from what Peel was prepared to offer. The most important of their policies was opposition to the Whigs' New Poor Law of 1834, which introduced the test of less eligibility for poor relief, and saw the erection of the hated 'bastilles' – or workhouses. Many Conservative operative associations were equally incensed at the Whigs' Factory Act of 1833 and sought a ten-hour working day; or else, they wanted adequate social provision for the ills produced by industrial capitalism.[62]

Local Conservative organisations were also quick to seize the consequences of electoral registration. This had been introduced by the Reform Act to establish exactly who – and how many people – had the right to vote. Legal minds turned themselves to the annual battle of the revising courts, where the claims of contending parties to be included on the register could be disputed with passion. As historians have recognised, this increased the sense of local partisanship in constituencies, and contributed significantly to the Conservative general election victory of 1841. It created a political apparatus and organisational mechanism that were to make the Conservative Party a living entity, not limited to the confines of Westminster.[63]

Not that Westminster was neglected either. In 1832, the Conservatives founded

62 David Walsh, *Making Angels in Marble. The Conservatives, the Early Industrial Working Class and Attempts at Political Incorporation*, London, Breviary Stuff Publications, 2012.

63 Philip Salmon, *Electoral Reform at Work. Local Politics and National Parties, 1832–1841*, Woodbridge, Boydell & Brewer, 2002.

the Carlton Club in central London. This was one of the great political clubs to be founded in the decade – pre-dating the Reform Club by four years. The Carlton acted as a central coordinating mechanism for peers, MPs and political wire-pullers, as well as providing a convivial place to meet and exchange political intelligence. The quiet, modest, but ruthlessly efficient figures of Francis Bonham and Lord Granville Somerset emerged as crucial in the political apparatus of the party, demonstrating an energetic commitment to organisation. Aspirant new MPs – including the young Disraeli – sought the imprimatur of the club's sanction, which made them the equivalent of official candidates at election time.[64]

The later 1830s demonstrated Peel's pragmatic approach to the terms upon which he would accept power. The general election that followed the accession of Queen Victoria in 1837 saw the Conservatives move within thirty seats of the government (314 to the Whigs' 344).[65] However, Peel's policy of 'governing in opposition' – helping the Whigs to pass measures with which the Conservative front bench were in broad agreement, in order to outflank the extreme wings of both parties – frustrated those who hungered for a swift return to office. Peel almost had his chance in May 1839, but found himself defeated in the so-called 'bedchamber crisis' by the obstinacy of Queen Victoria, whose openly avowed partisanship for Melbourne's government prevented the Conservatives playing the part of 1834–35 over again. Nor was Peel's relationship with Wellington, the indispensable leader of the Conservative peers in the House of Lords, as harmonious as it might have been. Though Peel and Wellington operated something of a dual leadership, in that each was *primus inter pares* in their respective chamber, miscommunication and misunderstanding threatened the equanimity of a partnership that was vital to Conservative success.[66]

---

64 Sir Charles Petrie and Alistair Cooke, *The Carlton Club 1832–2007*, London, The Carlton Club, 2007; Norman Gash, 'The Organisation of the Conservative Party, 1832–46, Part I: The Parliamentary Organisation', *Parliamentary History*, Vol. 1, 1982, pp. 137–59; Norman Gash, 'The Organisation of the Conservative Party, 1832–46, Part II: The Electoral Organisation', *Parliamentary History*, Vol. 2, 1983, pp. 131–52.

65 Crowson, op. cit., p. 38.

66 Richard A. Gaunt, 'Wellington, Peel and the Conservative Party', in C. M. Woolgar ed., *Wellington Studies V*, Southampton, The Hartley Institute, 2013, pp. 262–85.

GENERAL ELECTION, 1841

When the long-anticipated general election was finally called, in the summer of 1841, Peel brought his unrivalled economic expertise to bear in determining the issues upon which it was fought – and upon which his ministry would subsequently be judged. The Whigs' plan to revise the duties paid on sugar, and to replace the unpopular Corn Law with a moderate fixed duty, was designed to meet the country's growing financial deficit, which had intensified since the economic depression of 1837. In these circumstances, Peel based his appeal to the electorate upon the maintenance of protection, the defence of the union with Ireland, and the preservation of the Church of England against Whig and O'Connellite incursion.[67]

Though historians no longer argue that 'all turned upon the name of Sir Robert Peel', the reasons that sentiment gained ground during the election are unsurprising. Peel's increasingly personal identification with the Conservative Party – and the party's with Peel – had been solidified during the late 1830s through the increasing range of texts, images and artefacts bearing his name and profile. Any pronouncements by Peel, such as his set-piece orations on being installed as rector of Glasgow University in 1837 and at the Merchant Taylors' Hall in 1838, were promoted extensively in a variety of forms, including medals, portraits and caricatures.[68] The Conservatives also gained the crucial endorsement of *The Times* – its editor John Walter stood for Parliament as a Conservative on an anti-Poor Law platform. Though the party made advances in new areas, its electoral victory in 1841 (with a majority of seventy-six seats over its opponents) represented a revival in its pre-1830 heartlands – rural, Anglican constituencies and small boroughs with fewer than 500 electors. This was the body of opinion that had abandoned Wellington's ministry in

67 Betty Kemp, 'The General Election of 1841', *History*, Vol. 37, 1952, pp. 146–57; Edwin Jaggard, 'The 1841 British General Election: A Reconsideration', *Australian Journal of Politics and History*, Vol. 30, 1984, pp. 99–114.

68 Donald Read, *Peel and the Victorians*, Oxford, Basil Blackwell, 1987, pp. 63–96; Richard A. Gaunt ed., *Peel in Caricature. The 'Political Sketches' of John Doyle ('HB')*, Tamworth, The Peel Society, 2014.

the summer of 1830 in the face of economic distress and the growing demand for parliamentary reform, and returned to Conservatism with the desire to maintain agricultural protection and preserve the Anglican Church.[69]

PEEL GOVERNMENT, 1841–46

Peel's ministry of 1841–46 is rightly regarded, alongside Gladstone's government of 1868–74, as the most significant of the nineteenth century, in point of domestic policy. From the outset, Peel stamped his personal authority on the ministry by assuming responsibility for economic and financial affairs. His Chancellor of the Exchequer, Henry Goulburn, was unequal to challenging Peel's primacy in directing and presenting the course of government policy. The board of trade went, initially, to the former Chancellor and Dillyite Ripon, before providing Gladstone with his first major department of state. With Graham at the Home Office, Stanley at Colonies, Wellington in Cabinet without portfolio (he resumed command of the army in 1842), and the Earl of Aberdeen as Foreign Secretary, the Cabinet was one of the strongest ever formed, in point of past performance and future potential. Even the resignation of the Duke of Buckingham (formerly Chandos) over the government's 1842 Corn Law was rendered pyrrhic by his acceptance of the Garter.[70]

Yet from the outset, Peel's ministry contained within it the seeds of its own destruction. Much of this was the inevitable consequence of an election fought upon the narrow ground of agricultural protection and Anglican privilege. The 1842 Corn Law disappointed those expectations overnight by substantially modifying the sliding scale of duties (last revised in 1828) in the direction of free competition. A similar measure, applied to Canadian corn in 1843, and a deeply divisive proposal to modify the sugar duties in 1844 increased the disquiet of Conservative agriculturists. However, the most audacious plank

69 Crowson, op. cit., p. 38 lists 367 Conservatives, 271 Whigs/Liberals and twenty others.

70 Gaunt, op. cit., 2010, pp. 103–30; Bruce Coleman, '1841–46', in Seldon, op. cit., 1996, pp. 104–57.

in the ministry's economic programme was the re-introduction of income tax in 1842 at a rate of 7 pence in the pound on incomes over £150. This was consciously designed as a temporary expedient to offset drastic reductions in the rate of import duties paid on raw produce and manufactured goods. It was designed, in Peel's phrase, to make the country 'cheap for living' and to counteract the attractions of Chartism, which had been demanding further political reforms since 1838. After surviving the calamitous social conditions of 1842, trade recovered, finances improved and the ministry was emboldened to move further and faster in the direction of free trade – notably in its groundbreaking Budget of 1845.[71]

Ireland was exempted from the income tax, but the Queen was not. This was not political vindictiveness on Peel's part – his relations with Victoria were eased considerably thanks to judicious relations with her husband Prince Albert[72] – but part of a wider policy of mollifying and ameliorating Irish discontent by demonstrating the fair-minded and judicious nature of rule from London. In the face of O'Connell's 'Monster Meetings' for repeal of the Act of Union, Peel pursued a policy that looked, to his more sectarian followers, increasingly partial to Catholicism. There was the Charitable Bequests Act in 1844, a land commission under Lord Devon to investigate the root cause of Ireland's socio-economic grievances, and, most controversially of all, a tripling of the government grant to the Catholic training seminary of Maynooth in 1845. Peel's Irish policy sought to accommodate Conservatives to the reality of living in a kingdom of multiple religious identities. However, its short-term consequences were disastrous for his leadership. Facing a major campaign against the Maynooth Grant – and the revolt of half of his MPs – the measure only passed with opposition votes.[73]

---

71 See Gareth Stedman Jones, 'Rethinking Chartism', in his *Languages of Class: Studies in English Working-Class History, 1832–1982,* Cambridge, Cambridge University Press, 1983, pp. 90–178.

72 Richard A. Gaunt, 'A Power Behind The Throne? Sir Robert Peel, Prince Albert and the Making of the Modern Monarchy', *Conservative History Journal*, 11(2), 2014, pp. 50–54.

73 Donal A. Kerr, *Peel, Priests and Politics, Sir Robert Peel's Administration and the Roman Catholic Church in Ireland, 1841–1846*, Oxford, Oxford University Press, 1982; David Eastwood, '"Recasting Our Lot": Peel, the Nation, and the Politics of Interest', in Laurence Brockliss and David Eastwood eds, *A Union of Multiple Identities. The British Isles, c.1750–c.1850*, Manchester, Manchester University Press, 1997, pp. 29–43.

What Peel did not do was as significant for his leadership as what he did. Much to the chagrin of the Conservative operative associations and the likes of Walter, Peel continued the New Poor Law apparatus in 1842, and, in 1844, determinedly opposed the campaign of Ferrand, Ashley and Oastler to achieve a ten-hour working day for factory workers, which he regarded as an imposition on manufacturing output. Graham's attempts to legislate for the education of factory children in 1843 also came unstuck, because of differences between Anglicans and Dissenters over the religious basis of schooling. Within the party, ginger groups of political dissent – both on specific issues and over the course of government policy more generally – began to coalesce. Young England – a party of religiously minded, aristocratic MPs, who sought the revival of medieval chivalry and a paternalistic social order – found an articulate mouthpiece in Disraeli. Though disgruntled at his lack of preferment under Peel, Disraeli was more genuinely motivated by principle than subsequent historians have given him credit for. His *Sybil, or The Two Nations* (1845) portrayed an endemic social schism that was incapable of being alleviated by Peel's social and economic reforms.[74]

Peel's high-handed, authoritarian handling of opposition in the ranks, and his frequent recourse to the threat of resignation, was particularly grating to his followers. By the end of 1845, when news of the Irish potato famine began to reach England, he expressed himself in no mood to conciliate them:

> I am perfectly at ease in my own mind and conscience. Not only have I acted with the best intentions – but firmly believe that that which I have done is the best that under the circumstances could have been done. As to newspapers, every malignant and malevolent fellow who has been disappointed can write an article with a pompous 'we', as if he were speaking the public voice.[75]

---

74 For a reappraisal of Disraeli and Young England, see Richard A. Gaunt, 'From Country Party to Conservative Party: The Ultra Tories and Foreign Policy', in Jeremy Black ed., *The Tory World. Deep History and the Tory Theme in British Foreign Policy, 1679–2014*, Farnham, Ashgate, 2015, pp. 149–65; Richard A. Gaunt, 'Toryism and the Young England Movement', in Corinna Wagner, Joanne Parker and Nick Groom eds, *The Oxford Handbook of Medieval Victorianism*, Oxford, Oxford University Press, forthcoming.

75 Letter from Peel to his wife, 16 December 1845, in George Peel ed., *The Private Letters of Sir Robert Peel*, London, John Murray, 1920, pp. 273–4.

Peel met the Commons in January 1846 determined to repeal the Corn Laws. He had resigned office in December 1845, having failed to secure Cabinet backing for the policy, only to return to power more determined than ever, once the Queen found herself without an alternative ministry. It was, in one respect, the pattern of 1829 and 1834 all over again. It raised in Peel all his prejudice towards executive service in the face of insuperable obstacles – party considerations were discounted. Historians continue to debate the motivation and timing of the repeal; in particular, whether it was the culmination of a long-term policy he had deliberately kept from his followers, or the consequence of short-term contingencies stimulated by the Irish potato famine.[76] What is not in doubt is that, as months of Conservative opposition ensued (skilfully orchestrated by Lord George Bentinck and Disraeli), Peel's attitude towards the long-term survival of the party hardened to the point of attrition. Conservative agriculturists in the Commons were equally committed to upholding protection against, what they regarded as, the temporary and unproven troubles of Ireland. Honour to the party, and consistency to the pledges exacted in 1841, was, from their perspective, only part of what was at stake.[77] The bitterness of this internecine conflict was in marked contrast to events in the Lords, where Wellington skilfully marshalled a government victory for the bill in spite of his own doubts about the measure and the opposition of the protectionist peers, who looked to Stanley as their future leader.[78]

Peel had, to all intents and purposes, yielded the leadership of the Conservative Party by the end of 1845. Though Richard Cobden, the leader of the Anti-Corn Law League, wrote to Peel idealistically prophesying his future as leader of a progressive coalition that would realise the interests of

---

76 Boyd Hilton, *A Mad, Bad and Dangerous People? England, 1783–1846*, Oxford, Oxford University Press, 2006, pp. 551–8, argues the long-term view.

77 Anna Gambles, *Protection and Politics: Conservative Economic Discourse, 1815–1852*, Woodbridge, Boydell & Brewer, 1999.

78 Richard W. Davis, *A Political History of the House of Lords, 1811–1846: From the Regency to Corn Law Repeal*, Stanford, 2008, pp. 322–36.

the middle-class electorate inaugurated in 1832, the reality of the situation was not in doubt. Peel's government was defeated in the Commons on its Irish Coercion Bill on the same evening that the Repeal Bill passed in the Lords. Peel resigned office on Monday 29 June 1846 with a parting – and very deliberate – shot at the narrow-mindedness of his back-bench opponents (the same MPs on whose votes he had relied over the preceding five years). The immediate legacy was a schism in the Conservative Party, roughly in the proportion two-thirds protectionist to one-third Peelite.[79]

ASSESSING PEEL

In 1983, Ian Newbould argued that Peel's leadership of the Conservative Party from 1832 to 1841 represented 'a study in failure'. Peel failed to convert the party to Peelite principles, and the Conservatives' election victory of 1841 was secured in the old heartlands of pre-1830 Toryism. But, as Norman Gash rightly contended, 'failure is a relative term'. It would be as well not to judge Peel by criteria that are, in our own age, more exacting in determining political success and failure.[80]

However, to assess Peel against the political structures operating in his own day is complicated by the fact that such structures were clearly changing. The 1832 Reform Act underscored the demise of the methods by which governments had traditionally secured themselves in office – patronage, finance, and an appeal to support the King's chosen ministers. Governments had been supported by a mixture of ministerialists and office-holders (who had a stake in the administration's survival), partisans (who supported its policy for ideological and personal reasons), and a broad swathe of independent, country gentlemen (who prized the security and confidence of a government

---

79 Gaunt, op. cit., 2010, pp. 127–30.

80 I. D. C. Newbould, 'Sir Robert Peel and the Conservative Party, 1832–1841: A Study in Failure?', *English Historical Review*, Vol. 98, 1983, pp. 529–57; Norman Gash, *Sir Robert Peel* (revised edition), Harlow, Longman, 1986, pp. ix–x.

that enjoyed royal favour). From the 1830s, as the implications of the Reform Act hit home, the depleted resources of what radicals had castigated as 'Old Corruption' gave way to the emergence of political parties with increasingly sophisticated methods of exerting discipline.[81]

Peel certainly believed in and encouraged the Conservative Party's evolution during the 1830s. The 1841 general election exemplified the fact that a party with a majority in the House of Commons could overturn a ministry that enjoyed the confidence of the crown. Conversely, Peel's experience in 1834–35 showed that a government that enjoyed royal favour, but lacked adequate support in the Commons, could not stand for long. It was the dawn of the classic age of 'parliamentary government', upon which contemporaries looked back with satisfaction.[82]

However, Peel had an alternative understanding of the situation. Once a party had helped a government to achieve office, he believed that ministerial privileges – the superior knowledge derived from access to official papers, the traditional loyalty owed to the crown and resistance to factional interests – made party considerations secondary to those of the executive. In any case, the Conservative Party continued to represent a broad swathe of interests in this period, rather than acting as a monolithic bloc that moved in unison with the loudest dissenting voice. Not all ultras agreed on objects or tactics, just as the different groups of MPs who opposed Peel on different measures during the 1841–46 government did not constitute a permanent, unified opposition in themselves.[83]

The fragility of this situation was exposed by the crisis of 1846. Peel's concept of loyalty to the crown, in pursuit of a policy of his own devising, met an

81 For a shrewd exposition, see Norman Gash, *Lord Liverpool*, London, Weidenfeld & Nicolson, 1984, pp. 1–7; Peter Jupp, *The Governing of Britain, 1688–1848: The executive, Parliament and the people*, London, Routledge, 2006.

82 Angus Hawkins, '"Parliamentary Government" and Victorian Political Parties, c.1830–1880', *English Historical Review*, Vol. 104, 1989, pp. 638–69.

83 For the wider context, see David Eastwood, 'Peel and the Tory Party Reconsidered', *History Today*, 42(3), 1992, pp. 27–33; Norman Gash, 'Peel and the Party System, 1830–1850', *Transactions of the Royal Historical Society*, 5th ser., vol. 1, 1955, pp. 47–69.

equally strong opposition from Conservative MPs, who prized consistency to the platform upon which they had been returned to Parliament. It was a stand-off Peel was ill suited to meet, given his political history, and one the Conservative Party was increasingly unlikely to accept with equanimity.[84]

It was easy, in the aftermath of the repeal, for Peel to retreat back upon a predisposition against the party, and to await a call to serve the crown in a manner that did not rely upon its inconvenient necessity. In this respect, the most telling statement of Peel's attitude towards party leadership remains the fact that, even when a Peelite party was formed (in the aftermath of the repeal), to perpetuate his name and legacy, he explicitly refused to lead it.[85]

84 D. R. Fisher, 'The Opposition to Sir Robert Peel in the Conservative Party, 1841–1846', PhD thesis, University of Cambridge, 1970.

85 Gaunt, op. cit., 2010, pp. 131–42.

CHAPTER 5

LORD DERBY

ANGUS HAWKINS

Lord Derby is a relatively forgotten figure of Victorian Conservatism; curiously so, given he is the longest-serving leader of the Conservatives, and a three-time Prime Minister. Derby fought five elections as leader in the period between 1846 and 1868, operating as head of three minority governments, but never securing a parliamentary majority. Angus Hawkins argues that many of his strengths have been overlooked due to a mixed electoral record. His mantra of considered and sustained progress and reform went some way to healing many of the schisms in the party that had erupted prior to his leadership. Their principal cause – a policy of protectionism – was successfully abandoned, and the Conservative 'brand' was successfully rehabilitated to one of responsible and moderate government. Hawkins also argues that Derby was a successful manager of his party, marshalling disparate factions with little serious questioning of his authority. As a result, Derby's role in Conservative history is in need of revision and reassessment.

• • •

Edward Stanley (1799–1869), 14th Earl of Derby, was the first British statesman to become Prime Minister three times.[86] He headed Conservative governments in 1852, 1858–59, and 1866–68. Derby led the

86 Edward Stanley was styled Lord Stanley 1834–44. From 1844 to 1851, he sat in the Lords as Lord Stanley of Bickerstaffe. On the death of his father in 1851, he became Earl of Derby. For convenience, I have referred to him as Derby throughout this essay. What follows draws on: Hawkins, op. cit., 2007; and Hawkins, *The Forgotten Prime Minister, The 14th Earl of Derby: Achievement, 1851–1869*, Oxford, Oxford University Press, 2008.

Conservative Party for twenty-two years, from 1846 to 1868. He remains the longest-serving party leader in modern British politics. Derby's third ministry oversaw the passage of the 1867–68 Reform Acts. These extended the parliamentary electorate in the United Kingdom from 1,364,000 voters (20 per cent of all adult males) to 2,477,000 voters (33 per cent of all adult males). Under Derby's second government in 1858, Jews were allowed to become MPs, and the property qualification to be an MP was abolished.

These achievements alone might suggest that Derby was a significant and effective Conservative Party leader. Yet his place in the pantheon of Conservative leadership has been undistinguished. His contribution to the history of Victorian Conservativism has been overshadowed by Sir Robert Peel and Benjamin Disraeli. Under Derby, the Conservatives never won a majority at any general election. All three of his governments were minority ministries. His tenures of power were brief. Some historians, as a result, have seen the period between the electoral triumphs of 1841 and 1874 as one of Conservative despondency and ineffectiveness.[87] A more accurate assessment of Derby's record as Conservative leader requires consideration of his personal qualities, his political beliefs, and the unpromising circumstances under which he assumed leadership of the party.

As a young man, Derby was brought up in the staunchly Whig household on the extensive estates of Knowsley, Lancashire – the Stanley family seat since the fifteenth century. After Eton and Christ Church, Oxford, he entered the Commons as a promising and talented Whig MP in 1822. His evident intelligence, self-confidence, forceful oratory and aristocratic status won him political advancement. In 1827–28, he briefly served as under-secretary for the colonies in Lord Goderich's ministry. In 1829, he spoke in favour of Catholic emancipation. Aged thirty-one, in 1830, he became Chief Secretary for Ireland, and, in 1833, Colonial Secretary in Lord Grey's reform ministry. A prominent advocate of the 1832 Reform Acts, his policy

---

87 For example, Donald Southgate, in Norman Gash, Donald Southgate, David Dilks and John Ramsden eds, *The Conservatives: A History from their Origins to 1965*, London: Allen & Unwin, 1977, who describes this period of Conservative history as the 'dog days', and heads a chapter section 'The Incompetence of Derby' (p. 139).

in Ireland combined reform of national elementary education with an Irish Church Temporalities Act, reducing the cost of the Irish establishment, firmly protecting property rights and maintaining law and order in the face of rural violence over payment of the tithe. The Irish populist leader Daniel O'Connell dubbed him 'Scorpion Stanley'.[88]

Suffering his first attack of gout aged barely thirty-four, Derby became Grey's Colonial Secretary in April 1833. He immediately saw the legislation abolishing slavery in the British colonies through the Commons. His direct observation of slavery during his travels around the United States in 1824–25 had hardened his abhorrence of the moral corruption he saw as inherent in the slave system. But, by 1834, ministerial divisions over the appropriation of the Church of Ireland's revenue for lay purposes prompted Derby's resignation from Grey's government. Derby saw such appropriation as a fundamental violation of the rights of property. During 1834–35, he looked to form a party drawing together moderate Conservatives and Whigs – the so-called Derby Dilly.[89] However, by April 1835, the Derby Dilly had dispersed, and, during 1836–37, Derby migrated to Peel's Conservative Party.

By his mid-thirties, the core of Derby's political beliefs was clear and consistent. Moderate and judicious reform should respond to the advancement of a dynamic society, safeguarding progress. Yet the nation's historic institutions, while adapting to progress, should be preserved as the foundation of order and stability. The role of the aristocracy in providing enlightened leadership must be maintained. The rule of law and the sacrosanct nature of property rights must be upheld. The moral authority of the Anglican Church, as the nation's established Church, must be protected, while political entitlements should be extended to non-Anglicans – so might popular clamour and demagogic demands be held in check, while responsible reform answered justified grievances. Upon his installation as rector of Glasgow University in December 1834, Derby stated to his audience:

---

88 Hawkins, op. cit., 2007, p. 220.

89 This was O'Connell's dismissive term for the group, which was subsequently and quickly taken up by others.

> His will be a glorious destiny who knows how to direct and turn into the proper channels the energies of the people, and to conduct with propriety, at this period, the government of this great nation; but if he shall imagine himself capable of stemming and abruptly resisting its force onwards, he will be swept along with the torrent.[90]

This statement of political belief became known as the 'Knowsley Creed'.

Derby's beliefs reflected his personality. Always conscious of his social standing, he was never given to easy flattery of others and was sensitive to perceived slights. Those outside his family who did not share in his enjoyment of horse racing or *battue* shooting often encountered a personality seeming distant and aloof. From his mother, he acquired a moderate evangelical Anglican faith, which emphasised the responsibilities of wealth and public duty as a requirement of aristocratic privilege. As a young man, he published books on the Christian parables and the miracles of Christ. For Derby, political power was a natural obligation, not a prize for which to strive. Genuine effort was cloaked by a social manner of nonchalance. Exertion and earnestness were inappropriate matters of display. This manner prompted some, not in his confidence, to think he lacked political seriousness. A bluff sense of humour in social settings, often pricking the pomposity of others, disguised his convictions. Yet his commitment to politics was sincere and deeply felt – a commitment concealed by his disdain for vulgar indications of personal ambition.[91] Close colleagues recognised his clarity of thought, patience and resourcefulness, and acuteness of intellect powerful in debate. For relaxation, he translated French, German and Italian poetry. His rendering of Homer's *Iliad* into English blank verse was judged by that sternest of

---

90 *The Times*, 22 December 1834, p. 3.

91 As Derby reminded Disraeli in 1849: 'He who has put his hand to the parliamentary plough cannot draw back. I do not speak, of course, of the great majority of members of both Houses, who act as parliamentary units, giving numerical strength and nothing else, to the party to which they attach themselves, but of those whom talent, or station, or accident has placed in the foreground and enabled them to exercise, whether they will or not, an influence over numbers of their brother members. For them there is no retreat.' (Stanley to Disraeli, in William Monypenny and George Buckle, *The Life of Benjamin Disraeli, Earl of Beaconsfield, Vol. 3*, London, John Murray, 1914, p. 127.

Classical critics William Gladstone to be 'of very high excellence'.[92] These qualities led *The Times* to describe Derby as 'the only brilliant eldest son produced by the British peerage in a hundred years'.[93]

By 1838, Derby was established as a prominent member of Peel's Conservative Party. His former Whig colleagues, he declared, had become the complicit tools of radical designs. In 1841, Peel appointed him Colonial Secretary – the same office Derby had resigned seven years previously. Derby was the youngest member of Peel's Cabinet. As Colonial Secretary, he resisted the territorial expansion of Britain's existing colonies, while upholding international trading and commercial interests. Yet the decisions of local colonial administrators and the aspirations of commercial traders repeatedly ran counter to Derby's preferences. The Indian province of Sindh was annexed, the crown colony of Hong Kong was established, and Natal was annexed as part of the Cape Colony. At the same time, Derby confronted Lord John Russell over the government's policies in Ireland, and clashed with Lord Palmerston over foreign policy – while also suffering severe attacks of gout during 1843.

Colonial business proved less crucial to Peel's concerns after 1841, however, than the economy and domestic social tensions, despite Derby's part in securing tariff reform for imported Canadian corn in 1843. This fostered Derby's increasing sense of marginalisation in Peel's Cabinet. Colleagues such as Sir James Graham, Henry Goulburn and Gladstone became more prominent advocates of Peel's policies. That Derby's personal relations with the austere and formal Peel were never warm or relaxed exacerbated this sense. Their relative social status inhibited easy fellowship. Derby was heir to the pre-eminent noble family of Lancashire, with large, landed estates and a peerage title going back to 1485. Peel was the grandson of a Lancashire yeoman farmer, and his father had made a fortune in cotton textile manufacturing. Patrician self-regard kept Derby outside the charmed circle of Peel's admiring acolytes. In October 1844, at his own request, Derby left the Commons

---

92 Gladstone to the Duchess of Sutherland, 28 December 1864, in John Morley, *The Life of William Ewart Gladstone, Vol. 2*, London, Macmillan, 1903, p. 193.

93 *The Times*, 25 October 1869, p. 7.

to take a seat in the House of Lords. In the Upper House, he explained, he would be able to provide essential service in a broader range of government business, and support the increasingly frail and deaf Duke of Wellington as Conservative leader in the Lords.

So it was that Derby observed the bitter Conservative schism of 1846 over Corn Law repeal from the Lords.[94] Already, in December 1845, he had resigned from Peel's Cabinet over the Prime Minister's decision to remove the tariff on imported corn in response to the onset of a potato famine in Ireland. Derby's objections were twofold. First, he regarded total repeal, as opposed to adjustments in the tariff on imported corn, as largely irrelevant to the causes of suffering in Ireland. Second, he saw such a decision as a violation of good faith with the Conservative backbenchers who had been elected in 1841 on the basis of preserving the Corn Laws. His parting words to his ministerial colleagues were that they could 'not do this as gentlemen'.[95]

A dejected Derby was deeply distressed by Peel's determination to repeal the Corn Laws. With acute regret, he watched the anguished outcry of Conservative backbenchers against what they portrayed as Peel's apostasy. In May 1846, with opposition support, Peel secured repeal of the Corn Laws. A minority of 112 Conservative MPs accompanied the Prime Minister into the division lobby. Over 230 Conservative MPs refused to follow their front bench. Bitter acrimony tore Conservative ranks apart. Throughout the crisis, Derby retained hope that Conservative divisions might, in due course, be healed. From his Whig political apprenticeship, he had learned that cohesive party association was essential to the efficient workings of parliamentary government. Regard for back-bench opinion by party leaders was a requirement in maintaining necessary mutual relations of trust and confidence between those who led and their followers. Loyal back-bench votes gave a government authority. But Derby found himself reluctantly drawn into the role of

---

94 Stanley went up to the Lords with the title Lord Stanley of Bickerstaffe – the title used by his father to enter the Lords in 1832 during the lifetime of the 12th Earl of Derby.

95 Lord Broughton and Lady Dorchester, *Recollections of a Long Life by Lord Broughton, Vol. 6*, London, John Murray, 1909, p. 299.

party champion against a faithless leadership. Only the sustained courtship of protectionist peers in March 1846 prompted Derby to cautiously accept being their leader in the Lords. Not until May did he publicly affirm his overall leadership of the protectionists in both Houses. In the Commons, meanwhile, Lord George Bentinck's wild-eyed fury and Disraeli's razor-edged ridicule gave vent to Conservative back-bench outrage.

In a powerful three-hour Lords speech on 25 May 1846, Derby denounced Peel's government for pitting agricultural and manufacturing interests against each other, for adopting crude self-interested competition ('a reciprocity of evil'), for severing communal bonds, and for employing a dangerous rhetoric stirring pernicious class hatred in a cause irrelevant to Irish suffering.[96] Yet Derby's oratorical triumph was a political failure. Repeal of the Corn Laws passed into statute. On 28 June, Conservative back-bench MPs took their revenge by combining with the Whig and radical opposition in rejecting Peel's Irish Coercion Bill. On 29 June, Peel announced his resignation as Prime Minister.

The circumstances under which Derby assumed the protectionist party leadership in 1846 were fraught with exceptional difficulty. Bitter resentment, particularly in the Commons, flowed unabated. Many protectionist MPs, moreover, adopted a violent anti-Catholic rhetoric fired by Peel in 1845, enlarging and making permanent the Maynooth Grant. Hoping for eventual Conservative reunion, Derby advocated a restorative calm, and restraint from vindictive attacks on the Peelites. But such a strategy proved beyond the capacity of many of his followers. The protectionists appeared a party of atavistic and aggrieved rural protest, some espousing a vehement anti-Catholicism threatening to inflame sectarian conflict.

Derby's major achievement as Conservative leader after 1846 was gradually rehabilitating the party as capable of moderate and responsible governance. The hostile perception of the party, shorn of Peelite talent, as a gathering of backwoods bigots was slowly shed. Derby gave the Conservatives a future. In

96 Lord Stanley, 25 May 1846, Hansard, 3rd ser., vol. 86, col. 1128–76.

the 1847 general election, in which religious issues as well as free trade were prominent, about 250 protectionist MPs were returned to the Commons. Derby then resumed, with demurring on the part of some, the party label 'Conservative', rather than 'protectionist'. This change was significant. It denoted links with the party of the 1830s that had espoused moderate reform associated with the defence of the nation's historic institutions; the party Derby had crossed the floor of the Commons to join. At the same time, Derby, in close collaboration with J. W. Croker as editor of the *Quarterly Review*, sought to distance his leadership from Protestant anti-Catholic bigotry. The protectionist outrage of Conservative MPs was held in check. Derby looked to rescue the party from a fate of embittered reaction.

A major difficulty for Derby in the late 1840s was the absence of reliable and effective leadership in the Commons. The volatile Bentinck, who leapt to the forefront of protectionist ranks in 1846, stirred animosity and division; in December 1847, Bentinck resigned the Commons leadership.[97] Desperate short-lived expedients were attempted. The young Lord Granby proved a broken reed. The elderly John Herries was past sustained exertion. It was in these circumstances that Derby found himself forced to acknowledge the talent and ambition of Disraeli. Though recognising Disraeli's power in debate, Derby distrusted Disraeli's mercurial temperament, eagerness for acclaim, and uncertain judgement – reservations compounded by Conservative back-bench mistrust of Disraeli's exotic background and manner. Yet, in the absence of alternatives, Disraeli had become de facto leader of the Commons by 1849.

Derby's wariness of Disraeli also arose from the obstacle Disraeli placed in the path of Conservative reunion. Disraeli's devastating attacks on Peel in 1846 remained a bitter memory for some Peelites. Nonetheless, Derby continued to hold open a door through which Peelites might return to the Conservative ranks. Over time, this proved effective. During the late 1840s and 1850s, over seventy of those Peelite MPs who supported Corn Law repeal

---

97 Bentinck had been a member of the Derby Dilly in 1834–35.

eventually re-joined the Conservative Party under Derby's leadership. A much smaller, if distinguished, number of Peelites – notably Gladstone – ultimately joined the Liberal Party.

From the late 1840s, Derby also entertained the hope of an eventual Conservative merger with moderate Whigs alienated from their colleagues by radical influence. In correspondence with Earl Fitzwilliam and Lord Ponsonby in 1851, he suggested that they all came from the same political stable – those formerly described as 'old constitutional Whigs'. As such, they were to be distinguished from present-day Whigs like Russell, who were abandoning the aristocratic landed interest to demagogic urban forces. From the early 1850s, Derby looked to Whig ranks for accessions of support. Unlike the return of penitent Peelites, however, this strategic aim remained largely a hope, rather than becoming a reality. When forming his second government in February 1858, Derby wrote to the 3rd Earl Grey, inviting him to join the ministry. But Grey declined because of 'the wretched leaders' Derby had for his party, particularly Disraeli in the Commons.[98] Nonetheless, sixteen Whig and Liberal MPs voted with the Conservative government in the early hours of 1 April 1859, unsuccessfully opposing Russell's motion criticising the ministry's Reform Bill. In *The Times*, Grey published a letter describing Russell's motion as superfluous and vague.[99]

During 1860–61, Derby maintained private communication, through intermediaries, with the Liberal Prime Minister Palmerston, supporting the premier in resisting the policies of his radical colleagues and his Chancellor of the Exchequer, Gladstone. When forming his third government in July 1866, Derby offered office to Lord Clarendon and the 'Adullamite' Liberal MPs Edward Horsman and Robert Lowe. All three, however, declined.

During 1867, Liberal disarray followed resentment at being browbeaten by Gladstone, differences over reform, and fear of dissolution. Divided Liberal and radical MPs then played a crucial part in the ultimate success of

98 Hawkins, op. cit., 2007, p. 161.

99 Hawkins, op. cit., 2007, p. 209.

the Conservative Reform Bill. Yet the lasting merger of Conservatives with Whigs and moderate Liberals desired by Derby never transpired. Not until after 1886, when Irish home rule shattered the Liberal Party, did the coming together of Conservatives with Liberal Unionists finally give form to the realignment of parties long anticipated by Derby.

These party calculations framed Derby's central aim in the 1850s and 1860s of re-establishing the Conservative Party as capable of responsible and moderate government. His first ministry, following a general election in July 1852 that returned a free trade majority to the Commons, formally abandoned protection as party policy. Law reform, self-government for New Zealand, resolution of the militia issue (which had occasioned Russell's ejection from office earlier in the year), consideration of the renewal of the East India Company's charter, and support for public health legislation for London were undertaken. In foreign policy, the London Protocol (resolving the dispute between Denmark and the German states over Schleswig-Holstein) was signed, and friendly British relations with Austria were restored in the wake of the Erskine Mather affair.[100] In concert with Russia and Austria, British diplomacy defused the crisis threatened by the suspicion of France's intention to annex Belgium. In contrast to Palmerstonian bluster, Derby described his foreign policy as 'a calm, temperate, deliberate, and conciliatory course of conduct, not in acts alone, but in words also'.[101]

Upon forming his second government in February 1858, Derby declared: 'In politics, as in everything else, the same course must be pursued – constant progress, improving upon the old system, adapting our institutions to the altered purpose they are intended to serve, and by judicious changes meeting the demands of society.'[102]

Whigs and Liberals, he insisted, did not possess a monopoly on progressive

---

100 Erskine Mather was a British subject assaulted by officials in Florence.

101 Hansard, HL deb., 27 February 1852, vol. 119, col. 893. The fall of Derby's government in December 1852 brought to a sudden end negotiation with France over a commercial treaty seeking a mutual reduction of tariffs. This anticipated the famous Cobden–Chevalier Treaty of 1860. If signed, it would have been a significant political coup for the Conservative ministry.

102 Hansard, HL deb., 1 March 1858, vol. 149, col. 41.

wisdom. During 1858–59, Derby oversaw the resolution of the Orsini affair with France (which had just forced Palmerston's resignation from office), reform of the government of India following the mutiny of 1857, a sale and transfer of Irish land measure, and legislation giving Catholic chaplains in the British Army permanent rank and salary. He secured the passage of a bill allowing Jews to become MPs, and legislation abolishing the property qualification to be an MP (a Chartist demand). Against French naval expansion and the building of steam-driven ironclads, Derby, despite the protests of Disraeli as his Chancellor of the Exchequer, increased expenditure on the Royal Navy. He also framed a parliamentary Reform Bill in 1859, proposing a uniform £10 householder suffrage in all constituencies, with 'merit franchises' for those borough voters who possessed £60 in a savings bank, a government pension or a university degree, or who were members of the learned professions.

On becoming Prime Minister for a third time in July 1866, Derby advocated: 'Safe and steady progress, strengthening, rather than subverting, the institutions of the country, and maintaining that balance between the various parts of our constitutional system ... the consequence of which has been a progressive improvement in our legislation according with the temper and character of the times.'[103]

During the recess of 1866–67, Derby led his ministerial colleagues towards proposing the parliamentary Reform Bill, establishing a rated household suffrage in the boroughs and a £15 annual rental qualification in the counties. In its final amended form (the county qualification, for example, being reduced to £12), the Reform Act passed in August 1867, creating over 930,000 new voters in England and Wales, and increasing the electorate by 88 per cent. Liberal opponents characterised this as a product of Disraeli's cynical dexterity in appropriating their own principles. Certainly, between March and July 1867, Disraeli had skilfully dissected the Liberal opposition. But the 1867 Reform Act was, in a broader sense,

103 Hansard, HL deb., 9 July 1866, vol. 174, col. 744.

the natural outcome of Derby's desire to affirm the Conservatives as a responsible party, deserving the confidence of the nation.

In a speech at the Free Trade Hall in Manchester in October 1867, Derby declared that the morality of the working classes had persuaded him that 'boldness was safety' and that the rate-paying household suffrage in the boroughs was a sure definition of urban respectability.[104] By rewarding the moral virtues of the working man with the vote, his government had strengthened that mutual respect and essential trust cementing the nation's loyalty to its institutions. A cordial union had been preserved between labour and capital – that harmony between employers of labour and the employed previously threatened by radical agitation and divisive Liberal rhetoric. Moreover, it was a settlement of the complex parliamentary reform question that had proved beyond the capacity of the Liberal Party – their claim to the sole possession of progressive wisdom thereby being refuted.

The complement to Derby's rehabilitation of the Conservatives as a responsible party of government, while in office, was his containment, while in opposition, of the extreme opinions of his ultras. He distanced himself, for example, from the visceral anti-Catholicism of MPs such as Charles Newdegate. Defence of the established Church, he maintained, was distinct from anti-Catholic bigotry. The anti-Catholic national club, largely Conservative in membership, he regarded as 'a mischievous body whose extreme pretensions and views must not be encouraged'. This was to be achieved 'by the negative means of avoiding in debate, or in meetings of the party', language that 'may unnecessarily *frossier* their … views'.[105] Better, he believed, to avoid raising such disruptive cries, so as to allow divisions within Whig, Liberal and radical ranks to come to the fore, in the absence of Conservative initiatives providing their opponents with common ground. Derby described this opposition strategy as 'masterly inactivity', 'armed neutrality' or 'killing with kindness'. As he instructed Disraeli in April 1857: 'To foment divisions and jealousies between

104 *The Times*, 18 October 1867, p. 10.

105 Derby to Disraeli, 14 November 1853 (Derby Mss 182/1, Liverpool City Archives).

the discordant elements of the government, majority must be our first object; while we should carefully avoid multiplying occasions for their voting in concert in opposition to motions brought forward by us.'[106]

Amid reports in June 1860 of an imminent breaking up of Palmerston's Cabinet, Derby declared: 'We ought to adhere, as far as possible, to our policy of making every *obstructive* motion come from the Liberal side of the House.'[107] Tellingly, in 1851, 1855 and 1858, it was radical motions that prompted Whigs and Liberals to resign from office. In 1852 and 1866, Liberal governments were dismissed by Commons motions moved by those on the Whig and Liberal benches. This affirmed Derby's belief in the deep divisions inherent among his opponents. It also gave plausibility to his hopes of eventual party realignment.

Passivity in opposition was a difficult strategy to maintain while keeping the party together. Back-bench frustration or disillusionment could sour party morale. Distrust of Disraeli often proved a convenient lightning rod, diverting flashes of dissatisfaction away from Derby himself. Yet, at other times, it could trigger complaints about Derby's inactivity, seeming disinterest or incapacity because of illness. But, repeatedly – for example, in January 1852, April 1853, January 1854, February 1855, February 1857, June 1859 and March 1866 – Derby's direct appeals to the parliamentary party elicited enthusiastic support and immediately restored Conservative resolve. Despite heading the Conservative Party for twenty-two years, Derby never faced a serious challenge to his leadership. His patrician embodiment of mid-Victorian Conservative sensibilities gave him an undisputed authority. Hardly any Conservative leaders have retired at moments of their own choosing. Many have been pushed; far fewer have jumped. Derby is a member of the latter select group.

In March 1867, severe illness forced Derby to pass effective leadership of the government over to Disraeli. During July, Derby rallied himself to take the Conservative Reform Bill through the Lords. This exertion immediately

106 Derby to Disraeli, 24 April 1857 (Hughenden Mss B/XX/S/148, Bodleian Library, Oxford).

107 Derby to Pakington, 28 May 1860 (Derby Mss 188/2, Liverpool City Archives).

forced him back to his sick bed. In February 1868, a frail Derby resigned the premiership, and Disraeli succeeded him. Until his death at Knowsley in October 1869, Derby became a venerated, if somewhat spectral, presence hovering over Disraeli's shoulder. Derby spoke in the Lords for the last time in June 1869, opposing Gladstone's bill disestablishing the Church of Ireland. It was legislation, Derby declared, in which political folly was only matched by moral injustice. On leaving the chamber and passing by Lord Cairns, he tersely remarked: 'I have nothing left but to go away.'[108]

After his death, Derby rapidly became seen as the gifted aristocratic adornment of a past political age. The 'popular' politics of the 1870s, in the wake of the 1867 Reform Acts, proved a very different political world from that familiar to Derby. As Walter Bagehot observed in the introduction to his 1872 edition of *The English Constitution*: 'The change since 1865 is not a change in one point, but in a thousand points; it is a change not of particular details, but of pervading spirit.'[109] Derby was the last of those whom Bagehot called 'the pre-1832 statesmen' (the others being Palmerston and Russell) to hold power.

As the product of an earlier generation, Derby's abilities and temperament did not match those qualities required of party leadership from the 1870s. As convention decreed, as a peer in the Lords, he did not engage in popular extra-parliamentary speeches or campaigning. He possessed, his elder son noted, 'a strong dislike of being made the object of public curiosity'.[110] Beyond Westminster and St James's, it was royal visits, agricultural shows, museum openings and Conservative Party banquets that were the occasion of Derby speaking directly to the local community. Gladstone's election campaign in South West Lancashire in November 1868, when he delivered six open-air speeches over three days, Derby regarded as 'balderdash and

108 Granville to Queen Victoria, 22 July 1869, in: G. E. Buckle ed., *The Letters of Queen Victoria, Second Series, Vol. 1*, London, John Murray, 1926, p. 621.

109 Walter Bagehot, 'Introduction to the Second Edition 1872', in Paul Smith ed., *The English Constitution*, Cambridge, Cambridge University Press, 2001, pp. 194–5.

110 John Vincent ed., *Disraeli, Derby and the Conservative Party: The Political Journals of Lord Stanley, 1849–1869*, Sussex, Harvester Press, 1978, p. 48.

braggadocio'.[111] Yet, by the 1870s and 1880s, public campaigning was seen as a necessary requisite of effective party leadership. Following Gladstone addressing an audience of 25,000 at Greenwich in 1871, Bagehot wrote that 'it will be one of the most important qualifications of a Prime Minister to exert a direct control over the masses'.[112] Derby remained an essentially Westminster politician. He expended little effort in cultivating the press, despite the expansion of political journalism from the 1850s. To the suggestion, shortly before he died, that the Conservatives raise a subscription to purchase *The Globe* his response was blunt: 'I cannot conceal from you that, in my opinion, even in a political sense, there is no more unsatisfactory mode of spending money than the purchase of a second-class newspaper.'[113] He never acknowledged the growing power of the press, and this disdain was reciprocated by journalists, giving further encouragement to the neglect of Derby by posterity.

From the 1870s, middle-class politicians such as Gladstone and Disraeli became public celebrities, personifying the titanic popular clash between Liberals and Conservatives. Peers such as Lord Hartington and Lord Salisbury, and sons of the peerage such as Lord Randolph Churchill, from the 1870s addressed public audiences enlisting popular support. The political parties established centralised national organisations recruiting a mass membership. Professional party agents became active in the constituencies, replacing amateur, part-time, local solicitors. The introduction of voting by ballot in parliamentary elections in 1872 ended the public declaration of votes. Parties in Parliament became more rigidly aligned, disciplined blocs of votes. Enacting legislation became seen as a primary purpose of Parliament. As a result, the sovereignty of Parliament, central to the notion of parliamentary government prevalent from the 1830s to the 1860s, was gradually supplanted

111 Derby to Disraeli, 22 November 1868 (Hughenden Mss B/XX/S/505, Bodleian Library, Oxford).

112 Walter Bagehot, 'Mr Gladstone and the People', in N. St John-Stevas ed., *Bagehot's Historical Essays*, London, 1971, p. 268.

113 Derby to Colville, 12 September 1869 (Derby Mss 197/2, Liverpool City Archives).

by a notion of electoral sovereignty. The concept of the 'electoral mandate' was recognised by the 1880s. General elections – rather than party dynamics within the Commons – made and unmade governments. This was a political world far removed from that inhabited by Derby – one he would have undoubtedly regarded with patrician disdain.

Derby offered little inspiration to later generations of Conservatives. No multi-volume 'tombstone' biography was produced, such as that written for Disraeli by W. F. Monypenny and G. E. Buckle. Disraeli's memory and aphorisms were readily evoked by later Conservatives – initially Lord Randolph Churchill, creating, what he called, 'Tory democracy'. In 1924, Stanley Baldwin added the term 'one-nation' Conservativism to the party lexicon.[114] During the twentieth century, historians burnished the memory of Peel. Despite Peel twice 'reneging' on his party (over Catholic emancipation in 1829 and the Corn Law repeal in 1846), he became, for Norman Gash, 'the founder of modern Conservatism'. From the 1970s, the memory of Lord Salisbury offered some historians and politicians – deeply sceptical of liberal truisms and progressive pieties – the ideal of an authentic, acerbic Conservative intelligence.[115] But remembering Derby failed to excite the aspirations of his successors.

As a result, the historiography of mid-Victorian Conservatism has been largely written through the eyes of Disraeli – the view from Hughenden, rather than from Knowsley Hall. From that perspective, Disraeli's genius was suppressed by the dead weight of Derby's apathy and uninterest. Only after Derby's death was the alchemy of Disraeli's rhetoric able to turn the base metal of social reform into the gold of party triumph, and convert the formerly alien coin of imperialism into a powerful, patriotic sense of national destiny. This concealed the extent to which Disraeli's often precarious Commons leadership was critically dependent upon Derby's endorsement. It also

114 Disraeli never used the term 'one-nation' Conservatism, but did, of course, write in his 1844 novel *Sybil* of England being divided into 'two nations' that knew nothing of each other – a social chasm that needed to be healed.

115 In 1978, the historian Maurice Cowling, the philosopher Roger Scruton, and others formed the Salisbury Group. See: Maurice Cowling ed., *Conservative Essays*, London, Cassell, 1978. The *Salisbury Review* launched in 1982.

obscured the intelligence and commitment informing Derby's command of the party and Conservative policy from 1846 to 1868.

An assessment of Derby's achievement as Conservative leader, released from Disraelian myth, restores an understanding of a critical and difficult period in the party's history. Under his leadership, the Conservatives never won a majority in the Commons, and all three of his governments suffered from being minority ministries. As a peer leading the party from the Lords, he did not address those extra-parliamentary audiences Palmerston and Gladstone spoke to from the 1850s. The political press he regarded with disdain. In 1846, he hesitantly agreed to lead an aggrieved minority party committed to a policy – protection – but it proved a political liability. Yet he personified a patrician Conservatism, possessing an innate wariness of strident jingoism, an allergic sensitivity to divisive ideology, and an overriding sense that the nation wished to be at ease with measured progress.

Derby's major achievement was to gradually rehabilitate the Conservatives as a party capable of moderate and responsible government. From being seen as an enraged body of atavistic rural protest, he slowly restored the party to a credible custodian of judicious progress. This enabled the party to survive, and gave it a future. Here, his early Whig political education – under the 12th Earl of Derby (his grandfather) and the 3rd Marquess of Lansdowne – was key. A disposition to preserve and an ability to improve, he believed, were the hallmark of successful statesmanship. He also held a lifelong conviction that political power rested on an association of mutual trust and confidence between backbenchers and party leaders in Parliament. Shepherding, not driving or defying, party opinion was the requirement of effective leadership. Unlike Peel or Disraeli, Derby never succumbed to contempt for his followers. In 1867, with characteristic audacity, Disraeli claimed to have 'educated' the Conservative Party. But it was Derby who bequeathed his successors a party seen as capable of moderate government – rescued from blinkered reaction and embittered rural nostalgia.

CHAPTER 6

BENJAMIN DISRAELI

ROBERT SAUNDERS

Disraeli's leadership operated during an era when, as Robert Saunders points out, governments continued to be made and unmade more frequently on the floor of the Commons than via the electorate. His astute management of the Conservative parliamentary party was consequently particularly significant. His electoral record is more mixed, with defeats in 1868 – months after gaining the leadership – and 1880 – in economic circumstances, Saunders argues, that were partially of his own making. That said, his second election as leader, in 1874, saw the Conservatives achieve their first outright victory since 1841. This was due to a popular, national appeal that embraced, rather than cowered away from, an electorate expanded by the Reform Act he skilfully shepherded through Parliament in 1867. His belief in the plausibility of a cross-class Toryism that occupied the centre ground means his leadership is now seen as particularly influential in providing a mould for future Conservative electoral success.

• • •

Benjamin Disraeli was the most unlikely leader the Conservative Party ever produced. He was a Jew, a dandy, a scoundrel; and a failed poet, who squandered a fortune in South America and entered Parliament to escape his creditors. He slept with aristocratic women while defrauding their husbands, got drunk with Turkish soldiers, and plotted in Paris with the King of France. It was a life of sex, drugs and Roquefort – a literary fantasy played out at the highest levels of

British politics. A self-proclaimed 'adventurer', Disraeli was not by race, temperament nor character in the conventional mould of Conservative leadership. Yet he never doubted his vocation for power or his destiny to govern the affairs of men.[116]

Disraeli had strong views on leadership, which he expressed in a series of caustic judgements on his contemporaries. Lord Liverpool was 'the arch mediocrity', entirely lacking in 'the happy properties of a leader'.[117] Sir Robert Peel was 'a burglar of others' intellect', able to 'give to his friends no guiding principle, for he had none'.[118] Lord Derby knew 'nothing of the management of men', while Lord Palmerston was an 'old painted pantaloon', whose 'false teeth ... would fall out of his mouth when speaking, if he did not hesitate and halt so in his talk'.[119] The leaders Disraeli admired were men of destiny: patriot kings, like Richard the Lionheart; or the Machiavellian figure of Prince Klemens von Metternich, who governed half of Europe from Vienna, and whose portrait hung on Disraeli's wall.

Disraeli led his party in the House of Commons from 1851 to 1868, and served either as Prime Minister or Leader of the Opposition from 1868 to 1881. In 1874, he steered the Conservative Party to its first general election victory since 1841, ending the wilderness years of Lord Derby's lethargic and ineffectual leadership. Yet his importance as a leader does not rest principally on his electoral success – a test that, for this period, would be distinctly anachronistic. Nor does it depend on his legislative record, despite the Second Reform Act and the social reforms of the 1870s. Disraeli's importance lies rather in a new vision of political leadership – a popular Toryism that would endure long after his death. As a novelist, Disraeli was

116 The terms 'Conservative' and 'Tory' had slightly different inflections in this period. Disraeli preferred to describe himself as a 'Tory', but, as both terms were applied to the party he led, I use them here interchangeably.

117 Benjamin Disraeli, *Coningsby; or The New Generation, Vol. II*, London, Dunne, 1844.

118 Hansard, HC deb., 15 May 1846, vol. 86, col. 675; also 'The Character of Sir Robert Peel', in Benjamin Disraeli, *Lord George Bentinck: A Political Biography*, London, Constable, 1905, p. 201.

119 Robert Saunders, *Democracy and the Vote in British Politics, 1848–1867: The Making of the Second Reform Act*, Farnham, Ashgate, 2011, p. 197; Robert Blake, *Disraeli*, New York, St Martin's Press, 1967, p. 363.

peculiarly alert to the narratives that shape political alignment, and he set out to reimagine his party not as a narrow and suspicious elite, but as 'the national party of England'.[120] It was Disraeli who taught Conservatism to be comfortable with popular politics, laying the foundations for a democratic Toryism that would shape the politics of the twentieth century.

'WITH WORDS WE GOVERN MEN': THE POET IN POLITICS

Disraeli was born in 1804, the son of a Jewish writer and historian. He was circumcised as a child and attended synagogue with his family. Practising Jews were barred from the House of Commons until 1858, but, when Disraeli was thirteen, his father fell out with the Jewish authorities and had his children baptised into the Church of England. The teenage Disraeli found himself, rather unexpectedly, a member of the established Church, though it has never been very clear what he privately believed.

Disraeli was convinced from childhood that he was destined for greatness, but it was not, at first, political eminence to which his ambitions were directed. His youthful hero was Lord Byron, the poetic genius. At the age of thirty, Disraeli published his own volume of poetry, *The Revolutionary Epick*, which he hoped would establish him as the inheritor of Byron's mantle. In the preface, he explained that each age of man produced a single genius, who gave tongue to the spirit of the age. It was a role that had been fulfilled in the past by Homer, Virgil, Dante and Milton; but the modern age – the revolutionary age – had not yet found its representative genius. Disraeli offered himself, in what he modestly described as a spirit of 'sincere humility'.[121]

The Revolutionary Epick was not a critical triumph. In more than 3,000 lines of verse, one reviewer commented that 'there is not one' that 'deserves the name of poetry', and that its chief service to letters was probably the fact

120 Saunders, op. cit., p. 70.

121 Benjamin Disraeli, *The Revolutionary Epick*, London, E. Moxon, 1834, p. iv.

it extinguished Disraeli's poetic ambitions for ever.[122] Nonetheless, with its emphasis on the supremacy of the imagination, the poem articulated an idea that would become central to Disraeli's conception of leadership:

> *Fling to the heady wind*
> *The tattered scroll of cold philosophy,*
> *That vaunts of human REASON: nobler far*
> *The faculty divine mankind impels,*
> *IMAGINATION on her airy throne*
> *Of Iris-painted clouds ...*
> *... Thus, in human life,*
> *Upon the mass the man of genius breathes*
> *His spell creative, thus their swelling hearts*
> *Rise to his charm!*[123]

This was to become the governing principle of Disraeli's politics. The truly great leader, in Disraeli's view, was not the Victorian 'man of business' – governing, like Peel, 'from behind a desk' – but 'the man of genius', who worked his 'spell creative' upon 'the mass'.[124] This was 'charismatic leadership' *avant la lettre* – a quasi-religious model of leadership that appealed to men's hearts rather than to calculated self-interest. As Disraeli put it, in a passage attributed to the angel of Arabia in his novel *Tancred*: 'Power is neither the sword nor the shield, for these pass away; but ideas, which are divine.'[125]

It was this, in Disraeli's view, that explained the chaotic politics of the 1830s and 1840s. Like his near contemporary Thomas Carlyle, Disraeli thought that the politicians of his own day had lost their vocation to lead, creating a vacuum that was filled by popular demagogues. 'Man', he wrote, 'is made to adore and to obey; but if you will not command him; if you give him nothing

---

122 'Mr Disraeli and his *Revolutionary Epic*', *The Spectator*, 21 May 1864, p. 9.

123 Disraeli, op. cit., 1834, pp. 73–4.

124 Norman Gash, *Mr Secretary Peel: The Life of Sir Robert Peel to 1830*, London, Faber, 1961, p. 4.

125 Benjamin Disraeli, *Tancred; or, The New Crusade, Book IV*, London, H. Colborn, 1847.

to worship; he will fashion his own divinities, and find a chieftain in his own passions.'[126] During the Chartist outbreak of the 1840s, when millions demonstrated for universal suffrage and democratic reform, Disraeli turned the blame onto his own back benches. He asked:

> Why are the people of England forced to find leaders among these persons? The proper leaders of the people are the gentlemen of England. If they are not the leaders of the people, I do not see why there should be gentlemen ... [You] must blame yourselves alone if you have allowed the power that has been entrusted to you by the constitution to slip from your hands.[127]

For Disraeli, what the Chartists wanted was not democracy but leadership. As a Chartist orator in one of his novels proclaims: 'If I saw a Simon de Montfort again I should be content to fight under his banner.'[128] For Disraeli, the great institutions of Church, monarchy and aristocracy were not brakes on popular power to be defended against a turbulent and volatile mass; they were popular institutions, which had only to appeal to the imagination of the people to stand on a firm foundation.

In this respect, Disraeli was the first great Tory populist. He believed neither in democracy nor in the 'pernicious doctrine' of 'natural equality' – the masses were to be *led*, not *followed*.[129] But he was confident that the great institutions of Tory England – the Church, the crown and the House of Lords – could capture the imagination and command the affections of the people, if they only had the wit to try. This was as much a matter of rhetoric as of policy: 'With words', he wrote, 'we govern men.'[130] His was a politics of theatre: of great speeches and extravagant gestures that would capture the imagination of the age. First, however, he had to attain power, in a party that viewed him with suspicion.

---

126 Benjamin Disraeli, *Coningsby; or The New Generation, Vol. IV*, London, Dunne, 1844, Chapter 13.

127 Hansard, HC deb., 20 June 1848, vol. 99, col. 964.

128 Benjamin Disraeli, *Sybil, or The Two Nations, Book IV*, London, H. Colborn, 1845.

129 Disraeli, op. cit., 1905, p. 323.

130 Vincent, op. cit., 1978, p. 46.

CLIMBING THE GREASY POLE

Disraeli entered the House of Commons in 1837, during the long ascendancy of Sir Robert Peel. The personal antipathy between the two men can sometimes disguise the extent to which they articulated different visions of Conservatism. Peel was a child of the French Revolution. The events of 1789 and their bloody aftermath became the consuming obsession of his life, and he built up one of the largest collections in England of French revolutionary literature. His formative ministerial years were spent in Ireland – always the most troubled part of the United Kingdom – and this combination of French and Irish precedents gave him a lasting horror of mob politics. Peel presented the reforms of the 1840s, with new taxes on the rich funding reductions in the duties on food, almost as a ransom payment – 'a cheap purchase of future security' – that would distract the attention of the masses from Westminster.[131] His goal, as he put it in 1846, was to anaesthetise popular politics, so that 'thoughts of the dissolution of our institutions should be forgotten in the midst of physical enjoyment'.[132]

This could hardly have been further from Disraeli's brand of popular Toryism. When Peel denied him ministerial office, Disraeli reinvented himself as Peel's tormentor-in-chief. He hounded his leader over the reduction of protection, the grant to the Catholic seminary in Maynooth, and – above all – the repeal of the Corn Laws, which triggered Peel's fall in 1846.

The break-up of the Tory Party in 1846 transformed Disraeli's prospects.[133] The former Prime Minister carried with him into exile almost all his senior Cabinet colleagues and most of the rising stars of the party.

---

131 Martin Daunton, *Trusting Leviathan: The Politics of Taxation in Britain, 1799–1914*, Cambridge, Cambridge University Press, 2001, pp. 80–81.

132 Hansard, HC deb., 22 January 1846, vol. 83, col. 95.

133 It also set the course of his relations with Peel's disciple William Gladstone. Having vacated his seat in 1845, Gladstone could only look on helplessly – like a young Obi-Wan Kenobi – as his master was cut down before his eyes.

Lord Derby assumed the leadership in the House of Lords, but the rump that remained in the Commons was so embarrassingly denuded of talent that it had little choice but to lean on Disraeli, as the last man standing who could go toe to toe with the Liberal front bench.

Nonetheless, it was not until 1851 that Disraeli was formally entrusted with the leadership in the Commons. From 1846 to 1848, he served under Lord George Bentinck – an orator of such limited ability that he considered hiring a barrister to speak in Parliament on his behalf. After Bentinck's resignation in 1848, Disraeli was installed in a joint leadership with John Charles Herries and the Marquess of Granby, an arrangement intended – as one observer commented – to place him 'like a sandwich between two pieces of bread ... in order that he might be made fit for squeamish throats to swallow'.[134] The arrangement was formally dissolved in 1851, yet Disraeli remained for the next two decades a leader on sufferance. His party accepted him because they could not function without him, but that would change if a viable alternative could be lured from the ranks of the Liberals. As a result, Disraeli's hold on the leadership was always precarious. His survival would require careful management of his troops and visible success in the House of Commons.

All this made Disraeli much more reliant on his party than was common in the nineteenth century. Unlike Gladstone or Palmerston or Derby (all of whom crossed the floor at some stage in their career), Disraeli did not have the financial independence, the aristocratic credentials or the personal following to prosper as an independent agent. If he wanted to exercise the power for which he considered himself destined, he needed to retain the support of the Conservative Party; but if he wished to lead that party into government, he had to broaden its electoral appeal. The tension between those impulses – one requiring him to cosset and reassure his followers, the other to challenge their prejudices and preconceptions – provided the dynamic for the rest of his career.

134 Monypenny and Buckle, op. cit., p. 139.

EDUCATING HIS PARTY

In the mid-nineteenth century, the success of a party leader was not measured principally in election results. Governments were made and unmade, not at elections, but on the floor of the House of Commons. Elections might refresh the materials from which the House was composed, but they were not yet the great tests of rival administrations that they later became. Between the First and Second Reform Acts, in 1832 and 1867, there were eleven changes of government, of which only one – the formation of Peel's second government in 1841 – followed directly from success at a general election. Not until the 1870s did it become customary for a party leader to campaign outside his own constituency; when Gladstone did so in 1866, he was accused by one of his own backbenchers of being an 'influence of terrorism'.[135]

In this context, leadership focused more on the management of forces within Parliament than on the construction of majorities outside it. This was a particularly difficult task in the decade after 1846, when party alignment was still disarranged by the break-up over the Corn Laws. Disraeli prided himself on his management of men, spending long hours meeting with backbenchers, flattering their vanities and assuaging their concerns. He liked to boast that *he* could have repealed the Corn Laws without splitting his party, though it is more likely that he would have sought a compromise more palatable to his supporters. As Chancellor of the Exchequer, his Budgets were political rather than strictly financial, constructed as much with an ear to the House as with an eye to the national balance sheet.

As Leader of the House of Commons during the minority governments of 1852, 1858–59 and 1866–68, Disraeli had to hold together a fractious Tory alliance, keep the opposition divided, and try to scrape together votes from independents and disaffected Liberals. He was intensely frustrated by Lord Derby's reluctance to assist in this endeavour, complaining that his leader

135 Hansard, HC deb., 26 April 1866, vol. 182, col. 2090.

knew 'nothing of the management of men'.[136] Unlike Derby, Disraeli was not temperamentally inclined to 'masterly inactivity'; nor did he mistake a lethargic acquiescence in opposition for playing the long game.

Disraeli was aware, however, that the Conservatives' exile from government could not be ended simply by manoeuvring in the political salons. In the aftermath of the Great Reform Act, they simply lacked the electoral base to be more than an occasional placeholder in office, holding the fort while the Liberal Party resolved its own internal divisions. By opposing the Reform Act, and then resisting the repeal of the Corn Laws, the Tories had allowed themselves to be marginalised as the party of a splenetic agricultural rump. If they were to do more than simply punctuate a run of Liberal administrations, they needed to 'lay the foundation of a national party' – requiring changes in both policy and presentation.[137]

The first task was to release the party from the millstone that had hung around its neck since 1846: its allegiance to agricultural protection. Talk of reintroducing the Corn Laws was electorally toxic, as successive defeats in 1847 and 1852 made clear. As Disraeli told a colleague in 1853: 'We must have our eyes opened at last to the futility of attempting to govern this country by merely the landed interest, and not even by its complete power.'[138] The Tories, he observed caustically, had 'stuck to protection 'til the country positively spat upon it', and the time had come to acknowledge political reality.[139] This process of political detoxification would require delicate handling. For many Tories, restoring protection was the fundamental purpose of Tory politics, and it was the repeal of the Corn Laws that had brought Disraeli himself to the leadership. Rather than abandon the policy outright, Disraeli sought to reframe the question by demanding 'compensations' for the agricultural interest in other parts of the tax system. Not until his second Budget was

---

136 Saunders, op. cit., p. 197.

137 Disraeli to Lord Malmesbury, 26 January 1853, in Michael Pharand et al. eds, *Letters of Benjamin Disraeli*, Toronto, University of Toronto Press, 1982, Vol. 9, Letter 2480, p. 463.

138 Saunders, op. cit., p. 94.

139 Disraeli to Lord Henry Lennox, 18 July 1852, in Pharand et al., op. cit., Vol. 6, Letter 2335, p. 93.

defeated, in December 1852, did he positively abjure protection. This drew a stern rebuke from Derby, but it was essential in clearing the party of an electoral incubus.

The larger task, however, was to restore the reputation of Conservatism as a national and progressive force. Ever alert to the power of symbols, Disraeli urged the party's rising star, Lord Stanley, to contest a great commercial seat like Manchester or the City of London. Victory in such a seat, he observed, would be 'a public and national announcement that the *old* Whig monopoly of Liberalism is *obsolete*' and would be worth more than 'ten small [boroughs]'. He proposed to Derby an ambitious scheme of administrative reform, modelled on Edmund Burke's plans in the 1780s. He was keen, too, to moderate his party's language, warning his constituents that they should never adopt 'the unfavourable position' of seeming 'opposed to all change'.[140]

For Disraeli, however, the key lay in the reform of Parliament. Ever since the Great Reform Act in 1832, reform had been viewed as a Whig or Liberal possession. The practical effects of the measure had been less destructive to the Tories than the political narrative it inspired: the perception that the Liberals were the party of reform while the Tories were fearful of popular politics. A second Liberal reform act, he foresaw, would entrench that idea; and, for this reason, he always resisted suggestions that the party cooperate in passing a moderate Liberal measure. By contrast, a *Tory* reform bill would break the association between Liberalism and popular politics, allowing the Conservatives to recast themselves as the friends of the people.

His opportunity came in 1866, when the Liberal government of Lord Russell and William Gladstone collapsed over the latest in a series of failed reform bills. Derby returned to the premiership at the head of a minority government, with Disraeli as Chancellor and Leader of the House of Commons. Derby concurred in the decision to table a new reform bill, but with the Prime Minister becalmed in the House of Lords and a martyr to gout, it

140 Saunders, op. cit., p. 107.

fell to Disraeli to shape the bill in its passage through the Commons. This was no easy task: over the previous thirty years, reform had established itself as the Bermuda Triangle of British politics, sinking every government that attempted passage. Ministerial reform bills had failed in 1852, 1854, 1859, 1860 and 1866, while numerous back-bench proposals sank beneath the waterline. The Tories, in 1867, were gravely outnumbered, and their previous attempt at reform, during the minority government of 1858–59, had succeeded only in reuniting the Liberal opposition.[141]

The ensuing crisis encapsulated all Disraeli's talents of party management. By opening up the bill to amendments from across the floor, he divided the Liberal opposition and played different factions off against one another. Gladstone complained, with some justice, that Disraeli seemed scarcely to mind what manner of measure was passed, so long as it was carried by a Conservative government. 'Disembarrassed of all political conviction', he wrote caustically, the Conservative leaders 'cared little more what were the clauses of their bill, than the porter at a railway station cares what may be the contents of the portmanteau on his shoulder'. Gathorne Hardy, one of Disraeli's Cabinet colleagues, worried likewise that his leader was 'always looking for what will suit others', rather than 'what is sound in itself'. Hardy thought this a 'fault', but as a method of carrying contentious legislation, it proved dazzlingly successful. Only four Tories voted against the second reading of the bill, and the third reading was sent to the Upper House without even the formality of a division.[142]

For Disraeli, the significance of the Reform Bill lay less in its consequences for the electoral system than in the message it sent about the Conservative Party. It was the ultimate act of political rebranding: a public declaration that the Tories were a popular and national party, not afraid to appeal to a mass electorate. Disraeli boasted to a friend, shortly before the crucial vote, that he had 'achieved the dream of my

---

141 For the history of reform since 1848, see Saunders, op. cit.

142 Ibid., pp. 266, 273.

life' – 're-establishing Toryism on a national foundation'. As he modestly observed in the autumn, he had 'educated' his party in the ways of popular government, with the result that 'the Tory Party has resumed its natural functions in the government' – for 'what is the Tory Party unless it represents national feeling? If it does not represent national feeling, Toryism is nothing.'[143]

AT THE TOP OF THE GREASY POLE

Disraeli's triumphant management of the reform crisis secured him the full leadership of the party after Derby's retirement in 1868 – something that had been far from certain in the three or four years previously. His first premiership lasted only a matter of months, as the Liberals – with reform now settled – reunited under the leadership of William Gladstone. At the following election in 1874, however, Disraeli led the Conservative Party to its first majority since 1841. The reform gamble had paid off, the new electorate bringing to an end the long electoral exile of the Derby years.[144]

Disraeli became Prime Minister for a second time in 1874, this time at the head of a stable majority. At sixty-nine years of age, with his health failing, Disraeli was not an especially active premier. He slept through meetings of the Cabinet and, after the death of his wife in 1872, spent much of his time writing infatuated letters to younger women. Richard Cross, who became Home Secretary in the new administration, was astonished to discover how little thought had been given to the government's legislative agenda, with the result that there was some difficulty

143 Ibid., pp. 276–8.

144 Despite the deserved upturn in Derby's reputation, it is worth noting that both his predecessor Sir Robert Peel and his successor Benjamin Disraeli spent more time in office in a single sitting than he managed over a period of twenty years. No other Conservative between the Duke of Wellington and William Hague has led the party into a general election without ever winning a majority.

in composing the Queen's Speech. Cross had 'quite expected that [Disraeli's] mind was full of legislative schemes', 'but such', alas, 'did not prove to be the case'.[145]

Nonetheless, Disraeli's second government was to leave behind a substantial body of legislation. While this owed much to the energy of his ministers, Disraeli could plausibly claim to have set the strategic direction for the administration during his years in opposition. With the Liberal Party abandoning the centre ground, under the energetic and controversial leadership of William Gladstone, a new political space was opening up for a party of constitutional defence and moderate, pragmatic reform. In a series of speeches as Leader of the Opposition, Disraeli had identified three key principles on which to found the new Conservatism. The first was the maintenance of 'the English constitution': the defence of Church, the crown and the House of Lords against Gladstone's allegedly menacing intentions. The second was 'the condition of the people', especially 'the labouring classes', through careful attention to 'the health of the people'. The third principle was the defence of Britain's imperial power against the alleged neglect and incompetence of Liberal ministers.[146]

This was not, by any means, a novel body of ideas. Social reform had been a cross-party concern since at least the 1840s, and neither the empire nor the constitution was under any serious parliamentary attack. What was new was Disraeli's willingness to bind these themes together into a vision of popular Conservatism, packaged to appeal to a mass electorate. Disraeli was by no means the first politician to take pride in Britain's global power; but he was the first to make the empire expressly partisan, wrapping himself and his party in the flag of imperial patriotism. Social reform may have been principally of value as a distraction from the more radical reforms of the Gladstonian Liberal Party ('We came in', Disraeli noted, 'on the principle of not harassing the country'), but it also played

145 Paul Smith, *Disraeli: A Brief Life*, Cambridge, Cambridge University Press, 1996, p. 175.

146 'Mr Disraeli at the Free Trade Hall', *Manchester Guardian*, 4 April 1872.

to the image of the Conservatives as the 'national party', legislating in the interests of all classes.[147]

This vision set the direction for the government of 1874–80. The heroic reforms of the Gladstone administration gave way to smaller, more cautious measures of social reform: the Artisans' Dwelling Act, the Public Health Act, the Sale of Food and Drugs Act, the Factory Act, the Education Act, and the Employers and Workmen Act (which laid the foundations of modern trade union law). With the exception of the latter measure, the practical importance of these bills should not be overstated. Most were merely permissive, granting powers to local authorities – which most chose not to exercise. The attraction of a 'policy of sewage' was partly its capacity to sideline more contentious issues of constitutional reform, affecting the Irish Church, the rights of property or the organisation of the tax system. Nonetheless, it left behind a body of useful reforms, while buttressing the claims of the Conservative Party to govern in the national interest.

Imperial policy provided a more attractive field for one of Disraeli's temperament. Though he never visited any of the major colonies, the empire appealed to his love of colour, dash and popular spectacle. The first half of his premiership saw a series of grand, imperial gestures: the purchase of the Suez Canal shares; the proclamation of Victoria as Empress of India; and the 'Imperial Durbar' of 1877. Disraeli's brinkmanship with Russia in 1875–76 – sending the fleet to Constantinople to defend the Turkish Empire – fired the starting pistol on popular 'jingoism', with music-hall crowds singing: 'We don't want to fight, but, by jingo, if we do, we've got the guns, we've got the boats, we've got the money too!' The result, in the short term, was a diplomatic triumph at the Congress of Berlin in 1878. The German Chancellor Otto von Bismarck was mightily impressed: '*Der alte Jude*,' he proclaimed; '*Das ist der Mann!*'[148]

Yet imperial policy was a double-edged sword. Compelled to raise taxes

147 Smith, op. cit., 1996, p. 175.

148 Blake, op. cit., 1967, p. 646.

to fund imperial wars he had never wanted, Disraeli left himself vulnerable to the financial and moral assault launched by Gladstone in the Midlothian campaign. An economic recession weakened his position further still, and the government suffered a landslide defeat in the election of 1880. 'We can but die like gentlemen,' Disraeli reflected, before doing precisely that the following year.[149]

CONCLUSION

After the failure of *The Revolutionary Epick*, Disraeli wisely confined his poetic ambitions to a series of love poems, written each year on the anniversary of his marriage. In one of these odes, he reflected upon his life in Parliament, amid:

> *The blaze of factious senates ... where the prize*
> *Is power o'er the powerful, and to sway*
> *The race that sways the world.*[150]

Unlike most of his successors, Disraeli never pretended that his ambition was to serve. His pursuit of power was undisguised and unabashed; leadership, in his view, was a noble ambition and the natural reward of genius. From unpropitious beginnings, he led his party in the House of Commons for a quarter of a century, serving twice as Prime Minister. But how does he fare when measured against the criteria in this book?

Electoral success is a doubtful test for a Victorian statesman; only after the Second Reform Act in 1867 did the general election emerge as the crucible of British politics. Disraeli's record in this area was mixed: in 1874, he led the Conservatives to their first parliamentary majority since 1841;

149 Smith, op. cit., 1996, p. 209.

150 Ibid., p. 83.

but he was defeated in 1868, and again in 1880. His record as an election-winner was superior to Derby's and comparable to Peel's, though it would be comfortably exceeded by Lord Salisbury later in the century. Disraeli could, nonetheless, claim to have been ahead of his time in his understanding of electoral politics, appreciating the importance not just of good organisation, but of a compelling narrative that reached beyond an existing base.

Uniquely among the statesmen of his day, Disraeli owed his political position entirely to the support of his party. He proved a highly effective party manager, despite possessing none of the modern instruments of party discipline. He had little influence over the selection of party candidates, minimal control of party resources and was in charge of a party whose commitment to politics often lagged behind its enthusiasm for country sports. The 'apathy of the party' was a constant source of complaint: 'a sharp frost' in the hunting season, he noted caustically, 'would make a difference of twenty men'.[151] The challenge was to maintain the cohesion of the parliamentary party while expanding its appeal in the country – a test that brought Disraeli his most brilliant success in the passage of the Second Reform Act. This was both a triumph of party management and an act of political rebranding, giving the Conservatives their first great parliamentary victory since the days of Peel.

Disraeli governed in difficult times, though these were partly of his own making. It was Disraeli, as much as anyone, who had destroyed the party of Peel and driven it into the backwaters of agricultural protection. Yet it was Disraeli, too, who most clearly analysed the party's problem after 1846, and the need to find support beyond the agricultural interest. The Liberal alliance of the 1850s and 1860s – combining, as it did, the constitutional conservatism of Palmerston, the financial rectitude of Gladstone, and the radicalism of John Bright and Richard Cobden – left little political space for a popular Conservative alternative; but once Gladstone took the party into more turbulent waters after 1865, Disraeli was quick to reposition the Conservatives on the centre ground. A Conservatism that combined

---

151 Ibid., p. 110.

constitutional defence with imperial adventure and limited social reform had considerable potential, providing the template from which Salisbury would build in the 1880s and '90s.

For Disraeli, leadership was an end in itself, not simply a means to other goals. He was always more interested in the gladiatorial combat of politics than in the policies of the governments he led. Yet his conviction that the people really *could* be led, and that the future of Conservatism lay in its ability to win popular support, laid the foundations for a popular Toryism that would define the party for much of the twentieth century. The two phrases most commonly associated with Disraeli – 'one-nation Conservatism' and 'Tory democracy' – were never actually used by the man himself, but they captured something that was authentically Disraelian: a call to popular leadership and a conviction that Conservatism could reach across class boundaries. It was Disraeli's achievement, as he put it in 1870, to recognise that 'imagination in the government of nations' was 'a quality not less important than reason'.[152] No Conservative leader has shown a surer feel for the theatre of British politics, or exerted such a lasting hold on the popular imagination.

152 Ibid., p. 157.

CHAPTER 7

LORD SALISBURY

T. G. OTTE

Lord Salisbury was a long-serving and, Thomas Otte argues, extremely effectual leader of the Conservative Party. Fourteen of his twenty-one years as head of the party were spent as Prime Minister. His time as leader encompassed periods in opposition (1881–85 and 1892–95), but the Liberal Party never won an overall majority opposing Salisbury. This was due both to effective electoral strategies, particularly evident in the landslide victories of 1895 and 1900, but also an ability to adapt to his political and strategic environment. His 'negative' statecraft, Otte believes, played a significant role in sealing the rift in the Liberal Party, which, ultimately, saw Liberal Unionists join Salisbury's Conservatives in a coalition government. This meant he often showed acute skills of negotiation and tactical manoeuvrability. His active political mind waned as his time in office progressed, but his philosophical underpinnings of pragmatic opposition to fundamental reform found a legacy in twentieth-century Conservative statecraft.

• • •

Few political figures have been more overlooked and underestimated for longer than the 3rd Marquess of Salisbury, Robert Cecil. Few have been more successful leaders than he, if leadership is taken to mean articulating 'a sense of direction … projecting electoral appeal and putting together a winning coalition of effective support'.[153] It was little wonder that

153 P. F. Clarke, *A Question of Leadership: Gladstone to Thatcher*, London, Hamish Hamilton, 1991, p. 3.

Clement Attlee, who knew a thing or two about leadership, thought Salisbury the best Prime Minister in his lifetime.[154]

Lord Salisbury led the Conservative Party for twenty-one years and two months – at first, after 1881, in uneasy cohabitation, but from 1886 as sole leader. It made him the second longest-serving Tory leader, beaten only by the 14th Earl of Derby, but easily leaving his predecessor but one behind in the premiership stakes. Salisbury headed governments three times for a total of thirteen years and nine months. His electoral record was impressive, too. The narrow win in the 1886 general election was followed by landslides in 1895 and 1900. The 1892 election produced a draw, with the Liberals in office but without a majority, and only the 1885 contest was a clear defeat, though one that paved the way for victory the following year. Salisbury secured the long Tory ascendancy in the late Victorian period, and laid, at least in part, the foundations of the party's dominance in the twentieth century.

SALISBURY'S PHILOSOPHY

Salisbury, the politician, eludes easy labelling. An aristocrat 'with illustrious [Tory] forebears, [he] came from the class among which the Conservatives wanted but rarely managed to find their leaders'.[155] And yet, as already contemporary commentators noted, there was nothing of 'the bluff, quick-tempered, rosy-gilled country gentleman' about him.[156] This large, shambling man was a highly strung, near-neurotic intellectual, 'who slowly grew a shell of taciturn obliviousness as his protection against intrusion'.[157] His political and scientific essays, written under the cloak of

154 John Gardiner, *The Victorians: An Age in Retrospect*, London, Hambledon, 2006, p. 57. The neglect has now been redressed, albeit sometimes noisily, in: E. D. Steele, *Lord Salisbury: A Political Biography*, London, UCL Press, 1999; and Andrew Roberts, *Salisbury: Victorian Titan*, London, Weidenfeld & Nicolson, 1999.

155 P. Marsh, *The Discipline of Popular Government: Lord Salisbury's Domestic Statecraft, 1881–1902*, Aldershot, Gregg Revivals, 1993, p. 152.

156 F. D. How, *The Marquis of Salisbury*, London, Isbister, 1902, p. 3.

157 P. F. Clarke, op. cit., p. 44.

anonymity, and for money rather than to prove himself as a theoretician, testify to the range and depth of his intellectual interests. His social and political commentary, mostly dating from the 1860s, although not flawless, is remarkable for its unflinching cynicism and remorseless logic, free of any sentimental cant and moralising humbug.

Salisbury was one of the few intellectuals to lead a party that was 'weakest among the intellectual classes, as is natural'[158] – a party that only rarely let itself be led by such a type. Later twentieth-century attempts at defining various Tory 'isms' may fill a handful of history's footnotes, but no other Conservative leader has had serious works dedicated to his political thought and its intellectual milieu.[159] And yet, 'nearly all his opinions were wrong ... nearly everything he thought about his own times was proved wrong'.[160] Salisbury was a steely and stubborn, yet subtle, defender of the aristocratic order, although he himself succeeded to the marquessate only by accident. The *leitmotif* of his essays was his opposition to democracy and reform:

> Political equality is not merely a folly – it is a chimera ... every community has natural leaders, to whom, if they are not misled by the insane passion for equality, they will instinctively defer ... They are the aristocracy of the country ... woe to the community that disposes of them altogether![161]

Having failed to prevent reform, Salisbury thought his views an impediment 'to work[ing] heartily with the moderate Liberals – it is only under their leadership

---

158 Derby to Disraeli, 15 August 1875 (Hughenden MSS, Bodleian Library, Oxford, Dep. Hughenden 112/2).

159 J. F. A. Mason, 'Lord Salisbury and the *Saturday Review*', *Bulletin of the Institute of Historical Research*, xxiv(1), 1961, pp. 36–54; Michael Pinto-Duschinsky, *The Political Thought of Lord Salisbury, 1854–1868*, London, Constable, 1967; Paul Smith, 'Introduction', *Lord Salisbury on Politics: A Selection from His Articles in the Quarterly Review, 1860–1885*, Cambridge, Cambridge University Press, 1972, pp. 1–109; Elie Kedourie, 'Tory Ideologue: Salisbury as a Conservative Intellectual', *Encounter*, Vol. 225, 1972, pp. 45–53; Michael Bentley, *Salisbury's World: Conservative Environments in Late-Victorian Britain*, Cambridge, Cambridge University Press, 2001.

160 Richard Shannon, 'Disraeli and Salisbury', in A. B. Cooke ed., *The Conservative Party: Seven Historical Studies, 1680 to the 1990s*, London, Conservative Political Centre, 1997, p. 41; also, Donald Southgate, *The Conservative Leadership, 1832–1932*, London, Macmillan, 1974, pp. 103–5.

161 Robert Cecil, 'The Confederate Struggle and Recognition', *Quarterly Review*, Vol. 112, 1862, pp. 535–70.

that a Conservative Party in the future could be formed. Pure "squire" Conservatism is played out.'[162] Yet he adjusted with ease to the mass politics ushered in by the 1867 franchise reform: 'The commonest error in politics is sticking to the carcass of dead policies.'[163] Privately, he continued to complain of 'the great democracy we all have to obey', with its 'ill-informed and unbridled impulses'.[164] In practice, he proved a highly effective political leader who sought to channel these 'impulses' through a mixture of rational exposition and oratorical appeals to imperial and patriotic sentiments. Appearing in public was increasingly distasteful as to him – his niece described him memorably as looking like 'a badger seeking its hole'.[165] Yet he understood the value of such mass organisations as the Primrose League, whose local habitations gave the party a broader national presence, and whose activities – an idiosyncratic mixture of music-hall and church flower festivals – connected it with sections of society beyond its traditional hinterland in the shires.[166]

Salisbury's conception of politics was unashamedly class-based and materialist. His language, indeed, had almost Marxian overtones. People's thoughts and actions were determined by 'material interests alone'. The function of government was 'to define and secure in some form or other the distribution of property'. This was the true battlefield of politics: 'A ... class of those who have little see their way to getting more by means of a political convulsion.'[167] He was driven by a fear of 'the beginning of a serious war of classes'.[168] And

162 Salisbury to Carnarvon, 24 April 1868 (Carnarvon MSS, British Library, Add. MSS. 60758); also, Gwendolen Cecil, *The Life of Robert, Marquis of Salisbury, Vol. 1*, London, Hodder & Stoughton, 1921–32, p. 294.

163 Salisbury to Lytton, 25 May 1877 (Lytton MSS, Hertfordshire Record Office, Hertford, D/Ek/C36).

164 Salisbury to Lytton, 2 November 1877 (ibid.); also to Acland, 9 April 1896 (Acland MSS, Bod., MS Acland d. 74). See: Robert Taylor, *Lord Salisbury*, London, Allen Lane, 1975, p. 135.

165 'Much of his speech was amusing to listen to, but I don't expect it w[oul]d be so amusing to read,' Alice Blanche Balfour's diary, 4 May 1898 (Whittinghame Muniment MSS, National Archive of Scotland, Edinburgh, GD 433/2/224). The 'dying nations' speech can be found in *The Times*, 5 May 1898.

166 Martin Pugh, *The Tories and the People, 1880–1935*, Oxford, Blackwell, 1985, p. 29; Janet Robb, *The Primrose League, 1883–1906*, New York, Columbia University Press, 1968, pp. 87–105.

167 Robert Cecil, 'The House of Commons', *Quarterly Review*, Vol. 116, 1864, pp. 265–6. Salisbury had some superficial knowledge of Marx.

168 Salisbury to Balfour (10 April 1880, Balfour MSS, BL, Add. MSS. 46988).

yet, just as he had demonstrated an unexpected capacity for democratic leadership, so the atavistic, aristocratic, class warrior won over sections of the newly enfranchised middle classes – the villa voters – without the support of whom the Conservatives could not have maintained themselves in office. A liberal sprinkling of honours and peerages helped, and so did his effective use of the Primrose League and the party organisation under its redoubtable principal agent Capt. Richard 'The Skipper' Middleton.[169]

Defeated in 1867, Salisbury took the fight to Gladstone and the Liberals in 1884, because further franchise extension was unavoidable. If cleaving to dead policies was a cardinal error, then so was fighting a lost cause in the last ditch. Extension, however, could be turned to the Conservatives' advantage. After all, the 1880 Liberal victory had depended largely on the decisions of 2,000 voters in marginal constituencies.[170] To squeeze any benefit out of further reform, then, it had to be accompanied by redistribution, redrawing constituency boundaries and establishing single-member seats of equal size – and he forced it on Gladstone in a bold stroke.[171]

The move not only increased Tory numbers in Parliament – there were more county seats, and newly created suburban divisions in the major provincial cities – it also enabled Salisbury to stamp his authority on the party. Even so, Salisbury's politics were informed by a powerful, pessimistic, intellectual current: all 'institutions ... must die, like all other things, when their time comes'.[172] The world could be going to the dogs, but that did not mean the Conservatives ought 'simply to keep things as they are' – that was impossible. Besides 'there is much ... it is highly undesirable to conserve'.[173] But he understood that change would always incite

---

169 Richard Shannon, *The Age of Salisbury, 1881–1902: Unionism and Empire*, London, Longman, 1996, pp. 60–62.; also, J. V. Beckett, *The Aristocracy in England, 1660–1914*, Oxford, Blackwell, 1986, pp. 460–67.

170 Anon. [Salisbury], 'Ministerial Embarrassments', *Quarterly Review*, Vol. 302, 1881, p. 541.

171 Lord Salisbury, 'The Value of Redistribution: A Note on Electoral Statistics', *National Review*, Vol. 10, 1884, pp. 145–57. For the high politics dimension, see A. Jones, *The Politics of Reform 1884*, Cambridge, 1972, pp. 196–222.

172 Salisbury to Austin, 29 April 1888 (Austin MSS, Bristol University Library, DM668/Austin).

173 Anon. [Salisbury], 'Disintegration', *Quarterly Review*, Vol. 312, 1883, p. 562.

resistance: 'The army of so-called reform, in every stage of its advance, necessarily converts a detachment of its force into opponents. The more rapid the advance the more formidable will the desertion become, 'til at last ... the balance between the forces of conservation and destruction will be redressed.'[174] As de Tocqueville before him, so Salisbury understood that the moment of greatest danger was the point at which concessions were made to those demanding change. Conservatism, then, was 'a fighting retreat' – slow, steady and tenacious – permitted very occasionally to rest on that fragile balance between the forces. Whatever skirmishes Salisbury expected to win, ultimately he knew that his cause was lost: 'The game was to lose slowly and to lose hard.'[175]

There was no battle Salisbury fought harder or more fiercely than that in defence of the established Church. It was at the core of his resistance to what he saw as the sustained and concerted assault on authority and property by the allied forces of religious dissent and radicalism. Nonconformist chapels and meeting houses were 'earthworks and blockhouses for the maintenance of an untiring political guerilla', and dissenting ministers were 'ready-made electioneering agents ... natural adepts in all the low stratagems of political warfare'.[176] Salisbury's very personal form of Anglicanism was devout and deep-rooted, and it holds the key to the cynicism and worldliness of his statecraft. His Christian belief endowed him with a sense of fatalism that enabled him to accept the fell blows of providence.[177] Providence was unfathomable; but in this impermanent, imperfect and inadequate world,

---

174 Robert Cecil, 'The Past and Future of Conservative Policy', *Quarterly Review*, Vol. 127, 1869, pp. 551–2.

175 Smith, op. cit., 1972, p. 106. For an instructive parallel with de Tocqueville see Lord Salisbury, 'The Programme of the Radicals', *Quarterly Review*, Vol. 135, 1873, p. 560.

176 Robert Cecil, 'Conservative Reaction', *Quarterly Review*, Vol. 115, 1860, pp. 270–71; for a detailed examination of Salisbury's views on Church matters, see: Bentley, op. cit., pp. 188–219; and A. L. Kennedy, *Salisbury, 1830–1903: Portrait of a Statesman*, London, John Murray, 1954, pp. 10–25.

177 His speeches and essays were peppered with phrases such as 'fate ordained' or the 'mad and bloody pranks' of human contrivance. Robert Cecil, 'Four Years of a Reforming Administration', *Quarterly Review*, Vol. 113, 1863, p. 256; Robert Cecil, 'Democracy on Its Trial', *Quarterly Review*, Vol. 110, 1861.

choosing the lesser of several evils was the most attainable to man. And it absolved Salisbury from rigid morality, precisely because salvation was not of this world.[178]

LIBERAL PARTY MANAGEMENT AND THE 'IRISH QUESTION'

Salisbury's religious belief was a licence to be ruthless and vengeful when he deemed it necessary to be. Even so, the nature and the limits of his statecraft cannot be properly appreciated unless placed against the background of a fragmenting Liberal Party. A combination of factors was slowly weakening the grip of the once seemingly natural party of government on the electorate. *Pace* Salisbury's own pessimistic prognostications, reform had brought villadom into the Tory orbit, with various religious and sectional interests reducing the attraction of Liberalism for it. In Ireland, the Liberals had ceded their electoral dominance to the Nationalists, and the Irish Brigade's support was to be had only at a heavy price. Foreign and imperial complications also intruded upon the internal dynamics of the party, causing friction between those ready to carry on in a Palmerstonian groove and those favouring retrenchment.

It was the Irish Question, however, that drove a wedge between the different parts of the Liberal Party, and would keep it divided for the next quarter of a century. Salisbury's role was by no means passive in this. On the contrary, he manipulated Liberal divisions the more deeply to entrench them. Gladstone, with his moral, crusading instincts, had fastened onto home rule for Ireland as the elixir for reviving his party. Decanting the potent Irish beverage into the Liberal bottle, he broke it. Salisbury, with his ruthless instinct for power and expediency, made sure the bottle could not be glued back together again. He did so through a mixture of parliamentary manoeuvres,

---

178 For some suggestions, see: Bentley, op. cit., pp. 188–9.

substantive offers to renegade Liberals, and public rhetoric designed to resonate with an electorate sceptical of the merits of home rule.

Salisbury's caretaker government (June 1885 to January 1886) was never likely to last for long. But given the inconclusive result of the November election, Salisbury boldly played the 'Orange card' to maximum effect. His Irish Coercion Bill of January 1886 booby-trapped the door to No. 10. As anticipated, the measure ran into the buffers of Liberal–Irish opposition, and Salisbury had to relinquish the premiership. But the Liberal Party had fractured, with seventy-four Liberal MPs having decided to abstain and eighteen having joined the Tories in the division lobby.[179]

Under such circumstances, Gladstone's third administration was doomed. The Whig leader Lord Hartington (later 8th Duke of Devonshire) refused to join it; and the leading light among the radicals, Joseph Chamberlain, was hostile to home rule, though he accepted office.[180] Neither 'Harty-Tarty' from outside the Cabinet nor 'Brummagem Joe' inside it could neutralise Irish devolution. In June 1886, Whig and radical anti-Gladstonians joined forces with the Conservatives to defeat home rule. Gladstone dissolved Parliament once more to seek an electoral mandate for Irish devolution – and failed. The 1886 general election was an emphatic rejection of home rule. The Liberals were reduced to a rump of 191 MPs – 125 fewer than the Conservatives – though the Tories were some twenty seats short of a majority (316). Parnell's Nationalists had retained their stranglehold on the majority of Irish seats (eighty-six), but they no longer held the balance at Westminster. That role now fell to the seventy-eight anti-home rule Liberals.

In retrospect, there was a curious irony about the convulsions of 1884–86. Returned to office, Salisbury and senior Tories were doubtful 'whether the country *can* be governed, nowadays, by people holding opinions you and I

179 W. C. Lubenow, *Parliamentary Politics and the Home Rule Crisis: The British House of Commons in 1886*, Oxford, Clarendon Press, 1988; also, Peter Davis, 'The Liberal Unionist Party and the Irish Policy of Lord Salisbury's Government, 1886–1892', *Historical Journal*, 18(1), 1975, pp. 85–104.

180 C. H. D. Howard ed., *Joseph Chamberlain: A Political Memoir, 1880–1892*, London, Batchworth Press, 1953, pp. 193–4.

should call even moderately Conservative'.[181] Yet, whatever their private pessimism, they were on the brink of establishing a Tory ascendancy that was to last for a generation. Given the distribution of forces in 1886, a Tory–Liberal Unionist alliance was the only practical course. Indeed, Salisbury was prepared to offer Hartington a formal coalition, even at the price of accepting him as Prime Minister.[182] Hartington declined, as Salisbury may well have anticipated. The Liberal Unionists agreed to oppose home rule, but they had little else in common. If the pace were forced, the work of destruction might remain incomplete. The Whigs would enter a pact, but the two dozen Chamberlainites would be left in no man's land.[183] Only the vexed Irish issue stood between them and mainstream Liberals, while Chamberlain's social reform ideas remained an obstacle to an alliance with Salisbury's Tories.[184]

The peculiarities of the Liberal disintegration, then, made for caution on Salisbury's part. They did not necessitate a change of course, however. Salisbury proceeded tentatively, but remained attuned to the needs of the dissenting Liberals, and never ceased to indicate his 'general hopes of an understanding' among Unionists of all stripes.[185] As long as there was no formal coalition, Salisbury was 'reduced to making bricks without straws, but if I fail, my taskmaster [the electorate] will only say, "You are idle."'[186] Ideally, refraining from domestic legislative activism was his *beau idéal*. It was, after all, the 'feebleness of our government' that guaranteed the status

---

181 Hicks Beach to Salisbury, 25 December 1886 (Salisbury MSS, Hatfield House, 3M/E/Hicks Beach, original emphasis); for the not-always-easy relations between the two, see Thomas Otte, '*Black Michael*': *Sir Michael Hicks Beach and the Problems of Late-Victorian Conservatism*, Tunbridge Wells, Conservative History Group, 2006, pp. 8–10.

182 Brett's journal, 29 January 1886 (Esher MSS, Churchill College Archive Centre, Cambridge, ESHR 2/7); Steele, op. cit., pp. 202–9.

183 According to Salisbury's Chief Whip, there were about twenty-one Chamberlainites in the Commons. Viscount Chilston, *Chief Whip: The Political Life and Times of Aretas Akers-Douglas, 1st Viscount Chilston*, London, Routledge & Kegan Paul, 1961, p. 84.

184 Michael Hurst, *Joseph Chamberlain and Liberal Reunion: The Round Table Conference 1887*, London, Routledge, 1967.

185 Salisbury to Akers-Douglas, 9 January 1886 (Chilston MSS, Kent Archive Office, Maidstone, U564/18); also, Shannon, op. cit., 1996, p. 193.

186 Salisbury to Austin (private), 29 July 1886 (Austin MSS, DM668/Austin).

quo.[187] But, in the real world of Westminster politics, abstention was not an option if the renegade Liberals were to be won over. To secure it and to cement some form of Unionist alliance were key objects of Salisbury's statecraft. That he succeeded was the result of a fortuitous combination of deliberate moves on his part and of favourable circumstances.

Like other political leaders before and after him, he had always appreciated the uses of divisive issues: 'Like a battlefield in actual war, they derive their significance not from the value of the ground itself, but from the importance of the country to which they open access.' Successful statecraft depended on identifying and exploiting dividing lines. History taught 'that parties range themselves … on some one great issue by which men's minds were turned … The great question of the day [home rule] has been accepted as the dividing line … and men have joined together, by reason of their agreement on that great question.'[188] Salisbury emphasised that 'dividing line' in his public utterances. He was 'confident that the longer the matter is under consideration, the more emphatic this determination of the national opinion [to oppose home rule] will become.'[189] Fortune had dealt him the Orange card, and he played it for all it was worth: 'This was the … real battle that we are fighting.'[190] To that end, he mobilised anti-Catholic and imperial sentiments. Devolution, he expounded at a major pre-election rally in 1892, meant:

> Setting up an ultra-protectionist island, which will be protected by England in the adoption of those theories. (Cheers.) England is the Protestant nation of the world … You are going to create an ultra-clerical state under the archbishops Croke and Walsh. (Hear, hear.) … You are going to give

187 Salisbury to Balfour, 29 March 1886, in Robin Harcourt Williams ed., *The Salisbury-Balfour Correspondence, 1869–1892*, Hertfordshire, Hertfordshire Record Society, 1988, p. 138.

188 Hansard, HL deb., 27 January 1887, vol. 310, col. 32.

189 Salisbury to Walsingham (president of the Eastern Union of Conservative Associations), 27 May 1887 (Walsingham MSS, Norfolk Record Office, Norwich, WLS/LX/47/14).

190 'Lord Salisbury in Edinburgh', *The Times*, 30 November 1888.

> ... all that is backward, all that is unprogressive, all that is contrary to civilisation and enlightenment in Ireland, power over all that is enlightened, civilised and progressive. (Cheers.) But ... if we allow ourselves to be deceived by hollow sentimental follies, which are, in reality, only excuses for weakness and want of courage, the days of our power will be set, and slowly we shall recede from the great position that was handed down to us.[191]

If Salisbury played the ball, he also played the leading men on the Liberal side, and this proved cripplingly effective. There was, in Tory circles, a widespread belief that the Liberal leader had gone mad, and Salisbury amplified such fears. In his public speeches, invariably laced with his own special brand of sarcasm, he disparaged both Gladstone's sincerity and his practical sense, often with a less-than-delicate suggestion of mental instability. Salisbury warned an Edinburgh audience in 1888 that Gladstone, having now convinced himself he had always supported home rule, had other ideas 'generating in the recesses of that teeming brain'.[192] If it was not the 'GOM' (Grand Old Man) himself, then it was his acolytes – men such as John Morley – who found themselves the target of such barbs. 'Mr Morley's nerves ... [have] been the subject to this prophesied [Irish] agitation,' Salisbury suggested in 1893.[193]

The combination of dividing lines and personal invectives proved effective. Salisbury's statecraft was not wholly negative, however, and also consisted of courting the seventy-eight non-Gladstonian Liberals with warm words and offers of policies and office. 'The path of a man who attempts coalition', he noted in early 1887, 'is beset with pitfalls.'[194] Yet, for someone who had so openly evinced a disdain for modern politics, Salisbury proved remarkably

---

191 Ibid., 3 February 1892.

192 Ibid., 1 December 1888. Unsurprisingly, Gladstone complained in January 1889 that Salisbury had 'behaved very ill to him' – Frederick Hamer ed., *The Personal Papers of Lord Rendel*, London, Benn, 1931, p. 67.

193 'Lord Salisbury at Cardiff', *The Times*, 29 November 1893. For some thoughts on Salisbury's rhetorical devices, see Bentley, op. cit., pp. 295–305.

194 Salisbury to Smith, 23 January 1887, as quoted in Bentley, ibid., p. 292.

skilled at party and, more especially, coalition politics. He heaped flattery on Hartington with an industrial-sized shovel, lauding him as a great patriot – 'one of the most disinterested men who ever lived'.[195] This was the more easily done, since Hartington was without any personal ambitions – unless they took the shape of quadrupeds at Newmarket or the Duchess of Manchester. But it helped to cultivate closer ties with all non-Tory Unionists.

Just how useful this was became apparent when Randolph Churchill's star imploded at the end of 1886. Salisbury had only reluctantly appointed his quarrelsome leadership rival as Chancellor of the Exchequer; Churchill's self-destruction allowed him to put his stamp on the Tory Party. By filling the vacancy at the Treasury with George Joachim Goschen – a decidedly conservative Liberal – he bound the dissentient Liberals to the administration, even though their leader himself remained aloof. The new Chancellor, indeed, decided to accept the office because it would 'increase the appearance of coalition rather than conversion [of Liberal Unionists to Toryism]'.[196]

Showering Liberal Unionists with praise and making one of them Chancellor was one part of Salisbury's statecraft, the other being substantive policy concessions. The stalemate at Westminster meant that government measures had to take on a Liberal Unionist appearance. This was a carefully calibrated element of Salisbury's domestic statecraft. There was a chance of forging a durable combination of all forces in defence of the social and political status quo, embracing Tories, Whigs and Chamberlainites. Salisbury had kept such a regrouping in view ever since home rule had erupted onto the scene. To secure it, the government's legislative programme contained various policies designed to appeal to Chamberlain and his followers. In ordinary times, free elementary education, elected parish councils and smallholder grievances would not have been Tory priorities. Times were not ordinary, however. What Salisbury had once called 'the floodtide of fortune' was with the Tories now.

---

195 *Annual Register 1888*, p. 5.

196 Goschen to Hartington, 2 January 1887 (Devonshire MSS, Chatsworth, 340.2133). For Churchill and Salisbury's leadership, see also: R. Quinault, 'Lord Randolph Churchill and Tory Democracy, 1880–1885', *Historical Journal*, vol. 22, no. 1, 1979, pp. 141–65.

To navigate it, and to fish in the swell of the rising tide, required more than traditional Tory policies. Moderate reforms allowed Salisbury to net and land the Chamberlainite fry. Their leader was not unaware of this. Indeed, he had made 'more progress ... with the practical application of my political programme', and this he owed 'entirely to [his] former opponents'.[197] His parliamentary alliance had yielded practical results, and this gave him grounds for continuing it. Commentators, indeed, spoke of a coalition without a coalition ministry.[198]

FOREIGN AFFAIRS COMPETENCE

Foreign affairs also played a prominent role in Salisbury's statecraft. Disraeli's imperial rhetoric had proved its electoral potency, and Salisbury was not shy in deploying it. The Tories were the patriotic party and that of empire, and they laid claim to a particular competence in foreign affairs. It was attributed to Salisbury personally, not least by himself. Here, the Gladstone government's ineptitude abroad was the perfect foil for Tory attacks, and Liberal incompetence was a prominent theme in Salisbury's speeches: 'It is not adverse fortune abroad that has condemned all their efforts to failure, but adverse imbecility at home.'[199] What a contrast with his own stewardship of foreign affairs: 'I cannot help remembering what the state of the world was at that time ... and how much British policy ... was foiled. I think we have a right to look with something of satisfaction at the contrast in general affairs between that time and this. (Loud cheers.)'[200]

---

197 Chamberlain to Dale, 1 May 1890, as quoted in Denis Judd, *Radical Joe: A Life of Joseph Chamberlain*, Cardiff, University of Wales Press, 1993, p. 173.

198 P. W. Clayden, *England Under The Coalition: The Political History of Great Britain and Ireland from the General Election of 1885 to May 1892*, London, T. F. Unwin, 1892, pp. 56–60, 106–7.

199 Hansard, HL deb., 18 May 1885, vol. 298, col. 690–93; for the connection of patriotism and empire see Pugh, op. cit., 1985, pp. 91–2.

200 'Lord Salisbury at Carnarvon', *The Times*, 11 April 1888; instructive on this, Cammarano Fulvio, *Strategie del conservatismo britannico nella crisi del liberalismo: 'National Party of Common Sense' (1885–1892)*, Bari, Lacaita, 1990, pp. 102–13.

Whatever its practical uses in terms of foreign policy, the idea of 'empire' was central to Salisbury's statecraft. Not the least advantage of the imperial theme was that it lent itself to suggestions of drive and energy when, in the domestic sphere, he wished to keep things quiescent. Disraelian rhetorical stardust was useful, but Salisbury offered red meat, too. Although decrying 'any ambitious schemes of constitution-making', he suggested greater cooperation between Britain and the white settler colonies, 'namely a union for purposes of mutual defence'. Such an arrangement would facilitate 'the drawing closer and closer and closer of those bonds … created by a common origin, a common history, and a common allegiance'.[201]

Salisbury's public utterances were characterised by the frequent deployment of the themes of empire, peace and prosperity, just as the navy, patriotism and empire were staple items of Tory platform rhetoric. The party and its leader sought to monopolise defence for the Tories. Its strategic and diplomatic logic aside, the 1889 Naval Defence Act was also a useful instrument for implying Liberal weakness on defence. The Gladstonian rostrum of retrenchment meant 'to disarm [and] … to drop out of [our] position as a great power and never to regain it'.[202] To maintain the country's international position required an active foreign policy, as Salisbury impressed on a gathering of Tory activists in language that would probably lead to his expulsion from the modern Conservative Party. 'That spirit of haughty and sullen isolation, which has been dignified by the name of "non-intervention",' would lead Britain into a cul-de-sac – 'we are part of the community of Europe, and we must do our duty as such. (Hear, hear.)'[203]

---

201 'The Colonial Conference', *The Times*, 5 April 1887. For some further thoughts on Salisbury's '*Kriegsverein*' speech, see Thomas Otte, '"We are part of the community of Europe": The Tories, Empire and Foreign Policy, 1874–1914', in Jeremy Black ed., *The Tory World: Deep History and the Tory Theme in British Foreign Policy, 1679–2014*, Farnham and Burlington, Ashgate, 2015, pp. 216–17.

202 Hansard, HC deb., 20 May 1889, vol. 336, col. 549. For the electoral uses of the imperial theme, see also: Thomas Otte, '"The Swing of the Pendulum at Home": By-elections and Foreign Policy, 1865–1914', in Thomas Otte and Paul Readman eds, *By-elections in British Politics, 1832–1914*, Woodbridge, Boydell & Brewer, 2013, pp. 121–50.

203 For an assessment of his foreign policy, see Thomas Otte '"Floating Downstream"?: Lord Salisbury and British Foreign Policy, 1878–1902', in Thomas Otte ed., *The Makers of British Foreign Policy: From Pitt to Thatcher*, Basingstoke and New York, Palgrave, 2002, pp. 98–127.

Emphasising Tory foreign policy competence helped to define Salisbury's public persona, and so strengthened the party's position with the voters. The risk it entailed was that it raised unrealistic public expectations. Any perceived slight abroad had the potential to recoil on the party and its leader. This was especially so during Salisbury's third administration after 1895, when the international landscape was less benign, and Liberal candidates had learned to use imperial rhetoric as an effective weapon against the Conservatives.[204]

Defence and empire played well with the electorate. But such themes were also useful for hardening the adhesion of the Liberal Unionists. Luring Chamberlain to his side was part of Salisbury's statecraft. It changed the internal Liberal Unionist dynamics. The differences between radicals and Hartingtonians were on the wane, and, when Hartington succeeded to the Devonshire title, Chamberlain was the undisputed leader of the Liberal Unionists in the Commons. His return to the Liberal mainstream was now all but impossible, and the prospect of a formal alliance drew nearer.

OPPOSITION AND RE-ELECTION, 1892–95

Salisbury's manoeuvres and formidable coalition-building skills were not enough to prevent defeat at the ballot box in 1892. But the result of the general election was far from conclusive. The Conservatives lost fifty-two seats (268) and the Liberal Unionists held on to two-thirds of theirs (forty-seven). Their combined strength, however, was only twenty-one votes short of a majority. Gladstone's forces were marginally stronger than their Tory opponents (273), but his fourth and final administration was once more dependent on Irish Nationalist support. The 1892 election was a narrow defeat, but it held out the prospect of renewed victory before too long.

The Liberal interlude, indeed, helped to fuse the Unionists more tightly

204 For a detailed discussion, see Thomas Otte '"Avenge England's Honour": By-elections, Parliament and Foreign and Imperial Policy in 1898', *English Historical Review*, vol. 121, no. 491, 2006, pp. 385–428.

together. When Rosebery's Liberal administration collapsed in June 1895, Salisbury reassembled the Unionist coalition, which fought a joint campaign in the subsequent general election in July. Defence of the constitution, anti-home rule rhetoric and appeals to imperial sentiments – the staple items of Unionist platforms – once more proved their worth. There could be no doubt about the electorate's verdict in 1895. The Unionists won by a landslide. The Tories, indeed, increased their tally by seventy-three (to 341 seats), which gave them a working majority of twelve – the first Tory majority in twenty-one years. The Liberals received a drubbing even worse than in 1886. No fewer than ninety-six of their MPs went down to defeat, among them potential future leaders. With seventy MPs, the Liberal Unionists nearly recovered their position of 1886. They no longer held the balance and Salisbury could have governed alone, but he chose not to. Formalising the alliance between the two Unionist groups had several advantages, not least in terms of parliamentary arithmetic. Combined, the Unionists had 411 MPs, which gave them a majority of 259 – the largest Commons majority since 1832. It also made the task of preserving the alliance easier.

Short-term benefits aside, Salisbury's statecraft was guided by longer-term strategic calculations. The 1895 result seemed to indicate a fundamental shift in the political landscape. Decades of reform agitation had come to a sudden halt. The 1867 and 1884 Reform Acts had not, after all, undermined the country's institutions. As Salisbury observed in a rare moment of public triumphalism: 'The result has turned out exactly the other way.'[205] Church and constitution were safe; 'Liberal pessimists in general, and home rulers in particular,' remained useful whipping boys for the delectation of Unionist audiences, but home rule itself had played out.[206] Britain had settled into the status quo, and that was what Salisburian statecraft now offered: a quiet life in place of strife, unmolested by strident appeals to moral crusades. 'The country was scarcely hungering and thirsting after reform,' as one Tory-leaning paper concluded.[207]

205 'Lord Salisbury at Watford', *The Times*, 31 October 1895; see also Marsh, op. cit., 1993, pp. 246–7.

206 'Lord Salisbury at the Guildhall', *Pall Mall Gazette*, 11 November 1895.

207 Ibid.

CONSERVATIVE—LIBERAL UNIONIST COALITION

As for Salisbury, the unexpected sense of security dulled his political instincts. There was, indeed, some tension between Conservative and Chamberlainite constituency organisations.[208] Salisbury recognised the inherent fault lines between his traditional Toryism and the urban masses, over whom Chamberlain seemed to hold sway with his mixture of social reform and imperialism. He could not afford to lose Chamberlain. If 'Joe' were 'to put [his] philosophy in the lumber room,' he hoped, 'this little breeze will very speedily be forgotten'. As for the Unionist alliance:

> We were imitating the statecraft of the potentates of the Congress of Vienna, who strove to establish the balance of power, by exchanging slices of territory, certified to contain so many million souls ... these marketable souls would, in the end, have the deciding voice, whether the bargain ... should endure or not. We were guilty of the same miscalculation.[209]

Some of the 'marketable souls' among Tory backbenchers, indeed, took a dim view of the new arrangements: 'Our fellows complain [that] the LUs [Liberal Unionists] have got too much,' Salisbury's son-in-law was warned.[210] And so they had. With five of the twenty-four Cabinet posts in their hands, they occupied a more prominent position than their strength in Parliament warranted. But for Salisbury, it was imperative to maintain the alliance and to bind Chamberlain to the government. His statecraft had always been pragmatic and free of any delusions. The aloof and aristocratic Salisbury could never attain real popularity. But Chamberlain's formidable Birmingham electioneering machine, the popular appeal of his social imperialist platform, and his personal charisma made him indispensable.

---

208 G. N. Curzon, 'Two Demagogues: A Parallel and a Moral', *New Review*, vol. 12, no. 71, 1895, pp. 363–72.

209 Salisbury to Selborne (private), 13 April 1895 (Selborne MSS, Bod., MS Selborne 5).

210 Brodrick to Selborne, 4 July 1895 (ibid.).

In the run-up to the 1895 general election, Salisbury made accommodating noises when Chamberlain launched a reform manifesto – an attempt to preserve some leverage over the Tories with the spectre of 'Radical Joe' redivivus. Salisbury's concessions were sufficient to placate Chamberlain, but he was warned that 'much care [and] consideration' were needed if the programme was to be implemented.[211] Salisbury was fluent enough in the language of social reform when he needed to speak it. He emphasised his government's endeavours 'to ameliorate the condition of the people'. In practice, however, 'there [was] not much to be done'.[212] If anything, domestic legislation was much diluted by an admixture of Tory water. In 1895, this did not matter, as, much to Salisbury's surprise, Chamberlain asked for the Colonial Office, rather than a senior domestic department of state, when joining the government.[213]

For Salisbury, Chamberlain's imperial conversion was the political equivalent of Pandora's box, and this appreciation shaped his statecraft. Imperialism was attractive to the electoral coalition that had borne the Conservatives into office, and it was key to their remaining there. But, in the longer term, it had a potentially corrosive effect on Unionist cohesion.

Salisbury's aloofness, presiding over his administration from the Olympian heights of the red benches in the Lords, helped to contain Chamberlain's destructive potential. Moreover, the unlikely partnership of 'Joe' and Arthur Balfour – Salisbury's nephew and Leader of the House of Commons – kept the Unionist alliance on the rails. Whatever frictions and irritations office brought, their 'system of ... dual control' ensured that the government survived more or less intact, and the coalition passed largely unscathed through the storms created by the Jameson Raid at the end of 1895 and the early reverses of the Boer War.[214]

---

211 Wolmer (later 2nd Earl of Selborne, Salisbury's son-in-law) to Chamberlain, 15 October 1894 (Chamberlain MSS, all extracts by kind permission of Birmingham University Library, JC 5/74/1).

212 Hansard, HL deb., 15 August 1895, vol. 36, col. 19, 54.

213 Roberts, op. cit., pp. 599–603.

214 Arthur Baumann, *The Last Victorians*, London, Benn, 1924, p. 124.

By then, Salisbury was no longer the force he had once been. Ill health and his wife's death in 1899 had taken their toll. To the younger members of the government, he was a liability – 'a strange, powerful, inscrutable, brilliant, obstructive deadweight at the top'.[215] When the tide of war turned in the summer of 1900, Salisbury no longer led, and the power vacuum at the heart of government increased Chamberlain's influence. It was he who persuaded the Cabinet to dissolve Parliament to reap the harvest sown on the Transvaal *veldt*.[216] Salisbury resisted such blatant opportunism, but ultimately yielded. It was the first time a government had decided to dissolve Parliament early to take advantage of favourable circumstances. Mafeking and Pretoria secured a Unionist victory, which, in the ordinary run of things, was not likely to have occurred.

The decision to don 'khaki' in 1900 was Chamberlain's, and so, in a sense, was the Unionist victory. Unionist rhetoric since 1895 had significantly increased the appeal of the imperial idea. The scrape with the Boers enabled the Unionists to drape themselves in the Union Jack and parade, to the steady drumbeat of war, as the 'national party'.[217] By any standard, it was a nasty campaign, but its outcome vindicated Chamberlain's calculations. It left unchanged the broad contours of the political landscape. The Conservatives lost seven seats (down to 334) – so they could no longer govern on their own, had they wished to – and the Liberal Unionists lost two seats (down to sixty-eight). Their combined tally, however, still stood at 402, and no government since 1832 had been re-elected with an enlarged majority. Although the campaign had raised Chamberlain's profile, success yielded only limited political profit. It did not provide him with 'Joe's mandate'. For that, Salisbury's powers of resistance remained too strong.[218]

---

215 Curzon to Brodrick (confidential), 19 July 1900 (Midleton MSS, BL, Add. MSS. 50074).

216 Chamberlain to Salisbury, 31 August 1900 (Chamberlain MSS, JC 11/30/198).

217 Paul Readman, 'The Conservative Party, Patriotism and British Politics', *Journal of British Studies*, 11(1), 2001, pp. 107–45.

218 James Cornford, 'The Parliamentary Foundations of the "Hôtel Cecil"', in Robert Robson ed., *Ideas and Institutions of Victorian Britain: Essays in Honour of George Kitson Clarke*, London, Bell, 1967, pp. 268–311.

In July 1902, Salisbury eventually relinquished the premiership, having seen the South African War to its end. His retirement from politics, and Balfour's succession to the premiership, did not affect the cohesion of the Unionist alliance. But, following the election, it used its self-proclaimed 'patriotic mandate' to enact a raft of partisan and increasingly unpopular measures. The tide was now running against the Unionists.

ASSESSING SALISBURY

Salisbury was a highly effective leader. In essence, his statecraft was negative. He was – indeed, as he himself put it – '*der Geist, der stets verneint!*'[219] He sought to retard the advance of progress, and, to that end, he settled down to a dogged and hard fight. He did not, however, resort to reactionary nostalgia or an equally cheap imitation of radical populism – both of which were advocated by some Tories. Neither struck Salisbury as realistic.

Circumstances undoubtedly favoured him – Gladstone was a gift to the Conservatives. But Salisbury skilfully exploited the opportunities presented by Gladstonianism, and, in so doing, he widened and deepened Liberal divisions, fatally weakening Liberalism as a political force. Conversely, Salisbury inculcated the Conservatives with a more coherent sense of their own creed than either of his predecessors had bequeathed or Randolph Churchill's 'Tory democracy' platitudes could ever offer.

It is an ironic twist to Salisbury's career that his success as leader stood in sharp contrast to his own gloomy prognostications. The war of the classes he so feared never materialised. But he and his twentieth-century successors – men like Stanley Baldwin – made effective use of the spectre of class warfare to mobilise opposition to reform. In this, he, and those who followed in his

219 Salisbury's entry in Rosebery's autograph book, as reported by Matthew Arnold. See Arnold to his daughter, 17 March 1885, in G. W. E. Russell ed., *Letters of Matthew Arnold, 1848–1888, Vol. 3*, London, Macmillan, 1904, pp. 204–5. The quote, of course, is from Goethe's *Faust* (1.6). Salisbury frequently used it in his correspondence.

footsteps, preserved the position of the propertied classes, and secured the political ascendancy of the Conservative Party into the twentieth century – and, perhaps, beyond it.

CHAPTER 8

ARTHUR BALFOUR

NIGEL KEOHANE

Whichever way you do the arithmetic, the electoral record suggests Arthur Balfour's leadership constitutes a period of unremitting failure for the Conservatives. Inheriting a party that, under Salisbury, had achieved a majority of 130 in 1900, the Conservative Party went down to a landslide defeat in 1906 that led to the loss of 246 seats. This was followed by two narrower defeats in 1910, but, nevertheless, still led to a significant anti-Conservative majority in the Commons. Nigel Keohane's portrait of Balfour digs deeper, but finds little to redeem his time as leader. There was an underestimated and hard-fought unity among Conservatives over home rule, but, in general, he managed an unruly party. His inability to formulate a winning electoral strategy was linked to a weak record of governing competence. In both areas, he showed a lack of flexibility and betrayed an unwillingness to focus on his, and his party's, electability. His legacy was a weak party, divided but still intact.

• • •

On 12 July 1902, the keys to No. 10 Downing Street were handed over from one generation of Cecils to the next. It was a family inheritance that, for Arthur James Balfour, cannot have been unexpected. This was, after all, the height of the 'Hotel Cecil', with Prime Minister Lord Salisbury counting among his government a son and a nephew as junior ministers, in addition to a son-in-law and two nephews (one of them Balfour) as Cabinet ministers. Formally, the change was made by the King on Salisbury's recommendation. But care had been taken to smooth any malcontent among potential contenders, with Salisbury sounding out Joe Chamberlain and the Duke of Devonshire (leaders of the Liberal Unionist wing of the Conservative Party) in advance.

The transition was smooth. *The Spectator* noted: 'As no one objected much less resisted … the new arrangement, though it is a transfer of the supreme direction of the empire, it was effected as easily as a transfer of Consols.'[220] In some ways, it matched Balfour's apparently effortless progression through his political career to that point. Born in 1848, he entered Parliament in 1874 at the age of twenty-six. As if presaging his leadership takeover, Balfour took his seat in Hertford unopposed at the beginning of his career. Judiciously, though, he subsequently and deliberately sought out a Manchester seat to contest, so as to signal both his willingness to fight and his capabilities. His rise was swift, achieving Cabinet rank in 1886, becoming Chief Secretary for Ireland in 1887, and assuming the roles of Leader of the House of Commons and First Lord of the Treasury from 1891. Salisbury had, at this juncture, worried whether a member of the Cecil family leading both Houses of Parliament would be perceived negatively. But there is nothing to suggest that the promotion was nepotistic rather than meritocratic, nor that the handover in 1902 was any different.[221] Balfour's appointment was met with general approval both among the party, who rubber-stamped his appointment a week later, and by the Conservative press.[222] This is probably just as well, given there was no alternative means of selecting the party leader.

It has become a near truism to describe Balfour as enigmatic. Historians have been stumped by the tall, handsome and sociable man, who remained a lifetime bachelor. Monikers given to him by contemporaries provide a sense of the breadth, as well as the inscrutable nature, of his character: once dandy (the 'scented popinjay'); then fragile ('pretty fanny'); then Machiavellian

220 *The Spectator*, 19 July 1902.

221 Roberts, op. cit., pp. 562–5.

222 John Ramsden, *The Age of Balfour and Baldwin, 1902–1940*, London, Longman, 1978; R.J.Q. Adams, *Balfour: The Last Grandee*, London, John Murray, 2007.

(the 'artful Arthur'); then affected snob ('more a mannerism than a man' to Lloyd George); then ruthless administrator ('Bloody Balfour' in Ireland). If any party leader might benefit from a framework of analysis, it is Balfour.

BALFOUR'S STATECRAFT AND LEADERSHIP

Balfour led the Conservatives and Unionists[223] from July 1902 until autumn 1911, serving as Prime Minister from 1902 to 1906, and the Leader of the Opposition from 1906 to 1911.

If statecraft is the art of winning elections and maintaining power, Balfour's tenure as Conservative Party leader was an unmitigated disaster. Balfour is one of the few prime ministers, and certainly the longest-serving Conservative Party leader, who managed neither. Under his leadership, the party lost three successive general elections. Hardly surprisingly, many historians have seen the Edwardian era as the nadir of the Conservative Party.[224] Few party historians have excused Balfour's role,[225] and neither have many biographers (with the principal exception of his niece).[226]

The details are gory, but they matter. In the 'khaki election' of 1900, under Salisbury's leadership, the Conservative Party won 402 seats to the Liberal Party's 183. In the 1906 election, after four years of Balfour's premiership, the Conservative tally dropped an astonishing 246 seats, ending with only 156 to the Liberals' 399 (and the erstwhile Labour Party on twenty-nine). The Conservative share of the vote dropped 7 per cent to 43.4 per cent – the lowest proportion of votes since 1880. Remarkably, only three Conservative Cabinet members retained their seats (Balfour not being one of them). In a mathematical sense, the catastrophe of 1906 was followed by more limited

223 Hereon referred to as the Conservative Party, for the purpose of simplicity.

224 For instance, E. H. H. Green, *The Crisis of Conservatism, 1880–1914*, London, Routledge & Kegan Paul, 1995.

225 See, for instance: David Dutton, *'His Majesty's Loyal Opposition': The Unionist Party in Opposition, 1905–1915*, Liverpool, Liverpool University Press, 1992.

226 Blanche Dugdale, *Arthur James Balfour*, London, Hutchinson, 1936.

defeats in 1910. In January/February 1910, the party won 272 seats to the Liberals' 274. But this apparent deadheat in fact represented a runaway victory for the anti-Unionist cause: the Irish Nationalists continued their dominance across the Irish Sea (eighty-two seats); the Labour Party grew its share of MPs to forty. In December 1910, the Conservatives won 271 seats to the Liberal Party's 272. But the same balance of power prevailed. If the Conservatives' appetite was for power, they were far from being sated. And, though historians have perceived ascendancy in the party's fortunes by the First World War, this movement upwards occurred after Balfour's movement outwards.

The remainder of this chapter discusses five dimensions of his leadership to assess whether the electoral arithmetic provides a rounded view of Balfour's leadership, and what explains that outcome: personal failure or factors beyond his control.

DEMONSTRATING GOVERNING COMPETENCE

By 1902, the Conservative Party had dominated British politics for most of the preceding seventeen years. However, the government was less robust than the size of the khaki election victory of 1900 might have suggested. The administration's record suffered as the Boer War dragged on and as controversy grew with Lord Kitchener's concentration camps. And the controversy would not end there. A report in 1904 by the Inter-Departmental Committee on Physical Deterioration pointed to a wide range of social, environmental, economic and moral factors contributing to the poor physical condition of war recruits (and the wider population).[227] This was to spur the national efficiency movement – yet it was hardly a positive testament to two decades of predominantly Tory rule.

If the baton handed to Balfour by his uncle was as much leaden as golden, the new Prime Minister ran with it vigorously in a number of directions. As

227 HMSO, 'Report by the Inter-Departmental Committee on Physical Deterioration', London, 1904.

an exercise in legislative reform, Balfour's supervision of the Education Bill through Parliament was impressive, and the policy important. The reform showed that his government could pass major legislation.[228]

A second area in which the Balfour government displayed confidence was foreign affairs. Naval policy was pursued keenly under the innovative guidance of the First Sea Lord Admiral 'Jackie' Fisher. Alliances with the Japanese and French followed (not, on Balfour's part, an anti-German move) and Balfour established new methods of overseeing military strategy.

Despite these successes, it is questionable how far Balfour's administration conveyed governing credibility to the electorate. On the eve of the election, Balfour informed his private secretary Jack Sandars that the government could trumpet a list of accomplishments likely to resonate with the electorate: Ireland; foreign affairs; colonial policy; education; national defence; and social reform.[229] Three things might be said about that list.

First, imperial and foreign matters feature high. In the early twentieth century, they could be important determinants of electoral success, but not, of course, as resonant in peacetime as in times of jingoistic fever (such as 1900 or 1918). Equally important diplomatic achievements, and even naval armaments, paled against the fallout of the Boer War, and, in particular, the Chinese indenture controversy. In 1904, Lord Milner, then High Commissioner of South Africa, successfully lobbied London for permission to use indentured Chinese labour. The outcome was disastrous politically, providing, as it did, an easy cause against which radicals and Liberals could unite on both moral and economic grounds.[230]

Second, Balfour's claims were rather bold in at least two areas. On social reform, the record was thin (dramatically so in comparison with the 1906 Liberal administration that followed). On Ireland, the 1903 Wyndham Land Act – the latest attempt at 'killing home rule with kindness' – was a substantial

---

228 Max Egremont, *Balfour*, London, Phoenix, 1998.

229 H. C. G. Matthew and Ruddock Mackay, 'Arthur James Balfour', *Oxford Dictionary of National Biography*, Oxford, Oxford University Press, 2004.

230 Egremont, op. cit.

piece of legislation, and probably the 'kindest' of its type. But, the Conservative Party had broken down into internecine strife over a misjudgement by Chief Secretary for Ireland George Wyndham that had left some colleagues 'bubbling with wrath'.[231] The origin was Wyndham's appointment of Sir Antony MacDonnell as his under-secretary in Dublin. The only difficulty was that MacDonnell was a home ruler advising a Unionist administration. The predictable happened. In September 1904, *The Times* reported that a devolution scheme published by the Irish Reform Association had originated with MacDonnell. Despite initial protestations of innocence, pressure from hard-line Unionists revealed that Wyndham had indeed been party to the idea. Wyndham, his nerves shot, was hounded from the party, and the Conservative reputation on Ireland was tarnished.

Therefore, by the general election of 1906, critics of Balfour could justifiably point to many elements of incompetence to stand alongside undoubted statesmanlike activity.

DEVISING AND IMPLEMENTING AN ELECTORAL STRATEGY

The outcome of these four years as Prime Minister was an electoral rout, to be followed, four years later, by back-to-back defeats. If Balfour had an electoral strategy, therefore, it wasn't a winning one. But did he have one at all?

Certainly, Balfour's brand of pragmatic conservatism did not lend itself well to identifying or mobilising constituencies of political interest. As Prime Minister, he reacted woodenly to the rise of the Labour Representation Committee (later the Labour Party). The Taff Vale judgement of 1901 antagonised the labour movement by making strike action less effective and more risky for

231 Balcarres's diary, 24 February 1905, in John Vincent ed., *The Crawford Papers: The Journals of David Lindsay, 27th Earl of Crawford and Balcarres, 1871–1940 During the Years 1892–1940*, Manchester, Manchester University Press, 1984, p.79.

its members.[232] But Balfour did little to act to assuage trade union concerns, and instead offered the purgatory of a royal commission. The result was a series of by-election defeats to Labour candidates. The Progressive Alliance, agreed in 1903 between Ramsay MacDonald and Herbert Gladstone, was a new type of challenge. The combination seriously affected the outcome in many seats in 1906 and 1910 by consolidating the anti-Conservative vote.[233]

Balfour's action did not stem from a lack of awareness; he recognised the emerging threat of socialism. However, he did little proactively to seek to win over the labour movement. In part, this stemmed from his broad stance on social reform, which derived much from Salisbury's approach – one of 'quietism', with problems dealt with as they emerged.[234] This tactic contrasted markedly with his colleagues in the Chamberlainite and Milnerite wings of the party, who sought to counter the threat of socialism and the rise of the Labour Party with a programme of social reform funded by tariff reform. Therefore, while he could acknowledge the dangers of socialism, his response was reactive. For instance, Leo Amery MP, a follower of Lord Milner and a tariff reformer, noted resistance from Central Office to his attempts to form a Conservative Labour Party that would 'send a certain number of representatives to Parliament to counteract the claim continually made by the present Labour Party that they are the only true representatives of the working man's special point of view'.[235]

A second sign of his insensitivity was his alienation of Nonconformists over the Education Act. Not historically a community associated with the Conservative Party, the alliance with the Liberal Unionists had brought a new connection to Nonconformists. In an abstract sense, Balfour recognised the dilemma:

---

232 Andrew Taylor, 'The Party and Trade Unions', in Anthony Seldon and Stuart Ball eds, *The Conservative Century: The Conservative Party since 1900*, Oxford, Oxford University Press, 1994, pp. 500–501. It restricted the right to picket and exposed union funds to actions for damages.

233 Robert Blake, *The Conservative Party from Peel to Thatcher*, London, Fontana, 1985.

234 E. H. H. Green, 'The Conservative Party, the State and Social Policy, 1880–1914', in Martin Francis and Ina Zweiniger-Bargielowska eds, *The Conservatives and British Society 1880–1990*, Cardiff, Cardiff University Press, 1996, pp. 96–111.

235 Paul Kennedy, *The Rise of the Anglo-German Antagonism, 1860–1914*, London, Allen & Unwin, 1982.

> As long as there are some parents who want no religious teaching; others who want simple Bible teaching; others who wish their children to be taught the characteristic doctrines of the Church of England, or of the Church of Rome, or of the Jewish community, it is quite manifest that many cases must occur when their wishes cannot be carried out.[236]

This was all very well as a detached statement of fact. But, even though he made some modest efforts to assuage the effect on Nonconformists, the policy to put Anglican schools 'on the rates' led to widespread passive resistance, especially in Wales. Joe Chamberlain managed to allay concerns in his own hinterland of Birmingham, but elsewhere he could not stem the tide. He reported to Devonshire: 'Our best friends are leaving us by scores [and] hundreds [and] they will not come back.'[237]

Such political detachedness extended to Balfour's methods of political activism. As leader, Balfour made little attempt to enable or encourage the party organisation to adapt to an expanding electorate or to the changing nature of popular politics. Much research has shown the important role that popular politics and non-party organisations played on the right in the first decade of the twentieth century. The register is astonishing: the Navy League; the National Service League; the Anti-Socialist Union; the Tariff Reform League (plus the Women's Unionist Tariff Reform Union); the Union Defence League; the Imperial Maritime League; and the Budget Protest League. Such organisations were the most mixed of blessings. They expanded the potential support base for the Conservative Party and injected much-needed energy and new blood into the movement.[238] But Balfour could never be their man. He was now the establishment against which many of them railed, tainted by the social circles he moved in, as well as by his involvement in the 1910 cross-party leaders' conference (which, admittedly, he appeared to

---

236 Peter Catterall, 'The Party and Religion', in Seldon and Ball, op. cit. Also, Egremont, op. cit.

237 P. Marsh, *Joseph Chamberlain, Entrepreneur in Politics*, Yale, Yale University Press, 1994.

238 David Thackeray, 'Rethinking the Edwardian Crisis of Conservatism', *Historical Journal*, 54(1), 2011, pp. 191–213.

enjoy rather too much).[239] What was more, the methods of popular politics were anathemas to Balfour's style.

What worked in the House of Commons – his quickness of wit and widely recognised debating style – did not equip him well as a successful campaigner. Lord Balcarres's frustration was evident by mid-1911:

> I cannot get him to understand the intellectual requirements of those who require a lead, not once, but frequently, on the same subject. He says he cannot repeat his speeches, for, unless spontaneous, they bore him. Nonetheless, those who fight for us in the country, and have won us elections in the past, do require their political stimulants in repeated draughts, and they must be humoured.[240]

This aloofness made him an unnatural party manager. The party organisation developed in spite of, rather than because of, Balfour's involvement. Professor John Ramsden's research has shown that party reorganisation made a major contribution to the revitalisation of the party in the pre-war period. But this was a development felt after 1911, not during Balfour's tenure.[241] A stab was made at reform under Balfour, but it missed the heart of the problem. Sir Arthur Steel-Maitland, the party chairman from 1911, noted that, 'with all his gifts, we were never anything else but a scratch lot of individuals under Balfour'.[242] The party wasted a good crisis when, in the aftermath of the shocking 1906 general election defeat, the leader botched a much-needed reorganisation of the party structures. The proposals of Joseph Chamberlain to democratise the National Union and exert some control over Central

---

239 John A. Hutcheson, *Leopold Maxse and the National Review, 1893–1914*, London, Garland, 1989; Geoffrey Searle, 'Critics of Edwardian Society: The Case of the Radical Right', in Alan O'Day ed., *The Edwardian Age: Conflict and Stability, 1900–14*, London, Macmillan, 1979, pp.79, 96; Franz Coetzee, *For Party or Country: Nationalism and the Dilemmas of Popular Conservatism in Edwardian England*, New York, Oxford University Press, 1990.

240 Balcarres's diary, 9 September 1911, in Vincent, op. cit., 1984, p. 222.

241 Ramsden, op. cit., 1978.

242 Steel-Maitland to Arthur Glazebrook, 26 August 1913 (Steel-Maitland Papers, National Archives of Scotland, 159/6/15-18x).

Office were flunked. Balfour kept personal control of Central Office, while some of its functions (for instance, literature) were passed over to the National Union. The Tariff Reform League remained an appendage and the Liberal Unionists were still separate. The result was further confusion, lack of clear accountability and the persistence of amateurism.[243] Two more general election defeats were required before Balfour would be persuaded of the need for a further review.

In three important respects – his philosophical hesitancy to proactively seek out an electoral constituency; his aloof style; and his poor management of the party organisation – Balfour struggled to evolve an electoral strategy.

LEADING AND MANAGING THE PARTY

On succession to the leadership, commentators noted the paucity of alternatives. Through to 1911, no candidate challenged credibly for Balfour's position. Even on exiting his job, Balfour noted rather triumphantly that there were fewer contenders than others might have liked to think.[244]

A decisive factor was that Joseph Chamberlain was never a full-blooded or committed rival for the party leadership. In part, this was because he primarily sought influence not station. The myth of 'Radical Joe' can be taken too far: there is little doubt that in early 1906 – when Balfour suffered the ignominy of losing his seat – Chamberlain spied an opportunity to take the lead.[245] Three factors, though, kept him as first lieutenant.

First, he sought power as a means to prosecute the tariff reform campaign, and he was right in thinking that the party leadership was not always the best medium. This is evident in the range of tactics he deployed – from extra-parliamentary activity through the Tariff Commission and Tariff

243 Stuart Ball, 'The National and Regional Party Structure', in Seldon and Ball, op. cit.; Ramsden, op. cit., 1978.

244 Adams, op. cit., 2007.

245 See, for instance, Dutton, op. cit., 1992.

Reform League, and repeated attempts to capture the Conservative Party organisation, through to his grappling for parliamentary power after the 1906 general election.

Second, he was too much a Liberal Unionist, too radical and too Nonconformist to be palatable to the bulk of traditional Tories.

Finally, Chamberlain had the unfortunate knack of making himself absent at key moments – the first when he shipped off to explore Milner's South African government, before tariff reform had been adopted fully by the Cabinet in 1903; and later, more unhappily, when he collapsed physically, just as the tariff movement was reaching rude health. Chamberlain, therefore, was dangerous, less as a straightforward rival for the leadership, but more as an agitator of party disorder and new propositions.

Of the two main contenders for the leadership by 1911, Walter Long was sclerotic and neurotic, prone to waspishness, bad temper and ill judgement – no more so than when he rounded on his chief in late autumn 1911.[246] If his personality was one-tenth as ill-ordered and ill-mannered as his pen, then he would have made a terrible leader. Austen Chamberlain (Joe's eldest son and brother of Neville) was a decent imitation of his father physically, but a poor one temperamentally, lacking the vigour, the driving conviction and the sharpness that characterised Chamberlain Senior. Reflecting on why Chamberlain did not rise higher, Balfour said the truth that many would not: 'Don't you think it is because he is a bore?'[247]

If, in a straightforward sense, Balfour was fortunate to survive without a credible competitor, he was equally unfortunate to have to lead a hugely divided party. While the divisions stemmed, in part, from Balfour's own failings, they derived as much from the fluidity of party politics of the time and the inherent ideological and cultural divisions within the Conservative coalition.

---

246 Long's behaviour certainly affected Balfour. See, for instance, November 1911 note by Sandars (Balfour Manuscripts, British Library, MS 49772), folios 292–3.

247 David Dutton, *Austen Chamberlain: Gentleman in Politics*, Bolton, Ross Anderson, 1985.

From 1903 to the end of Balfour's reign, the party suffered appalling divisions. These surfaced most notably over tariffs and the House of Lords.[248] In 1903, the party divided between a small group of free traders and a growing corpus of tariff reformers (it was ironic that the leaders of both movements came from the smaller Liberal Unionist wing of the party).

Balfour's tactics throughout were to manage the split by concession, usually of the last-minute variety. In 1903, he argued for protection, but with no taxes on food or raw materials, and then for retaliatory tariffs rather than imperial preference. In 1904, he introduced the idea that a full tariff programme would have to be backed in two general elections before being introduced by a future Conservative government. In the autumn 1910 general election, he pledged that a full tariff programme would have to be agreed by the people in a referendum to assuage concerns of opponents. All were unsatisfactory and unconvincing compromises that placated neither side. It was hardly surprising that, by the end, the Chief Whip Acland-Hood advised that 'the main cry is "want of backbone" and "vacillating policy".'[249] The consequences throughout his tenure were painful: a culling of the free-trader Cabinet members in 1903; defections (eleven, including, most famously, Winston Churchill) to the opposition benches;[250] outright internecine warfare between the factions in ensuing by-elections and the general election; rivalries after the 1906 election loss;[251] and the evolution of rival extra-parliamentary organisations.

As the apparent vacillation wore on, parliamentarians, and even the party rank and file, rebelled against Balfour. Back-bench groups proliferated: the Confederates formed over perceived inattention to the empire, as did the Reveille.[252] Protectionists such as Leo Amery and George Lloyd wanted a

---

248 Alfred Gollin, *Balfour's Burden: Arthur Balfour and Imperial Preference*, London, Anthony Blond, 1965.

249 Egremont, op. cit., p. 121.

250 Adams, op. cit., 2007.

251 Bridgeman's diary, 2 February 1906, in Philip Williamson ed, *The modernisation of Conservative politics: the diaries and letters of William Bridgeman 1904-1935*, London, Historians' Press, 1988, p.15.

252 Larry Witherell, 'Sir Henry Page Croft and Conservative Back-bench Campaigns for Empire, 1903–1932', *Parliamentary History*, 25(3), 2006.

challenge to Balfour, disaffected by the lack of vigour in his tariff policy.[253] By 1911, Leo Maxse was making reference in the *National Review* to 'BMG' – 'Balfour Must Go'. Not too much should be read into this: Maxse also had 'AMG' (Asquith), 'CMG' (Curzon) and 'GMG' (Grey).[254] A better barometer was the fact that hostility had extended as far as the normally deferential constituency membership. In the last months of his leadership, a number of associations passed resolutions calling for stronger leadership, demanding:

> Party leaders at once declaring in favour of definite, constructive and fighting policy that will appeal to electors and on which they can be educated. This meeting believes the present Unionist policy – entirely negative, except as to tariff reform – will never create and sustain any enthusiasm in the party or prove successful at the next or any future general election.[255]

The Oxford Association went further, passing a resolution professing 'that the leading of the Unionist Party is lacking in energy, foresight and initiative and that, unless that is remedied, there is no reasonable prospect of the return of the party to power'.[256]

Balfour's torturous lack of leadership over tariffs might have been explained away as simply a symptom of the fiscal entanglement. However, he replicated many of its worst features over the House of Lords in 1910–11. Caught between utter opposition to socialistic measures in Lloyd George's Budget of 1909 and a desire to preserve legitimate authority in the second chamber, his leadership was rudderless. Though ultimately a more short-lived controversy, the divisions over the House of Lords were

253 John Charmley, *Lord Lloyd and the Decline of the British Empire*, London, Weidenfeld & Nicolson, 1987, p. 23.

254 Egremont, op. cit.

255 The same resolution was passed at Bewdley Conservative Association, Brecon Conservative Association, Bristol West Conservative Association, Hastings Conservative Association, and Maidstone Conservative Association.

256 Oxford Conservative Association papers, 4 October 1911.

no less visceral. As William Bull concluded: 'Balfour is by far [and] away the most brilliant debater and parliamentarian in the House of Commons. [But] he is the worst leader we ever had [and] he is getting worse ... He does not lead.'[257]

The House of Lords controversy illustrated well two features that undermined Balfour's party leadership in this period. First, it was little help to Balfour's fortunes that his aloofness was matched by Lord Lansdowne's hesitancy in the Lords. Both men were experienced administrators. Both were reluctant oppositionalists. After the Lords crisis, the feeling was against the two leaders.[258] Even Balfour described Lansdowne as 'very diffident'.[259]

Second, Balfour wore his diffidence on his sleeve. The first advice that the new whip Robert Sanders received from his fellow party managers in 1911 was: 'Remember, in dealing with [Balfour], always tell him what you want done; never ask what he thinks it ought to be.'[260] Yet too much weight can be put on this. Nearly thirty years previously, Gladstone had noted how the easily observed characteristics were not Balfour's only ones: he, 'for all his lackadaisical academic manner, has got ability and principles' and 'might yet lead the Conservative Party'.[261] No more was he soft. Lord Ashbourne – the long-serving Lord Chancellor of Ireland – thought that 'A.J. Balfour presided over the Cabinet with more directness and authority than Lord Salisbury, i.e. he kept the members more closely to what he wished to discuss.'[262] He could act with ruthlessness, all the more barbarous because of its calmness. Old friends Curzon and Wyndham were both left to the wolves (each deserved it, mind).

If Balfour's personal diffidence offers an incomplete explanation of his

---

257 Bull's diary, cited in John Kendle, *Walter Long, Ireland and the Union, 1905–1920*, Dublin, Glendale, 1992.

258 Lord Derby to Walter Long, 19 October 1911 (Long Papers, British Library, MS 62405), folios 115–16.

259 Egremont, op. cit., p. 163.

260 Sanders's diary, 23 March 1911, in John Ramsden ed., *Real Old Tory Politics: The Political Diaries of Robert Sanders, Lord Bayford, 1910–35*, London, The Historians' Press, 1984.

261 Conversation reported in Leopold Amery's diary, 22 March 1913, in John Barnes and David Nicholson eds, *The Leo Amery Diaries I: 1896–1929*, London, Hutchinson, 1980.

262 Alistair Cooke and A.P. W. Malcolmson eds, *The Ashbourne Papers, 1869–1913*, Belfast, HMSO, p. 31.

apparently weak leadership over tariffs, his emphasis on the goal of party unity provides a more compelling one. In January 1904, Balfour told his constituents: 'In all this controversy, I have had few interests nearer my heart than the interests of the unity of the great Unionist Party.'[263] The traditional reading is that Balfour demonised Peel too much and would have been better giving a straighter account of his views and a stronger lead, even if this would have risked a more severe schism within the party. But this misses two important dynamics.

First, looking back, it is easy to miss the flux between the Conservative and Liberal parties in the last two decades of the nineteenth century. As Professor Dutton has argued, since 1886, both major parties remained 'inherently unstable coalitions'.[264] A progressive imperialist coalition between Conservative free traders and Liberal imperialists had been mooted by some, and – though faced with huge obstacles – remained a possibility.[265] The differences between tariff reformers and free traders were, in many instances, absolute.

Second, the deep-seated differences within the party over tariffs have had the misfortune of concealing from historians the unity that Balfour achieved. His one, overriding party political success was to hand over a party that was able to pursue a forceful anti-home rule strategy – the pre-eminent task, after all, of the Conservatives and Unionists. In 1910, he turned down Lloyd George's proposals to form a cross-party National Government when faced with the proposition of a federal United Kingdom. He preserved enough commonality around the case to hold the vast bulk of Unionists together under one banner. If the Unionist cause was to resurge under the leadership of Andrew Bonar Law, the basis was a legacy from Balfour.[266]

---

263 E. H. H. Green, *Ideologies of Conservatism: Conservative Political Ideas in the Twentieth Century*, Oxford, Oxford University Press, 2002.

264 Dutton, op. cit., 1992.

265 Huw Clapton, 'How not to run a political campaign: the failure of the Unionist free traders 1903–06', *Parliamentary History*, 30(2), 2011, pp. 165–8.

266 For the post-Balfour Irish strategy, see Jeremy Smith, *The Tories and Ireland: Conservative Party Politics and the Home Rule Crisis, 1910–1914*, Dublin, Irish Academic Press, 2000.

WINNING THE BATTLE OF IDEAS: A BALFOURIAN LEGACY?

In contrast to leaders such as Disraeli and Thatcher, few have identified a particular strain of Balfourian Conservative thought. Indeed, if the idea had been put to the man himself, he would likely have ridiculed it.

But did this most philosophical of political leaders have a clear philosophy to impress on colleagues, the political establishment and the wider public? His critics have been quick to point to the first half of the title of his famous work *A Defence of Philosophic Doubt*, ignoring its subtitle: 'Being an essay on the foundations of belief'. As E. H. H. Green has argued, his position on the constitution and, indeed, on tariffs was internally consistent and logical. His 1903 party conference speech was an exposition of this, with a strong argument against the perfection of the free trade ideal, the need for *realpolitik* and a readiness to retaliate against countries with trade barriers:

> And did any man ever hear of a country going into negotiations for these other purposes, which ever came out of those negotiations with a trace of success, unless they had, in the course of those negotiations, something they could offer, and something, in case of necessity, they might withhold? (Cheers.)[267]

Despite possessing sound logic on protection, Balfour had little success at winning the competition of ideas in domestic policy, where he was often forced to act as the referee between divisive elements within his party. Successive compromises meant that an all-out unadulterated pro-tariff policy was not tested on the electorate in three successive elections, despite nominal leadership from the party. This allowed Conservative colleagues in 1906 and 1910/11 to draw contrary conclusions about the electoral success of tariff reform as a concept: free traders argued it contributed to defeat; reformers suggested that the diluted version issued confusion and undermined the punch of full tariff

267 Arthur Balfour, Sheffield speech to the party, October 1903.

reform.[268] Even after the demise of Joe Chamberlain, Balfour never sought leadership of the tariff issue, as he was insufficiently committed outwardly to be a strong figurehead for the concept. More broadly, unlike contemporaries such as Chamberlain, Milner, Steel-Maitland and other members of the Unionist Social Reform Committee, Balfour did not develop a reformist instinct to counter the rise of socialism.

In contrast, Balfour's record on foreign policy and defence strategy was of great consequence. Three factors lay behind this relative success. First, the policymaking environment was better suited to Balfour's skills: foreign affairs were typically designed and executed away from the gaze of popular politics, instead within the milieu of Balfour's wide and cross-party social circle. Second, it helped that the party was far more united on foreign and defence matters than on domestic policy.[269] The leader was also simply more comfortable on these topics. It can have been no coincidence that his most persuasive and logical arguments on tariff reform were framed in terms of international negotiation and relations rather than domestic political bargains. Likewise, many years later he would become famous as the author of the 'Balfour Declaration', which set an ambition of an Israeli homeland.

Even by 1902, he had past form as Foreign Secretary and experience representing Lord Salisbury in the Boer War. During his leadership, Balfour's name became closely associated with a number of ideas and practices.

First, he guided his Foreign Secretary Lord Lansdowne to alliances with France and Japan that would form the basis of British peacetime and wartime policy in the First World War and beyond. As Austen Chamberlain noted years later, 'it is safe to say that Lansdowne took no important step and sent no important despatch without first consulting [Balfour]'.[270] Indeed, the Liberal government often called on Balfour's expertise when he was opposition

268 See, for instance, the letter from Chamberlain to Balfour, 29 January 1910, and from Salisbury to Chamberlain, 2 February 1910 (Austen Chamberlain Papers, Birmingham University Library, AC8/5/1; AC8/5/6). For 1906, see Witherell, op. cit.

269 Frank McDonough, *The Conservative Party and Anglo-German Relations, 1905–1914*, London, Palgrave, 2007.

270 Austen Chamberlain, *Down the Years*, London, Cassell & Co., 1935.

leader: in 1908, Asquith invited Balfour to join the invasion sub-committee of the Committee of Imperial Defence.

Second, he was highly influential in establishing the Committee of Imperial Defence itself in 1902 – the decision-making body that dominated defence strategy for decades.

Third, by dint of his personal authority, his involvement in the founding of policy, and his social circle, his mode and type of foreign policymaking established a pattern that was to be followed. For instance, his handling of the Agadir Crisis in 1911, when he proactively sought to counteract perceived divisions within Liberal ranks, was replicated three years later by the Conservative leaders in the crucial dealings with a vacillating Liberal government in July and August 1914.[271]

Finally, his Conservative opposition forced the Liberal government to increase naval expenditure, following the championing of the 'two-power standard'. This led to the evolution of a powerful 'blue-water' policy, which would hold significant sway into the First World War. This then formed a basis for Balfour's ideological and administrative legacy as party leader.

BENDING THE RULES: BALFOUR'S POLITICAL LEGACY FOR THE CONSERVATIVE PARTY

In political terms, Balfour also left a dual legacy as party leader, stemming from his time as opposition leader. In the first place, the Conservative Party successfully fought off attempts to abolish plural voting. Plural voting entitled a person to a vote as a resident and a second vote as a business owner (if in a different constituency), and was widely recognised as favouring the Conservative Party. This would remain important for the party's electoral prospects into the 1920s.[272] At the time, it was considered to gain the Conservatives thirty seats and some 500,000 votes. The Liberal

271 Rhodri Williams, *Defending the Empire*, London, Yale University Press, 1991.

272 Nigel Keohane, *The Party of Patriotism: The Conservative Party and the First World War*, Farnham, Ashgate, 2010.

government sought twice to remove the plural voting privilege, but the party recognised the issue was of sufficient electoral importance to them – as well as insufficiently resonant with the person on the street – that the legislation could be blocked in the House of Lords.[273] In this case, it represented judicious use of the Conservative supremacy in the Upper Chamber – as a block on reform.

Research has shown the breadth of tactical and constitutional factors that led Balfour and Lansdowne to use the House of Lords in the way they did. Their broad strategy was to allow more moderate social legislation through the second chamber, while obstructing radical or constitutional reform. They also pursued this policy as an exposition of their belief in the constitutional role of the second chamber, as well as it being a tactic to obstruct the most radical legislation.[274] The House of Lords represented a second line of defence for big-'C' and small-'c' conservative principles. Exercising influence through the Lords may have stemmed from a natural governing instinct that Balfour could not jettison, noting that, whatever the Liberal government attempted, the Unionists 'should still control, whether in power or in opposition, the destinies of this great empire'. He claimed – dubiously, as R. J. Q. Adams notes – that such a policy could even strengthen the second chamber as an institution.[275] Perhaps here he had in mind the advance of Salisbury, whose star rose when pursuing an oppositional policy in the House of Lords in the 1880s.[276] But the risks were also clear.

There is insufficient space here to do justice to the nuances and turns of debate associated with the stand-off between the House of Lords and the House of Commons in 1910 and 1911. At the final call, Balfour judged that it would be less catastrophic to let the Parliament Act (which reduced the power of the second chamber) pass, than to have the King, at Asquith's

273 Martin Pugh, *Electoral Reform in Peace and War, 1906–1918*, London, Routledge, 1978, p. 31.

274 Jane Ridley, 'The Unionist Opposition and the House of Lords, 1906–1910', *Parliamentary History*, 11(2), 1992, pp. 235–53.

275 Adams, op. cit., p. 234.

276 Roberts, op. cit.

bequest, flood the Lords with new peers, thus loosening the Conservative grip there, as well as potentially fatally de-legitimising it. This judgement – though reached very late and at the cost of worse internal divisions – was the right one for the party.

CONCLUSIONS

Balfour's leadership will be remembered, above all else, for its disastrous electoral defeats and a divided party. But, as described above, his influence as Conservative Party leader is poorly reflected in the bare electoral arithmetic, and party rifts stemmed not only from personal character failings, but also contextual factors.

His successes were notable. He was able to sustain the Conservative Party's future political position by keeping some of the less democratic (and more favourable) aspects of the electoral and parliamentary system in place, if not fully intact. He carved out an important legacy of policies and practices on defence strategy, foreign alliances and naval policy that established the tone of British foreign and military strategy into the First World War – and, in some cases, way beyond.

Mass Cabinet resignations, defections, fighting in the constituencies, and the rise of pressure groups and parliamentary ginger groups revealed huge party divisions from 1903 over tariff reform. Yet, these were – in part, at least – the product of an age of party realignment. The Conservative Party could harmonise around the Unionist theme, as it did from the end of the decade, if in a rather discordant way. Conservatives also shared a concern for the defence of the rights of property. But, in many other spheres, the Conservative coalition mixed conflicting ideologies: free traders versus tariff reformers; Anglicans versus Nonconformists; social reformers versus traditional conservatives. Yes, this was ever thus, but it was rarely as marked as in this period. These schisms were evident even within the Cecil family itself, which became a microcosm of party strife. It is also too simplistic to suggest that the absence of a credible alternative leader served purely to the benefit of Balfour. The spectre of Chamberlain loomed large enough to distract attention and inspire rebellion, without ever allowing the closure that a full-on confrontation might have allowed.

It is also too easy for historians to overlook Balfour's achievement in seeing off the other spectre that haunted him – namely Robert Peel, and his legacy of a major, long-term split in the party. In retaining the integrity of a Conservative Party as an entity, Balfour performed what he perceived as the most important task of leadership: preserving the party and retaining its ability to fight home rule. This formed the basis for a vociferous Unionist campaign between 1911 and 1914, led by his successor Andrew Bonar Law.

But, despite these contextual factors and achievements, Balfour's leadership had fatal flaws. In the refined fencing competition that was parliamentary debate, he duelled with style, even panache. In taking the fight to the streets, however, his foil was an over-refined weapon when compared to the cudgels of the Lloyd Georges and Joe Chamberlains. Much to the frustration of MPs and party managers, he didn't change his weapon, but instead retreated from the engagement.

This detachedness was a symptom of his distaste for popular politics and his lack of empathy for the emerging political constituencies with which his party would have to engage. The latter also derived from the small-'c' conservative policy he pursued on constitutional and social reform. This limited the scope of his ambition – and may explain why he over-estimated the electorate's perception of the governing competence of his government up to 1906. Such philosophical and political detachment came with costs: a failure to address the labour question; an inability or refusal to grasp the wider implications of tariff reform; disconnection from the political realities of education reform. This characteristic also induced his vacillation at crucial moments, especially over protection.

When he resigned the leadership in 1911, Balfour handed down a party that was in a worse state than when he had inherited it. But it was still there. And, perhaps for Balfour, that was enough.

CHAPTER 9

ANDREW BONAR LAW

ANDREW TAYLOR

Andrew Bonar Law's electoral record is complicated by: his entanglement and cooperation with David Lloyd George; the context of the First World War; and a period as Prime Minister cut short by illness and then death, barely a year after coming to the premiership. Andrew Taylor places particular emphasis on the relatively complex electoral context Bonar Law faced. The simple fact remains that the two elections he fought as leader – the coupon election of 1918, and the election of 1922, which he fought independently – both saw the Conservative Party comfortably into government. Bonar Law was successful in managing his party through a transitional political landscape and the movement to 'class-based' politics. After 1918 he was convinced the country's overriding need was for 'tranquillity' that eschewed active leadership of the type associated with Lloyd George. This means that Andrew Taylor outlines a statecraft characterised by containment, and paints the picture of a strong and safe pair of hands – if little more.

• • •

Andrew Bonar Law became Prime Minister, aged sixty-four, on 23 October 1922. On 19 May 1923, diagnosed with inoperable throat cancer, he resigned, dying on 30 October. He was Prime Minister for 209 days, hence the title of Blake's biography: *The Unknown Prime Minister.*[277]

277 Robert Blake, *The Unknown Prime Minister*, London, Odhams, 1955. Recent biographies are: R. J. Q. Adams, *Bonar Law*, London, John Murray, 1999; Andrew Taylor, *Bonar Law*, London, Haus, 2006.

Entering Parliament in 1900, Bonar Law's career coincided with a period of political change that culminated in the replacement in 1924 of the Liberal Party by the Labour Party as the Conservatives' main competitor for office; for over half this period, he was leader of the Conservative Party. Between December 1916 and March 1921 (when he first retired), he was de facto Deputy Prime Minister, and successively Chancellor of the Exchequer and Leader of the House. He was instrumental in destroying two prime ministers (Asquith and Lloyd George) and in making a third (Baldwin), and he also faced the rise of socialism, the onset of Britain's relative decline, and the rise of the modern state.

PATH TO LEADERSHIP

Bonar Law was born in 1858 in the manse of his father, an Ulster Presbyterian minister, in New Brunswick, Canada. After his mother's death, he left Canada as a child for Scotland, and, rather than go to public school, he entered the family bank and then the Glasgow iron market. Financially independent by the 1890s, his thoughts turned to politics, and he won the Glasgow seat of Blackfriars & Hutchestown in 1900 (he subsequently became MP for Dulwich, Bootle and finally Glasgow Central). An opponent of Irish home rule and a supporter of protection, Bonar Law achieved junior ministerial office in 1902. Although defeated in 1906, as a rising Unionist star he was quickly found a seat at Dulwich, and his career seemed set fair.

Bonar Law's natural melancholia was exacerbated by personal tragedy. In his eulogy, Bonar Law's successor Stanley Baldwin opined: 'I think he never recovered from the loss [in 1909] of his wife. From the loss of the boys during the war, he certainly never recovered, and I think what changed him in the war was what changed many people.'[278] Bonar Law found solace in politics. Blake suggested Bonar Law lacked the killer instinct, and his indecisiveness was a frequent complaint, but both, in reality, reflected his desire to avoid

278 Hansard, 13 November 1923, col. 24.

precipitate action.[279] Political experience told him that judicious vagueness and an emphasis on maximising the common ground could not only avoid trouble, but also keep opponents guessing, thus increasing his room for manoeuvre. Bonar Law was ambitious and acted to realise his ambition, with A. J. P. Taylor describing him as 'the most formidable giant-killer of the century'.[280] It is perhaps significant that Bonar Law was an accomplished chess player. As Machiavelli recommended in *The Prince*, Bonar Law combined the fox and the lion: 'One must be a fox in order to recognise traps and a lion to frighten off wolves. Those who simply act like lions are stupid.' Bonar Law was not stupid.

Bonar Law's lodestar was his party and party unity.[281] But, on the other hand, he was a polarising figure. It was in the interests of Unionism that he deployed his frequently biting rhetoric, which was dubbed the 'new style' after he became leader. Criticised for his vituperative language and for coarsening politics, it is important to remember that – in a political context, where the Liberals' majority rendered the Conservatives powerless – language was Bonar Law's only weapon. Bonar Law's rhetoric sometimes, in the opinion of his opponents, verged on the treasonous, but his party liked his slashing style.[282] Bonar Law once declared he only really cared about two things in politics – tariff reform and Ulster – and others noted that he lacked many of the Conservatives' usual atavistic sentiments and loyalties, pursuing, as he did, an unsentimental and pragmatic Conservatism.[283] These qualities made him leader in 1911.

When Balfour resigned the leadership in November 1911, the candidates – Austen Chamberlain (a tariff reformer) and Walter Long (representing the

---

279 Blake, op. cit., 1955, p.279; A. Taylor, op. cit., 2004, p.13.

280 A. J. P. Taylor, *English History 1914–1945*, Harmondsworth, Penguin, 1975, p. 42.

281 Robert Rhodes James, *Memoirs of a Conservative: J. C. C. Davidson's Memoirs and Papers, 1910–1937*, London, Weidenfeld & Nicolson, 1969, pp.124,126.

282 Vincent, op. cit., 1984, p. 263; David George Boyce ed., *The Crisis of British Unionism:. The Domestic Political Papers of the 2nd Earl of Selbourne*, London, The Historians' Press, 1987, pp. 93–4.

283 John Maynard Keynes, *The Writings of John Maynard Keynes. Volume X, Essays in Biography*, London, Macmillan, 1972, p. 83.

Tory squirearchy) – promised a divisive succession battle, and continued wrangling over free trade, which had destroyed Balfour. When Bonar Law's name first emerged, senior party opinion was dismissive, but events flowed swiftly in his favour. As a moderate tariff reformer, he was less divisive than Chamberlain, while his hostility to the Liberal government made him attractive to Long's faction; although denigrated as the 'third-best man', Bonar Law could unite the party. Neither Chamberlain nor Long could win against the other, and neither would withdraw in favour of the other, although they would support a compromise candidate.

Some Conservatives were sniffy about Bonar Law's background (Canadian, Scottish *and* nothing more than middle class), his education (neither public school nor Oxbridge), the fact he had made his money in trade, and his cleverness. But he was effective and popular.[284] Bonar Law spent time in the smoking room with his MPs, which, given his prodigious consumption of tobacco (it eventually killed him), was no hardship, and he was also conscious of not being seen as intellectually superior. As someone with 'common opinions and uncommon abilities' (Bagehot's definition of a statesman), Bonar Law's statecraft rested on him reflecting his party's attitudes and 'voicing the conservative sense of the electorate'.[285]

COALITIONS, COUPONS AND COOPERATION WITH DAVID LLOYD GEORGE

In 1914 Bonar Law accepted war demanded national unity, but, equally, he and many Conservatives believed the Liberal government guilty of partisanship and incompetence. Bonar Law was anxious to minimise Conservative discontent with the Liberals and bolster the war effort, but this

284 Vincent, op. cit., 1984, pp.237, 245–56; Philip Williamson ed., *The Modernisation of Conservative Politics: The Diaries and Letters of William Bridgeman 1904–1935*, London, The Historians' Press, pp. 53–4.

285 Thomas Jones, *Whitehall Diary Vol. 1, 1916–1925*, London, Oxford University Press, 1969, p. 222.

proved unsustainable. Throughout, party unity was a central consideration. In May 1915, Bonar Law joined the Liberals in coalition as a junior partner and, in this period, Bonar Law and Lloyd George drew closer, united by concern over Asquith's conduct of the war. Bonar Law's support for Asquith had come under increased attack from his backbenchers and, by November 1916, Bonar Law was convinced the situation could be resolved either by an election (inconceivable in wartime) or by a reconstruction of the government. In December, Lloyd George, supported by Bonar Law (who had been offered the premiership by the King), removed Asquith, becoming Prime Minister, with Bonar Law as Chancellor of the Exchequer.[286]

Bonar Law recognised war would transform politics. The growth of the state – which Bonar Law, as Chancellor, funded – he saw as a temporary expedient, but one that, nonetheless, created a new, complex politics of consent, dependent on working-class opinion. War made the extension of the vote, and the transformation of politics, inevitable. The Conservative Party, Bonar Law believed, had a key role in managing this transformation:

> Our party, if it is properly conducted, has no reason to fear that the mass of the people of this country will not support it. If we cannot win that support, we may as well go out of business, and it is our duty ... to see that everything is done by us to make our party what Disraeli once called it – and what, if it is to have any existence, it must be – a really national party.[287]

However, were the Conservatives a truly 'national' party? Bonar Law conceded that his party's image was one of 'class interests, class privileges and ... re-action', and that, if this was not challenged, 'I can imagine nothing worse, not only for the party, but for the nation'.[288] Secret discussions on electoral cooperation between Bonar Law and Lloyd George began in March

286 For a brief account of these complex events, see A. Taylor, op. cit., 2004, Chapter 5.

287 Special conference on the Representation of the People Bill, 30 November 1917 (NUA2/1/35), p. 9.

288 National Union gleanings and memoranda, no. 56, November 1922, p. 499.

1918, and, by July they had agreed on a distribution of candidates and constituencies. Labour posed a serious threat, and confronting it required a national movement under a leader who united all anti-socialists, which meant Lloyd George, not Bonar Law, as Prime Minister. Lloyd George's supposed ability to win working-class votes was strategically important because tariff reform, the Conservatives' last appeal to the working class, had split the party and ranged the unions against it.[289] Again, we see the centrality of party unity. The scale of the coalition's victory worried Bonar Law ('too big to be wholesome') and Conservative preponderance in the coalition posed problems of party management.[290] Aware of these pressures and worried by the growth of extra-parliamentary protest, Bonar Law enthusiastically supported measures to increase the state's resilience, declaring a willingness (even enthusiasm) for deploying state power against troublemakers.[291] The coalition, with the Conservatives at its core, wanted to stabilise society and politics, but new issues were emerging (Labour's electoral gains, unemployment, rent control, industrial militancy and high taxation) with the potential to polarise politics and plunge the country into class conflict. Bonar Law was convinced 'the middle way' could mobilise a vast constituency in favour of stability, and the coalition could embody that constituency.[292]

The flaw was that party prejudice and feeling *was* strong and rising. This was due to a growing rejection of Lloyd George-ism, middle-class discontent, and the coalition's failure to block Labour. Between December 1918 and November 1922, twenty-eight seats changed hands in by-elections; twenty-one were coalition losses. Eleven seats were Conservative, of which

---

289 Bonar Law to Salisbury, 3 May 1912 (Bonar Law Papers 33/4/34).

290 T. Jones, op. cit., 1969, p. 82. Baldwin also worried about 'a lot of hard-faced men who look as if they had done very well out of the war'. For accounts of this period, see: Maurice Cowling, *The Impact of Labour 1920–1924*, Cambridge, Cambridge University Press, 1971; Chris Cook, *The Age of Alignment: Electoral Politics in Britain 1922–29*, London, Macmillan, 1975; K. O. Morgan, *Consensus and Disunity: The Lloyd George Coalition Government 1918–1922*, Oxford, Oxford University Press, 1995.

291 Hansard, 20 March 1919, for example.

292 National Union conference, 10–11 June 1920 (NUA2/2/36), pp. 34–5.

five were won by the Liberals and three by Labour. Coalition Liberals lost eight seats to Labour. Many Conservatives concluded from this that they would do better without Lloyd George. Prior to his first retirement in March 1921, Bonar Law remained staunchly loyal, even seeking fusion between his party and the Lloyd George Liberals, convinced of the coalition's value as a bulwark against socialism.[293] Throughout 1921 and 1922, anti-coalition pressures inside the Conservative Party accumulated and, in the face of (Bonar Law's successor) Austen Chamberlain's arrogance and ideological coalitionism, a clash was inevitable. This came at the Carlton Club in November 1922. Although Baldwin led anti-coalition opinion, Bonar Law's attitude was critical. Initially uncertain, Bonar Law eventually decided to speak against the coalition.[294] The meeting at the Carlton Club voted against the continuation of the coalition; Lloyd George immediately resigned, and Bonar Law was invited to form the first Conservative government since 1900. Significantly, he sought the party's approval before forming a government.

THE ELECTORAL FLUX OF 1910–24

Central to understanding Bonar Law's statecraft is the electoral instability of 1910–24. Bonar Law was an election winner, but elections must be seen in context, which, for Bonar Law, was defined by flux and uncertainty. In January 1910, the Conservatives won 273 and Liberals 275 seats; in December, both won 272, with the Irish Nationalists (eighty-two then eighty-four seats) holding the balance of power, and the Liberal–Irish accord over home rule dominating parliamentary politics. Bonar Law won two elections – 1918 and 1922. Neither 1918 nor 1922 were vote landslides (winning 50+ per cent of votes cast); only 1918 was a seat landslide (winning

293 National Union gleanings and memoranda, no. 55, January to June 1922, p. 281; also, Bonar Law to Balfour, 24 March 1920 (Bonar Law Papers 96/4/11).

294 National Union gleanings and memoranda, no. 56, November 1922 (pp. 491–3 for his speech).

60+ per cent of the seats); but both were power landslides. A power landslide is the difference between the winning party's vote and seat share, and, on this measure, the 1918 and 1922 elections constitute two of the biggest landslides in electoral history.[295]

The Representation of the People Act (1918) tripled the electorate's size from 7,700,000 to 21,300,000, and its composition shifted signififcantly, with men over twenty-one and women over twenty-eight receiving the vote. This new electorate offered the Conservatives rich pickings (the 3,500,000 votes and 335 Conservative MPs of 1918 meant there was no *arithmetical*, as opposed to *political*, need for Lloyd George), but electoral conditions were fluid and unstable due to the continuing rise of Labour (in 1910, Labour polled some 300,000 votes, winning forty-two MPs; in 1918, it won 2,300,000 votes and had sixty-three MPs). Crucial was the Liberal split dating from 1916. In 1910, the Liberals polled some 2,200,000 votes, producing 272 MPs; in 1918, they were divided between the factions of Lloyd George (1,200,000 votes and twenty-eight MPs) and Asquith (1,400,000 and 133, respectively). This indicated a considerable pool of Liberal support. After 1918, the Conservatives were the dominant party, but the Liberals and Labour were *potentially* equal challengers. Electoral politics in the 1920s were, in the political science lexicon, at a non-Duvergerian equilibrium – a situation in which multi-party competition in a single-member plurality electoral system creates more than two potential competitors for office.[296] In these conditions, the electoral system could deliver a power landslide (as in 1922) but it could also (as in 1923) produce a situation where the Conservative, Labour and Liberal parties enjoyed equal voting power in the House of Commons. An election might produce, *inter alia*: a Conservative majority; a minority Conservative government; an anti-Conservative Labour–Liberal coalition; an anti-Labour Conservative–Liberal coalition;

295 See: Iain McLean, *Rational Choice and British Politics: An Analysis of Rhetoric and Manipulation from Peel to Blair*, Oxford, Oxford University Press, 2001, pp. 29–30.

296 Gary Cox, *Making Votes Count: Strategic Coordination in the World's Electoral Systems*, Cambridge, Cambridge University Press, 1997, pp. 85–9.

a minority Labour government; or, possibly, horror of horrors, a majority Labour government.

Turbulence meant Conservative dominance was not preordained, and, in 1922, Bonar Law was uncertain of Conservative victory.[297] The non-Duvergerian equilibrium raised complex strategic and tactical questions for Bonar Law and the Conservatives, because Labour, an avowedly socialist party, posed a more serious threat than the pre-1914 Liberals – so, how to respond to Labour's rise? Reaction? There would always be a 'reactionary element' in the Conservative Party, but if it was 'the sole element, our party is absolutely lost'.[298] This implied an anti-socialist coalition (a variation is the fusion of anti-socialists in a new party), a non-socialist progressive alternative, or else making the Conservative Party into *the* home for anti-socialists. The first and second options foundered on their potential to split the Conservative Party (as in November 1922, and with Baldwin's declaration for protection in 1923) and they risked electoral defeat; the third was more promising, but required a Conservative Party united and committed to destroying the Liberals, which was not yet thought feasible or, by some, desirable. All three hinged on anti-socialism, but was negative anti-socialism and a hostility to Labour a sustainable electoral appeal capable of delivering political hegemony? What would anti-socialism look like? Bonar Law was well aware of electoral arithmetic, noting: 'There is not one of my colleagues in the last House of Commons, and there will be none in the next, who could have his seat unless he had … the support of the mass of the people.'[299] Bonar Law saw his party as *the* anti-socialist party, but he was unable to develop a coherent electoral strategy and popular appeal. This was achieved by his successor. Bonar Law's electoral success was, therefore, contingent, occurring at a time when Labour was not fully established, the Liberals were divided, and there was a reaction against Lloyd George-ism.

297 T. Jones, op. cit., 1969, p. 222.

298 National Union gleanings and memoranda, no. 56, November 1922, pp. 491–2.

299 Speech at Leeds, 14 November 1922, in A. Taylor, op. cit., 2004, p. 114.

THE 1922 GENERAL ELECTION CAMPAIGN

The starting point for an understanding of Bonar Law's statecraft is his 1922 election manifesto. An election was necessary because of the coalition's collapse, but the speed of its collapse made it 'impossible' to develop detailed responses to 'the many questions with which we have to deal'.[300] This, however, was presented as a virtue:

> The crying need of the nation at this moment – a need that, in my judgement, far exceeds any other – is that we should have tranquillity and stability, both at home and abroad, so that free scope should be given to the initiative and enterprise of our citizens, for it is in that way, far more than by any action of the government, that we can hope to recover from the economic and social results of the war … [Recovery] will not be by attempts from above, it will be by the work of the people of the country; and my idea … is to leave free play to individual initiatives; to avoid attempts at improvement, which, at another time, would be very desirable and very necessary.[301]

At the time of the Chanak Crisis (September 1922), symptomatic of adventurism and over-reach, Bonar Law felt 'the prevention of war and massacre in Constantinople and the Balkans is not especially a British interest. It is in the interests of humanity … We cannot alone act as the policeman of the world.'[302] The main domestic problem was unemployment, on which action would be taken, but: 'The first essential is to reduce expenditure to the lowest attainable level in the hope that the taxpayer may find some relief from the burden of taxation, which not only presses so heavily upon individuals, but is the greatest clog upon the wheels of national industry.'

Bonar Law's government aspired to roll back the scale, scope and cost

---

300 Iain Dale ed., *Volume One: Conservative Party General Election Manifestos 1900–1997*, Abingdon: Routledge, 2013, pp. 23–6.

301 National Union gleanings and memoranda, no. 56, November 1922, p. 500.

302 *The Times*, 7 October 1922.

of Lloyd George's state, pursue a policy of tranquillity at home and abroad, and encourage lower expectations of government. Bonar Law avoided any policy – trade union reform, House of Lords reform, widening the franchise for women – that threatened the 'tranquillity' theme. A good example is protection. Amery, a convinced tariff reformer, argued the election was about changing government, whereas Bonar Law initially sought to keep the door open by reserving the right to increase tariffs for revenue purposes.[303] Bonar Law eventually committed himself to *not* changing the country's fiscal regime without another general election, because 'any violent change would be bad at this present time ... this parliament will not make any fundamental change in the fiscal regime of this country'.[304] Neville Chamberlain noted Bonar Law would enter No. 10 'not hampered by any foolish promises'.[305]

The context of Bonar Law's statecraft was the war. The problem was that the war's legacy was so great, neither tranquillity nor normalcy could be guaranteed. Bonar Law's task was straightforward in conception but complex in realisation: 'To govern competently and consolidate Conservative leadership of the anti-socialist forces without appearing reactionary in the process.'[306] Churchill derisively called Bonar Law's a 'government of the 2nd XI'. 'We may not have', Bonar Law declared, 'a monopoly of first-class brains, but we are ... composed of men with good judgement ... a government of first-class loyalty.'[307]

PARTY MANAGEMENT

Bonar Law became leader because of a breakdown in party management, so it was inevitable these considerations would loom large in his leadership.

---

303 Barnes and Nicholson, op. cit., 1980, p. 307; T. Jones, op. cit., 1969, p. 215.

304 National Union gleanings and memoranda, no. 56, June to December 1922, p. 548.

305 Neville Chamberlain to Hilda Chamberlain, 19 November 1922, in Robert Self ed., *The Neville Chamberlain Diary Letters: Vol. 2, The Reform Years, 1921–1927*, Aldershot, Ashgate, 2000, p. 132.

306 M. Cowling, op. cit., 1971, p. 245.

307 National Union gleanings and memoranda, no. 53, January to June 1921, p. 7.

Party considerations led him to secure the party's approval before forming his government. In fact, party management proved to be the least of Bonar Law's problems. The departure of leading coalition ministers (for example, Austen Chamberlain, Lord Birkenhead, Arthur Balfour and Robert Horne) created a potentially powerful group of dissidents, who remained committed to coalitionism and who expected Bonar Law's government to fail. Chamberlain's attitude to Bonar Law was unforgiving (Bonar Law had, after all, twice blocked his route to the premiership). Convinced Bonar Law would fail, and being committed to coalition, Chamberlain intended to keep the way open for 'a new coalition, if such becomes necessary (and I think it will), by not letting go of Lloyd George'.[308] This was precisely why Bonar Law, not Chamberlain, was leader. Aware of Chamberlain's inhibitions (party loyalty, fear of Labour gains if the government fell, and unpopularity in the party), Bonar Law could ignore him and his supporters, although he remained keen to win Chamberlain back.

Conservative diehards – those opposed to coalition and Lloyd George's Irish Treaty – were a potential source of trouble. Before 1914, Bonar Law had made his reputation as a defender of Ulster Unionism, and this, together with his broader political reputation, led many diehards to regard Bonar Law as one of their own. Before his retirement in 1921, Bonar Law, albeit with some misgivings, supported the Irish Treaty, and committed his government to ratification before the 6 December 1922 deadline. The treaty was an act of Parliament that 'had been before the country at a general election, when no responsible opposition to it had been raised', and, consequently, 'the government had no alternative' but to ratify it.[309] With Ulster's interests secured by partition, Bonar Law lost interest in the Irish Question.[310] Partition – a desire to remove Ireland from mainland politics – and the fact that the diehards had nowhere else to go meant ratification was a non-issue in party management. But Bonar Law was also strong enough to ignore the party grass roots anyway.

---

308 Austen Chamberlain to Ida Chamberlain, 18 November 1922 in Robert Self ed., *The Austen Chamberlain Diary Letters*, Cambridge, Cambridge University Press, 1995, p. 208.

309 November 1922 (CAB/23/29, 22), p. 1.

310 T. Jones, op. cit., 1969, p.165; Bonar Law to Croal, 21 November 1921 (Bonar Law Papers 107/1/83).

For example, the political levy and trade union political funds had long infuriated the party's grass roots. Attacking union political funds seemed an obvious way to damage Labour, but no action was forthcoming because 'the government have been too pre-occupied', although Bonar Law added that 'when they have less on their hands', they would consult the unions 'and try to get an arrangement that would seem fair to reasonable members of trade unions'.[311] This reflected Bonar Law's attitude to leadership. The party selected its leaders, who in turn chose the party's policy – 'if the party does not like the policy, they have to get another leader'.[312]

In February 1923, Davidson noted Bonar Law's mastery of the Commons, believing his government was 'shaping well'.[313] His majority was sufficient to see him through to 1927, and Clark sees the party as rejuvenated, concluding: 'All should have been set fair.'[314] However, events undermined his and his government's reputation for competence, which, when combined with persistent concerns about Bonar Law's health, gave his government a distinctly provisional feeling.

POLITICAL ARGUMENT HEGEMONY

The weakest element by far in Bonar Law's statecraft was political argument hegemony. The brevity of Bonar Law's premiership and the turbulence of the times militated against long-term strategic thinking. The failure to develop an argument was particularly serious because of the Labour Party's emergence as a credible competitor, deploying a set of arguments that was proving increasingly electorally persuasive. Notwithstanding, we can discern an embryonic argument in favour of limited government and of

311 21 March 1923 (CAB/23/45/16), p. 3.

312 A. Taylor, op. cit., 2004, p. 107.

313 Rhodes James, op. cit., 1969, pp. 140–41; Blake, op. cit., 1985, p. 209.

314 Alan Clark, *The Tories: Conservatives and the Nation State 1922–1997*, London, Weidenfeld & Nicolson, 1988, p. 13.

bringing resources and commitments more into line in order to focus on core national and imperial interests. The development of a hegemonic appeal was left to Baldwin, but it is interesting to speculate on the political and electoral viability of Bonar Law's approach. Fundamental to Bonar Law's appeal in 1922 was establishing a tone in politics distinct from both Lloyd George and Labour.[315] The government's determination to operate at a lower level of activity was reflected in a minimalist legislative programme; Amery described the King's Speech as 'like Bonar's customary ginger ale [Law was tee-total], rather dry and uninspiring but it will serve its purpose.'[316]

Symptomatic of Bonar Law's aspiration to enhance governability was his government's attitude towards unemployment. Bonar Law conceded unemployment was 'horribly bad', but asked: 'What can government do? It is easy to say [it] is the business of government to put it right. How exactly can they put it right?'[317]

In 1918, the yearly average unemployed was 0.8 per cent. In 1919, it was 6.0 per cent, falling in 1920 to 3.9 per cent, but averaging 16.9 per cent in 1921. When Bonar Law took office, it was 12.8 per cent. Ministers distanced the government from Lloyd George's interventionism. In response to a National Unemployed Workers' Committee rally in London (19 November 1922), where speeches of a 'seditious character' were made, the Cabinet agreed Bonar Law would not meet a deputation. This was the responsibility of the ministers of health and labour, and the government could not be seen to respond to extra-parliamentary pressure. Bonar Law's parliamentary secretary J. C. C. Davidson and the Metropolitan Police were to publicise 'the communist character' of the march's leaders, but there would be no prosecutions, in order not to inflame working-class opinion or give publicity to the marchers' cause.[318]

315 M. Cowling, op. cit., 1971, p. 243.

316 9 February 1923 (CAB/23/45/8), p. 1; Barnes and Nicholson, op. cit., 1980, p. 320.

317 Deputation from the Miners' Federation of Great Brtiain on distress in mining areas, 2 December 1922 (Bonar Law Papers 116/3/2).

318 Conclusions of a conference, 20 November 1922 (CAB/23/29), p. 1.

The 'abnormal circumstances' of the two previous winters meant 'it [had] been necessary to make considerable provision for unemployment'. Convinced unemployment was the result of wartime dislocation, high taxation and government spending, 'the extent to which government assistance can be given must ... be strictly limited, in view of the need of reducing the financial burden on the country'.[319] Central and local government would help, but 'as much stress as possible [should be laid] on the importance of stimulating private enterprise'.[320] The Cabinet approved various schemes, but reiterated that the solution lay in expanding trade, led by private businesses, and that unemployment benefit 'should be substantially less than the sum the individual could earn if he obtained employment'.[321] In attempting to engage Bonar Law with the unemployed during the election, Thomas Jones, for his pains:

> Listened to a long exposition of the virtues of individualism and the motives that moved mankind on the usual lines proper to a Glasgow businessman. I begged him to shew [*sic*] some real sympathy with the Glasgow unemployed, described the groups of half-starved men I had seen at the street corners ... and how I [had] been told that birds were nesting in the cranes on the banks of the Clyde.[322]

Bonar Law and his ministers were convinced there was little they could, or should, do.

Bonar Law's government made no coherent or sustained attempt to dominate the ideological debate or develop a programmatic response. Governance was directed at managing the pressures of post-war politics and the demands of politically and electorally significant groups, and lowering the political temperature. Amery described the government's responses

---

319 25 May 1923 (CAB/23/45/21), Appendix.

320 26 January 1923 (CAB/23/45/3), p. 2.

321 14 February 1923 (CAB/23/45/9), p. 9.

322 T. Jones, op. cit., 1969, p. 221.

to unemployment as 'makeshifts'; Neville Chamberlain, by then Minister of Health, agreed with Amery on 'the need for looking ahead and having some policy on social reform'.[323]

GOVERNING COMPETENCE

The Franco-Belgian occupation of the Ruhr in 1923 was intended to compel Germany to pay reparations. Bonar Law's government opposed the invasion, but did nothing so as not to jeopardise the alliance with France – the cornerstone of British foreign policy. Britain could do little other than express its doubts, appeal for calm, and call for a conference to finally resolve the reparations issue, accompanied by hints that Britain might withdraw its Rhine garrison (which no one believed).[324] Sensitive to the domestic political consequences of other trouble spots (for example, with Turkey over the Treaty of Sèvres, Polish–Russian tensions over Memel, and the British position in Iraq), ministers were keen to minimise both foreign and domestic troubles.

Bonar Law's government was vulnerable to the accusation that the coalition had betrayed its 1918 commitment to 'homes fit for heroes'. A Cabinet committee was created to deal with this politically sensitive question, but, despite the weaknesses of the 1919 Housing Act, the government refused to build houses directly. Government would subsidise local authorities, but 'should lay as much stress as possible on the importance of stimulating private enterprise'.[325] The decontrol of private rents, especially for the middle class, proved politically explosive. The original proposal was that decontrol on higher-rent houses would take place in June 1923, but this issue became central to the Mitcham by-election.[326] Electoral concerns led to the postponement of the decontrol

323 Barnes and Nicholson, op. cit., 1980, pp. 231, 352.

324 29 December 1922 (CAB/23/32/9), p. 3, for example.

325 26 January 1923 (CAB/23/45/3), p. 2.

326 Arthur Griffith-Boscawen, the Minister of Health, lost his seat in the general election, but was parachuted into Mitcham, where he lost the by-election as a result of rent decontrol.

of higher-rate rents until June 1924, with all rent control ending in June 1925 – neither of which saved Griffith-Boscawen from defeat, nor improved the government's image of competence.[327]

These issues caused political problems, but the deal over war debts with the United States, negotiated by the Chancellor Stanley Baldwin, triggered a major Cabinet crisis. After extensive negotiations in Washington, Baldwin cabled Bonar Law on the American offer, concluding this was the best deal available. The deal was endorsed by the Treasury, the Bank of England and the City, but the Cabinet was 'unanimously of [the] opinion that this is an offer we cannot accept'. The interest rate was 'intolerably unjust', acceptance would stimulate 'much hostility, and, at the best, there would be attacks upon America', which would inevitably worsen relations.[328] On 29 January 1923, Baldwin arrived in Southampton, where he blurted out his conviction that this was the best available deal. Next day (30 January), the Cabinet discussed the deal, and Bonar Law seemingly threatened to resign if it were to be accepted. Cabinet agreed to continue their discussion the next day. Only two Cabinet members supported Bonar Law, but, if Bonar Law carried out his threat, the government would fall.[329] On Wednesday, 31 January, the Cabinet agreed that the deal, though unsatisfactory, had to be accepted, as the alternative (default, which Bonar Law favoured, at least as a threat) entailed massive adverse economic and political consequences. Notwithstanding this phalanx of opposition, Bonar Law believed: 'We should repudiate our debt rather than burden the coming generation.'[330] Faced by a united Cabinet and no support from the City, Bonar Law conceded, limiting himself to writing in protest as 'Colonial' to *The Times*. Bonar Law took the pragmatic decision to back down, in

327 9 February 1923 (CAB/23/45/10), p. 5; 14 February 1923 (CAB/23/45/9), p. 5; 24 February 1923 (CAB23/45/12), p. 2.

328 15 January 1923 (CAB/23/45/2); T. Jones, op. cit., 1969, pp. 225–6; also, Bridgeman's diary, note on 1923, 15 December 1923.

329 30 January 1923 (CAB/23/43/4), p. 2; 31 January 1923 (CAB/23/45/5), p. 1; T. Jones, op. cit., 1969.

330 Rhodes James, op. cit., 1969, p. 143.

order to avert a Cabinet crisis that would have precipitated a general election and could have brought Labour to office. The concession reduced further Bonar Law's enthusiasm for the premiership.

In February, the government's majority fell to twenty-two on a motion supporting universal old-age pensions; in April, it was defeated on a vote on the employment of ex-servicemen, and, also in April, Austen Chamberlain rebuffed an overture to join Bonar Law's government. By-elections, then, as now, were referendums on a government's competence, and Bonar Law's record was not good.[331] At Willesden East (3 March 1923), a Conservative majority of 1,319 was transformed into a Labour majority of 5,176. At Mitcham (also 3 March), where Griffith-Boscawen's political career died, a Conservative majority of 5,036 became a Labour majority of 5,176. At Liverpool Edge Hill (6 March), the Conservative majority of 4,616 became a Labour majority of 1,050. These results stimulated criticism of Bonar Law's leadership. Amery felt the absence of Cabinet discussion meant ministers 'settled on the usual unsatisfactory compromise'; Chamberlain's verdict on the rent-control fiasco was that it accurately reflected the government's 'perpetual wobbling'.[332]

MANAGING PRIME MINISTERIAL POWER

Bonar Law believed Lloyd George's 'presidential' style of government was unconstitutional and dangerous. During the election, Bonar Law appeared to commit himself to abolishing the Cabinet Secretariat (nearly provoking the Cabinet Secretary's resignation), but he also opposed Lloyd George's personal bureaucracy, known as the 'garden suburb', and its unsavoury reputation – and this he did abolish.[333] The saga over the No. 10

331 In 1922–23, the Conservative tally was won one, lost four. The Liberals won three, lost one. Labour won two, lost none.

332 Barnes and Nicholson, op. cit., 1980, p. 321; Neville Chamberlain to Hilda Chamberlain, 24 February 1923, in Self, op. cit., 2000, p. 149.

333 T. Jones, op. cit., 1969, p. 219.

bureaucracy indicates Bonar Law's concern for 'normality', but Bonar Law agreed the secretariat (albeit reduced in size) and the ministerial rulebook should remain in force. The Prime Minister was to instruct the Cabinet Secretary as to the content of the Cabinet agenda, and minutes were to record only decisions.[334] Another significant decision was that no bill could be introduced without the Prime Minister's specific authority. These actions, part of a long process of increasing prime ministerial power, represent a significant reinforcement of that power.

Concern over public spending, a £65 million deficit, and high taxation enhanced Treasury control (with Bonar Law's endorsement), although whether this benefited the Chancellor or the Prime Minister in the long run is a moot point. Spending would be determined by bilateral negotiations between departments and the Treasury. The Treasury insisted 'the financial bearings and feasibility of all questions of policy should be comprehensively examined' and no spending proposal would come to Cabinet before agreement with the Treasury had been secured. Neither the PM nor the Cabinet would be involved in resolving spending disputes or in bilateral negotiations; spending decisions would focus on 'getting the best value for money and of making sure that there is money available'. The Treasury was responsible for 'taking a bird's eye view' of policy, which required early, close and continuous consultations with departments that had become accustomed to evading these consultations.[335]

Despite his desire for a return to the Prime Minister as *primus inter pares*, Bonar Law increased the Prime Minister's power and authority by discouraging debate and referring issues to committees. Cabinet debate was curtailed, there was 'very little talk, and things are largely cut and dried ... with all his mildness of demeanour, Bonar is really much more of an autocrat than LG [Lloyd George]'.[336]

334 Instructions to the Cabinet Secretary, 1 November 1922 (CAB/23/32/1), Annex III, p. 11.

335 11 January 1923 (CAB/23/45/1), p. 2; 21 March 1923 (CAB/23/45/16), pp. 11–12.

336 9 February 1923 (CAB/23/45/3), p. 4; Barnes and Nicholson, op. cit., 1980, pp.312, 313. Ministers were also instructed not to write signed press articles on current topics.

ASSESSING ANDREW BONAR LAW

Bonar Law was a transitional figure, leading the party into the era of class politics. His signal achievement was to keep the party 'in the political game at the highest level', and his doing so suggests that 'Bonar Law should be included in the pantheon of the party's greatest leaders'.[337] During his time, two shifts were under way: the replacement of the Liberal Party by Labour, and the redistribution of the Liberal votes. Evidence gathered in the mid-1960s showed 'only a minority of historic Liberal support went to Labour'.[338] Large numbers of middle- and working-class Liberals converted to Conservative voting in the inter-war period – partly because few came from Labour-supporting families (only 25 per cent of the pre-1918 cohort identified their father as Labour) – and the tendency of working-class Liberals to vote Conservative was strongest in the pre-1914 and inter-war cohorts. From 1918–24, these voters faced a Labour Party that was not fully established but they nonetheless saw Labour as a threat, and so were drawn to Conservative voting.

Bonar Law's primary object was to capture anti-socialist voters, who were not (as yet) Conservatives, in an anti-socialist parliamentary front. The party's re-assertion of independence in 1922 reduced the options to one: the Conservative Party as *the* anti-socialist front. Whether this would work was uncertain. The neutralisation of Ireland ensured a Conservative, not Unionist, identity (except in Ulster), but this identity's content was, as yet, an open question. Symptomatic of the difficulty of responding to these shifts was Bonar Law's appeal in 1922. In the immediate political context, tranquillity was appropriate, but, as many Conservatives (including Bonar Law) recognised, the conditions rendering tranquillity electorally attractive were temporary. Bonar Law's former Chief Whip was surprised when Bonar Law proved so

---

337 John Ramsden, *An Appetite for Power. A History of the Conservative Party*, London, HarperCollins, 1998, p. 246.

338 David Butler and Donald Stokes, *Political Change in Britain*, London, Macmillan, 1974, p. 168.

electorally popular, but the 'vapid' notion of tranquillity would not survive contact with reality, or evolve into a governing strategy.[339]

With the coalition's demise, the Conservative Party was poised to emerge as the mass anti-socialist party. If the modern Conservative Party was born between 1918 and 1922, Bonar Law was the midwife. Bonar Law's actions hinted at a strategy of popular anti-socialism, but, by the spring of 1923, Bonar Law lacked the political and physical energy necessary for such a feat of creativity. Throughout his life, Bonar Law was sceptical that the political space existed for a programmatic, socially aware Conservatism; he frequently expressed the view that if the voters wanted social reform, they would not vote Conservative.[340] Fiscal responsibility and economic orthodoxy (endorsed by the City, industry, the party and the press) were moral, political and economic goods, symbolising the new relationship between state and citizen that Bonar Law hoped to develop. But it was an essentially passive governance.

Despite his majority and control of his party, Bonar Law entered No. 10 facing considerable personal and political uncertainty. The Earl of Crawford was convinced Bonar Law would fail in his attempt to isolate his government from the new democratic dynamic, commenting: 'It is already apparent that high affirmation of principle, which was to guide this government instead of the opportunism of LG and co., has already been dispersed to the winds.'[341] Bonar Law's appeal in 1922 originated in reaction to Lloyd George, but the real target was Labour. Portraying socialism and communism as an alien threat to national unity pushed the party on a journey, which was completed by Baldwin in 1924. Bonar Law's reputation as a political hard man excited some adverse comment, but, over time, Bonar Law conveyed the impression of a man with strong convictions, weakly held. Bonar Law recognised that a party system built around the Conservative and Labour parties was pregnant with possibilities, but he did little to realise these possibilities. The emphasis

339 Vincent, op. cit., 1984, p. 465.

340 Bonar Law to Fabian Ware, 29 September 1908 (Bonar Law Papers 18/8/10), for an early instance.

341 Vincent, op. cit., 1984, p. 476.

on tranquillity and economic orthodoxy circumscribed his options, and his conviction that governments could, and should, play a limited role rendered him incapable of formulating a long-term electoral and governing strategy. This did not apply to other leading Conservatives.

Baldwin thought Bonar Law 'did greater service in preventing the doing of things it would be wiser not to do, rather than initiating things that ought to have been done'.[342] Baldwin's somewhat backhanded compliment goes to the heart of Bonar Law's statecraft. Bonar Law was an accomplished chess player – a game that spoke to his strengths and weaknesses as a politician. Keynes drew a direct connection between Bonar Law's politics and chess, conjecturing:

> The pieces on the board constituted the whole premises of the argument: that any attempt to look too far ahead was too hypothetical and difficult to be worthwhile, and that one was playing the game in question *in vacuo,* with no ulterior purpose except to make the right move in that particular game.[343]

Does this speak to Bonar Law's supposed caution and his inability to think strategically? Or does it point to his tactical acuity and doggedness? Bonar Law had a reputation for common sense, candour and integrity, but also for cunning and, when required, ruthlessness.

Enoch Powell believed political careers invariably end in failure. Entering No. 10, ill and exhausted, Bonar Law lacked the political vitality to develop a statecraft for a world irrevocably changed by war; notwithstanding Bonar Law proved a successful leader. As Lloyd George expressed it: 'He played a great part in great events.'[344]

---

342 Hansard, 13 November 1923, col. 24.

343 Keynes, op. cit., p. 34.

344 Hansard, 13 November 1923, col. 28.

CHAPTER 10

AUSTEN CHAMBERLAIN

DAVID DUTTON

David Dutton describes Austen Chamberlain's brief, tumultuous period as leader of the Conservative Party as an undiluted failure of statecraft. Chamberlain, who led the party from March 1921 to October 1922, never had his electoral mettle tested in a general election. He held a clear, and not inherently flawed, electoral strategy, and his principal diagnosis of the need to capture anti-socialist support, through alignment and cooperation with a struggling and split Liberal Party, was a theme pursued long beyond his time as leader. Yet Chamberlain's tin ear for the views of his party, his aloof style, and his inability to seek or listen to counsel led to widespread disillusionment among backbenchers and the Conservative rank and file. Quite simply, a failure of party management meant his political strategy remained unattainable and untested. Dutton describes a path to leadership that gave some hint of the leader's flaws (and the difficulties to come), though acquiring the leadership appears to have damaged, rather than enhanced, Chamberlain's political antennae.

• • •

Austen Chamberlain's leadership of the Conservative Party, or, strictly speaking, of the party in the House of Commons, is easily overlooked. Inheriting the position from the ailing Andrew Bonar Law in March 1921, he surrendered it back to the same man just nineteen months later, in October 1922. Moreover, Chamberlain was the last leader before William Hague whose tenure was not crowned by a period as Prime Minister. In some ways, his inconspicuous leadership mirrors his political career as a whole. Austen is the least celebrated of the three members of his family who held high office between the 1880s and the beginning of the Second World War. Though he enjoyed a distinguished ministerial career in his own right, with two spells at the Exchequer and a constructive term as Foreign Secretary, in a Commons sojourn of forty-five years, he still sits somewhat uncomfortably between the dynamic figure of his father Joseph – a man who, as Churchill put it, made the Victorian weather[345] – and that of his half-brother Neville, whose controversial politics have exercised an irresistible and unending attraction for historians. While Austen's death led to appropriate tributes in Parliament, the process of eclipse began immediately, with few sensing the passing of a truly major figure. 'I was saddened by how the House of Commons reacted to his death,' recorded the Conservative MP 'Chips' Channon. 'People just shrugged their shoulders, saying: "It's not too good a seat"; "He only held it by about forty in 1929." Little more.'[346] If, then, Chamberlain is remembered at all, it tends to be for the most negative of reasons: as the Tory who failed to rise to the top of Disraeli's 'greasy pole', or, more damagingly, as the politician who always played the game and always lost it.[347]

Yet Chamberlain's tenure of leadership is not without interest or significance, not least in illustrating the limitations of the power attached to the post. It also highlights the difficulties of serving strictly party interests – especially to the satisfaction of backbenchers and the Tory rank and file – within the context of a coalition government. Additionally, although Chamberlain, as leader, never fought a general election, his spell at the top of his party was dominated by the issue of how the Conservatives could best engage in, and emerge victorious from, such a contest. Finally, Chamberlain is unusual, though not unique, in enjoying a significant ministerial career *after* relinquishing the reins of leadership.

345 Winston Churchill, *Great Contemporaries*, London, Butterworth, 1937, p. 57.

346 Robert Rhodes James ed., *Chips: The Diaries of Sir Henry Channon*, London, Weidenfeld & Nicolson, 1967, p. 117.

347 The quip is variously attributed to Churchill or Lord Birkenhead.

As has often been noted, Austen Chamberlain was born into politics. His entire upbringing and education were designed to prepare him to carry the family name into a second generation of political distinction, and, one day, to the highest office of state. Not since the time of Chatham and Pitt the Younger had a father devoted so much attention to the political education of his son.[348] The remark, attributed to Joseph, that Austen 'was born in a red box, brought up in one, and would die in one' conveys something of the same meaning.[349] But it also suggests that the father came, in time, to see the limitations of the son and, belatedly, to pin his hopes on Neville, rather than Austen, to fulfil his dreams. 'You know,' he confided to a friend in 1902, 'of my two boys Neville is really the clever one, but he isn't interested in politics; if he was, I would back him to be Prime Minister.'[350] For all that, it was Austen who received the meticulous training for greatness. Rugby School and Trinity College, Cambridge, where he read history, were followed by experience of contemporary Europe, particularly France and Germany, where his father's renown gave him access to some of the leading political figures of the day. And it was Joseph's influence that helped secure his adoption as Liberal Unionist candidate for East Worcestershire – a constituency only just outside the control of the Chamberlainite caucus in Birmingham. In 1895, Austen, not quite thirty-two years of age, gained his first ministerial appointment as Civil Lord of the Admiralty in a government in which Joseph took the critical Cabinet post of Colonial Secretary. It would be unfair to suggest that Austen had not, independently, shown the talent and ability to merit advancement; but, at the same time, it would also be reasonable to argue that he did owe something to what the *Daily Mail* once called 'the inestimable advantage of being the son of his father'.[351]

Not surprisingly, Austen's relationship with his father developed into the most important of his political life, and one that endured long after Joseph's

---

348 Charles Petrie, *The Chamberlain Tradition*, London, Lovat Dickson, 1938, p. 130.

349 Thomas Jones, *A Diary with Letters 1931–1950*, London, Oxford University Press, 1954, p. 318.

350 Julian Amery, *The Life of Joseph Chamberlain, Vol. 4*, London, Macmillan, 1951, p. 275.

351 *Daily Mail*, 17 April 1918.

death in 1914. Even during the last year of his own life, the centenary celebrations of his father's birth became one of Austen's greatest preoccupations. The emotion of the occasion was almost too much for him and he became 'so moved that, at one moment, I feared he might break down'.[352] He had evidently 'worked himself into an appalling condition of nerves beforehand', and it was not surprising that, 'when the time came to speak, even a strong whisky and soda was insufficient to restore his control completely'.[353]

To have lived out the first forty years of his life in the same house as the magisterial figure who was his father left a profound impression upon him. Austen wanted to interpret the relationship entirely positively: 'My choice of a political career combined with my late marriage has given me an intimacy and friendship with my Father, which I think are rare in such a relationship, and certainly make it very beautiful and precious in our case.'[354] Yet, while parental influence no doubt opened many doors for the aspiring politician, in the longer term, Austen almost certainly suffered for being his father's son. His half-sister Hilda argued that Joe's anxiety to smooth Austen's path, by giving him the advantages that had been absent from the first stages of his own career, proved, in the end, a disservice, not obliging Austen early on to grapple with everyday difficulties. In addition, there were always those who insisted on comparing his performance with that of his father – and they invariably found the younger man wanting. Austen suffered, according to one historian, 'from being the over-groomed offspring of an outstanding personality'.[355]

He even seemed to cultivate his father's physical appearance. To dress like Joseph in the 1890s was one thing, but to favour the same outfit – frock coat, silk top hat, orchid and monocle – forty years later, by which time such attire had become mannered and dated, was, to say the least, curious. But, as

---

352 L. Amery, *My Political Life, Vol. 3*, London, Hutchinson, 1955, p. 201.

353 Neville to Hilda, 11 July 1936 (Chamberlain MSS, NC18/1/969).

354 Austen to Mary Carnegie, 30 March 1913 (Chamberlain MSS, AC/4/1/968).

355 Peter Rowland, *The Last Liberal Governments, Vol. 1*, London, Macmillan, 1968, p. 50.

Austen himself fully realised, this surface resemblance disguised important differences between the two men. Joseph 'has been more ambitious for me than ever I have been for myself ... and that is the only point on which I have ever had to resist his counsels'.[356] Whereas his father was a born political fighter, relishing the challenge of controversy and battle, Austen was, by nature, a man of compromise and conciliation. Harold Macmillan, who observed him in the 1920s and '30s, judged him 'very unlike his father ... respected, but never feared'.[357]

There was, moreover, one aspect of his father's character that Austen was privately determined *not* to emulate. 'Pushful Joe' was not an epithet he sought to inherit. While his devotion to his father's memory remained profound, there lurked in Austen's mind the uneasy, if largely unspoken, knowledge that Joe had not been entirely a gentleman. This would have a lasting impact on the younger man's long and sometimes anguished path towards the leadership of the Conservative Party, and on his conduct once he was installed. 'He had quite a good opinion of himself,' judged Leo Amery. 'But he had an exaggerated fear of being regarded as pushful ... or other than scrupulously correct and loyal in all his personal dealings.'[358]

Developments in 1903 and 1906 subtly modified the relationship between father and son, while apparently bringing Austen appreciably closer to the position of leadership. In September 1903, Joe resigned from the government of Arthur Balfour in order to campaign for, and educate the nation on, the merits of tariff reform from the comparative freedom of the Commons back benches. Meanwhile, at the early age of forty, Austen was promoted to the senior Cabinet post of Chancellor of the Exchequer. This rapid advance was widely interpreted as a means for Austen to act as a bridge between the Prime Minister and his father, ensuring the former's broad commitment to the policy of tariff reform.

---

356 Austen to Mary, 7 May 1911 (Chamberlain MSS, AC4/1/651).

357 Harold Macmillan, *The Past Masters*, London, Macmillan, 1975, p. 128.

358 L. Amery, op. cit., 1955, p. 386.

Three years later, with the Unionist coalition relegated to the ranks of opposition, following the disastrous 1906 general election, the elder Chamberlain suffered a severe and crippling stroke, which marked the effective end of his public life. It now fell to Austen to take over the leadership of the Liberal Unionists in the Commons, and, more informally, of the tariff campaign in the country. For the father, the cause of tariff reform had been an almost spiritual crusade; for the son, it was primarily a matter of filial duty and much less a question of intellectual conviction. Austen's new role placed him in the most difficult of positions. At a time when he should have been ready to fashion his own distinctive political identity, he was called upon to be a sort of surrogate version of his father – to be even more Joe's son than hitherto. It was near to being a no-win situation. While he failed to maintain the wholehearted commitment of those Chamberlainites who would have laid down their political lives for Joe, he still attracted the hostility of those for whom the elder Chamberlain represented a dangerous and distasteful innovation in Unionist politics.

By the autumn of 1911, Balfour's position as Unionist leader had become precarious, not least because of his own waning enthusiasm for the role. His electoral record was unenviable, having led the Unionists to three successive defeats. Inevitable criticism within the party was exacerbated by Balfour's hesitant and ambiguous leadership during the constitutional crisis that had culminated in the passage of the Parliament Act that summer. In these circumstances, the announcement of his resignation on 8 November was scarcely a surprise.

No one candidate stood out as the departing leader's obvious and undisputed successor, but Austen Chamberlain's claims were clearly strong. For Amery, Chamberlain's general ability, debating power, and parliamentary and administrative experience made him an obvious choice.[359] The Chief Whip focused on Chamberlain's already wide political career – 'Whip, Treasury, Postmaster General, Admiralty, Exchequer – quite a large range.'[360] Yet Balfour's secretary pointed to the debit side of Chamberlain's CV – 'That he comes from

359 Ibid., p. 385.

360 Vincent, op. cit., 1984, p. 238.

Birmingham, that he is a Liberal Unionist, that he is not allied by family tradition or landed estates with the traditional Conservative Party.'[361] The first of these impediments was perhaps the most important. 'Birmingham' implied far more than a geographical derivation. It was a contemptuous shorthand description of a new and distasteful form of politics. According to one MP, the 'Birmingham mind ... would run an empire on the principles of retail trade', while, for Lord Balfour of Burleigh, 'the Birmingham influence ... was pursuing things that by no stretch of the imagination can be described as Conservative'.[362] In many ways, this was unfair on Chamberlain. He was by inclination – and certainly evolved into – a conventional Conservative. Harold Macmillan, as conscious as most of social standing, later judged that 'there was not really much of Birmingham about him'.[363] Being a Liberal Unionist in 1911 was not quite the handicap it would have been a decade before. After all, Conservatives and Liberal Unionists would formally amalgamate the following year. Yet Chamberlain's political pedigree remained suspect, and his recent association with the Halsbury Club, whose members had been openly critical of Balfour, could only confirm misgivings. In the circumstances, it was almost inevitable that the Conservatives of 'family tradition' and 'landed estates' would rally round an alternative candidate, Walter Long, as an unequivocal representative of these historic interests.

Chamberlain's contemporary comment that he wished there were 'another Balfour ... obviously marked out for the post', to whom he would gladly 'play second fiddle', should not be taken at face value.[364] Looking back on these events six years later, he admitted that his ambition had been fired, and that he 'dreamed, like others, of being head of a ministry that should make some history, domestic and imperial'.[365]

The truth lay somewhere between these two assessments. Chamberlain

---

361 J. Sandars's note of the events leading to Mr Balfour's resignation (Balfour MSS, Add. MS 49767).

362 Bowles to Sandars, 11 November 1911 (Balfour MSS, Add. MS 49862); Balfour of Burleigh to Long, 5 December 1907 (Balfour of Burleigh MSS 30).

363 Macmillan, op. cit., p. 128.

364 Austen Chamberlain, *Politics from Inside*, London, Cassell, 1936, p. 381.

365 Austen to Ida, 4 November 1917 (Chamberlain MSS, AC5/1/45).

would have been happy to accept the leadership, had it been offered to him on a plate; but, unduly sensitive 'to the slightest suggestion of self-advancement', it was not something for which he was prepared to fight.[366] In short, he 'lacked that ultimate hardness, without which men seldom reach supreme political power'.[367] As a result, as soon as Balfour's resignation became public, Chamberlain absented himself from the Commons, 'repelled by even the faintest suggestion of canvassing for support'.[368]

Most well-placed contemporaries believed that Chamberlain would have emerged victorious from a contested election, perhaps on a second ballot. After all, he enjoyed the backing of the majority of the shadow Cabinet, the Chief Whip, the party chairman, the Halsbury Club and Sir Edward Carson, who had, at one time, seemed ready to throw his own hat into the ring. At the same time, the strength of opposition to Chamberlain among Long's supporters made a contest inevitable, with the prospect of later recriminations, and a possible damaging split in the party's ranks. Granted Chamberlain's mindset, he was always going to be susceptible to the idea of a compromise third candidate, capable of reconciling Unionism's warring factions. Once the impossibility of his own overwhelming victory became apparent, Chamberlain wrote to Long to stress that serious fissures in the party would be inevitable if the choice between them went to the indignity of a vote. He proposed, instead, that both candidates should withdraw in favour of the relatively unknown Andrew Bonar Law, whose interest in the position had hitherto been regarded as no more than laying down a marker of his possible future ambitions. With Long agreeing to follow Chamberlain's lead, Bonar Law's election became a formality.

By his actions in 1911, Chamberlain established, in many minds, the reputation of a man of unimpeachable rectitude. Others, however, judged that he had merely confirmed a basic political incapacity, which would always

366 P. Marsh, *The Chamberlain Litany*, London, Heinemann, 2010, p. 249.

367 Blake, op. cit., 1955, p. 72.

368 Marsh, op. cit., 2010, p. 109.

circumscribe his career in public life. In terms of his future prospects, it probably did Chamberlain no favours that members of his close family encouraged his belief in the first of these interpretations. 'We are all very proud of you,' reported his sister Beatrice, 'you are a little too good for this world.' His half-sister Ida was of the same mind: 'One must be prepared to pay the penalty for having a higher moral standard than one's neighbours.'[369]

In the years that followed, Chamberlain remained a leading figure in the Conservative hierarchy. In private he made it clear that he did not necessarily regard the 1911 decision as final, and that, should the occasion arise, he would have no hesitation in standing again for the party leadership.[370] Indeed, if history judges Chamberlain a perpetual loser, he was not necessarily a good one. He nursed a lasting resentment towards Bonar Law – 'I don't think that, if our positions had been reversed, I could have acted as he did' – and consistently underestimated the new leader's political skills.[371] Of Bonar Law's performance in Asquith's wartime coalition, he later reflected that 'we could not have been ... more inadequately represented by any leader'.[372] But the crucial relationship in determining Chamberlain's remaining in contention for the Tory leadership, should a vacancy occur, was not with any Conservative, but with Asquith's successor as coalition Prime Minister, the Liberal David Lloyd George. Here, Chamberlain's initial hostility – 'quite untrustworthy ... doesn't run crooked because he wants to but because he doesn't know how to run straight' – was transformed into a growing trust and personal regard: 'No living Englishman can compare with him and, when the history of these times comes to be written, can you doubt that he will stand out like the younger Pitt, if not with the effulgence of Chatham?'[373]

Thus, having accepted appointment for a second term as Chancellor of

---

369 D. R. Thorpe, *The Uncrowned Prime Ministers*, London, Darkhorse, 1980, pp. 5, 51.

370 Sandars to Balfour, 10 November 1911 (Balfour MSS, Add. MS 49767).

371 Austen to Mary, 10 November 1911 (Chamberlain MSS, AC4/1/728).

372 Austen to Ida, 4 November 1917 (Chamberlain MSS, AC5/1/45).

373 Austen to Hilda, 14 December 1916; 6 February 1921 (Chamberlain MSS, AC5/1/3; AC5/1/191).

the Exchequer in January 1919, he was well placed to succeed Bonar Law – albeit in the continuing context of a coalition government still headed by a non-Conservative – when illness forced the Tory leader's resignation in March 1921. Chamberlain took over the party leadership in the Commons (Curzon retaining the position in the Lords) without a contest. This was fortunate from his point of view. As in 1911, he was not prepared to fight for the post. He later explained his position to J. C. C. Davidson, saying that he had:

> A great horror of anything that savours of intrigue or pushfulness on the part of a possible candidate, and felt then as I felt ten years ago ... that the only right thing to do was to keep quiet and leave members to make up their own minds without either courting their favour or shunning responsibility if their choice fell upon me.[374]

The political climate that confronted Chamberlain on assuming the party leadership was very different from the one within which he would have operated had he become leader a decade earlier. To his credit, he was fully aware of the transformation that had taken place. As Chamberlain put it: 'The man who thinks he can take up his life again in 1921 where he left it on 4 August 1914 is a man who might as well be dead and buried.'[375] The Liberal Party that had entered the war as the party of government was now shattered and divided. Meanwhile, Labour had risen from its pre-war status as a party of protest to become a genuine contender for power. Moreover, these changes had taken place in the context of an expanded electorate – something like three times its pre-war size – from which the Conservatives could not take for granted their own credentials as an ongoing party of government. For a brief period, while Labour rose and the Liberals fell, Britain entered a genuine era of three-party politics, adding new complexities to the

374 Rhodes James, op. cit., 1969, p. 103.

375 Self, op. cit., 1995, p. 149.

parliamentary landscape and the political lexicon alike. Against this background, Chamberlain developed into one of the more thoughtful observers of a changed world, and, in particular, of the 'impact of Labour'.

Chamberlain's overriding objective was to restructure the political system in such a way as to bar Labour's route to power. His innate conservatism made him want to maintain the country's existing social and economic structure 'against real, potential or imaginary threats from the working class'.[376] The last days of the war had found him looking forward apprehensively to a future 'full of difficulty and danger, strikes, discontent and much revolutionary feeling in the air when the strain and patriotic self-repression of the last few years are removed'.[377] Labour represented 'a serious menace to the nation ... because of its difference from every other party ... in being directed and controlled from outside Parliament'.[378] This inevitably meant reassessing the pre-war antagonism that had kept Conservatives and Liberals apart. 'A new party has come into existence,' he wrote in 1922, 'and this party ... is divided from both the old parties on what are likely to be the greatest issues of the next few years, for it challenges the basis of our whole economic and industrial system.'[379] The issues that now confronted politicians were largely economic and social questions upon which the older parties had usually been agreed. The practical conclusion to this line of reasoning was the need to maintain the post-war coalition with Lloyd George's wing of the Liberal Party and, once 'hostility and prejudice ... old habits and rivalries' had been 'softened or removed', probable fusion.[380]

Of course, Chamberlain's understanding was not perfect. It was also open to the Conservatives to improve their electoral prospects by the adoption of

---

376 Margaret Morris, '"*Et l'honneur?*" Politics and Principles: A Case Study of Austen Chamberlain', in Chris Wrigley ed., *Warfare, Diplomacy and Politics*, London,: H. Hamilton, 1986, p. 83.

377 Austen to Ida, 9 November 1918 (Chamberlain MSS, AC5/1/112).

378 Chamberlain to R. Cecil, 26 April 1921 (Chamberlain MSS, AC24/3/16).

379 Chamberlain to Madge, 26 January 1922 (Chamberlain MSS, AC33/1/21).

380 Chamberlain to Churchill, 8 April 1921, in Martin Gilbert, *Winston S. Churchill, Vol. 4* (companion part 3), London, Heinemann, 1977, p. 1434.

progressive new policies tailored to the interests of the expanded electorate. 'While Austen looked to Liberals to produce the margin of victory,' writes Peter Marsh, 'Neville looked to social reform to enhance the Conservative appeal.'[381] That said, capturing the 'Liberal vote' would remain, in one form or another, at the heart of Conservative electoral strategy for the following three decades. But Chamberlain's goal would strain his relationship with the Conservative Party almost to breaking point. The difficulty lay not in his analysis of the problem, but in his failure to persuade a majority of his party of the correctness of his diagnosis. This failure derived directly from the personal shortcomings of his leadership.

Leadership brought out the worst features of Chamberlain's character. The dignity and integrity that he had long cultivated transmogrified now into an aloof pomposity that made him difficult to approach, let alone influence. In a revealing confession, Chamberlain wrote: 'I wonder whether I can cultivate pleasant colloquial habits. To be hail fellow well met with all my "followers".'[382] In fact, there is no evidence that he made any effort in this direction. Far from frequenting the Commons smoking room, Chamberlain increasingly lost contact with the party he led. His attitude towards the leadership became ever more authoritarian. No doubt drawing upon the example of his own public loyalty to Bonar Law over the preceding decade (notwithstanding the 'contemptuous spleen' readily vented in private[383]), Chamberlain expected the party's MPs and rank and file to abide by the policy determined by the leader and to keep any criticism or reservations to themselves. 'A[usten] does not readily take suggestions either on gardens or politics,' Neville had wryly noted as early as 1918.[384] It is surely revealing that Chamberlain interrupted his regular correspondence with his half-sisters Ida and Hilda for several weeks before and beyond his loss of office in October 1922. While there may

381 Marsh, op. cit., 2010, p. 189.

382 Austen to Hilda, 20 March 1921 (Chamberlain MSS, AC5/1/194).

383 Self, op. cit., 1995, p. 28.

384 Neville to Hilda, 20 July 1918 (Chamberlain MSS, NC18/1/177).

be some truth in his protestation that he had been 'too busy, too tired or too *bruised* to write', it seems also probable that he was consciously avoiding family advice with which he would not agree.[385] Fatally for a political leader, his skin was of the thinnest kind. He did not so much *take* offence as seemingly grasp it with open arms, no matter how innocuous or well-intentioned the proffered dissent. Sustained by the agreement of a small but important group of Cabinet colleagues, Chamberlain never understood that good leadership derived from the cross-fertilisation of ideas and opinions, rather than being inflexibly imposed from above. As one critic put it: 'He seemed to feel that it was not consonant with his position to seek to induce the recalcitrant group to join him. Rather it was for them to offer loyal obedience.'[386]

The gap between leader and led widened steadily over the course of Chamberlain's tenure. As recent experience has shown, one of the difficulties facing a political leader in coalition is to convince his followers that their own party interests are being sufficiently upheld within the government's policies and priorities. Under Chamberlain, a growing number of Conservatives regarded the coalition in general, and Lloyd George in particular, as diminishing, indeed spent, assets. Whatever might have been the case at the time of the coupon election of 1918, Tories found it increasingly difficult to accept subordinate status in the government, despite their numerical dominance in the Commons. The perception that Chamberlain exercised less influence than Bonar Law merely exacerbated matters. Individual initiatives, most notably Lloyd George's Irish settlement and latterly his foreign policy, progressively eroded the confidence of sections of the party in the government as a whole. Chamberlain personally saw his goal with some clarity. He told Lloyd George:

> My object has been to lead the Unionist Party to accept merger in a new party under the leadership of the present Prime Minister and including

385 Austen to Ida, 18 November 1922 (Chamberlain MSS, AC5/1/250).

386 Memorandum by Pollock on the fall of the coalition government (Pollock MSS, d432).

> the great bulk of the old Unionists and old Liberals so as to secure the widest and closest possible union of all men and women of constitutional and progressive views.[387]

But, in so far as the Conservatives as a whole understood this strategy, they did not like it, fearing the loss of their own identity and feeling increasingly confident in their ability to prevail at a general election without Liberal support.

Chamberlain seemed to wilfully underestimate the forces that ranged against him. Even when a meeting of 200 Conservative MPs on 14 March 1922 expressed grave concern over coalition policy and came close to repudiating his leadership, he dismissed it as of 'no real significance', insisting that, except among a 'small "die-hard" section', support for Lloyd George and himself remained strong.[388] In truth, there was, by this stage, no excuse for Chamberlain's failure to appreciate the strength of party feeling against him. The party chairman, whose ears were better attuned to the grass roots than Chamberlain's, had warned him in January of the 'growing number of candidates and constituency chairmen who say that they won't support the coalition beyond the life of the present parliament'.[389] But Chamberlain carried on regardless, seemingly bent on his own destruction, 'more short-tempered, more inflexible and more imperious' in his conviction that he alone knew what was best.[390] By the late summer, 184 MPs and candidates had declared that they would stand at the next election as independent Conservatives rather than supporters of the coalition. Yet, on 17 September, government leaders took the disastrous decision to go to the country as a coalition once the foreign situation allowed. In acquiescing in this step, Chamberlain was ignoring the advice of party managers, elder statesmen, junior ministers and backbenchers. His wilful disregard of those whom he nominally led represented 'a breach of the understanding upon which the

387 Memorandum by Chamberlain, 6 January 1922 (Chamberlain MSS, AC32/2/27).

388 Chamberlain to Lloyd George, 15 March 1922 (Lloyd George MSS, F/7/5/8).

389 Younger to Chamberlain, 30 January 1922 (Chamberlain MSS, AC32/3/4).

390 Ramsden, op. cit., 1998, p. 243.

allegiance of the ... party to its leaders depends'.[391] Figures such as the Chief Whip, party chairman and principal agent owed a primary loyalty to the party 'as a concept and a whole, rather than to any particular leading figures'.[392] George Younger, the party chairman, could not have been blunter: 'It is a question of either breaking the party or breaking you, and I intend to do the latter.'[393]

Undeterred, Chamberlain produced his prediction for the general election, showing – to his own satisfaction, at least – that no government was possible without coalition and that coalition was only possible under Lloyd George.[394] Having seen the strength of anti-coalition feeling at the two previous party conferences, he determined to bypass the one scheduled for November by calling a meeting of Conservative MPs at the Carlton Club on 19 October – the timing designed to allow for the result of a by-election in Newport (where an independent Conservative was standing against a Liberal) to offer proof of Chamberlain's thesis. A seat lost to Labour would greatly strengthen his argument.

His mood was belligerent. He intended 'to tell them bluntly that they must either follow our advice or do without us, in which case they must find their own chief and form a gov[ernmen]t *at once*. They would be in a fix.'[395]

In the event, all Chamberlain's calculations unravelled. His speech at the Carlton Club was 'very rigid and unbending, needlessly so'. It 'left no exit for those who sincerely wished to find some escape from passing a vote of censure'.[396] The Newport seat had been won by the Tory candidate and the question of an alternative leader was resolved by the presence of Bonar Law, apparently restored to good health. Indeed, at Bonar Law's entrance, Chamberlain's 'face blanched with surprise and anticipation of what it meant'.[397]

391 Ibid., p. 3.

392 Stuart Ball, *Portrait of a Party*, Oxford, Oxford University Press, 2013, p. 514.

393 Ibid., p. 500.

394 Austen to Ida, 24 September 1922 (Chamberlain MSS, AC5/1/249).

395 Chamberlain to Birkenhead, 12 October 1922 (Chamberlain MSS, AC33/2/52).

396 Vincent, op. cit., 1984, p. 453.

397 Memorandum on fall (Pollock MSS., d432).

Bonar Law's own speech warned of the dangers of repeating the mistakes of Peel over the Corn Laws – always a telling argument in Conservative circles – and he stressed the importance he attached to keeping the party united, something that no longer seemed possible under Chamberlain's leadership. By a vote of 185 to eighty-eight, the party opted for independent action at the election. The size of the majority showed that far more than (what a later generation would style) the 'usual suspects' had opposed their leader. Support had ebbed away among a swathe of mainstream and normally loyal MPs.[398] Chamberlain and Lloyd George immediately resigned their positions and, on 23 October, Bonar Law was unanimously re-elected as party leader.

It was a dramatic end to a catastrophic episode in the history of the Tory leadership. Chamberlain had been 'quite stupid and obstinate with an impossible conceit that would smash anyone in public life'.[399] The man who, in 1911, had supposedly been driven by an overriding concern not to split the party, behaved, in 1922, as if intent on doing just that. The potential for lasting damage was considerable. Indeed, for the first time since the mid-nineteenth century, there now existed two rival sets of Conservative leaders and 'the distinction between pro- and anti-coalitionists remained the most significant fault line in Conservative politics for the next nine years'.[400] Yet the impact on the party was contained. Key party managers remained in place and Bonar Law quickly led the Conservatives to an overwhelming general election victory – though the fact that he did so on just 38 per cent of the popular vote gave no guarantee of future success and showed that Chamberlain's analysis of the electoral scene was not entirely without merit.

Chamberlain himself does not need to be remembered as the Tory leader who failed to become Prime Minister. Lloyd George offered to step down in his favour in February 1922; Chamberlain had only to say yes. The question is whether a Chamberlain premiership would have been any more successful

---

398 Stuart Ball, op. cit., 2013, p. 341.

399 Younger to H. Cecil, 11 December 1923, cited in Self, op. cit., 1995, p. 15.

400 Stuart Ball, 'The legacy of coalition: fear and loathing in Conservative politics, 1922–1931', *Contemporary British History*, 25(1), 2011, p. 65.

than his party leadership. That seems unlikely. Chamberlain simply lacked the necessary skills. 'Nature intended him', wrote the perceptive Leo Amery, 'for a good lieutenant and eventually an elder statesman.'[401] He did indeed enjoy a political renaissance in the very different post of Foreign Secretary (1924–29), where he said Prime Minister Baldwin largely left him 'to go my own way, pursue my own policy and face my own difficulties'.[402] Finally, as elder statesman in the 1930s, Chamberlain could happily operate from a position of dignified isolation – a respected survivor of an earlier age, his unfortunate term as party leader largely forgotten.

---

401 L. Amery, 1955, p. 71.

402 Austen to Mary Carnegie, 20 September 1925 (Chamberlain MSS, AC4/1/1264).

CHAPTER 11

STANLEY BALDWIN

ANNE PERKINS

Despite a far from unblemished electoral record, Anne Perkins argues that Baldwin's fourteen years as Conservative leader give him a strong claim to being one of the most successful exponents of political statecraft in the party's history. He lost the office of Prime Minister twice to minority Labour administrations, following the elections of 1923 and 1929. However, he regained it with a majority of almost 200 in 1924, and again in 1935, when replacing Ramsay MacDonald as head of the National Government he had co-created. His desire to re-shape the electoral environment led successfully towards a clear two-party choice between a mainstream left and a right with cross-class appeal. This led to tactically supporting the formation of Labour governments and a self-consciously moderate attitude towards the General Strike of 1926. While Baldwin was unchallenged as leader as much due to a lack of alternatives as to his effective party management, Perkins argues his political strengths were in evidence until his resignation in 1937.

• • •

Stanley Baldwin, who led the Conservative Party from 1923 until his laurel-wreathed retirement in 1937, is arguably the most successful Prime Minister of the twentieth century. He re-shaped Conservatism, rescuing it from the hard-faced men who had done well out of the war, by conjuring up a particular idea of Englishness, of which he seemed to be the embodiment. For all its platitudinous sonority, it persuaded enough people that this was who they were to call upon to keep Britain calm and united

– when much of Europe was losing its head to fascism or communism – through depression and war.

Baldwin gave his name to an era of economic stagnation. Yet he lived through an age of transformation: political, cultural and economic. When he was born in 1867, Disraeli had yet to become Prime Minister for the first time. When he died eighty years later, Clement Attlee was in No. 10 at the head of a Labour government with a handsome majority. Baldwin lived through the turbulent, often painful birth of the modern era – two world wars, the Russian Revolution, the introduction of universal suffrage and the rise of the Labour Party. He was in Parliament from 1908 until 1937 – a time when, across Europe, democratic politics struggled against the dictators.

His critics say that Baldwin did not so much set the political weather as try to smother it. Had the mechanisms for unseating a Tory leader been more explicit, he might – after needlessly calling and losing an election in 1923 – have been unseated almost before he started. For those who like their politics activist, energetic and confrontational, Baldwin's passive and conciliatory style, his seeming lack of ego and his frequent prolonged silences often seemed the antithesis of leadership. But after his death, his sternest critic Winston Churchill described him as 'the most formidable politician I ever encountered in public life'.[403]

The Baldwin family were prosperous iron masters in Worcestershire. By the time Stanley inherited his father's parliamentary seat in 1908, at the age of forty, he was, in today's terms, a millionaire several times over. After the war, he was left very much richer. But he was not only a businessman. His mother's family had close links with the world of literature and the arts. Rudyard Kipling was both a first cousin and a close friend. He made much of his distaste for intellectuals, but, staying with a young colleague Rab Butler in 1935, it emerged that he had read all the classicist Gaston Boissier's commentaries in their original French.

---

403 Keith Middlemas and John Barnes, *Baldwin: A Biography*, London, Weidenfeld & Nicolson, 1969, p. 1072.

It was in a similar spirit that Baldwin liked to present himself as an accidental Prime Minister. But his politics were driven by a sense of mission that, after some uncertainty about his potential for public life in his early years as an MP, became clear to him during the Great War. It is commonplace to accuse him of being bogus – of affecting the political persona of the paternalistic chairman of the nation. Yet, from both his personal correspondence and from the faith suggested by his early leaning towards a career in the Church, it is clear that his purpose was genuine, if sometimes burnished for advantage. He saw himself as the midwife to mass democracy, charged with educating the new electorate so that they understood their new political right was accompanied by an equal duty – the duty to consider the consequences of their actions in the context of the good of the country. There was a parallel duty on political leaders, too: to conduct their business with honesty and transparency.

1922–24

The tone of Baldwin's long leadership of the Conservative Party was set by his arrival on the public stage. This happened not when he became an MP, nor even when he entered the coalition Cabinet under Lloyd George as president of the board of trade in 1921, but rather the following year, when he emerged as the leader of a revolt against the coalition. His boldness then defined him as a man of principle, motivated by a moral sense that both found Lloyd George's dubious personal and political conduct unpalatable, and rejected the compromises implicit in coalition. 'It is strange so simple and modest a man', reported *The Times* on the day of the Carlton Club coup, 'should have had so important a share in the making of modern history.'[404]

He was not alone in wanting to end the coalition. The Conservative

404 *The Times*, 20 October 1922.

Party chairman Sir George Younger – feeling his authority slipping away as constituencies rushed in mounting numbers to select their own, rather than coalition, candidates – had been arguing for it since January. But for the Conservative members of the coalition government, their alliance with the Liberals was all that stood between power and the new and rapidly growing Labour Party. In the previous four years, Labour candidates had won fourteen by-elections – more than all the other parties combined. The party had all the appearance of the political wing of an industrial movement that was shaping up to threaten the empire. In 1921, the ending of wartime controls had led to the threat of a miners' lockout by the owners, and, in response, the restoration of the triple alliance of transport, dockers' and miners' unions. The choice was between Conservatives like Baldwin, who wanted to confront the threat openly, or those who supported the coalition's attempts to try to buy it off, as Lloyd George was accused of doing, in order to keep Labour from power.

The immediate grievance, however, was military adventurism. On holiday in Aix – Baldwin's customary late summer holiday destination – he was alerted by a newspaper hoarding of talk of a war against Turkey. Appalled that colleagues could contemplate the human and financial cost of a war so soon after the end of the war to end all wars, he rushed home. By the time he reached London at the end of the first week in October, the threat had fizzled out. However, Austen Chamberlain, the Conservatives' leader, had, meanwhile, secretly agreed to a snap election and to the continuance of the coalition. Baldwin resolved at once that this was the issue on which he would fight. At a meeting of Conservative Cabinet ministers, he warned that he would resign if the party went into the election as part of the coalition.

A few days later, at the meeting of the parliamentary party – reluctantly summoned by Chamberlain at the Carlton Club – Baldwin announced himself as the leader of the rebels and made an emotional speech against the continuance of the coalition. It was not the speech that carried the day – that came from Andrew Bonar Law, Chamberlain's predecessor as party leader, who had been forced to quit due to ill health. But Bonar Law's presence at the

Carlton Club that night was down to Baldwin's power of persuasion. Baldwin had gone on a personal mission to his old friend to harry him out of retirement, accusing him of 'leaving the white men on the beach'. He went on: 'It means we shall just all sink out of politics and we shall leave it to those who are not as honest.'[405] Loyalty to a higher purpose regardless of the personal cost was one of Baldwin's supreme values. The tone of his attack on Bonar Law was echoed a decade later in an election address of 1931, when he dismissed Labour MPs, who had brought down their own government rather than make cuts, as the people who 'brought us to the verge of ruin and then ran away because they had not the courage to face up to the crisis'.[406]

With Bonar Law at their head, the dissidents stormed to victory against the coalitionists, and, at the general election the following month, the Conservatives won 345 seats – a majority of nearly 100. But the result belied the political realities. The country was in a state of flux. The Conservatives had won only 38.2 per cent of the vote. They were fewer than ten points ahead of Labour. From this point on, it was clear that elections would be won on the centre ground. The question was whether Liberals or Conservatives would occupy it.

Baldwin became Chancellor of the Exchequer. Leading coalitionists – Chamberlain, Churchill, Birkenhead – stayed away. Within six months, he was Prime Minister, for, in May the following year, Andrew Bonar Law was diagnosed with cancer of the throat. With the coalitionists still outcasts, the choice of leadership lay between Lord Curzon, the Foreign Secretary – and acting Prime Minister, for Bonar Law had resigned immediately – and Stanley Baldwin, Chancellor of the Exchequer. While Curzon's claims to the role, in brilliance and years of service, were theoretically great, both his personal manner and, more pragmatically, his membership of the House of Lords (where Labour had no representatives) made him, it was widely felt, unfit. The King sent for Baldwin.

---

405 Middlemas and Barnes, op. cit., p. 121.

406 Transcribed from a piece of newsreel footage.

Baldwin had become convinced of the necessity to revisit the issue of tariffs, on which the party had split fewer than twenty years earlier. He believed protecting key industries would be both a way of stimulating the economy and tackling unemployment. But the party was committed not to introduce them without a second general election. It was a first test of his idea of political leadership: a choice between honesty and transparency, or another cynical fudge.

Baldwin never admitted to making political calculations. He was, he often insisted, an ordinary man – one of you, not one of us; 'a plain man of the common people'.[407] The political calculations must have seemed as sound as the moral objective of straightforward dealing with the voters. Clearly, to keep Labour out of power, the anti-Labour vote had to be united. An appeal to protection risked reuniting Asquithian and Lloyd George Liberals, but that had its own virtue: it would end speculation about a Conservative–Liberal realignment and smooth the path for the return of the refuseniks from the coalition – in particular, Austen Chamberlain and Winston Churchill. Baldwin would win his own mandate and silence those critics who could not understand how he had become leader.

Famously, the plan backfired. In a three-horse race, the Conservatives finished in front, but well short of a majority. Labour, for the first time, emerged as the second largest party. For a brief period, Baldwin's future was uncertain. He himself thought he would have to resign as party leader as well as Prime Minister. There was a short-lived move by his critics to try to make a new coalition with the Liberals. He survived in much the same way as he had become leader in the first place: there was no alternative who commanded support.

Even in a tight corner, Baldwin saw political advantage. There was to be no backstairs deal to keep Labour out, for that would allow the workers' party to claim the capitalists had allied against them. He would wait for the Commons to meet, where, without Liberal support (which was not forthcoming),

---

407 Philip Williamson, *Stanley Baldwin: Conservative Leadership and National Values*, Cambridge, Cambridge University Press, 1999.

a minority Labour government was guaranteed. The Liberals would take the blame for letting in Labour, thus completing the split between coalition Conservatives and Liberals.

Baldwin intended to construct a future where voters chose only between right and left. He wanted Labour as a partner in democracy, not as a threat to it. This first Labour government would be a controlled experiment in power, but on licence – a minority government that could be turfed out of office on the whiff of an attempt to bring in, say, the capital levy (the wealth tax promised in Labour's election programme that had struck fear into the heart of the property-owning classes). But Baldwin would lead a constructive opposition, and he withdrew his proposal for tariffs in recognition of its defeat.

He used the period of opposition to make a series of interventions away from Parliament that promoted his version of the Conservative Party – a movement that was national, patriotic and open to all. These were the opening shots in a quiet campaign that, his critics later asserted, was to freeze the country in a kind of time warp, making Conservatism the enemy of modernism. The most distinctive and, to a modern audience, the least familiar of Baldwin's tropes in those early years of establishing his political identity were already being defined. There was Baldwin himself, a simple man 'called to special work',[408] inspired by the idea of service. And there was the fragile treasure of democracy, young and new and in need of tender care. And there was England – or, occasionally, Britain – the setting for this great work of social responsibility and economic stewardship. Baldwin's England – most famously described in a St George's Day tribute – was the country, 'and the country is England'.[409] As for the east wind of German socialism, Russian communism and French syndicalism, they merely befogged the true Englishman. How much better to rely on the native common sense and political sense 'that has never failed our race'?

Baldwinian Conservatism was contrasted with socialism. Conservatism

---

408 Williamson, op. cit., 1999, p. 137.

409 Stanley Baldwin, *On England, and Other Addresses*, London, P. Allan, 1926, pp. 6–9.

was solid, traditional, universal, rooted in place and slowly shaped by history. Conservatism had an ideal. Socialism had an ideology – an intellectual, foreign-influenced, rule-bound, conflictual plan to remake society on materialistic class lines. Baldwin devoted most of his speeches to explaining and promoting his Conservative view, but, when the opportunity arose, he was swift to frame socialism in the context of the 'other' – alien and un-British.

1924–26

The only question about Ramsay MacDonald's first government was how many weeks it would last. Baldwin was anxious it should have a chance to prove itself, and to experience the realities of power. He was also anxious, as Labour plans to restore diplomatic and trading relations with Soviet Russia began to mature, that dealings with Russia should be the grounds on which to defeat MacDonald and force a new election. In fact, an internal Labour scandal brought down the government before relations with the Soviets could. But the 1924 election was always the 'red' election, and it is still remembered for the Zinoviev letter, published by the *Daily Mail* just before polling day as evidence of Russia's indirect control over the Labour Party (and established as fraudulent only many years later).

The result of the 1924 election gave Baldwin not just the mandate he desired, but a result that appeared to be a vindication of his disastrous decision to go to the country the year before. The Conservatives won 46.8 per cent of the vote – a result distorted by first-past-the-post electoral chance into a majority of over 200. Labour was clearly second, with a 33.3 per cent share of the vote, and the Liberals were a distant third, with 17.8 per cent and a mere forty seats. It seemed that Baldwin had even won the two-party politics he sought.

He was determined to be magnanimous in victory. He faced down those in his own party who wanted to defeat and destroy Labour. In March 1925, he denied government support to a back-bench bill seeking to end the trade union levy, on which Labour funding depended:

> We stand for peace … we want to create an atmosphere, a new atmosphere in a new parliament for a new age, in which the people can come together … I know there are those who work for different ends from most of us in the House, yet there are many of all ranks and all parties who will re-echo my prayer: 'Give peace in our time, O Lord.'[410]

Britain's long period of industrial discontent was approaching a climax. Baldwin again tried to avoid a confrontation. By the mid-summer of 1925, a miners' strike threatened again. In July, faced with an expanded industrial alliance of the biggest trade unions in support of the miners' claims and the threat of a general strike, he agreed to provide a subsidy to support pay for the next nine months to allow the two sides to reach a deal. Later, when the strike had been successfully resolved, Baldwin claimed that it had been necessary to prepare public opinion (which tended to sympathise with the miners): 'Democracy has arrived at a gallop in England and I feel all the time it is a race for life. Can we educate them before the crash comes?'[411]

This was a double education. First, it was an education in industrial relations. The government would not intervene again to help find a resolution. One of Baldwin's fiercest criticisms of Lloyd George was that he put off hard choices and allowed people to escape the consequences of their actions. He prided himself, as an employer through the family firm Baldwin Ltd, on a large workforce, with whom he enjoyed good relations, and on his respect for the working masses. He spoke of trade unions as part of the same tradition as friendly societies – a 'peculiarly English growth. Democratic and indigenous.'[412]

Second, it was an experiment in the political education of the nation. Baldwin wanted the general strike to be understood, not as a powerful gesture

410 Middlemas and Barnes, op. cit., p. 297.

411 Philip Williamson and Edward Baldwin, *Baldwin Papers: A Conservative statesman 1908–1947*, Cambridge, Cambridge University Press, 2004, p. 196.

412 Philip Williamson. *National Crisis and National Government. British Politics, the Economy and Empire 1926–1932*, Cambridge, Cambridge University Press, 1992, p. 350.

of working-class solidarity using their only weapon against unscrupulous employers, but as an attempted coup against a properly elected government – an attempt by an unelected minority to take power from the majority. This was the tenor of one of his most famous radio broadcasts, on the fifth day of the nine-day strike. Speaking in the slow, informal style he had deliberately adopted, Baldwin argued that a general strike was 'a direct attack on the community ... [by] a body not elected by the voters of the country ... without consulting the people, without consulting even the trade unionists ... to dislocate the life of the nation ... starving us into submission'.

Baldwin's carefully moderate statements were in contrast to the atmosphere of hysteria and alarm at an impending revolution, fanned by arrests, rumours and newspaper headlines as the start of the general strike approached. MI5 leaked reports of plans for civil war. The threat of mutiny was taken seriously. Quasi-fascist organisations and local militia were allowed to form to defend civil society. Tanks rolled down Oxford Street in an unnecessary show of strength. But the Trade Union Congress (TUC), which always wanted to negotiate rather than strike, was soon ready to abandon the miners. Almost in an instant, the popular press discovered just how good-hearted even trade unionists were – not only the thousands of volunteers who had joined up to lend a hand, but the strikers themselves were discovered to be properly English, open to compromise and common sense: Baldwinians.

1929–31

The leader of the Conservative Party in Baldwin's time was a powerful figure. He had control of the party organisation, where he had installed his closest political ally J. C. C. Davidson as party chairman. Particularly in government, he had power of patronage, and, even after the advent of the Conservative Research Department by Neville Chamberlain in 1929, he maintained control over party policy.

In 1929, the Conservatives suffered another shock defeat under Baldwin's leadership. It followed a full parliamentary term in which his light-touch leadership and modest reforms, driven mostly by Chamberlain, extended support to the unemployed, improved health and housing and, with Churchill as Chancellor, restored economic order as defined by the Treasury. It was as catastrophic as it was unexpected, changing the shape of the party and leaving it geographically reduced to southern England, with a newly dominant element of businessmen and professionals, and a die-hard rump of right-wingers. For the first time, Baldwin had to address the challenge of leading a party in opposition in a way that pacified his southern critics without alienating voters in northern cities, whose support had to be won back if the Conservatives were to win power again.

For any leader of a political party, electoral defeat – especially when victory has been confidently anticipated – provokes challenge. In the Conservative Party of the 1920s, where leaders emerged through an undefined process and exercised powers that had few formal boundaries, challenge could come in several forms.

After a defeat that was a national rejection of both party and leader – the campaign was called the Safety First campaign ('Baldwin's security mixture', one poster called it, playing on the Prime Minister's fondness for pipe-smoking) – Baldwin again considered resignation as he had in 1923, was again persuaded out of it, and again faced a challenge to his leadership. But his first decision, in keeping with his political persona, was that, in contrast to his decision then to wait until he was defeated in the Commons, this time he would accept the voters' rejection like 'a good sportsman' – as he told the King's private secretary Lord Stamfordham – 'who has had his run, been beaten and takes his beating like a man'.[413]

Once Baldwin had decided to stay as party leader, factors operated in his favour: a hung parliament meant another election fairly soon was likely.

---

413 Stuart Ball, *Baldwin and the Conservative Party: the Crisis of 1929–1931*, New Haven, Yale University Press, 1988, p. 27.

Not one of his ministers, despite surviving an election that had cost more than 150 colleagues their seats, was inclined to see the fault in themselves or Baldwin. They preferred to interpret it as understandable but ill-informed enthusiasm for a giveaway Labour government – a view that made it all the easier to hold Labour feet to the fire after the Wall Street Crash in October 1929 precipitated a global slump.

In vain, activists demanded a more thorough investigation of the reverse. But Baldwin's ally, the party chairman J. C. C. Davidson, set up a national inquiry and allowed it to run quietly into the sand. Later, as the wolves howled at the door, Davidson was sacrificed and his successor Neville Chamberlain showed how a more hostile chairman could use his power. Chamberlain warned Baldwin that he had seen research showing that the party leader had forfeited the confidence of the party's volunteers – an argument that appears to have been as unfounded in research as Davidson's earlier attempt to explain defeat had lacked diligence, but one that came close to having the desired effect of prompting Baldwin's resignation.

Chamberlain's move came as the two press barons Lords Beaverbrook and Rothermere, whose creation and amplification of public opinion through their national papers the *Daily Express* and *Mail* were a perpetual goad, nearly succeeded in bringing Baldwin down. They responded to the popular belief that a programme of tariff reform could have won the election, and had now become essential, by launching their own campaigns. Soon they were even standing their own candidates under the banner of the United Empire Party, trying to box in Baldwin's policy options by framing Britain's future as a choice between playing the leading role in a private, tariff-protected empire or being a small island nation against the world. It was all the easier to diminish Baldwin because of his profound but controversial convictions that relations with India needed to be modernised and that India should be set upon the path to dominion status. The conflation of the two issues created the greatest threat Baldwin faced.

Baldwin was lucky in his enemies. Churchill's opposition to Baldwin's

India policy was a matter of high politics that did not interest the wider electorate. Nor did his critics share an alternative vision. The only common point of resistance to Baldwin was frustration at his extraordinary inertia, and even that was mitigated by his personal charm and the affection even the most exasperated of his critics continued to feel. Even so, he might have gone had he not a rare ability, at moments of profound crisis and great drama, to produce exceptional speeches. In 1930, he survived the loss of the South Paddington by-election to a Free Trade candidate, and then, at the St George's by-election with an independent Conservative candidate standing on an anti-Baldwin ticket, he considered resigning and standing himself. Persuaded out of it, he produced a devastating attack on the press barons, culminating in his charge that 'what the proprietorship of those papers is aiming at is power, and power without responsibility – the prerogative of the harlot through the ages'.[414]

By 1931, the crisis in Britain's trading position and the over-valued pound had brought the economy to the point of bankruptcy. Labour's modest attempts at introducing welfare measures to ease the poverty of the long-term unemployed and their families were declared unaffordable. The bankers made it clear no further loans would be forthcoming until cuts were approved. Ramsay MacDonald appealed for support against his own party. But Baldwin, determined that Labour should make the cuts itself, refused to help form the National Government that would, in his eyes, have to take the blame for what he wanted voters to identify as Labour extravagance. Only after the MacDonald government had split and fallen did Baldwin lead the Conservative Party into the National Government.

Even – or, perhaps, particularly – economic catastrophe could be exploited as another useful lesson in the Baldwinian education in democracy. And, in case it failed, the National Government was a useful device for blocking the risk of a popular triumph for a Labour Party determined not to impose austerity.

---

414 Williamson and Baldwin, op. cit., p. 258.

1931–37

Baldwin's final period at the heart of power – serving in the National Government as Lord President to Ramsay MacDonald's prime ministership, and then, from May 1935 until June 1937, as Prime Minister again himself – was a period of unchallenged dominance. Paradoxically, it is this period of relatively little internal challenge that was subsequently to cause his reputation such harm. He was the unquestioned leader of the Conservative Party and, to a significant extent, of the country as well – a national figure, carefully sustaining his non-partisan image; the embodiment of the best of traditional English virtue, which he reflected back onto the people themselves.

Yet, despite his authority, his extreme caution in pursuing a policy of rearmament – even after he had personally become persuaded of its necessity – and his reluctance to challenge Neville Chamberlain's obsessively secret management of the Foreign Office have been condemned since the moment of the 1940 publication of 'Guilty Men'. This was the final revenge of Lord Beaverbrook – who sponsored the short book, written by, among others, Michael Foot (himself a victim later of hysterical press opposition) – that finally succeeded in orchestrating the winning blow in the long and largely hostile relationship.

This last period in power was dominated by two concerns. First, the rise of Hitler. Baldwin was deeply reluctant to pitch Britain into another war that he expected to be ruinous of the nation and of Europe more broadly – morally, economically and culturally. Second, he was confident that British voters were equally, if not more, hostile towards the prospect of war. Both considerations illustrate the limits of a style of leadership that chooses to deliberately keep in step with the mass of public opinion. That is the sentiment Churchill so infamously dismissed as the sacrifice of principle for power. Yet, the truth of Baldwin's assertion that a democracy is always two years behind the dictator is surely unquestionable.

In Baldwin's defence, the spirit of the times, for at least the first half of the decade, was passionately in favour of peace through multilateral action, orchestrated by the League of Nations, and of disarmament – into both of which much political effort was expended. And when the case for re-armament came to be made, its leading political advocates were Churchill – permanently alienated from Baldwin and the Conservative Party over India – and a group of Churchill's younger acolytes – Harold Macmillan, Duff Cooper and, to a lesser extent, Anthony Eden, whom Baldwin scarcely knew.

Nor did re-armament appear an affordable option in the first half of the 1930s. Spending more on defence meant borrowing more, raising taxes or even deeper cuts to spending on health and welfare. In the end, by 1939, re-armament was to involve all of the above. At the time, income tax was reduced, although not until after the cuts Labour had had to make in 1931 were reversed, and it did not go up until 1936 – the year that defence spending outstripped spending on health and welfare for the first time.

The final months of Baldwin's political career were also its apotheosis. In January 1936, George V died, and the abdication crisis – which was to play out in a few intense weeks at the end of the year – began.

Edward VIII, whom Baldwin knew fairly well from a joint trip to Canada in 1927, had had a series of mistresses. It was assumed – or, at least, hoped – that he would smarten up once he became King. His mistress at the time, Wallace Simpson, was married, and therefore considered 'safe' – although there was disquiet about reports that Edward and Mrs Simpson were increasingly seen without Mr Simpson. Then, in September, reports surfaced in America (and, consequently, in Canada too) that she was to divorce her husband.

In October, returning from a long, enforced absence caused by a nervous collapse, Baldwin came to realise the matter was out of hand. He met the King secretly and pressed him, to no avail, to intervene to stop the divorce. In November, himself under pressure from the Cabinet, he warned the King that the British press would break the story any day – at which the King announced that he intended to abdicate in order to marry Mrs Simpson.

For the next six weeks, Baldwin worked tirelessly to achieve a series of objectives. First, secrecy had to be maintained. Second, the dominions needed to be kept informed and consulted where necessary. The ultimate objective was to avoid a confrontation that risked a constitutional crisis, or the very real danger of allowing circumstances to develop where public opinion was split. That meant enabling the King to abdicate in a way that was clearly his own choice and taming some of the more morally affronted members of Cabinet, led by Neville Chamberlain, who wanted to force the pace. It also meant heading off a plan – rumoured to be brewing between Churchill and his old chums in the *Mail* and the *Express* – to allow a crisis to develop over the prospect of the King's suggestion of a morganatic marriage, thus forcing the government to resign and letting in a Churchill-led coalition. Baldwin won every battle, but they were the last he fought in public life. Shortly after the coronation of George VI, he retired, garlanded with honours.

Baldwin made Conservatism not about politics, but anti-politics; not about the harsh and damaging divisions of partisanship, but the reflection of the shared understanding and sentiment of a 'free and patriotic people'. It was not a new understanding of Conservatism – it owed much to Baldwin's own hero Disraeli – but it was one that had a new force in the aftermath of war and revolution, and, later, in economic crisis. His skill was to appropriate for Conservatism, at least in his lifetime, mass democratic support, and to create for Labour and the wider labour movement the space and climate in which to develop into an entirely constitutional political force.

CHAPTER 12

NEVILLE CHAMBERLAIN

STUART BALL

Neville Chamberlain, as Stuart Ball notes, was untested as leader of the Conservative Party on the electoral stage. However, the historical consensus, and every available indicator, suggests that the National Government's large majority was under little threat prior to the Second World War. Similarities to his half-brother Austen do not end with their lack of electoral pedigree as leader. An aloof style and intolerance of opposition was a significant factor in Neville's downfall; but, unlike Austen, it was also, in part, a source of strength, both within the party and in the wider country. While infamously linked to the policy of appeasement, the loss of faith in his prime ministership was due to wider military failures. His domestic policy in peacetime was largely defined by a lack of dissent and by widespread support within the Conservative Party, the National Government which he led, and the country at large. By May 1940, the first remained true, while the others had dissipated as his flaws as a statesman were exposed. However, on the whole, Ball suggests some reassessment of Neville Chamberlain's leadership skills is overdue.

• • •

Neville Chamberlain is one of three Conservative Party leaders who did not contest a general election during his term of office (his half-brother Austen Chamberlain and Iain Duncan Smith being the other two), and he is unique in being the only Conservative Prime Minister not to have led the party in an election. However, historians are agreed that he was on course for a comfortable victory if the expected peacetime election in either the autumn of 1939 or the summer of 1940 had taken place – the National Government might have lost a few seats to Labour, but its substantial overall majority was not in danger. The causes of Labour's landslide victory of 1945 are to be found in the impact of the Second World War and the changing public mood after Dunkirk, especially in 1940–42. It is certainly the case that the opprobrium heaped by the end of the war upon the record of the pre-war National Government, and therefore on its leaders, over not only the failures of appeasement and the shortcomings of re-armament, but also the government's management of the economy and mass unemployment, played a significant part in the rejection of the Conservatives in 1945. In that retrospective sense, Chamberlain was perhaps the most prominent of those who might be blamed for the defeat, but this was a development that took place after he ceased to be Prime Minister in May 1940, and, indeed, mostly after his death six months later.

Neville Chamberlain came relatively late to a parliamentary career and the national stage, but – in common with his predecessor as party leader Stanley Baldwin – he rose rapidly during the political turmoil of the early 1920s.[415] He had the advantages of a famous name (with the recognition and connections that brought) and a regional power base. Born in March 1869, he was the younger of the two sons of Joseph Chamberlain – a charismatic and controversial figure who had 'made the political weather' in late Victorian Britain, first as a radical within the Liberal Party, and then by breaking with Gladstone over Irish home rule in 1886 and creating the Liberal Unionist Party (which moved into coalition partnership with the Conservatives in 1895

---

415 The authoritative life of Chamberlain is Robert Self, *Neville Chamberlain*, Aldershot, Ashgate, 2006. There are also shorter biographies: Nick Smart, *Neville Chamberlain*, Abingdon, Routledge, 2009; H. M. Hyde, *Neville Chamberlain*, London, Weidenfeld & Nicolson, 1976; Iain Macleod, *Neville Chamberlain*, London, F. Muller, 1961. The original authorised life remains useful: Keith Feiling, *The Life of Neville Chamberlain*, London, Macmillan, 1946. Chamberlain's career is also discussed in: Graham Stewart, *Burying Caesar: Churchill, Chamberlain and the Battle for the Tory Party*, London, Weidenfeld & Nicolson, 1999; Peter Clarke, 'The businesslike approach: Neville Chamberlain', in *A Question of Leadership: Gladstone to Thatcher*, London, Hamish Hamilton, 1991, pp. 107–124; Alan Beattie, 'Neville Chamberlain', in J. P. Mackintosh ed., *British Prime Ministers in the Twentieth Century: Vol. 1*, London, Weidenfeld & Nicolson, 1977, pp. 219–71. For the historiography, see David Dutton, *Neville Chamberlain*, London, Arnold, 2001.

and eventually merged with them in 1912). The Chamberlains dominated the politics of Birmingham and its region, but, while his elder half-brother Austen was groomed for leadership and became an MP in 1892 at the age of twenty-eight, Neville was originally destined for a business career (to secure the family fortunes) and a more modest role in local government. Whereas Austen went to Oxford University, Neville's higher education was the practical curriculum of Mason College in Birmingham. His first independent managerial role, overseeing a sisal plantation in the Bahamas from 1891 to 1896, was a failure Chamberlain took very personally. However, the long and lonely struggle cemented his characteristics of hard work and stubborn determination. He returned to Birmingham, and, by 1914, had established a prominent position in the city's business and public life. He served as Lord Mayor in 1915–16, after which, in December 1916, he accepted a national role as director-general of national service. However, he was left unsupported and, after seven months, was effectively forced to resign – a bitter experience that left him with a lasting loathing of Lloyd George.

Chamberlain entered the House of Commons for the Ladywood division of Birmingham in the post-war election of December 1918 (later transferring to the safer seat of Edgbaston in 1929). Loyalty to his half-brother Austen, who succeeded Bonar Law as leader of the Conservative Party in the House of Commons in March 1921, muted his hostility towards Lloyd George and his increasing disaffection from the coalition. However, the latter was shared by the majority of the Conservative Party below the level of the Cabinet, and, by October 1922, it was Neville rather than Austen who was firmly in the party mainstream. Chamberlain was overseas at the time of the Carlton Club meeting of Conservative MPs on 19 October, which decisively rejected his half-brother's strategy of continuing the existing coalition under Lloyd George, and, after which, both Lloyd George and Austen resigned, with Bonar Law becoming Prime Minister and Conservative Party leader.

As most of the former leaders were holding aloof, the new premier needed capable ministers in the House of Commons, and he offered Neville Chamberlain the position of Postmaster-General, outside the Cabinet. After a moment of fraternal strain, Chamberlain accepted, and his effectiveness in debate led to a swift promotion to the Cabinet in March 1923 as Minister of Health. Five months later, as a consequence of Bonar Law's retirement and replacement by Baldwin, Chamberlain was appointed to fill the vacancy at the Treasury.

Although he was only to be Chancellor of the Exchequer for a few months due to the Conservative defeat in the general election of December 1923, Chamberlain had most definitely arrived at the front rank of politics, and a powerful position in the Conservative Party. In the 1924–29 Baldwin ministry, rather than returning to the Chancellorship, he chose the Ministry of Health, where he implemented a major series of reforms of local government, which enhanced his reputation for competence and drive. By 1929, he was often spoken of as the likely successor to Baldwin, but his position as unquestioned heir apparent was confirmed during the troubled period in opposition during the second Labour government of 1929–31, and, especially, by his formidable performance as party chairman from June 1930 to April 1931. When the Labour government collapsed under the pressure of the financial crisis of August 1931, it was Chamberlain who accompanied Baldwin to the key meetings with Labour leaders, and it was Chamberlain who was one of the four Conservatives in the emergency ten-man Cabinet formed on 24 August. After the decision to continue the National Government, and its massive electoral victory in October 1931, Chamberlain succeeded the former Labour Chancellor of the Exchequer Philip Snowden at the Treasury. He played a major part in the implementation of the protectionist tariffs and the imperial preference first advocated by his father in 1903, and his unflinchingly orthodox control of the national finances saw the government through the height of the depression in 1932–33. His Budget of April 1934 was able to restore the 1931 cuts in benefits and the pay of state employees, and, by the time of the November 1935 election, unemployment had fallen below the two million mark. Chamberlain remained Chancellor during Baldwin's final term as Prime Minister in 1935–37, and, during the latter's nervous exhaustion in the summer and autumn of 1936, deputised for him extensively, including giving the leader's speech at the party conference. Chamberlain was already ranging over wide areas of the government's activity – particularly in foreign policy – before Baldwin's retirement. 'Firm, unemotional and calm under criticism,'[416] he was the inevitable successor, becoming Prime Minister on 28 May 1937, and, following coronation at a party meeting, leader of the Conservative Party on 31 May.

PRIME MINISTER AND CONSERVATIVE LEADER IN PEACETIME: MAY 1937 TO SEPTEMBER 1939

The transition of power was smooth and accompanied by only a minor reshuffle to replace the promoted and retiring ministers, in which the main consideration was to keep the balance between the various component parties of the National Government.[417] At the age of sixty-eight, Chamberlain came to the office of Prime Minister with a reputation established over nearly fifteen years for executive capacity and legislative achievement, and possessing the redoubtable political strengths of being 'strong of will, firm of purpose, [and] unyielding in controversy'.[418] A former Cabinet colleague described him as 'a man of action', while the Attorney General noted in his diary in June 1937 that Chamberlain 'will be a tower of strength and consistency'.[419] Parallels have often been made with Margaret Thatcher as a conviction politician of inflexible drive – authoritarian in Cabinet and publicly pre-eminent above colleagues; intolerant of critics and contemptuous of doubters. Certainly, in the words of one Cabinet colleague, Chamberlain 'stood out entirely above the

416 The view of the wife of a long-serving back-bench MP: Margaret Beamish's diary, May 1937 (East Sussex Record Office, Chelwood MSS, CLW/3/1/1/1).

417 Amery's diary, 27 May 1937, in John and David Nicholson eds, *The Empire at Bay – The Leo Amery Diaries, II: 1929–1945*, London, Hutchinson, 1988, pp. 441–2; Self, op. cit., 2006, pp. 262–4.

418 Unpublished memo by David Margesson, 'Chamberlain – A Candid Portrait', no date but circa October 1939 (Churchill College Archives Centre, Margesson MSS, MRGN/1/5/1-5).

419 Amery to Beaverbrook, 13 July 1938 (Parliamentary Archives, Beaverbrook MSS, BBK/C/7); Somervell's journal, June 1937 (Bodleian Library, Somervell MSS, Eng.c.6565, f.90).

"Yes Men" and small fry of the Cabinet'.[420] However, this pre-eminence left him in a position of solitary exposure in the event of failures, and encouraged his characteristic tendency to regard himself as uniquely capable of resolving the problems of the day. As Headlam observed after Chamberlain's fall, he had been 'too much convinced that he could stand alone' – a trait that also led to his tendency to personalise issues and differences.[421]

Chamberlain's manner in Cabinet meetings was not dictatorial; instead, he exerted control through his clarity of thought and mastery of both the wider issues and the practical details – usually expressed through his summing-up of discussion – and 'he was always ready to take a decision'.[422] There was no room in his character for self-doubt. David Margesson, who, as Chief Whip, had attended many Cabinet meetings, observed that the Prime Minister 'has great patience and will listen without interruption to the lengthiest exposition of opinions with which he does not agree – but they never have the slightest effect on his own judgement'.[423] Chamberlain acknowledged this himself in a public speech in 1939, in which his jest was synonymous with reality: 'I am the most reasonable of men and I never object to opposition so long as I can have my own way.'[424] The Prime Minister certainly intended to be in control of his government, and, 'in his own Cabinet, after he had got rid of one or two tiresome members, his was the only will that ever prevailed'.[425] He was particularly determined in his conduct of foreign policy – the key area in which he believed he could achieve a resolution – and this led to the resignation in February 1938 of the Foreign Secretary he had inherited from

420 Comment of Winterton in Amery's diary, 8 October 1938.

421 Headlam's diary, 1 July 1940, in Stuart Ball ed., *Parliament and Politics in the Age of Churchill and Attlee: The Headlam Diaries 1935–1951*, Cambridge, Cambridge University Press, 1999, p. 210; Neville to Hilda Chamberlain, 15 April 1939, in Robert Self ed., *The Neville Chamberlain Diary Letters: Vol. 4, The Downing Street Years 1933–1940* [hereafter *NCDL*], Aldershot, Ashgate, 2005, p. 406.

422 Somervell draft memoirs (Somervell MSS, Eng.c.6565, f.246).

423 Margesson, 'Chamberlain – A Candid Portrait'.

424 *The Times*, 10 June 1939; Neville to Ida Chamberlain, 4 December 1938, *NCDL*, p. 366.

425 Margesson, 'Chamberlain – A Candid Portrait'; Neville to Hilda Chamberlain, 27 March 1938, *NCDL*, p. 311; Maurice Cowling, *The Impact of Hitler: British Politics and British Policies 1933–1940*, Cambridge, Cambridge University Press, 1975, pp. 262–4.

Baldwin, Anthony Eden. However, Chamberlain was pragmatic on many domestic issues and, here, he left much more scope to departmental ministers. Two aspects of his character were significant factors in his eventual downfall. Firstly, his personal manner often appeared 'aloof, with a touch of arrogance', and 'he could not conceal his contempt for insincerity and "hot air"'.[426] Secondly, his Chief Whip noted that, 'while he is the complete master of the clear and logical exposition of a case, he has no charm of manner or command of rhetoric'.[427] On the other hand, Chamberlain's stubborn determination and intolerance of opposition were the very qualities that led many MPs to see him as a strong, clear-sighted and capable leader, in whom they had confidence.

When he became Prime Minister and leader of the Conservative Party, Chamberlain was the dominant figure on the national scene.[428] The Labour leader Clement Attlee was unable to compete in stature and experience, and his party had made only limited progress in developing a credible or attractive programme. Chamberlain had no rivals within his Cabinet – his most senior ministers lacked credibility and support from MPs. The Chancellor of the Exchequer Sir John Simon – the leader of the small National Liberal Party contingent – was an unpopular figure, thought to be lacking in conviction, and he had been an unsuccessful Foreign Secretary in 1931–35. The new Home Secretary Sir Samuel Hoare possessed a manner to which few warmed, and his reputation for competence and judgement had been badly damaged by the fiasco of the Hoare–Laval Plan, which had led to his resignation as Foreign Secretary in December 1935, and by his over-eager quest to return to office a few months later.

Chamberlain's two foreign secretaries were much more respected. Anthony Eden was a glamorous figure from a much younger generation, and might have become a threat but for his poorly presented resignation in February

426 Somervell's draft memoirs (Somervell MSS, Eng.c.6565, f.246–7).

427 Margesson, 'Chamberlain – A Candid Portrait'.

428 M. Cowling, op. cit., 1975, pp. 257–9.

1938, which was followed by a deliberate avoidance of attacks on Chamberlain and a conciliatory speech in the debate on the Munich Agreement. Eden's replacement Lord Halifax was widely admired for his qualities of character, but his position in the House of Lords, his conception of his role as the loyal executor of Chamberlain's policy, and his relative lack of personal ambition made him instead a pillar of support.

The rising younger members of the Cabinet either had flaws or had yet to establish themselves. Oliver Stanley had, for some time, been the foremost, but there had been doubts about his resilience ever since his panic during the Unemployment Assistance Board crisis of early 1935. Walter Elliot was seen by many as a leader in future years, but his positions at the Scottish Office and then the Ministry of Health gave only modest scope, and his vacillation over resignation during the Czech Crisis in 1938 damaged his reputation with both pro- and anti-appeasers. Sir Thomas Inskip had been touted at one point as the possible successor to Baldwin, but was now mired in the unrewarding role of Minister of Defence Coordination. Duff Cooper was an effective debater, but was proving to be much less so as a departmental chief. William 'Shakes' Morrison was also failing to confirm his early promise. In fact, as one junior minister told his sister: 'We have some terribly dud ministers, both in the Cabinet and among the under-secretaries', with the inevitable consequence that 'the PM towers above us all and has to answer on every big debate'.[429] This remained a weakness throughout Chamberlain's government, and was due to the lack of strong rising talents as much as it was to the Prime Minister's reluctance to include them.[430] In consequence, instead of strengthening the ministry, promotions to the Cabinet were widely regarded as 'the nadir of mediocrity',[431] and reshuffles always tended to

429 Bernays to Brereton, 16 March 1938, in Nick Smart ed., *The Diaries and Letters of Robert Bernays 1932–1939*, Lewiston, E. Mellen Press, 1996, pp. 346–7.

430 Neville to Hilda Chamberlain, 11 December 1938, *NCDL*, p. 367-8.

431 Crookshank's diary, 16 May 1938 (Bodelian Library, Crookshank MSS, Eng.Hist.d.359, f.205). Although this judgement came from a junior minister resentful of being passed over, it was widely shared.

disappoint. In April 1940, the latter was a significant factor in Chamberlain's downfall.[432]

Parliamentary dissent on the government benches was minimal during the peacetime period, and its impact was almost non-existent. It was confined to the related aspects of the government's foreign policy of 'appeasement' towards Germany and Italy, and the progress of re-armament. Contrary to the later heroic myth, the criticisms of the anti-appeasers were occasional and muted, often hesitant and sometimes apologetic.[433] Their opposition was rarely carried to the point of abstention in a division, and hardly ever to voting against the government. The most substantial dissent was in the debate on the Munich Agreement on 6 October 1938, when twenty-two Conservative MPs abstained. Given that the government's overall majority was ten times that figure, this was hardly a serious threat. The Duchess of Atholl, the one critical MP who first resigned the government whip and later her seat, lost the resulting by-election at Kinross & West Perthshire in December 1938 in a straight fight with an official Conservative candidate.[434] During the winter following the Munich Agreement, the other anti-appeasers wisely kept their heads down, but, even so, several of them – including Churchill – were in some danger of de-selection by their constituency associations. The pressure on the dissidents eased as the appeasement policy lost credibility after March 1939, but it still seemed to most government MPs to offer the best chance of avoiding war, and the solidity of Conservative back-bench support for Chamberlain was hardly affected by the setbacks of the spring and summer of 1939. One factor in the containment of parliamentary dissent throughout the period was the efficiency and effectiveness of Margesson as Conservative and government Chief Whip. He had held this office since 1931, and had

432 Amery's diary, 15 March 1939; Euan Wallace's diary, 4 April 1940 (Bodleian Library, Wallace MSS); Zetland to Linlithgow, 1–2 May 1940 (British Library, Zetland MSS, D609/12).

433 N. J. Crowson, 'Conservative parliamentary dissent over foreign policy during the premiership of Neville Chamberlain: myth or reality?', *Parliamentary History*, 14(3), 1995, pp. 315–36; Neville Thompson, *The Anti-Appeasers: Conservative Opposition to Appeasement in the 1930s*, Oxford, Clarendon Press, 1971, pp. 7–26.

434 Stuart Ball, 'The politics of appeasement: the fall of the Duchess of Atholl and the Kinross & West Perth by-election, December 1938', *Scottish Historical Review*, Vol. 69, 1990, pp. 49–83.

a close working relationship with Chamberlain. By 1937, Margesson was at the height of his reputation and authority, and was delivering a high level of cohesion and discipline. This was not by dictatorial or confrontational methods; on the contrary, as Churchill later willingly admitted when retaining him in his post in 1940, Margesson had avoided deepening rifts and had aimed to contain dissent rather than stamp it out. Under him, the Whips' Office in this period was a smooth-running and effective machine.

During Chamberlain's leadership of the Conservative Party in peacetime, he was also the Prime Minister of a coalition government.[435] However, he did not face the problems and tensions of his half-brother Austen in 1921–22. Formed during the financial crisis of August 1931, and confirmed in office by general elections in October 1931 and November 1935, by 1937, the National Government was a stable and harmonious combination, without policy or personality fissures on party lines. It provided the best of both worlds: there were enough remaining Liberal (and a few Labour) figures at Cabinet level for it to retain credibility as having a broader basis than the Conservative Party alone, and to therefore attract wider electoral support, but there were no significant disagreements on principles or programme, nor any desire from its constituent parts to break up. The Liberal element was too weak and too dependent upon the electoral pact to strike out on its own, and had no incentive to do so. Conservative MPs and grass-roots members were equally content with the arrangement: unlike 1922, the coalition was headed by an authoritative Conservative Prime Minister, who was following policies that ranged from the acceptably necessary to the strongly approved, in an improving economic climate, without substantial or supported internal party dissent. Up to the spring of 1939, the parliamentary anti-appeasers were few in number, divided between different cliques, lacking a convincing or appealing alternative policy, and facing considerable grass-roots hostility. Even after Hitler's repudiation of the Munich Agreement by the seizure of Bohemia in March 1939, the rank and file remained strongly supportive

435 Nick Smart, *The National Government 1931–1940*, Basingstoke, Macmillan, 1999, pp. 148–223.

of Chamberlain, with a wide range of local associations passing resolutions of unabated confidence and support. Similarly, the depth of support from the mainstream majority of Conservative MPs – the critical core element for any party leader – remained almost undiminished, and, indeed, the worsening international situation worked to suppress public criticism rather than encourage it.[436] There was an unquestioned presumption that the National Government in its present form would collectively contest the next election, and the parliamentary critics of its foreign policy – including Churchill – were not opposed to this, nor did they dissent from its domestic policies.

One reason for this was that the National Government had an effective domestic record that it could put forward with confidence.[437] It was presiding over a stable and secure economy, which was making evident progress out of the Great Depression. Unemployment was still high, but the trend was clearly downwards, only in part due to the re-armament programme: the yearly average fell from 2,100,000 in 1935 to 1,800,000 in 1936 and 1,600,000 in 1937, although it rose to 1,900,000 in 1938, before returning to 1,600,000 in 1939. Furthermore, the worst levels of unemployment were concentrated in 'black spots', which, in any case, were Labour heartlands, and the government's developing regional policy since the Special Areas Act of 1934 was seeking to tackle this, creating the Special Areas Reconstruction Association in 1936. The number of people in work increased each year, rising from 13,500,000 in 1935 to 15,900,000 in 1939. Most importantly for the Conservative Party, this was a decade of low middle-class unemployment, which kept the party's core supporters contented. Even more than that, for those in work (especially white-collar and skilled manual workers), it was a period of rising living standards, with a rapid expansion in the numbers of private cars and home ownership – in the latter case, it was a boom period, with 1,600,000 new houses built in 1935–39, largely by the private sector. Alongside this, the

436 Stuart Ball, op. cit., 2013, pp. 216–17, 236–9, 364–7.

437 Geoffrey Fry, *The Politics of Crisis: An Interpretation of British Politics 1931–1945*, Basingstoke, Macmillan, 2001, pp. 68–80.

slum clearance programme, which had begun in 1933, had been accelerated in 1938, and was affecting about 25,000 houses per month.

The National Government had not only provided fiscal stability and relatively cheap money, it also had a creditable record of domestic reforms.[438] Since the 1935 general election, its measures had included the Public Health Act and the Midwives Act – which established maternity services funded by local government – as well as the extension of national insurance to agricultural workers, and legislation for holidays with pay. The Factory Act of 1937 raised health and safety standards for seven million workers, and brought a further four million under its terms for the first time, and there was some progress in the depressed state of agriculture due to the development of the marketing boards introduced earlier in the decade. Moreover, by 1939 there was a system of guaranteed minimum prices for many of the main products of both arable and livestock farming. The Coal Bill, introduced in January 1938, aroused some Conservative opposition due to its apparent extension of state direction, but it was amended and was, in any case, the sign of an active government willing to take bold steps that were in keeping with the contemporary interest in planning, rationalisation and efficiency. Although an increase in pensions was ruled out on the grounds of cost in July 1939, Chamberlain was determined to pursue further social reforms. Proposals under consideration for the manifesto of a potential 1940 election included the introduction of family allowances and the extension of health insurance to dependants.[439]

THE PROSPECTS FOR THE NEXT GENERAL ELECTION

The standing of Chamberlain personally, and of his government, was such that he could have called a general election whenever he wished

438 Ramsden, op. cit., 1978, pp. 362–3.

439 Ramsden, *The Making of Conservative Party Policy: The Conservative Research Department since 1929*, London, Longman, 1980, pp. 91–2.

to do so.[440] Some voices urged swift capitalisation upon his enormous popularity after his return from the Munich Conference on 30 September 1938. Relieved and grateful crowds lined the route from Heston airfield to Downing Street, and a survey of public opinion by Mass-Observation gave 54 per cent in favour of Chamberlain's actions, and only 10 per cent definitely opposed. Was this a missed opportunity to secure a victory? The fact that Conservative Central Office had some doubts encouraged hesitation, but the sound political reason Chamberlain did not request a dissolution was that it was still too early in the life of the parliament to be justifiable on any basis except the snatching of a cheap party advantage, and so 'it would have been bad tactics'.[441] The moment of national unity and thanksgiving was not the time to exacerbate divisions, and exploiting public relief for such a purpose would have tarnished his image of statesmanship and have conflicted with the Conservative Party's ethos of patriotic sacrifice.

Instead, it was the sign of a strong and confident government that the general election would be held either in the autumn of 1939 (after four years in office, following the same interval as in 1935), or in the late spring or early summer of 1940.[442] All the evidence points in the same direction: if peace had been preserved, the Conservative Party would have been in a very strong position to contest this election, in terms of both its internal condition and the external political environment. Chamberlain had a long-standing connection with the party organisation: he had been party chairman in 1930–31, during which time he had secured the loyal support of leading officials, and especially of the general director Robert Topping. He had also been chairman of the Conservative Research Department, effectively since its establishment in 1930, and had a close relationship with its director Joseph Ball, who, in the late 1930s, was engaged in both manipulation of the press and the monitoring of dissenters

---

440 Neville to Ida Chamberlain, 3 April 1938, 12 February 1939, 23 April 1939, *NCDL*, pp. 313, 381, 410.

441 Neville to Hilda Chamberlain, 15 October 1938, 11 December 1938, *NCDL*, pp. 356, 368; Ramsden, op. cit., 1980, p. 91.

442 Neville to Ida Chamberlain, 12 February 1939, *NCDL*, p. 381; Bernays to Brereton, 5 January 1939, in Smart, op. cit., 1996, pp. 385–6; Hoare to Astor, 12 June 1939 (Cambridge University Library, Templewood MSS, X4).

on behalf of his chief. The party chairman Douglas Hacking had been in his post since March 1936, and had the support of a cohesive and experienced team of senior headquarters officials. While there had been spending cuts in the early 1930s, much of this had eliminated waste and produced a fitter and more efficient and focused organisation. Some previous services had been devolved to the local associations, which could now stand on their own feet, and, certainly, there were no complaints from the grass roots about a lack of support or efficiency. In 1936–39, national party expenditure stabilised at around £125,000 annually, and, in 1938, there were 145 staff at Central Office and a further twenty-four in the twelve regional area offices in England and Wales. The Conservative Party's finances were in good shape nationally, and there was not likely to be difficulty in raising a substantial election fund. The local membership was remaining steady – estimated at around 1,250,000 – and, in most areas, the constituency associations were functioning effectively as a long-accustomed part of local public and social life.[443]

Chamberlain and appeasement enjoyed strong support across the spectrum of the Conservative press, particularly in *The Times* and *Daily Telegraph* (with which the *Morning Post* had merged in 1937). He did not suffer as Baldwin had from the antagonism of the press barons – their mass-circulation newspapers gave him strong support. The influential Conservative regional press was also firmly behind Chamberlain, apart from some criticism of appeasement from the *Yorkshire Post*, which duly suffered a backlash from aggrieved Conservatives. The Liberal press was in decline, and its two popular titles merged into the *News Chronicle*, which took a more neutral stance. The Labour Party did have the support of the *Daily Herald* – widely popular at the time due to an injection of trade union funds and effective marketing – but it was still heavily outsold by the combined circulations of the *Daily Express* (owned by Lord Beaverbrook) and the *Daily Mail* and *Daily Mirror* (both owned by Lord Rothermere). The National Government's time in office does not appear to have turned opinion against it. Labour was still

443 Stuart Ball, op. cit., 2013, pp. 165–6, 195–6, 283, 297–9.

identified with failure, the economic crisis of 1931, and the alarming aspects of its shift to the left in 1931–35. The National Government had weathered the economic storms of the early 1930s and turned the corner towards recovery; it also appeared to have the most credible strategy and clear will for peace, while prudently proceeding with re-armament.

By 1939, the National Government had become an accepted fact of life. Not only most Conservatives, but also most of the public, saw no need to make a change and run risks at home and abroad; indeed, the threatening international situation enhanced the need for a strong leader and a stable government. Chamberlain himself was physically fit, mentally sharp and eager for the fray; he had also become an effective communicator through the new mass media of cinema newsreels and radio broadcasts. Despite his age, there was no doubt in his followers' minds that he was the best possible leader for both the approaching general election and the next government, or about his willingness to continue.[444] Although there were setbacks in his foreign policy, Chamberlain retained undisputed command over his government and the Conservative Party, and had the vigorous support of a very large majority of its MPs, especially on the right wing and in the mainstream centre.[445] A young and newly elected MP attending the dinner in Chamberlain's honour given by the 1922 Committee in March 1939 found his leader's address 'a great speech and very heartening', and Chamberlain enjoyed debating successes in the House of Commons up to the very eve of war.[446]

There were no signs of a significant further advance for the Labour Party in the period between the 1935 general election and the declaration of war, either at local government level – where, after gains in 1932–35, the party seemed to have reached a plateau of support – or in parliamentary by-elections. During Chamberlain's peacetime premiership, the National Government defended

---

444 Neville to Ida Chamberlain, 12 March 1939, Neville to Hilda Chamberlain, 15 July 1939, *NCDL*, pp. 392, 429.

445 Thomas, copy of letter, 12 April 1938 (Carmarthenshire Archive Service, Cilcennin MSS, Cilc.coll.40).

446 Christopher York's diary, 28 March, 24/29 August 1939 (courtesy of Edward York, Hutton Wandesley Hall, Long Marston, Yorkshire); Hoare to Astor, 1 August 1939 (Templewood MSS, X4); note by Beamish on Chamberlain's speech of 1 September 1939 (Churchill College Archives Centre, Beamish MSS, BEAM/3/3).

forty-three seats, of which it retained thirty-four. One of the losses (at Bridgwater in November 1938) was in special circumstances to an independent Progressive candidate, and the other eight were to Labour. However, all of the latter were constituencies Labour had previously won in either 1923 or 1929 (or both), when the party had achieved minority government but fallen short of an overall majority. Furthermore, four of the eight Labour gains were in London, and a fifth (Dartford) was on its periphery; but, elsewhere in the south of England, Labour made no gains in the other fourteen contests; in the Midlands and East Anglia it made two gains in eleven by-elections; in the north of England and Scotland it did not gain any of the seven government seats being defended. Crucially, the Labour Party did not win a single seat that would have expanded on its high-water mark of 1929 and thereby have indicated even a faint chance of defeating the National Government, which, in 1935, had enjoyed a majority of 254 MPs over the Labour and Liberal parties combined.

To have overturned this would have required a massive swing, of which there was no sign either electorally or in the early opinion polls. The very first Gallup survey of voting intentions in October 1937 excluded the undecided, and simply stated 'for the government, 68 per cent; for the opposition, 32 per cent'.[447] Their three later polls did include a 'don't know' category; the first of these in February 1939 found the narrowest gap, with 50 per cent supporting the government and 44 per cent the opposition, but thereafter the opposition fell back, with an increase in the proportion of undecided eroding its support and not the government's. The poll in December 1939 recorded 54 per cent for the government and 30 per cent for the opposition, while in February 1940 both government and opposition dipped by three points, to 51 per cent and 27 per cent respectively.[448] In all of the samples, support for the National Government remained remarkably close to its

447 Anthony King and Robert Wybrow eds, *British Political Opinion 1937–2000: The Gallup Polls*, London, Politico's, 2001, p. 1.

448 These three polls are omitted from the compilation of Gallup data in King and Wybrow, op. cit., but are given in David Butler and Anne Sloman eds, *British Political Facts 1900–1979*, London, Macmillan, 1980, p. 234. Curiously, the December 1939 poll is absent from the later edition: David Butler and Gareth Butler eds, *Twentieth-Century British Political Facts 1900–2000*, Basingstoke, Macmillan, 2000, p. 265.

53.3 per cent share of the poll in 1935. In October 1938, Gallup began asking electors whether they were 'satisfied' or 'dissatisfied' with the Prime Minister, and continued to do so monthly until July 1939. During this period, Chamberlain maintained a positive lead of between nine and seventeen percentage points, with a higher rating in the months after the German seizure of Bohemia (the figures for April to July 1939 ranging between 52 and 55 per cent satisfaction) than in the winter after the Munich Agreement (the figures for October 1938 to March 1939 varying from 48 to 54 per cent).[449]

When to this picture is added the mixed messages of the Labour Party in 1937–39 over foreign policy and re-armament,[450] and its internal disunity over the idea of a 'popular front' that would include communists (which led to the expulsion of Sir Stafford Cripps and Aneurin Bevan in January 1939), it is hard to see how the opposition could have made up ground in peacetime.[451] Equally crucial was another factor: the weakness of the independent Liberal Party, which nominated candidates in only twelve of the fifty-three by-elections from June 1937 to September 1939. In three cases, it did not contest seats it had fought in 1935, when it had stood in only 161 constituencies and won a mere twenty-one. The further decline of the Liberals since then ensured that there would no repeat of the pattern of 1923 and 1929, when a reinvigoration of the party had led to many three-way contests and consequent Conservative losses. In May 1939, the Home Secretary considered that 'if there was an election, it looks as if the majority would not be much altered';[452] this was after the German seizure of Bohemia, and there were no further serious setbacks for the government during the remaining months of peace. The likely scenario for 1940 therefore lay in the range between a close repeat of the 1935 result and the recovery by Labour of some of the seats it had held in 1923 or 1929, perhaps taking its total to around the 200 mark,

449 King and Wybrow, ibid., p. 183.

450 Bernays to Brereton, 21 October 1938, in Smart, op. cit., 1996, p. 376.

451 Neville to Hilda Chamberlain, 19 February 1939, *NCDL*, p. 384; John Swift, *Labour in Crisis: Clement Attlee and the Labour Party in Opposition 1931–1940*, Basingstoke, Macmillan, 2001, pp. 151–2.

452 Hoare to Sassoon, 13 May 1939 (Templewood MSS, X4).

but leaving the government with a majority of between 100 and 150 at worst. There seems to be no reason to doubt that the judgement expressed by the experienced senior officials at Conservative Central Office in February 1939 also applied to the whole of Chamberlain's peacetime premiership: 'If we went to the country now, we should romp in.'[453]

THE FALL OF CHAMBERLAIN: SEPTEMBER 1939 TO MAY 1940

Neville Chamberlain's fall from office as Prime Minister was due to the factor that has caused the departure of the largest number of Conservative leaders since 1900: the erosion of confidence and support in the parliamentary party. This has also led directly to the dismissals of Austen Chamberlain, Heath, Thatcher and Duncan Smith, led indirectly, but clearly, to Balfour and Douglas-Home deciding to quit, and contributed at least as much as the immediate trigger of health to the resignations of Eden and Macmillan. It is only with Major in 1997 that the practice began of falling upon the sword immediately after electoral defeat, which is now a customary expectation after emulation by his successors in 2001 and 2005. Age and illness have been more frequent causes than electoral failure, and account for the remaining four leaders – Salisbury, Bonar Law, Baldwin and Churchill – as well as facilitating the removal of Eden and, to a lesser degree, Macmillan. However, in Neville Chamberlain's case, there are three distinguishing features of his departure. Firstly, he did not lose the crucial vote in numerical terms, although he had clearly done so in the political context that mattered – a distinction he shares with Thatcher. Secondly, while Chamberlain lost the office of Prime Minister, this did not entail his resignation as Conservative Party leader. Thirdly, and uniquely among Conservative leaders, this all took place in wartime.

Chamberlain's party leadership is divided into two contrasting parts by

453 Neville to Ida Chamberlain, 26 February 1939, *NCDL*, p. 387.

the outbreak of war in September 1939.[454] In peacetime, he was the dominant director of a cohesive ministry, exuding drive and clarity. In wartime, his touch often appeared hesitant or maladroit, with complacency replacing assurance, and his inflexibility and imperviousness to criticism transformed from an asset to an anxiety. Within a few months, to an increasing number of his supporters, Chamberlain no longer looked like the right man for his job: uncomfortable with the demands of war; unimaginative in response to them; and uninspiring to a nation nervously apprehensive of the coming onslaught.[455] The Chief Whip noted in October 1939 that 'his manner is dry; his speeches cold; his prose colourless'.[456] The outbreak of war damaged Chamberlain's position, although this was due less to the evident failure of his policy of appeasement and more to mishandling the immediate situation and misjudging the mood of the House of Commons and the country. The delay in declaring war after the German attack on Poland was due to French requests (which could not be revealed) for time to complete their mobilisation, but, together with other mixed signals, it appeared that Chamberlain was willing to negotiate with Hitler at Polish expense, in a manner similar to the now discredited Munich Agreement. The Prime Minister's lacklustre and non-committal speech on the evening of 2 September 1939, thirty-six hours after the invasion began, 'left the House aghast',[457] with 'all except a few ultra-government men utterly dismayed and disgusted'.[458] Members of the Cabinet were 'horrified', and the speech was followed immediately by a virtual Cabinet revolt, which demanded the issuing of an ultimatum to Germany that would expire before the House of Commons met the next day – otherwise the government might fall.[459]

---

454 Stuart Ball, op. cit., 2013, pp. 492–7.

455 Self, op. cit., 2006, pp. 391–3; Paul Addison, *The Road to 1945: British Politics and the Second World War*, London, Cape, 1975, pp. 63–71.

456 Margesson, 'Chamberlain – A Candid Portrait'; Harold Nicolson's diary, 20/26 September 1939, 2 November 1939, in Nigel Nicolson ed., *Harold Nicolson: Diaries and Letters 1939–1945*, London, Collins, 1967, pp. 35, 37, 45.

457 Crookshank's diary, 2 September 1939.

458 Amery's diary, 2 September 1939; Zetland to Linlithgow, 4–6 September 1939 (Zetland MSS, D609/11); Nicolson's diary, 2 September 1939, in Nicolson, op. cit., pp. 418–20.

459 Wallace's diary, 2/3 September 1939; Amery's diary, 3 September 1939.

There was some recovery after this, and Chamberlain retained a strong basis of support among Conservative MPs until the end of his premiership.[460] This appears to have been the case with the public as well, although allowance must be made for the crude sampling methods of the early opinion polls. It was perhaps natural for the Prime Minister's support to increase in the first months of war, from both a rally of patriotic sentiment and an abatement of opposition attacks. According to Gallup's monthly survey, satisfaction with Chamberlain rose to 68 per cent in November 1939, and, although it then slightly diminished, in March 1939, it was still at 57 per cent, with only 36 per cent dissatisfied.[461] However, there was no poll in April, and the May figures revealed a striking collapse, with only 33 per cent satisfied and 60 per cent dissatisfied. While there is no evidence that this directly influenced Conservative MPs, the synchronicity of timing is striking. During the tense but anti-climactic months of 'phoney war' from September 1939 to April 1940, in which British land and air forces barely engaged the enemy, parliamentary confidence in Chamberlain was eroded by poor debating performances, ineffectual reshuffles that retained or even promoted weak and unpopular ministers,[462] and misjudged assessments, such as his declaration in a speech on 4 April 1940 that Hitler had 'missed the bus' – which was swiftly followed by the German seizure of Denmark and Norway.[463] The dismissal of the high-profile Secretary of State for War Leslie Hore-Belisha in January 1940 may have become unavoidable, but it was poorly presented. Chamberlain and Margesson 'did the right thing in the clumsiest way',[464] and left the impression of

460 Croft to Chamberlain, 2 September 1939 (Churchill College Archives Centre, Croft MSS, CRFT/1/8/ch56); Wallace's diary, 22 November 1939, 19 March 1940; Nicolson's diary, 19 March 1940, in Nicolson, op. cit., pp. 63–4.

461 King and Wybrow, op. cit., pp. 183–4.

462 Inskip's diary, 16 December 1939 (Churchill College Archives Centre, Inskip MSS, INKP/1/2); Nicolson's diary, 3 April 1940, in Nicolson, op. cit., pp. 65–6; Wallace's diary, 31 March 1940, 4 April 1940; Zetland to Linlithgow, 1–2 May 1940 (Zetland MSS, D609/12); Self, op. cit., 2006, pp. 413–14.

463 This was not the first example of Chamberlain's tendency to make complacent statements that were swiftly proven wrong: a year previously, he had given an over-optimistic interview to the Lobby press only a few days before the German seizure of Bohemia; Amery's diary, 15 March 1939.

464 Bracken to Cooper, 15 January 1940 (Churchill College Archives Centre, Duff Cooper MSS, DUFC/3/6).

sacrificing an energetic reformer to the hostility of hidebound generals. After less than two months of war, one Cabinet minister noted in his diary that 'one hears little else but criticism of the government wherever one goes'.[465] Alongside this, the government's Home Policy Committee considered 'that the political situation was deteriorating rapidly from the government point of view' due to the opposition parties continuing to hold public meetings, while the Conservative Party forbore from responding due to their much stricter interpretation of the wartime political truce.[466] While naturally the standing of the government rose and fell according to events, much of the news was discouraging, and there was growing concern over ministerial complacency and the continuation of peacetime methods.

When the first serious military clash, resulting from the German invasion of Norway, revealed a lack of resources and coordination – ending in failure and withdrawal – these doubts crystallised, and the 'underlying feeling of considerable anxiety' found expression in the ensuing parliamentary debate on 7 and 8 May 1940.[467] Chamberlain's opening speech was 'a very obvious flop',[468] and the War Minister Oliver Stanley was ineffectual and unconvincing, although the Chief Whip 'thought we had had a reasonably good first day in an admittedly difficult situation'.[469] At the start of the second day of the debate, sensing that support for the Prime Minister was crumbling, the Labour Party announced that they were making it a vote of confidence. In reply, Chamberlain immediately declared he would rely on his 'friends' for support – this was deemed a personalisation of a national issue, and 'a tactless performance' that 'greatly annoyed many of our people'.[470] Once again,

---

465 Wallace's diary, 24 October 1939.

466 Wallace's diary, 15 November 1939.

467 Zetland to Linlithgow, 9 May 1940 (Zetland MSS, D609/12); Stuart Ball, op. cit., 2013, pp. 366–7, 496–7, 503, 505; Self, op. cit., 2006, pp. 420–25; Nick Smart, 'Four days in May: the Norway debates and the downfall of Neville Chamberlain', *Parliamentary History*, 17(2), 1998, pp. 215–43; Kevin Jefferys, 'May 1940: the downfall of Neville Chamberlain', *Parliamentary History*, 10(2), 1991, pp. 363–78; Addison, op. cit., pp. 93–8.

468 Amery's diary, 8 May 1940. This was not only his view, but also that of the pro-Chamberlain correspondent of the *Birmingham Post*.

469 Wallace's diary, 7 May 1940.

470 Amery's diary, 7 May 1940; Wallace's diary, 8 May 1940.

when under pressure, Chamberlain equated party cohesion with loyalty to him, in a confrontational manner that suggested he regarded himself as infallible and irreplaceable.[471] Although questions could have been raised about Churchill's decision-making in charge of the navy during the Norwegian debacle, the government's critics were primarily concerned not with operational detail, but with the attitudes and methods of the government, as revealed by the first major clash of arms. The unstated text of the debate was that it was about the future more than the past, and, specifically, the need for a broader coalition including the Labour Party that could establish a genuine national consensus and possess the authority to mobilise both capital and labour, direct the workforce, plan the economy and increase production.

The division at the end of the debate on the evening of 8 May 1940 was a victory for Chamberlain by 281 votes to 200, and it must be remembered that the large majority of Conservative MPs continued to support him – in some cases, passionately. However, the fall in the government's normal majority was fatally damaging: thirty-nine National Government MPs (of whom thirty-three were Conservatives) had voted against, and approximately a further forty had attended the debate but abstained.[472] Crucially, the rebels extended beyond the predictable critics and included previously loyal MPs in the party's mainstream, such as Quintin Hogg, defender of appeasement in the Oxford by-election after the Munich Agreement of 1938. During the months following the outbreak of war, many younger Conservative MPs had joined their reserve units and become aware of deficiencies in readiness, which were at variance with ministers' complacent reassurances. Sixteen of the MPs who voted against the government had pointedly attended the debate in uniform.[473] Ultimately, as in

471 Nicolson's diary, 8 May 1940, in Nicolson, op. cit., p. 78. Chamberlain had taken a similar attitude on previous occasions, such as the issue of adjourning the House of Commons for the recess in August 1939: Nicolson's diary, 2 August 1939, Nicolson, ibid., pp. 407–8.

472 Although eighty-eight government MPs did not vote, it has been established that fifteen were paired and a further thirty-two were unable to attend the debate, so the number of deliberate abstentions by MPs who were present can be no more than forty-three, and was probably slightly less. See: J. S. Rasmussen, 'Party discipline in wartime: the downfall of the Chamberlain government', *Journal of Politics*, Vol. 32, 1970, p. 385.

473 By January 1940, sixty-two government MPs were serving in the armed forces. See: Addison, op. cit., p. 69.

1916, the fall of the Prime Minister was due to military setbacks and not failures of party leadership. Indeed, it was Chamberlain's fatal weakness in May 1940 that he was too much of a party figure: his maladroit appeal for support to his 'friends' had seemed narrow and polarising, while, crucially, the Labour Party would not serve under him, and so he could not form a government of all-party national unity, which was now an imperative necessity.

For the first time, there was also a credible alternative in Churchill, who, since his unavoidable readmittance to office at the outbreak of war, had been the one minister to impress both the House and the public with his aggressive quest to take the war to Germany by all available means and with his determined commitment to the pursuit of victory.[474] After consultations over the following two days, including a final confirmation that Labour would not join a government headed by him, Chamberlain resigned as Prime Minister on 10 May 1940. However, this did not entail his resignation as Conservative Party leader, and he retained that crucial role until the onset of terminal cancer – wholly undetected in May 1940 – led to his resignation on 3 October and his death on 9 November 1940. If this entirely unforeseeable development had not occurred, there was no reason why Chamberlain could not have continued as Conservative leader for the duration of the war – and, indeed, beyond (as Asquith did of the Liberal Party after 1916, although that is not a very comforting precedent). Chamberlain retained the support of a large majority of Conservative MPs, as they vocally demonstrated when he first entered the House of Commons after resigning the premiership.[475] Churchill was well aware of this political reality, and immediately after becoming Prime Minister he wrote to Chamberlain acknowledging that 'to a very large extent I am in your hands'.[476] However, he was reassured by the effective partnership that they had forged during the previous few months, by Chamberlain's sense

474 Wallace's diary, 26 September 1939.

475 Channon's diary, 13 May 1940, in Robert Rhodes James ed., *Chips: The Diaries of Sir Henry Channon*, London, Weidenfeld & Nicolson, 1967, p. 252.

476 Churchill to Chamberlain, 10 May 1940 (Birmingham University Library, Neville Chamberlain MSS, NC/7/9/80).

of honour and loyalty, and by his crucial commitment to continuing the war despite the fall of France; it was Halifax, not Chamberlain, who wavered over Hitler's peace offers.

CONCLUSION

At first glance, Neville Chamberlain is atypical of Conservative leaders and prime ministers, having never contested a general election, and falling from power in wartime. However, there are themes and circumstances that he has in common with other leaders, not only during the peacetime period.[477] The first and most obvious of these is the part played by an improving economic picture – especially in the Midlands and the south of England, and for the middle class and the skilled (particularly self-employed) working class. Combined with a broadly centrist social programme, such a climate will, in general, maximise the Conservative Party's appeal. It is possible for the party to win substantial majorities without one of these two factors – as in 1924 (Baldwin's moderate 'new Conservatism') or 1983 (economic recovery) – but retaining office when in government generally requires both: compare the successes of 1935, 1955, 1959 and 1992 with the defeats of 1906, 1923, 1929, 1964, February 1974 and 1997. Of course, attaining power from opposition is most likely to succeed when there is an inversion of the economic factor – a recession, or, at least, the perception of stagnation – but success is still most likely with a more inclusive agenda: hence recovery in 1931, 1950, 1951, 1970 and 2010, but further defeat in 1966, minimal progress in 2001 and little better in 2005. It might seem that Thatcher's victory in 1979 conflicts with this, but the economic factor was very strong and the party's programme was still quite moderate and far from fully fledged Thatcherism.

477 For a comparative discussion of the nature of Conservative Party leadership, see Stuart Ball, op. cit., 2013, pp. 459–76.

Secondly, the leader's pre-eminence in the government is an asset when things are going well: it gives coherence and clarity, and the leader is a recognised and generally respected figure, even when arousing above-average antagonism among the opposition parties. However, when the government hits turbulent waters, it leaves the leader exposed in solitary eminence, and likely to become a lightning rod for popular frustration. What seemed like strengths are now perceived as flaws: determination becomes inflexibility; command becomes arrogance; confidence becomes complacency; and decisiveness becomes a failure to listen. This was the almost identical process that undermined the leaderships of Austen Chamberlain, Heath and Thatcher, and several of its features also appear in the decline of Macmillan's position in 1961–63.

Thirdly, there is the importance of keeping control of the parliamentary party. The defeat, which the rebel MPs of the Norway debate feared that the continuation of Chamberlain's premiership would lead to, was a much graver one of national defeat in war, but the impulse was similar to the anticipation of the electoral defeat that removed Thatcher and Duncan Smith, and encouraged the departure of Macmillan and Douglas-Home. This might seem an obvious point, but the record shows how easy it is for a Prime Minister to lose touch with the party: Macmillan in 1961–63; Heath in 1972–75 did so fatally; and Baldwin came close to grief in 1929–30.

Finally, there is the personal factor of physical health, stamina and mental resilience. Although sixty-eight years old when he became Prime Minister, Chamberlain was seen as the most vigorous figure in the Cabinet, possessing a mental acuity that made him the master of his brief in debates, able to range widely across the government's work and coordinate and expound it. Although Chamberlain was to be seventy-one in the spring of 1940, before the outbreak of war, no one had any doubts about his capacity to lead the government to an election victory and continue as Prime Minister for most of the next parliament. He shared these personal characteristics with Bonar Law in 1911–21, Churchill in 1940–51, Macmillan in 1957–61, and Heath and Thatcher for nearly all of their leaderships – a list that includes the majority of the Conservative Party's most successful twentieth-century leaders, and thus company in which Neville Chamberlain might not often be thought to be placed.

CHAPTER 13

WINSTON CHURCHILL

JOHN CHARMLEY

Churchill's electoral record shows two defeats – one by a landslide in 1945 and the other by a narrow margin in 1950 – and a single slender victory in 1951, in seats but not in the popular vote. As John Charmley notes, Churchill was unique in being given a third attempt after twice failing electorally. If not counter-intuitively, then certainly against the enduring common perception, Charmley argues that his leadership of the Conservative Party was more negative than this mixed record suggests. His electoral strategy was bereft of fresh ideas in 1945, and any reforms in organisation of the party's platform emanated from below, rather than from his leadership. Charmley contends that Churchill's management of the party was, at best, 'light touch', and, at worst, non-existent. In domestic policy debate, the Conservative Party did little to shift debate onto their terms; though, in foreign policy terms, his influence continued to be felt throughout the post-war period. Churchill's record as a party leader is, on balance, one of failure.

• • •

Churchill would, of course, be delighted to have known that the 'statecraft framework', designed by Toby James and Jim Buller, fits him hardly at all; he would have expected no less. When Asquith's daughter once opined, 'We are all worms', Churchill's response was, 'But I do believe that I am a glow worm.'[478] Churchill's lustre, as the fiftieth anniversary of his

---

478 Violet Bonham Carter, *Winston Churchill, As I Knew Him*, London, Eyre & Spottiswoode, 1965, p. 16.

death in 2015 showed, has not been dimmed by the passage of time; he is the opposite of a 'here today, gone tomorrow' politician. However, if 'statecraft' is to be measured by success in winning elections and holding on to power, then Churchill was pretty much a failure. He won only one general election – and on a minority of the popular vote at that, with a narrow parliamentary majority. In terms of providing a 'winning electoral strategy', his contributions were, at best, mixed. In terms of 'governing competence', there is more to be said on the positive side, but, when we include 'party management', the best that can be said is that Churchill did not get in the way of those better equipped than himself to undertake that thankless task. As for 'augmenting political hegemony', one might ask precisely whose hegemony he augmented, in what Paul Addison has called 'Attlee's consensus'. Only when it comes to 'bending the rules of the game' could Churchill be awarded a straight alpha plus, but, since he did not think the rules applied to him, that is hardly surprising. For all of this, however, Churchill remains the pre-eminent Conservative politician of the last century, and is one of the few to whom historians return again and again. He is one of only two about whom film-makers have bothered, and his historical immortality is assured. Nonetheless, as a party politician, and as a political leader, his record is distinctly mixed – but that should cause no surprise.

If we are talking context with Churchill, it is wise to bear in mind that the context that mattered most to him was the one inside his head. Most successful political leaders have something of the sociopath about them, which is more neutral than saying they are ruthless pragmatists who would sacrifice their own grandmother in order to attain and keep power. It was rightly said of Churchill that the only political party to which he was loyal was the one gathered under his hatband. Political parties like to use people, but tend to object when people use them. Churchill was one of the very few political figures of the first rank to return the favour, having not only 'ratted' from the Conservatives to the Liberals in 1905, but're-ratted' to the Conservatives in 1924. Between 1903 and 1905, and again twenty years later, he tried to find a middle 'Liberal/Conservative/constitutionalist' position, and there is no doubt that, however fruitless that was in terms of finding a political berth, it more accurately described his instincts. In 1923, he very much looked forward to a 'hung' election and to leading a group of right-wing Liberals into coalition with the moderate Baldwin. Only when the Red Scare of that year brought the Tories back with a majority did he formally agree to re-join the party he had left in 1903. This is worth mentioning because it reflects his attitude towards the Conservative Party, which was, at best, ambivalent – something that spilled over into his party management.[479]

After Baldwin's defeat in 1929, Churchill had tried to seize the party leadership, allying himself with the imperialist right – a tactic that earned him exile from the National Government formed in 1931.[480] His attacks on its India Bill, again from the far right, sent him further into the political wilderness, from which he emerged only thanks to the efforts of Herr Hitler in September 1939. Neville Chamberlain needed a public demonstration of his determination to prosecute a war he had neither wanted nor knew how to manage, and the news that 'Winston is back' at the admiralty did the trick. But it was, again, Hitler who finally brought Churchill to the position he had long desired. The failure of the Norwegian campaign Churchill had planned led to a vote of confidence in Chamberlain's government, which coincided with the Nazi assault on the Western Front. When Chamberlain lost it, Churchill became, in the absence of any alternative, Prime Minister. Again, the circumstances of his accession to the premiership matter in terms of the 'statesmanship framework', because he became Prime Minister before he became leader of the Tory Party. It is worth noting that, on his first appearance in the House as premier, the Tory benches were silent, exploding into approval only when Neville Chamberlain, their leader, came into the chamber. That silence spoke volumes.[481] Had anyone predicted at that point that Churchill would have been Conservative leader fifteen years later, they would have been dismissed out of hand. He was sixty-five, drank and smoked too much, took no

479 Robert Rhodes James, *Churchill: A Study in Failure*, London, Weidenfeld & Nicolson, 1970, pp. 148–52.

480 Stuart Ball, op. cit., 1988.

481 John Charmley, *Churchill: The End of Glory*, London, Hodder & Stoughton, 1993, pp. 396–400.

exercise, and would have found life insurance expensive – all of which goes to show how unpredictable politics is.

The parallel in Churchill's mind in 1940 was with the position of Lloyd George in 1916, when Asquith had remained leader of the Liberal Party – that had not ended well for the Great War leader. With that in mind, when, only a few months later, in October, Chamberlain stood down because of cancer, Churchill immediately accepted the leadership of the Conservative Party. In the circumstances of October 1940, it was inevitable; but neither he nor his party imagined it would be a long-term arrangement. In many senses, this feeling is key to Churchill's period as leader: it meant neither he nor the party planned for what would happen after the end of the war; and, later, it would mean that those discontented with the old man were wary of trying to oust him, not just because of his great fame after 1945, but because it hardly seemed worth the effort when he was over seventy and prone to strokes. Yet his willpower proved formidable.

During the war itself, Churchill was, of course, the leader of a national coalition – something that suited his temperament admirably. He liked being the 'father of the nation', and he loved directing the war. He was very happy to let the self-effacing Attlee chair most of the Cabinet committees dealing with the Home Front, and to let Bevin and Morrison get on with whatever it was they needed to do in terms of mobilising labour and local government. Churchill knew these things mattered, but had no interest in them when there was a war to win. Churchill was incredulous when Rab Butler elected to go to the board of education, rather than the War Office, in 1943 – it confirmed him in the thought that Butler was rather 'wet'.[482] This would not have been quite as fatal for the Conservatives as it was to prove in 1945 had his deputy Anthony Eden been a bit more interested in the party; but he was not, detesting large sections of it almost as much as Churchill himself. The result was that the once formidable party election machine suffered neglect; some of that was the natural result of the war, but the lack of interest from Churchill and Eden played its part as well.

482 Anthony Howard, *Rab*, London, Jonathan Cape, 1987, pp. 109–10.

In the circumstances of 1945, none of this seemed to matter. Churchill had no intention of calling a party political election, and neither did Attlee. Both men recalled well what had happened in the khaki election of 1918, when the triumphant Lloyd George had gone to the country at the head of a coalition and slaughtered the opposition. But, when it came to it in May 1945, the Labour Party conference refused to continue with the coalition. Churchill was hurt at what he took to be the waspish tone of Attlee's rejection, but it is indicative of his approach that he refused to form a purely Conservative government.[483] Instead, as he would in 1951 when he finally won an election, he formed what he called an 'all-party' government. Although the Liberals refused to join, the former National Liberal Party leader Lord Simon did, and stayed on as Lord Chancellor. The former civil servant Sir John Anderson remained at the Exchequer, and Lord Woolton – a non-party figure, who had been a great success as Minister of Food – joined the Cabinet as Lord Privy Seal. Along with a smattering of other independent or 'national' ministers, the caretaker government was a declaration of Churchill's intention to form something less than a purely Conservative administration.

James and Buller remind us that part of the context within which we have to judge leaders is a collective one. Leaders rarely tower above the political scene, to the extent that, before their first election victory, they have anything approaching total dominance. That was not true of Churchill in 1945. Indeed, as one David Low cartoon – which pictured Brendan Bracken, in the uniform of the First Lord of the Admiralty, and Lord Beaverbrook, in his usual 'crusader' outfit, in a boatyard with a figurehead of Churchill – commented: 'We've got an admiral, we've got a figurehead, and, with a bit of luck, they won't notice we don't have a ship.' But, as the result showed, 'they' did.

The Conservatives suffered from a number of disadvantages in 1945 – none of which the presence of Churchill was sufficient to outweigh. Indeed, he was, in some ways, one of them; although the question of whether anyone could have done better only has to be posed to suggest that the context

483 Martin Gilbert, *Winston S. Churchill, Vol. 8*, Boston, Houghton Mifflin, 1988, pp. 20–21.

of the 1945 election was not one favourable to the Conservatives. Easy – and, in some senses, correct – as it is to note the factors against which no Conservative leader could have prevailed, it is necessary, in the context of measuring Churchill's success as party leader, to point out his own peculiar failings as well.

As early as 1942, Lord Beaverbook had noted that, just as Liberalism had been the main victim of the Great War, Conservatism would be the victim of this one.[484] The causes were not far to seek: the war was a collective war, one in which the state mobilised all its resources to win. A statist party would present that as the way to build the 'land fit for heroes' that Lloyd George had promised and failed to deliver. It was a collective war in which the communist bogey that had served the Conservatives so well since 1917 was being put to rest (for a while, as it turned out) by the success of Soviet arms, and in which an appeal to the common people had been made – along with promises about welfare for the future – that, again, a socialist party would appear to be better equipped to deliver. On top of the toxic legacy of the Depression (which, whatever revisionist historians now tell us, seemed to have been very real to those who had lived through it) and of appeasement (which, by 1945, not even those Conservative and Labour MPs who had supported it at the time remembered supporting), there was also the fact that Churchill took very little interest in his party or, indeed, in electioneering. There was a powerful tide running against the Conservatives, but their leader did nothing to help them – mainly because he assumed the party would continue to provide him with a platform for power and, given his lack of interest in it, he failed to realise it needed his help.

One very common complaint encountered in the diaries and letters of their contemporaries is that neither Churchill, nor his deputy and putative successor Anthony Eden, were 'real' Conservatives, or 'party' men. Eden disliked electioneering almost as much as he disliked most of his fellow Conservatives. He was, understandably, distracted by the fact that his eldest son

---

484 John Charmley, *A History of Conservative Politics Since 1830*, Basingstoke, Palgrave, 2008, p. 133.

was missing in action, and pondering whether to become head of the new United Nations. Churchill, who took equally little interest in the mechanics of electioneering, simply expected things to work as they always had, taking no account of the effect of the war on local party organisation, and paying no attention to those like Rab Butler, who were cognisant of the fact.

The closest Churchill came to having a winning electoral strategy was to assume that his reputation as 'the man who won the war' would win him the election. The war against Japan was not over, and Churchill was sure the electorate would want him to 'finish the job' and negotiate a successful peace settlement.[485] Never knowingly weary of a war himself, Churchill seems to have been blissfully unaware that, for most of his fellow countrymen, its ending was a blessed relief. The thing they looked forward to was the thing that bored him – the details of post-war reconstruction. Harold Macmillan, in his first ministerial post (Secretary of State for Air), was a lone voice in urging Churchill to 'go full steam ahead with the programme of social reform prepared by the coalition government', and to 'abandon clumsy anti-socialism'. His advice fell on deaf ears.[486]

Even if Churchill had heeded Macmillan's good advice, his own pre-war record – like that of his party – would have rendered them unconvincing harbingers of the New Jerusalem, not least in the face of a set of more plausible candidates. Labour's leaders – national figures because of the role they had played in the coalition – had far more political credibility than they would have had in 1940, when they had been out of power for nearly a decade. The old Tory tactic of claiming Labour lacked experience of governing could not be deployed against Attlee, Bevin and Morrison. With the sole exception of Butler, no Conservative minister was associated with the Home Front, and, when it came to – as it did – a competition to decide which party would build the New Jerusalem, there was little doubt.

There were clear signs during the election campaign that playing the

---

485 Gilbert, op. cit., 1988, p. 9.

486 D. R. Thorpe, *Supermac*, London, Chatto & Windus, 2010, p. 237.

khaki election card was not a winner. Late in the campaign at Walthamstow, Churchill found himself at the receiving end of abuse from crowds chanting: 'What about jobs? What about houses?'[487] His one memorable utterance in the general election was when he referred to Labour needing a 'Gestapo' to implement its policies; even Martin Gilbert could find nothing in that to praise.[488] It was an important blunder, because it played to the Labour narrative that Churchill, although a great war leader, was an old man, out of touch with what the ordinary people needed.

Here Churchill's dominance was something of a curse. It was easy enough for the opposition to paint him as the great war leader who would be a poor peacetime one, and his standing was such that none of the other leading Tories could even come close to him. Eden, the only other figure of any stature, was much more interested in emphasising the need to finish the war against Japan and to keep the peace in Europe than combating Labour on the front that mattered – housing and prosperity.[489] The fact that the Conservative manifesto placed 'home affairs' in fourth place, after 'the world', 'the empire' and 'defence', spoke of where Churchill's real concerns lay.

When all the results were in on 26 July 1945, the Conservatives had suffered their greatest defeat since 1905, with only 215 seats against Labour's 395. Twelve million had voted for Labour; only ten million for the great war leader. Even in Churchill's own seat of Woodford, an independent had polled more than 10,000 votes. Churchill had spectacularly failed to repeat the success of his old friend Lloyd George.

The defeat landed the Conservative Party with a problem it proved unable to solve, which preoccupied its leading figures for the next decade. The ideal thing would have been for Churchill to have retired and to have been replaced by Eden, who was younger, more liberal and more photogenic, but the old man showed no sign of wanting to go. Had he actually shown signs of

---

487 A. Horne, *Macmillan, Vol. I*, London, Macmillan, 1988, p. 286.

488 Gilbert, op. cit., 1988, p. 39

489 Anthony Eden, *Freedom and Order, selected speeches 1939–1946*, London, Faber & Faber, 1947, p. 347.

wanting to lead the party, there might have been something to have been said for his staying, but the difficulty was that he showed no such sign, preferring to spend his time writing his lucrative war memoirs and wintering in warmer climates. As his one significant ('Iron Curtain') speech in 1946 at Fulton, Missouri, showed, he had also found a new cause – the struggle against the Soviet Union. This, allied to his determination to reverse the humiliation of 1945, ensured that Churchill remained in position. His fame, and his age, created a situation whereby Eden – Churchill's most likely replacement – felt unable to ask him to go, or to plot his removal.[490] What, after all, was the profit in trying to remove an aged legend, who surely, Eden thought, must, in the way of things, go soon? If Eden, as the main beneficiary, would not try to remove the old boy, no one else would try to do so either. The result was that Churchill stayed where he was. The Conservative Party, as was its wont, found a way of working around this major problem by producing policy documents to which Churchill, rather reluctantly, gave his imprimatur.

Churchill came from a political tradition that did not believe in setting out detailed plans in opposition – something his own experience suggested offered hostages to fortune. But Rab Butler, at the head of the revived Conservative Research Department, put forward a series of 'charters', designed to show that the Tories were 'modern' and able to combat Labour on the Home Front.[491] Churchill is said to have looked at the Industrial Charter, which accepted most of Labour's nationalisation measures, and have commented that, with policies like that, Attlee would lose. Butler persuaded him to endorse it all the same. Whatever the truth of that, it embodied, like many political legends, a greater truth. Many of the younger and more liberal Conservatives, like Harold Macmillan, had lost their seats in 1945, and it was the older and more right-wing who had kept theirs. Butler could have had real trouble with free marketeers such as Churchill's friend Brendan Bracken, so Churchill's consent, however ill-informed, was vital. In this negative sense,

490 D. R. Thorpe, *Eden*, London, Chatto & Windus, 2003, pp. 416–20.

491 A. Howard, op. cit., pp. 153–63.

Churchill played a part in allowing Conservative policy to be re-shaped. His own lack of interest in domestic policy helped this process, as did the fact that world affairs increasingly preoccupied his attention.

If we can acquit Churchill of any part in shaping Conservative policy on the domestic front, the same is not true of foreign affairs. Whatever the rule that foreign affairs rarely abut on general elections, the 1940s and early 1950s were an exception to it. Churchill, like Attlee and Labour, had wanted a post-war world where cooperation with the USA and the USSR would be possible, but, even before the coalition of 1945 had ended, it was becoming clear that Stalin did not trust his allies to give him the sort of territorial settlement to which he felt entitled. His idea of what that should be was not one acceptable to a country that had gone to war to stop one power dominating Europe. Opposition ought to have meant that Churchill played little part in the emergence of a policy of containment, but his role transcended that of party leader. It suited both the Truman administration and Attlee and Bevin that he should have delivered the stern warning contained in the 'Iron Curtain' speech in March 1946 at Fulton, Missouri, and, while both groups distanced themselves from its 'war mongering' at the time, a year later they were happy to have used the speech as an indicator of the way the wind was changing. If, as some have argued, there was an 'Attlee consensus' after 1945, its foreign policy component was, at least in part, Churchill's doing. That 'Atlanticist' consensus would outlast the social democratic one by many decades.[492]

In one sense, one might have thought that the growing perception of the USSR as a threat might have helped shift things Churchill's way as the election of 1950 approached. One of the few consistencies to be found in his career was his opposition to communism, against which, as Lloyd George had once said, his grand ducal blood revolted. But with Bevin having overruled Attlee's more cautious approach to the USSR, and with Labour being able to claim credit for NATO and 'the bomb', it was hard to pin the appeasement label on them. However, the now Labour-supporting *Daily Mirror* did not

---

492 John Charmley, *Churchill's Grand Alliance*, London, Hodder & Stoughton, 1996, pp. 117–30.

find it hard to pin the 'war monger' label on Churchill at that election, so it may be doubted how far geo-political circumstances played to his advantage.

Opinion polls played very little part in anyone's election strategy back in 1950, although they showed Labour in with a good chance of holding on to power. With major changes to the constituencies – eleven new seats added, six abolished and 170 changes in all – along with the abolition of plural voting, it is hard to commute how far these things factored into the result, which gave Labour a slender lead of five (with 315 seats to Churchill's 297, on a higher number of votes).[493]

Historians, not least Conservative ones, have paid much attention to the Conservative Research Department and Rab Butler's 'charters', and they certainly played a part in allowing the Conservatives to suggest that they were not going to turn the clock back to the 1930s. But it is hard to know what part that played in the Tory revival. The charters were a sign of something that was important: the reform of local Conservative associations opened them up to young men of talent like Ted Heath, Iain Macleod and Enoch Powell – men who, in the past, would have been fortunate to have found a winnable seat first time around. With the Woolton reforms to expand and energise the party, and with the 'Attlee terror' providing plentiful targets, the local associations grew in size and helped mobilise the Conservative vote as of old. So, it is likely it was the faltering performance of an exhausted Attlee government, and disappointment with the slowness of the transition away from wartime privation, that tipped the balance of an election in which Labour still obtained more votes.[494]

Had the Conservatives not come so close, the demands for Churchill to have gone might have been irresistible; at the age of seventy-six, five more years of opposition would have been beyond him, and, whatever he had thought, others would reach that conclusion. But few thought Attlee would labour on with so small a majority, and so, in anticipation of another election in the near future, no challenge to Churchill emerged.

---

493 Anthony Seldon, *Churchill's Indian Summer*, London, Hodder & Stoughton, 1981, pp. 5–21.

494 Ibid., pp. 5–70

The narrowness of the Conservative defeat also encouraged party unity, and Eden, the heir apparent, was convinced that the 'old man' would go once he had finally erased the defeat of 1945. So it was a united party that went into the election Attlee called in early 1951. Labour collected a quarter of a million more votes than Churchill and the Liberals, but too many of them were in safe Labour seats, so they ended up with 295 seats compared to Churchill's 321.

It is indicative of Churchill's mindset, however, that he had tried to woo the Liberals, and that, when he formed his government, he invited in non-party figures such as Lord Alexander and Lord Monckton. The role of Conservative Party leader sat uneasily on Churchill – unlike the role of Prime Minister, a post to which he hung on for another four years. Despite another major stroke, Churchill was still in post in 1955, and it was only the prospect of another general election that persuaded him to stand down and give Eden a brief period at No. 10 before winning the election of that year.

Was Churchill a successful party leader? The blunt answer has to be no. It was not a role he relished, nor was it one upon which he spent much of his time. But there were advantages to the party in this – at least between 1945 and 1951. Self-confident and uninterested in detail, Churchill's approval of Butler's various charters, and his rebranding of the party, stilled the right-wing discontent with Butler. How could one be more Conservative than 'Winston'? He allowed the necessary reforms to take place and bed down. He effortlessly commanded the attention of the press, the newsreels and radio, and, in the absence of any more 'Gestapo' gaffes, his prestige continued to lend the Conservative brand something it lacked, by way of gravitas.

Of course, Churchill stands quite independent of any success, or otherwise, as Tory leader: that is not what his fame is based upon, nor what he sought to be remembered for. We might note, in passing, that the one area of his career before 1945 he never wrote about was his time as Baldwin's Chancellor; domestic politics failed to interest him. And yet, as we have seen, he is unique among Conservative leaders in losing two elections and being allowed the time to win a third one. It is doubtful – even given the lack of mechanisms for selecting and deposing leaders – that any other Conservative leader would have been extended such an opportunity. Easy though it would be to conclude this chapter by saying he stood aside from and above the context, it is clear that the 1951 victory owed far more to others than it did to him. For all the Butlerite attempts to claim victory as a triumph for his reforms, it was as much a reaction to Labour's exhaustion and want of ideas as it was to anything else. Still, the horse had carried the jockey home and, for Churchill, that was enough.

For all his fame, Churchill's record as a party leader and election-winner confines him very firmly to the lower part of any league table based on success in these areas. That his fame will outlast that of all those who finish above him in such a table is, of course, simply proof of something Churchill always knew: the rules did not apply to him.

CHAPTER 14

ANTHONY EDEN

DAVID DUTTON

Anthony Eden's short but long-awaited period in office was bookended by electoral triumph and foreign policy disaster. The 1955 general election was, in many ways, a personal victory. As David Dutton points out, the Conservative Party's vote share has not been bettered since. Many in the Conservatives felt they were on the road to an electoral disaster under Churchill, and Eden's accession – coupled with his immediate decision to call an election, and a comfortable majority of sixty – was vindication for those who had long called for him to lead the party. Dutton charts Eden's slow and tumultuous rise to the leadership, illustrating that his frustrated ambitions – while not hampering his popularity – may have ultimately damaged his personal ability to govern, given his eventual ill health. His considered strategic distancing from appeasement is juxtaposed with the series of rash errors that made up the Suez Crisis, and culminated in his resignation. While Eden's short period in office means Dutton partially reserves judgement, his long-held ambivalence towards the Conservative Party, and disdain for its radical right fringes, did not bode well for effective party management in the long term.

• • •

With a tenure of just twenty-one months, Anthony Eden shares with Alec Douglas-Home the dubious distinction of being the shortest-serving leader of the Conservative Party in the twentieth century among those who rose to the premiership. Yet other statistics might seem to point, in sharp contrast to the experience of Douglas-Home, to a generally positive assessment of Eden's term as head of the party. He was, or at least should have been, one of the best prepared of all incoming leaders. For a total period of about seventeen years, interrupted only by a short interval around the outbreak of the Second World War, Eden was widely seen as the 'next Conservative leader'. When it finally came in 1955, his succession to Churchill was not contested. One of his ministers judged that no Prime Minister since Pitt had entered office with higher expectations of success.[495] Furthermore, all his time as leader was spent as Prime Minister. He fought one general election and won it decisively, increasing his party's strength in the Commons by twenty-three seats – the first time that an incumbent government had raised its majority since 1865. Yet few now deem the Eden premiership – not the same thing as his party leadership but, in the circumstances, closely analogous to it – as anything other than a disaster. Overshadowed by the Suez Crisis, it left the party, and indeed the country, at a very low ebb. At the end of the millennium, BBC Radio 4 conducted a poll among leading academics and politicians to construct a ranking list of the prime ministers of the twentieth century. Nineteen candidates were considered – the incumbent, Tony Blair, being excluded – and Eden filled the bottom place, beneath even the hapless Neville Chamberlain.

Anthony Eden was first elected to Parliament in 1923 for the safe Conservative seat of Warwick & Leamington. He rose rapidly and served as parliamentary private secretary to the Foreign Secretary Austen Chamberlain from 1926 to 1929. After the Tories' loss of office in the latter year, the outgoing Cabinet minister William Bridgeman judged Eden, along with Oliver Stanley, Robert Boothby and Harold Macmillan, to be the coming men in the Conservative Party.[496] Crucially, the patronage of the party leader Stanley Baldwin saw Eden appointed parliamentary under-secretary at the Foreign Office at the formation of the National Government in August 1931. By this

495 John Boyd-Carpenter, *Way of Life*, London, Sidgwick & Jackson, 1980, p. 122.

496 Philip Williamson ed., *The Modernisation of Conservative Politics*, London, Historians Press, 1988, p. 225.

move, he overtook other Conservatives of his generation on the ladder of ministerial advancement. He was just thirty-four years of age.

The 1930s were, of course, a time that ruined the reputations of a considerable number of politicians, especially those charged with the construction and conduct of Britain's foreign relations. Eden was very close to that process for most of the decade. From 1931 until 1935, he was the second-ranking minister at the Foreign Office. Then, in December 1935, he became the youngest Foreign Secretary of the twentieth century, holding the post until his resignation in February 1938. It would have been difficult for his later career to prosper had he not managed to distance himself from the doings of his ministerial colleagues while he held subordinate office, and from the Prime Minister he served as Foreign Secretary. To be seen to be *with* the 'appeasers', but not *of* them, was a considerable political achievement, but one that Eden pulled off. His subordinate status before 1935 was widely interpreted to convey distance rather than complicity. Eden became associated in the popular mind with a more wholehearted commitment to the internationalism of the League of Nations – and, in the first years of the 1930s, with the sincere espousal of disarmament – than was attributed to the government as a whole. His performance at Geneva, where he often deputised for the Foreign Secretary, made him the 'blue-eyed boy of the National Govt'.[497] Yet the popular perception of Eden's role suggested a far greater divergence between his views and those of the government than was justified. Similarly, his subsequent performance as Foreign Secretary was rather less heroic than was later suggested, not least by Eden himself. No fundamental difference existed between Foreign Secretary Eden and Prime Minister Chamberlain over the need to appease Nazi Germany.

Nonetheless, as far as the path to the leadership was concerned, Eden's most important act as a member of the National Government was to leave it – before its foreign policy went seriously wrong. That resignation was prompted by a relatively minor disagreement over the timing of negotiations with Mussolini,

497 Stuart Ball ed., *Parliament and Politics in the Age of Baldwin and MacDonald*, London, 1992, p. 264.

a significant difference over policy towards the United States, and a growing personal irritation at the increasingly obtrusive interventions of the premier in the realm of foreign policy. By this time, however, many observers – particularly among the young – had come to see in Eden the one hope for a more positive stance. Edward Heath, then a student at Oxford, spoke for many: 'The news left me speechless, and I returned to my room utterly despondent. With Eden, whom we so admired and revered, now gone, who would stand up to the dictators and prevent Europe being dragged into war?'[498]

By this time, Eden was widely seen as Chamberlain's most likely successor as Conservative leader. His more senior colleagues may have nurtured private ambitions, but each was handicapped by one serious impediment or another. To compound his widespread unpopularity, Samuel Hoare's reputation remained tarnished by the Hoare–Laval episode; Lord Halifax found himself in the wrong parliamentary chamber; and John Simon in the wrong political party. For some time, Eden's standing remained high. 'Chamberlain will be your leader for a short time,' Baldwin is said to have told Duncan Sandys, 'then Anthony will have a long reign.'[499] More than a year after his resignation, Gallup still found that 38 per cent of those asked named Eden as their preferred successor to Chamberlain, while a mere 7 per cent opted for Churchill. Among the political classes, however, Eden's departure from office initiated a process that rapidly undermined his future prospects. By his conduct after February 1938, he convinced many that he lacked the qualities of leadership that had hitherto been attributed to him. Determined not to kick away the political ladder by which he had risen so far and so relatively fast, Eden was careful to draw a distinction between criticism and disloyalty. But, in avoiding too overt a challenge to the Chamberlain government, and thereby escaping a charge of disloyalty, Eden ran a parallel risk of dissatisfying those who looked to him for a lead.

The problem began with his Commons resignation speech, which left

498 Edward Heath, *The Course of My Life*, London, Hodder & Stoughton, 1998, p. 50.

499 Nigel Fisher, *Harold Macmillan*, London, Weidenfeld & Nicolson, 1982, p. 172.

most observers confused over the precise issue upon which he had felt compelled to leave office. In the months that followed, he was frequently absent from Parliament, missed repeated opportunities to strike hard when he was there, and seemed determined to proceed tangentially, as in his repeated calls for a more broadly based government. In so far as he did criticise his former colleagues, the grounds for that criticism were progressively removed as the government's policy evolved, especially after the guarantee of Polish independence at the end of March 1939, and the subsequent decision, however unenthusiastic, to seek an alliance with the Soviet Union. A former MP sent a blunt warning of the consequences of Eden's timidity:

> During the last few months I have met many people who are beginning to lose confidence in you. Your stock has fallen appreciably … People say … 'Why doesn't he come out and fight in the open? … Does he expect the rank and file of the Tory Party to forsake the party machine and invite him to lead them when Chamberlain retires?'[500]

When, amid rumours of an imminent general election in the late summer of 1939, Eden began to hint at the possibility of forming a new party, even Lord Cranborne – probably his closest political colleague – was outraged. The likelihood was of war, not a political campaign, and 'talk of a general election seem[ed] slightly academic'.[501]

In time, all of this would be forgotten, at least by the general public, and Eden's 1938 resignation would re-emerge, even in the first historical assessments, as a decisive moment in British political history. Churchill himself would play a key role in this regeneration, writing of the 'one strong young figure standing up against long, dismal, drawling tides of drift and surrender'.[502]

---

500 Lord Davies to Eden, 9 September 1938 (Avon MSS, all extracts by kind permission of Birmingham University Library, AP14/1/725).

501 Cranborne to Eden, 17 August 1939, cited in Simon Ball, *The Guardsmen*, London, HarperCollins, 2004, p. 200.

502 Winston Churchill, *The Gathering Storm*, London, Cassell, 1948, p. 201.

His influential account of the 1930s heaped 'sweeping blame on everyone else, except Anthony Eden'.[503] In the short term, however, the effect upon the internal dynamics of the Conservative Party was dramatic. No precise moment can be identified when Churchill irrevocably overtook Eden as 'Conservative leader in waiting', but it was in the spring of 1939 that the latter's confidant J. P. L. Thomas issued a prescient warning: 'I have a feeling ... that among some of our supporters in the country, Winston's speeches are a bit dwarfing yours as he has been very good of late.'[504] Chamberlain did restore Eden to government at the outbreak of war in September 1939, but only in the relatively lowly position of Dominions Secretary. This necessarily involved his departure from the eponymous group of dissident MPs who had gathered around him at the time of the Munich crisis. Ironically, the Eden Group proved a more effective organisation in the absence of its leader.[505] When Eden did attend a group dinner in the spring of 1940, one attendee noted that 'somehow or other, Anthony is so fair-minded (or senselessly loyal) about his colleagues that his presence seems to deaden any constructive criticism'.[506] Not surprisingly, when, a few weeks later, it came to choosing Chamberlain's successor, Eden was, in the words of one of his own supporters, 'out of it'.[507]

As Prime Minister, Churchill promoted Eden to the War Office, though still without a formal seat in the War Cabinet. Only when the death of Lord Lothian offered Churchill the chance to transfer Halifax to the resulting vacancy at the Washington embassy was Eden restored to his former eminence as Foreign Secretary. 'How fortune aids some people', judged Cuthbert Headlam in a comment that echoed the sentiments of many Eden critics.[508] Nonetheless, Eden now rapidly reasserted himself as a leading figure in the

---

503 *Toronto Globe and Mail*, 28 June 1948, cited in John Ramsden, *Man of the Century*, London, HarperCollins, 2002, p. 381.

504 Thomas to Eden, no date (Avon MSS, AP14/2/97D).

505 David Dutton, 'Power Brokers or just "Glamour Boys"? The Eden Group, September 1939–May 1940', *English Historical Review*, Vol. 118, 2003.

506 J. Lancaster to Cranborne, 4 April 1940, cited in Simon Ball, op. cit., p. 201.

507 Nicolson, op. cit., p. 75.

508 Stuart Ball, op. cit., 1999, p. 233.

war government and, in June 1942, was formally anointed as Churchill's heir. The Prime Minister informed the King that, in the event of his own sudden death, he should summon Eden to succeed him as 'the outstanding minister in the largest political party in the House of Commons'.[509]

Objectively, the old cliché about being only a heartbeat away from supreme power assumed more than usual relevance. Eden might not have had long to wait to fulfil his ambitions. Quite apart from the inherent dangers of his wartime travels, Churchill was now in his sixty-eighth year and in less robust health than the public imagined. Over the years that followed, he would battle against heart failure, strokes and pneumonia. Yet, against all the odds, he would celebrate his eightieth birthday still holding the role of Tory leader (and the premiership). Eden's authorised biographer has identified 'at least seven occasions on which Churchill's resignation was anticipated, before it actually occurred'.[510] Not for nothing would Harold Macmillan later suggest that Eden's problem 'was that he was trained to win the Derby in 1938; unfortunately, he was not let out of the starting stalls until 1955'.[511]

As Foreign Secretary, until the Conservatives lost office in 1945, Eden largely got on with his job. He, like others, often found Churchill's ways irritating, but at heart he accepted that the country's great war leader would remain supreme, even in matters of diplomacy, for the duration. Then, he shared the widespread view that the unexpected Conservative defeat in 1945 afforded Churchill the appropriate pretext for a dignified withdrawal from public life. At an emotional final meeting of the caretaker Cabinet, Churchill declared that he, unlike Eden, would never sit at the Cabinet table again. He seemed to be stating no more than the obvious.[512] 'The old man won't be there much longer,' Eden assured a sceptical Thomas Barman.[513] In fact, Churchill, still determined to win the nation's formal endorsement, retained

509 Winston Churchill, *The Hinge of Fate*, London, Cassell, 1951, p. 337.

510 Thorpe, op. cit., 2003, p. 416.

511 Ibid., p. 430.

512 Lord Avon, *The Reckoning*, London, Cassell, 1965, p. 551.

513 Thomas Barman, *Diplomatic Correspondent*, London, Hamish Hamilton, 1968, p. 196.

the title of opposition leader, leaving to Eden most of the routine duties of that thankless post, while he honed his credentials as an international statesman and prepared his war memoirs for publication. The Tory victory in 1951 was accompanied by a renewed Churchillian promise of early departure. In fact, it would be a further three and a half years before Eden secured his inheritance.

Throughout the long years of waiting, Eden never really lost the position of heir apparent. Other luminaries shone brightly, though usually briefly, and Churchill was not above teasing Eden by reminding him of the qualities and ambitions of potential rivals. But in 1944, Gallup found that 55 per cent of the population wanted Eden to succeed once Churchill left office. No other candidate made double figures. By the end of that year, Eden had even overtaken Churchill as the popular choice to lead the country once the fighting was over. Of course, the Conservative leadership was not at the disposition of the electorate, but such statistics were difficult to ignore. Indeed, by the late 1940s, there was good reason to believe that Eden's leadership would improve the party's electoral chances. Surveys made by Conservative Central Office revealed that he was widely admired by Labour voters and the best-placed figure to attract the still considerable 'Liberal vote'.

As the years passed, Churchill became ever more ingenious in devising reasons to postpone his own retirement. Sometimes these were skilfully dressed up in stratagems supposedly designed to broaden Eden's experience of domestic politics. Increasing doubts about his chosen successor's abilities may also have been a factor. Meanwhile, Eden toyed with the idea of abandoning the struggle and exploring pastures new, be it the Indian viceroyalty in 1943, the secretary-generalship of the UN in 1946, or a career in the City in the early 1950s. The frustration on Eden's part was intense. Latterly, he seemed genuinely keen to quit political life. By 1954, he confessed that he was at the end of his tether and could not stand it much longer. 'I cannot go on like this with this old man. I must escape somehow.'[514] But what Eden would not do was act decisively to force Churchill's hand. It seems likely that

514 Private information.

the handover of power came just in time, before the anxiety of protracted expectation finally sapped his will to carry on.

Succeeding Churchill on 6 April 1955, Eden announced nine days later that the country would go to the polls on 26 May. It was self-evidently a brave decision. Eden felt the need to secure a personal vote of confidence from the electorate, but at the same time risked the ignominy of contriving one of the shortest administrations of all time. In the event, it appeared that he had shown not just courage, but also sound judgement. When the results were declared, the *Daily Mail* suggested that the Tory victory was 'above all ... a resounding personal triumph for the Prime Minister', despite the fact that foreign affairs, Eden's speciality, had played a smaller part in the campaign than in 1951.[515] The Nuffield electoral study aptly sums up his performance:

> He stressed the virtues of toleration and reasonableness, and the perils of national disunity. He said nothing memorable but said it very well. He stirred up no excitement but he made no enemies. The success of his performances, both on the platform and on television, vindicated those Conservatives who had argued that, in the current public temper, his leadership would be a greater electoral asset to the party than that of his predecessor.[516]

Adopting a style that would later be used to advantage by John Major, Eden took to making a series of impromptu addresses to small groups of voters at street corners. According to Harold Macmillan, the Prime Minister did not 'put a foot wrong'.[517]

By common consent, the election was the most boring of the post-war era. It was, judged Violet Bonham Carter, 'like being offered two plates of cold meat and asked, "Ham or tongue, sir?"'[518] The Nuffield study writes

515 David Butler, *The British General Election of 1955*, London, Macmillan, 1955, p. 158.

516 Ibid., p. 75.

517 Peter Catterall ed., *The Macmillan Diaries 1950–57*, London, Macmillan, 2003, p. 433.

518 Mark Pottle ed., *Daring to Hope*, London, Weidenfeld & Nicolson, 2000, p. 148.

repeatedly of 'apathy', though, in the light of figures for some more recent contests, the voter turnout of 76.8 per cent demands some modification of this assessment. Certainly, it was one of the least ideological of contests, not characterised by any great issues between the parties: 'More than in any contest [of the twentieth century to date] the choice lay between men rather than measures.'[519] The electorate gave a clear, if not wildly enthusiastic, vote of confidence to the incumbent government. In particular, it was evident that Labour's dire warnings, uttered during the far more partisan campaign of 1951, had proved unjustified. Peace had been preserved (with Eden, as Foreign Secretary, playing a notable role), full employment maintained, and the welfare state consolidated. Rationing and other controls had been removed, and taxation reduced in the Budgets of 1953 and 1955. Even the Labour campaign found it difficult to suggest that a further period of Tory rule would be a national disaster. Struggling to play down their own internal problems, and unsure how to develop their achievements of 1945–51, the best that Labour candidates could do was to compete with the Conservatives in terms of their ability to hold down prices and maintain the social services. In the context of mounting affluence, a Tory victory was, with reason, widely anticipated.

But if contemporaries and later commentators failed to be inspired by the 1955 election, victory was ultimately what mattered. Eden was ideally equipped to secure it. He appealed to an electorate that had perhaps had enough of major upheavals. Singularly unideological himself, Eden offered reassurance and a safe pair of hands. He was known for his high-profile diplomatic successes, going back over many years, and the imprimatur of being Churchill's chosen successor, rather than for any stance he had taken on domestic issues. The Conservative manifesto was an expression of the leader's personal qualities – 'liberally peppered with platitudes, high-sounding phrases, and cautious qualifications ... a maximum of rhetoric and a minimum of a programme'.[520] But it was what the electorate wanted.

519 D. Butler, op. cit., 1955, p. 17.

520 Ibid.

It is, moreover, easy to minimise Eden's achievement. Only then, noted R. A. Butler privately, had the party finally 'destroyed the myth that 1945 represented the beginning of some irreversible revolution'.[521] Reviewing a report by the party chairman in September 1954, when Churchill was still Prime Minister, Macmillan noted that 'an election now, under the present govt w[oul]d lead to disaster electorally'. Furthermore, 'nothing can avoid this result *next* year, except a complete change in the structure of the govt and a new PM'.[522] Not only was it an unusual achievement for a government to increase its majority, but the Conservative share of the vote, at 49.7 per cent, was the highest secured by any party since 1935. It has not been bettered since. And, from the perspective of the twenty-first century, it is striking that the Tories won a majority of seats in Scotland.

Of course, though the 1955 result confounded contemporary notions of the natural swing of the pendulum, the result of 1959 was to be even more impressive. For the fourth general election in a row, the Conservatives improved their position. Harold Macmillan's government boasted a Commons majority of 100 seats over all the other parties combined. For this outcome, however, Eden could claim little if any credit. The party whose leadership he resigned in January 1957 had been badly – some thought, mortally – wounded by the Suez affair. While many on the left of the party were outraged by the Anglo-French invasion of Egypt, whether or not they knew of or suspected the concomitant collusion with Israel, others on the right bitterly opposed the abandonment of the military campaign when apparently on the point of victory.

In the country, Eden's personal standing held up reasonably well. His approval rating among all voters stood at 52 per cent at the height of the crisis in November 1956, and actually increased to 56 per cent the following month – both figures significant improvements on his standing in the first half of the year. But the wider picture was more worrying. Peter Hennessy has well captured the enormity of the crisis in which Eden's leadership came to an end:

521 Ramsden, op. cit., 1998, p. 352.

522 Catterall, op. cit., 2003, p. 355.

> He had succeeded in alienating not just the Arab world, but President Eisenhower, the bulk of the Commonwealth and most of the major players at the United Nations. He had also succeeded in splitting his country, dividing his Cabinet and party, and causing the near collapse of the pound, while leaving Soviet influence uncurbed, and an untoppled Nasser's prestige in the Arab world hugely enhanced.[523]

The First Lord of the Admiralty, Lord Hailsham, was not alone among ministers in expecting that the government would fall in the aftermath of the British withdrawal from the canal.[524]

Succeeding Eden as party leader and Prime Minister, Macmillan saw his primary task as one of survival. 'I have', he told a colleague, 'taken on a very difficult job, in circumstances almost unparalleled in political history.'[525] For all his public *sang froid*, he felt obliged to warn the Queen that he 'could not answer for the new government lasting more than six weeks'.[526] Even out of office and out of Parliament, some of the damage Eden had inflicted upon his party threatened to be long-term. Lord Poole, the party chairman, warned that the Conservatives had now lost 'the Liberal vote', and that 'it may be some time, if ever, before we regain their confidence'.[527] This had been an important factor in the party's recovery since 1945. At the time of the 1955 election, even the *Manchester Guardian* had, albeit grudgingly, given the Tories its backing. Now Violet Bonham Carter confirmed Poole's analysis, admitting that she had almost persuaded herself in the early 1950s that Toryism was 'shading into Liberalism'. After Suez, however, she concluded that there was a 'reversion to type'.[528]

No man, least of all a political leader, is entirely the architect of his own destiny, and it is only right to devote some attention to the factors, essentially

---

523 Peter Hennessy, *The Prime Minister*, London, Penguin, 2000, pp. 217–18.

524 Peter Hennessy, *Muddling Through*, London, Indigo, 1997, p. 216.

525 Macmillan to Salisbury, 29 March 1957, cited in Simon Ball, op. cit., p. 330.

526 Harold Macmillan, *Riding the Storm*, London, Macmillan, 1971, p. 185.

527 Poole to Eden, 6 November 1956, cited in Hennessy, op. cit., 2000, p. 234.

528 K. O. Morgan, *The People's Peace*, Oxford, Oxford University Press, 1992, p. 155.

outside Eden's control, that contributed to the successes and failures of his leadership. The change of economic climate, which helped to contrast Labour austerity with Conservative prosperity, was a fortuitous bonus. The Tories had come into office in October 1951 facing a serious economic crisis, notwithstanding the very considerable achievements of the outgoing Labour government. Very quickly, however, the terms of trade moved decisively in Britain's favour. With the end of the Korean War, food and raw material prices fell so sharply that, by 1953, the country could buy 13 per cent more imports than in 1951 for the same volume of exports. Put simply, the British economy experienced significant gains, encouraging the maintenance of full employment and an expansion of the social services, without the Conservative government having to lift a finger. It is doubtful whether any subsequent government, of whatever political persuasion, has had the good fortune to operate in so benign an economic climate as that of 1951–55. When it came to the general election of 1955, voters were, on the whole, sufficiently content with their growing affluence to re-elect the Conservative government that Eden now headed: 'Change, it was felt, would be wrong, dangerous and unnecessary.'[529]

Eden was also lucky in terms of his political opponents. The resignation in April 1951 from the Labour government of three ministers, led by Aneurin Bevan, had initiated a period of deep divisions in the ranks of the Labour Party, which by no means had been fully healed by the time of the 1955 election. The party's lack of internal fraternity was graphically displayed at its annual conference at Morecambe in 1952, and undoubtedly contributed to some loss of support in the country. Clement Attlee had surprised many by not resigning the leadership after Labour's 1951 defeat. His primary purpose in staying on was to hold his disputatious party together. If this had the collateral effect of reducing Herbert Morrison's chances of the ultimate succession, so much the better. By the time of the 1955 election, however, Attlee was seventy-two years of age and had been in the post for two full

---

529 Bernard Porter, *Britannia's Burden*, London, Edward Arnold, 1994, p. 294.

decades. It was time for a change, and the contrast with the Conservatives, under their new and relatively youthful leader with his broad electoral appeal, was stark. The surprise, perhaps, is that the Tory margin of victory was not greater than it was.

As leader, Eden's good fortune soon ran out. Though once denied, it now seems incontrovertible that the state of his health was the single most important determinant in explaining the failures and mistakes of Eden's government.[530] The problem began with a botched operation for gallstones in 1953 and was never fully resolved for the rest of his life, notwithstanding periods of apparent good health. Robert Carr, Eden's PPS in the early 1950s, provides the useful commentary of one who was close to him at this time:

> He appeared to be getting very much better, but then, within the first six months of his premiership, he started getting the fevers again, two or three. The first one was generally written off as flu. Then there was another one ... It was quite clear to me by the end of 1955 that he was a far from well man.[531]

More conclusively, we have the analysis of David Owen, who was granted access to Eden's medical records. A letter from the Prime Minister's physician provides evidence that Eden 'was taking dextro-amphetamine, a stimulant that, combined with amylobarbitone, a sedative, is contained in Drinamyl. This combination ... used to be referred to as "purple hearts".'[532] Owen concludes that 'in relation to three crucial decisions – to collude with Israel, to mislead the American President and to lie to the House of Commons, even after the invasion – his judgement was seriously impaired and his illness and treatment made the major contribution to that impairment'.[533] Ironically, Eden's illness and medication had the effect of turning him into the sort of

530 See, for example, Thorpe, op. cit., 2003, p. 544.

531 Hennessy, op. cit., 1997, p. 211.

532 David Owen, *In Sickness and in Power*, London, Methuen & Co., 2008, p. 120.

533 Ibid., p. 140.

leader many of his critics wanted – bold, single-minded and decisive – albeit with tragic consequences. The Chief of Air Staff Sir William Dickson noted that, in the final days of the Suez adventure, Eden was like a 'prophet inspired, [who] swept the Cabinet and chiefs of staff along with him, brushing aside any counter-arguments and carrying all by his exaltation'.[534] This was not the patient, cautious, often hesitant diplomat of earlier years.

The circumstances of its ending make it impossible to judge Eden's leadership a success, irrespective of his unblemished electoral record. He resigned a genuinely sick man, although there had been open discussion of 'the succession' even before his departure to Jamaica in November 1956 to recuperate. Furthermore, there is some evidence that the Americans were consorting with the ambitious Harold Macmillan to secure what a later generation would call 'regime change', when the doctors' intervention secured their purposes for them.[535] One verdict, of course, is that it is impossible to judge fairly a man whose leadership of the party lasted less than two years. Eden's was a case of unfinished business, and we can have little idea of what the record of a full term would have looked like. Eden had no chance to re-fashion party policy according to his own inclinations, and failed even to construct a government that was distinctively his. The Conservative hierarchy in January 1957 remained essentially the one that Churchill had bequeathed. Eden delayed a major Cabinet reshuffle on coming to office out of sensitivity for the position of the Chancellor R. A. Butler, who had recently lost his first wife. And, when the governmental reorganisation did come, it was narrowly focused on Eden's desire to reassert his own control over the Foreign Office by appointing a figure, Selwyn Lloyd, whom he felt able to dominate. In policy terms, we have only tantalising hints as to how a more prolonged Eden leadership might have developed – a greater readiness perhaps to tackle the mounting scourge of inflation and a willingness to re-examine the extent of Britain's sprawling overseas commitments.

---

534 John Colville, *The Fringes of Power*, London, Hodder & Stoughton, 1985, p. 724.

535 W. S. Lucas, 'Suez, the Americans and the Overthrow of Anthony Eden', *LSE Quarterly*, 1(3), 1987.

Yet there is another possible scenario. Eden lacked many of the basic attributes of leadership, not least in his reluctance to delegate. His notorious temper, beneath a serene public demeanour, made him a difficult colleague and master. He was irredeemably 'unclubbable' and disinclined to spend time in the Commons smoking room, courting the support and friendship of back-bench MPs. And he was unusually sensitive to criticism, not least from the press, which rapidly turned against him after being broadly supportive during the election campaign. Above all, Eden's relationship with the Tory Party was always likely to be problematic. It is probably fair to say that it liked him more than he liked it. During the war he had found Labour colleagues in the Churchill coalition surprisingly congenial and, wondering whether he could not work with them in future, gave serious, if unstructured, thought to the creation of a new centre party as the best vehicle for the construction of a reformed post-war Britain. In 1943, he expressed his distaste for the Conservative Party – 'that is not where my supporters come from'[536] – and to his diary two years later confided that he was 'not really much use as a party man. I dislike our extreme right more than somewhat and I seem forever to be seeing the other fellow's point of view.' His hesitant conclusion – 'perhaps I could make something of the C[onservative] Party if I had it' – was short on conviction.[537] None of this suggests that a longer leadership would have brought significantly greater success than did Eden's brief and troubled tenure.

536 John Harvey ed., *The War Diaries of Oliver Harvey*, London, Collins, 1978, p. 258.

537 Eden's diary, 6 June 1945 (Avon MSS, AP20/1/25).

CHAPTER 15

HAROLD MACMILLAN

D. R. THORPE

The circumstances under which Harold Macmillan inherited the premiership in 1957, as head of a beleaguered Conservative Party in the wake of the Suez Crisis, were not grounds for electoral optimism. Yet Macmillan's sole vote-facing test as leader led to an overwhelming majority of 100 seats. D. R. Thorpe describes a prime ministerial focus that was on foreign affairs and the intertwining problems of de-colonisation, European integration and damaged Anglo-American relations. Macmillan's leadership story domestically is primarily one of success, defined by growing prosperity and a popular appeal that transcended class boundaries – epitomised by his inclusive brand of leadership. It was a decline in economic fortunes, and the renewal of Labour's opposition under Harold Wilson, that triggered the rash party management of the 'Night of the Long Knives', and a transition to retirement that was slowed, not driven, by the infamous Profumo scandal. Overall, Thorpe deems Macmillan's time as leader to be significant, and defined, in large part, by achievement at home and abroad.

• • •

Harold Macmillan succeeded Anthony Eden as Prime Minister on 10 January 1957 in the wake of the Suez Crisis. Both the nation and the Conservative Party were bitterly divided at the time, and Macmillan's task of restoring morale and unity seemed nigh impossible. Indeed, on his appointment, he warned the Queen that he did not think his government would last six weeks – a remark of which the Queen reminded him at his final audience six years and nine months later. Macmillan's path to the premiership was a long and tortuous one through the military, business and political worlds. After years as a rebellious backbencher in the 1930s, he had, eventually and belatedly, held eight ministerial posts before he entered 10 Downing Street, including those of Foreign Secretary and Chancellor of the Exchequer.

Macmillan was born in 1894, the third and youngest son of Maurice Macmillan – later to be, as Harold was, head of the family publishing firm Macmillan & Co. Harold was educated at Eton and Balliol College, Oxford, failing to complete his degree, as he was, in his own words, 'sent down by the Kaiser'. Gravely wounded at the Battle of Loos in 1915, he was one of the few of his Balliol contemporaries to survive the Great War. Oxford was for him, thereafter, a city of ghosts, exorcised only partially by 1960, when he became chancellor of the university. The memory of the sufferings of the Great War never left him.

After demobilisation, he joined the staff of the 9th Duke of Devonshire, Governor General of Canada, as his aide-de-camp. In Ottawa, he gained, as he recalled, 'his health and a wife'. He fell in love with the duke's third daughter, Lady Dorothy Cavendish, and they married on 21 April 1920 at St Margaret's, Westminster. The congregation included the Macmillan & Co. authors Thomas Hardy and Rudyard Kipling. Working at the family publishing firm, Macmillan was to have responsibility for the works of both Hardy and Kipling, as well as authors such as John Maynard Keynes (who advised Harold Macmillan on his own economic treatise *The Middle Way*, published in 1938), Sean O'Casey, Hugh Walpole and W. B. Yeats.

Macmillan was elected MP for the northern constituency of Stockton-on-Tees in the general election of 1924 – a seat he was to hold, apart from 1929 to 1931, until 1945. After his defeat in the general election that year, he was returned as MP for Bromley in a by-election in November 1945 – a seat he held until 2 October 1964 – though his political heart always remained in Stockton, as did that of his wife Lady Dorothy. The plight of the unemployed in Stockton-on-Tees during the depression in the 1930s had affected him deeply and moved him towards interventionist Keynesian economic thought. Macmillan became known as a rebellious backbencher, not only in economic matters, but in opposing Neville Chamberlain's appeasement policies. When Churchill became Prime Minister in May 1940, Macmillan at last received preferment, first as parliamentary under-secretary at the Ministry of Supply, and then, in February 1942, as under-secretary in the Colonial Office. However, in December 1941 he received real executive responsibility as Minister Resident in Northwest Africa, the so-called 'Viceroy of the Mediterranean', where he worked closely with General Eisenhower. This was the breakthrough in his political career that made the rest possible. In Churchill's caretaker government from May to July 1945, after the war, he served as Air Minister.

With the Conservative defeat in the July 1945 general election, Macmillan was prominent among those such as Anthony Eden and R. A. Butler in the task of rebuilding the Conservative Party and educating traditional Tories away from their prejudices. Although the Conservatives failed to dislodge the Labour government in the closely contested general election of February 1950, the party was returned with a majority of seventeen in that of October 1951. Macmillan then embarked on a series of increasingly important Cabinet posts over the next six years. His unequivocal success as Minister of Housing (1951–54) in fulfilling the Conservatives' pledge to build 300,000 houses a year was an achievement that made him a nationally recognised figure. He served as Minister of Defence from October 1954. When Eden succeeded Churchill as Prime Minister in April 1954, Macmillan became Foreign Secretary – a post he held until December 1955, when, to his disappointment, he was moved from the Foreign Office to the Treasury. In his one Budget of April 1956, he introduced Premium Bonds – denounced by the Archbishop of Canterbury Dr Geoffrey Fisher as a 'squalid enterprise'. Yet the scheme was to go from strength to strength over subsequent decades. From July 1956, Macmillan's time at the Treasury was dominated by the complications and controversies of the unfolding Suez Crisis. When Eden resigned as Prime Minister owing to ill health in January 1957, Macmillan was the preferred choice (over R. A. Butler) of the Cabinet, as well as of Winston Churchill, as

Eden's successor. Contrary to inaccurate mythology, the party's MPs were consulted – even those who were away on European business in Strasbourg.

Macmillan entered Downing Street at a low ebb in the fortunes of the Conservative Party – it was five points behind the Labour Party in the opinion polls. His achievement in leading the Conservatives to a landslide victory of 100 seats in the general election of October 1959 was one of the most remarkably swift and comprehensive revivals achieved by any political party in the twentieth century. He gave back to the party's MPs a sense of purpose, raising morale at every opportunity, and, as a priority, mended relationships with Eisenhower and Washington. Macmillan timed the election to perfection. Sitting in the garden at his Sussex home Birch Grove in the hot summer of 1959, one of his young grandsons complained about the noise of all the aircraft leaving nearby Gatwick airport. Macmillan pointed out that people were now enough well off to afford overseas holidays and would return refreshed and happy, voting the Tories back again in the autumn. And so it proved. Before the October campaign Macmillan told all the candidates to remember the story of G.K. Chesterton when speaking in a northern town before the war. The mayor had promised Chesterton that a band would be welcoming him at the station. Chesterton told him not to trouble himself, as he would be bringing his own trumpet! Macmillan urged the Tories to do likewise, as they campaigned in their constituencies. The resulting landslide was built on a 49.4 per cent share of the popular vote, a figure never since remotely equalled. Welcoming the MPs back to Westminster after the electoral triumph he told the newcomers not to be afraid of being rebels, after all he had been a back-bench rebel in his day, but only on one issue at a time 'otherwise it confuses the whips'.

Macmillan's success was built on a combination of full employment and a stable economy. When he said in a speech at Bedford on 20 July 1957 that 'most of our people have never had it so good' he was accused by some of his opponents of complacency. But some critics had not read the text carefully enough. Macmillan was not celebrating smug materialism, but issuing a warning *against* complacency. He was also helped by overwhelmingly favourable press support, the absence of rivals for his job, sound party finances, a skillful advertising campaign for the 1959 election by Colman, Prentis and Varley (who devised the slogan 'Life's better under the Conservatives. Don't let Labour ruin it'), and the policy divisions in the Labour Party between Gaitskellites and Bevanites.

In foreign affairs, Macmillan brought vast experience to the many problems facing the post-war world, not least in the retreat from Empire and the move towards colonial independence and the growth of the Commonwealth. His 'winds of change' speech before a hostile South African government in Cape Town on Monday 3 February 1960, though it infuriated Churchill and traditional Tories, was one of the bravest and most far-sighted of his career. Similarly, Macmillan had the foresight to see that in the changed political climate of the time, Britain had to achieve some rapprochement with Europe after the failure, from 1955 to 1957, to embrace the vision of Jean Monnet of a unified Europe to stand as a world power between America and Russia. His relationship with the young John Kennedy from January 1961 was to be an unlikely and unexpected success, the experienced elder statesman from Eisenhower's generation and the young, thrusting and modern President, not least through their telephone contacts during the Cuban Missile Crisis in October 1962.

Other important issues included defence policy at a time when national service was still in operation. Macmillan was to end national service in the early 1960s, but with experience as a former Minister of Defence was acutely aware of all the controversial issues surrounding the nuclear deterrent and a leaner army — 'big bangs and small forces' as he called it. But on the 'bomb' he was unequivocal: 'we must rely on the power of our nuclear deterrent or we must throw up the sponge'. This policy was eventually to lead to great difficulties with the French President de Gaulle. In reality, Britain increasingly depended on America by cancelling the increasingly obsolete British Blue Streak Missile system and opting for Skybolt, being developed by the Americans. Indirectly this option, which was to culminate in the purchase of Polaris missiles for her own submarines, was to contribute to the disappointment of the common market application.

Since the time of the post-war Labour government much had been made of the three interesting circles of the United States, Europe and the Commonwealth, with Britain at the still centre of intersection. Macmillan was acutely aware of the difficulties membership of the common market would cause in Commonwealth countries and in 1958 he became the first British Prime Minister to undertake a full Commonwealth tour, bolstering his reputation for unflappability by leaving in the wake of the resignation of the Chancellor of the Exchequer, Peter Thorneycroft, and his treasury team, which he insouciantly dismissed as 'a little local difficulty'.

Macmillan's Commonwealth tour was concurrent with the granting of independence to many former colonies. Sudan had become independent in 1956. Ghana, formerly the Gold Coast, achieved independence in 1958. After Macmillan's appointment of Iain Macleod as Colonial Secretary, the pace seemed unstoppable with Kenya, Tanganyika and Zanzibar achieving independence. In 1953 Churchill's government had established the Central African Federation comprising Nyasaland and Northern and Southern Rhodesia. The problems of Southern Rhodesia were not to be resolved in Macmillan's time as premier and proved controversial for future governments after Ian Smith's Unilateral Declaration of Independence in 1965.

After Peter Thorneycroft's resignation as Chancellor, Derick Heathcoat-Amory became Chancellor for two years. Selwyn Lloyd succeeded Amory in 1960. Lloyd was a firm believer in sound money and resisted Macmillan's Keynesian instincts. In this battle there could only be one eventual winner. Lloyd had warned Macmillan on appointment that he would be an orthodox Chancellor on taxation and public expenditure. In fact, he was to prove highly innovative in other areas, but he was soon caught up in the conflict between Stocktonian Keynesianism on the one hand and Treasury orthodoxy on the other. With Macmillan's support Selwyn Jones established the National Economic Development Council in 1962, a tripartite organisation for government, employers and trade unions, which survived many changes in the political landscape until June 1992. Lloyd made the first steps towards an incomes policy and encouraged, with Macmillan's approval, the concept of long-term dirigiste expenditure planning by drawing on the lessons of the French Commissariat du Plan.

Lloyd's Chancellorship was to founder on the cumulative political difficulties that arose in the spring of 1962. The 'pay pause' (a freeze on wages) he had introduced in the sharply deflationary measures of July 1961 was particularly unpopular with nurses and teachers, who had a large measure of public support, and contributed over the next month to a series of by-election reverses, culminating in the spectacular defeat by the Liberals in Orpington in March 1962. Lloyd's other initiative, the National Incomes Commission ('Nicky'), was intended to manage wage restraint in the long-term, with reference to the growth of productivity. Its birth pangs were traumatic. Macmillan sacked Lloyd on Friday 13 July, the Night of the Long Knives, with six other Cabinet ministers in a reshuffle that destroyed for ever his reputation, always overstated, for unflappability. The Liberal MP Jeremy Thorpe observed cruelly: 'Greater love hath no man than this, that he lay down his friends for his life.' Lloyd never altered his opinion that Macmillan's gravest mistake was 'thinking unemployment a worse enemy than uncontrolled inflation'. Macmillan's premiership had passed its peak.

The last two years of Macmillan's premiership were to be dominated by financial issues and the move towards some form of European integration, following on the idea of a European Free Trade Association, pursued by Thorneycroft. Macmillan went further, deciding that entry to the common market itself would be vital for Britain's future financial prospects. But he reckoned without de Gaulle's opposition. President de Gaulle's veto in January 1963 against Britain's membership of the common market came as a bitter blow and removed the rudder from Macmillan's plans. As he wrote despairingly in his diary, 'All our policies are in ruins'.

Macmillan's premiership is not divided into pre-1959 and post-1959; the real divide came when, after Gaitskell's untimely death in January 1963, Harold Wilson was elected Labour leader in February. Macmillan had ill-disguised contempt for Gaitskell, a sanctimonious Wykehamist with gestures like an American shopkeeper, as he once described him. Harold Wilson was to prove a most formidable Leader of the Opposition from 1963–64, though even then he was only just able to scrape into Downing Street in October 1964 with a majority of four seats.

Macmillan and Wilson had many similarities and they respected each other's political skills. Both were in many ways outsiders in their parties, mistrusted by many of their own erstwhile supporters, and were prepared to cut corners and be ruthless. This had not always worked in Macmillan's favour, as shown by the aftermath of the Night of the Long Knives. As economic difficulties had increased in 1961–62, resulting in adverse opinion polls and the devastating loss of the 'safe' Conservative seat of Orpington (bordering Macmillan's own Bromley constituency) in March 1962, Macmillan had summarily sacked his Chancellor of the Exchequer, Selwyn Lloyd, and six other Cabinet ministers on Friday 13 July. Reginald Maudling, who followed a Keynesian economic policy and a 'dash for growth', replaced Lloyd as Chancellor. As Nigel Birch, one of Macmillan's persistent critics, was to remark, it was 'never glad confident morning' again.

Following de Gaulle's veto on Britain's application to join the common market in January 1963, Macmillan's thoughts turned towards an orderly transition to a younger leader, giving time for his successor to establish himself in the public consciousness before the general election due by October 1964. This plan was comprehensively de-railed by the Profumo scandal in June 1963, when John Profumo, the War Minister, resigned after admitting that he had lied to the House of Commons about the nature of his relationship with Christine Keeler. One of the persistent myths about these events is that the Profumo affair brought Macmillan's premiership to a premature end. In fact, it was the exact opposite. 'Profumo' prolonged Macmillan's premiership, as he could not be seen to be driven from office by what Lord Hailsham, the Lord President of the Council, described as a 'squalid affair between a woman of easy virtue and a proved liar'. In the end Macmillan was brought down in October 1963 by his prostate, not by Profumo.

Further inaccurate myths prevail about the events of the Conservative leadership contest of October, which resulted in Lord Douglas-Home, the

Foreign Secretary, disclaiming his title under the terms of the Peerage Act of July 1963 and becoming Conservative leader and Prime Minister. The real loser in the wake of Macmillan's delayed retirement was not Rab Butler, who knew in his heart of hearts that as John Morrison, chairman of the 1922 Committee of backbenchers, had told him in the summer that 'the chaps will never have you', but Reginald Maulding. His star had mysteriously waned by the autumn. Macmillan did not manipulate the soundings of the extensive consultation, which for the first time in the party's history involved the *extra*-parliamentary party as well as the MPs and the peers. As Vernon Bogdanor has rightly observed, 'The outcome, the selection of Lord Douglas-Home, cannot be said to have seriously misrepresented Conservative opinion at the time.'

Was Macmillan a great Prime Minister? In his study *Britain Since 1918*, the former Labour MP and SDP founder member Professor David Marquand thinks so. 'Harold Macmillan, that master of irony and specialist in ambiguity,' he writes, 'emerges from my story as the nearest thing to a great Prime Minister in the post-war years.' Macmillan *was* a great Prime Minister for much of his time in Downing Street, though not quite in the supreme category occupied by Lloyd George, Churchill, Attlee and Margaret Thatcher.

Malcolm Muggeridge said that, 'to succeed pre-eminently in English public life, it is necessary either to conform either to the popular image of a bookie or a clergyman'. Macmillan was pre-eminent among Britain's political bookies, most of whose bets were successful until the latter months of his premiership. Macmillan's decision to seek election for the Chancellorship of Oxford University in 1960 in a contest against Sir Oliver Franks was a prime example of his willingness to gamble. The Cabinet, especially Lord Kilmuir, the Lord Chancellor, had grave reservations, warning the Prime Minister that he had nothing to gain and everything to lose. 'You risk your neck for something you don't really need,' he said, to which Macmillan replied, 'You might say the same about fox-hunting.' His eventual victory at the time of ongoing controversies about alleged fraud in a ballot held by the Electrical Trades Union, led the Labour MP Anthony Wedgwood Benn to congratulate Macmillan with ill-disguised irony on 'having proved by his own tremendous victory in a ballot held in Latin, open for all to see, that the establishment has nothing to learn from the Electrical Trades Union'. Macmillan's face puckered in delight. 'Except this,' he replied, 'that I think that on this occasion the establishment was beaten.' So it was. Macmillan was initially the outsider candidate and the whole episode is a microcosm of much of his style, as was his decision to create life peerages in 1957. This was seen by many traditionalists at the time as the fatal thin end of a wedge, regarding the future of the Lords. What they did not realise was that Macmillan could 'see beyond the trees', as he admiringly said of President Kennedy, and that the reform was no Trojan Horse, but eventually a means of the Upper House's salvation. Just before the end of his premiership, the Test Ban Treaty, signed in Moscow, proved a last political example of a gamble coming to fruition.

The rollercoaster ride of Macmillan's career as Prime Minister closely followed the ups and downs of the economic indicators. The Labour government from 1945–51 was associated in the public mind with austerity, scarcity, rationing and queues; Macmillan's government was increasingly associated with prosperity, growing affluence and the good life. His abiding achievement, by a combination of the luck of the economic cycle and careful planning, was to be the Prime Minister who led Britain from that immediate post-war world of deprivation to the years of plenty and widening opportunities. It was only as economic difficulties increased in the early 1960s that the political tide turned.

Moreover, the welfare state was not curbed under Tory rule, as Labour activists had prophesied. If anything, the collectivist drive that Macmillan directed from the Ministry of Housing brought a new level of social provision, continued during his premiership, which not only improved living standards, but eroded the support that working-class people had traditionally given Labour. The political opportunity afforded by this important transition was one that Macmillan shrewdly did not let slip. He had style in abundance, was a star on the world stage, and for much time successfully disguised Britain's international decline. He knew that the special relationship with America was to a great degree a myth, but he recognised that it was a useful myth, brilliantly sustained by his friendships with both Eisenhower and Kennedy.

Above all, Macmillan appealed to a remarkably broad cross-section of British society:

- The deferential working class, who believed that the governing class knew their business, and that it was best to let them be about it.

- The military veterans, who admired Macmillan's Great War record in an age when MPs who had seen active service were referred to in the House of Commons as honourable and gallant.

- The aspiring lower-middle class, who wanted their children to have the educational opportunities that were denied to them in the pre-war days.

- The Rotary Club members in Macmillan's Bromley constituency, who thought that he was a Prime Minister who actually looked like a Prime Minister.

- The left-of-centre Keynesian economists, who saw the author of *The Middle Way* as a kindred spirit.

- The intellectual and university world (the demographic that was Gaitskell's strong point), which admired Macmillan's innate seriousness on the big issues.

- The business world, which knew that Macmillan was a man of vast commercial expertise and that he could actually read a balance sheet.

- Disraelian 'one-nation Conservatives, who wanted Tory men and Whig measures'.

- The world of letters, which was in reverence at Macmillan's links with writers such as Hardy and Yeats.

- The religious community (though not Archbishop Fisher), for Macmillan's loyal churchmanship.

- The patriots, who applauded Macmillan's unambiguous pursuit of British interests.

- What might be called the 'Chatham House' constituency, who admired Macmillan's approach to the second phase of decolonisation.

- The aristocrats, who saw Macmillan as one of their own, though he was really a Forsyte businessman who had married into the aristocracy, rather than being an aristocrat himself.

Macmillan's wit was legendary and often had rapier-like deadliness. 'The Liberals offer a mixture of sound and original ideas,' he observed. 'Unfortunately none of the sound ideas is original and none of the original ideas is sound.' But at the heart of his political character was a steel that had been fostered by his bitter experiences in the Great War, and the long-term effect of his wife's affair with Robert Boothby MP, known to the Westminster village but not to the general public. These two traumas put grit into the oyster, rather as Bonar Law's widowerhood at a relatively young age had made him seek consolation in the driven world of political work.

One of the Macmillan & Co. authors he much admired, C. P. Snow, wrote to him at the time, in 1963, saying that he was the butt of the emerging satirists:

> Prime ministers, in the long run, survive in history according to whether their intelligent contemporaries find them psychologically interesting. You are the only Prime Minister for a long time, Churchill excepted, who has

> evoked any such interest. That, of course, is why you attract some hostile attention for the revue writers and the like: but if you didn't, there would be something very wrong.

Macmillan always remained a psychologically interesting Prime Minister, and his survival in history is assured. Walter Bagehot wrote: 'A great premier must add the vivacity of an idle man to the assiduity of a very laborious one.' Macmillan was both vivacious and assiduously laborious – those seemingly contradictory two requisites that Bagehot felt so necessary to sustain a great premiership. Macmillan's final *envoi* to the nation, written in May 1973 at the end of his last volume of memoirs (*At the End of the Day*), was one of guarded optimism:

> Nothing in my long experience or in my observations of the youth of today makes me fear that the people of Britain, in every walk of life, will shrink from the new challenge or fail to rise to the level of events. But to do so they must restore and strengthen the moral and spiritual, as well as the material, base on which they have rested for so many generations through so many troubles and tribulations.

Time has not eroded the relevance or the essential truth of Macmillan's message.

CHAPTER 16

ALEC DOUGLAS-HOME

ANDREW HOLT

Alec Douglas-Home was Conservative leader between October 1963 and July 1965, and Prime Minister for a shade under a year until the general election of October 1964. He led the party in that election to a slim defeat, Harold Wilson's Labour Party holding a majority of four due to a fairly large swing away from the Conservatives. While any lasting legacy is limited by a short tenure as leader, of Britain as well as the Conservative Party, Andrew Holt argues Alec Douglas-Home is unduly dismissed, holding under-recognised competencies and strengths. The context of his leadership and the hand he was dealt were particularly challenging and constraining. Equally, the closed-door and elitist nature of his path to the leadership was a burden, epitomising a shifting political culture to which he never truly became accustomed. Although his strength was foreign policy, he had little success in shifting the electoral debate to his advantage, and his time as Leader of the Opposition exposed his political weaknesses. While Douglas-Home had little patience for parliamentary discontent, and even less ability to manage it, his party organisational changes showed a sure touch and created a long-term legacy.

• • •

Despite a long and distinguished political career, Alec Douglas-Home has been called the 'unremembered Prime Minister'.[538] A perfect illustration of this came when, in retirement, he found

538 Hennessy, op. cit., 2000, p. 274.

himself conversing with an elderly couple on a train en route to Berwick-upon-Tweed. 'My husband and I think it was a great tragedy that you were never Prime Minister,' remarked the lady. 'As a matter of fact, I was,' Douglas-Home replied, 'but only for a very short time.'[539] Holding office for just 363 days and having his tenure in No. 10 bookended by Harold Macmillan and Harold Wilson did not help Douglas-Home leave a lasting impression on the public's consciousness. He has also attracted less scholarly attention than his contemporaries. As Anthony Seldon once wrote: 'Home's is the least-written-about career of any twentieth-century Prime Minister.'[540]

Born in Mayfair in the summer of 1903, the young Alec (then known by the courtesy title of Lord Dunglass) studied at Eton and Christ Church, Oxford. He remains the only Prime Minister to have played first-class cricket, averaging over sixteen with the bat, and a wicket for every 30.25 runs conceded with his medium-paced, out-swinging bowling.[541] Motivated by an old-fashioned aristocratic sense of duty, Douglas-Home first entered Parliament in 1931,[542] becoming parliamentary private secretary to Neville Chamberlain in 1936 and serving him loyally throughout the appeasement period, albeit with minimal involvement in policymaking.[543] Shortly after Chamberlain resigned the premiership in May 1940, Douglas-Home elected to undergo an operation for spinal tuberculosis. The procedure left him encased in plaster for almost two years, but was ultimately successful. His career suffered a further setback when he became one of many Conservatives swept from the Commons by the Labour landslide in the 1945 election.

539 D. R. Thorpe, *Alec Douglas-Home*, London, Sinclair–Stevenson, 1996, p. 8.

540 Keith Robbins ed., *The Blackwell Biographical Dictionary of British Political Life in the Twentieth Century*, Oxford, Blackwell, 1990, p. 209.

541 'Sir Alec Douglas-Home', in ESPN Cricinfo, accessed 22 January 2015 (http://www.espncricinfo.com/england/content/player/12295.html).

542 Lord Home, *The Way the Wind Blows: An Autobiography*, London, Collins, 1976, pp. 45, 187; Home to Fraser, December 1963 (M.48H/63, PREM 11/5006); Kenneth Young, *Sir Alec Douglas-Home*, London, Dent, 1970, p. 26.

543 John Dickie, *The Uncommon Commoner: A Study of Sir Alec Douglas-Home*, London, Pall Mall Press, 1964, p. 44.

Although Douglas-Home regained his seat in 1950, he was forced to vacate it upon inheriting the earldom of Home from his father in July 1951.

When the Conservatives returned to power in October 1951, Prime Minister Winston Churchill appointed Douglas-Home to the newly created post of Minister of State for Scotland. Promoted by Anthony Eden to be Commonwealth Secretary in 1955, Douglas-Home's extended tour of the Commonwealth between August and November of that year increased his prestige in Cabinet and led to his views being sought on wider foreign policy and defence issues.[544] The addition of the roles of Leader of the House of Lords and Lord President of the Council to Douglas-Home's portfolio under Harold Macmillan left him feeling further empowered to play a greater role in policymaking.[545] He handled these extra responsibilities with aplomb, and was regarded as 'the best of the lot' in comparison with other post-war incumbents of the Commonwealth Office.[546] In 1960, Macmillan surprised the nation by making Douglas-Home, who still had a low public profile, Foreign Secretary. The media storm surrounding the appointment soon dissipated, however. The *Daily Mail* summed up the changing mood the following summer, admitting: 'How *wrong* we were about Douglas-Home.'[547]

Despite this experience and success, Douglas-Home's appointment as Prime Minister on 19 October 1963 was a controversial one. He became the first peer to hold the premiership since the third Marquess of Salisbury, and subsequently the only man in modern times to do so without a seat in either house of Parliament, having renounced his title under the Peerage Act to fight a by-election. To the public, Douglas-Home's appointment represented a political upset. He had maintained a relatively low profile at the Foreign Office, where 'he had done good by stealth' and been happy to stand in the shadow of Macmillan.[548]

544 Thorpe, op. cit., 1996, p. 168.

545 Dickie, op. cit., p. 108.

546 Thorpe, op. cit., 1996, p. 160.

547 *Daily Mail*, 23 June 1961. Emphasis in original.

548 Thorpe, op. cit., 1996, pp. 106, 214, 228; Andrew Holt, 'Lord Home and Anglo-American Relations, 1961–1963', *Diplomacy and Statecraft*, Vol. 16, 2005, pp. 699–722.

In political circles, however, there was a wave of indignation. The leader of the Liberal Party, Jo Grimond, complained that the appointment was 'carrying the cult of the amateur too far', while Wilson called Douglas-Home 'an elegant anachronism'. The commentator William Rees-Mogg described it as 'turning aside from progress'.[549]

THE CHALLENGES FACING DOUGLAS-HOME

The circumstances under which Douglas-Home became Prime Minister cast a long shadow over his premiership. Indeed, Michael Hill has argued that Douglas-Home's position as leader from October 1964 was undermined not only by his electoral defeat, but also by the toxic legacy of the events that took place a year earlier.[550] These events, which played out at the October 1963 party conference in Blackpool, remain controversial. In the wake of Macmillan's sudden decision to resign due to ill health, there was no obvious successor. Chancellor Reginald Maudling's star was already fading, and a lacklustre speech reduced further his chances of becoming leader. The party therefore appeared to be faced with a choice between the right-wing Lord Hailsham, and the moderate and experienced Rab Butler. Hailsham had seemed rather too eager for the job, quickly announcing his intention to renounce his peerage and return to being known as Quintin Hogg. 'Q' (for 'Quintin') badges were soon being distributed among delegates by Randolph Churchill, Winston's son, while Hailsham was photographed very publicly feeding his baby daughter. He also aroused unease among Britain's American allies after his conduct during negotiations for the 1963 Test-Ban Treaty.[551] Butler had missed out twice already – in 1955 and 1957 – and still suffered the legacy of the Suez Crisis and his handling of the break-up of the Central African Federation.

---

549 Dickie, op. cit., pp. xiv, 193; *Sunday Times*, 20 October 1963.

550 Michael Hill, 'Alec Douglas-Home', in Timothy Heppell ed., *Leaders of the Opposition: From Churchill to Cameron*, Basingstoke, Palgrave, 2012, p. 68.

551 Thorpe, op. cit., 1996, pp. 267, 286.

It was in this context that Douglas-Home entered the contest. He came to be seen as the only candidate capable of uniting the Conservative Party. He appealed to both the traditional landed Conservative right wing and the younger, more radical Monday Club element – hostile to the decline in Britain's imperial role – without arousing the antagonism of the moderate One Nation Group.[552] He was straightforward in his approach, believing that 'in the complexities of modern politics the electors must be given a simple clear lead'.[553] He was also popular with the party rank and file. Maudling later wrote that they 'regarded him as the sort of man they would like to be themselves: a good athlete, not brilliant, but intelligent; a man of charm, integrity and balance'.[554] Douglas-Home was a reluctant Prime Minister. Though not without some private ambition, it was duty that again motivated him to enter the leadership contest.[555] There is likely something in Peter Hennessy's suspicion that: 'Part of Douglas-Home ... never wanted the demands of the premiership to disrupt his contented and measured life.' Nevertheless: 'It was a mixture of duty and ambition that forced him to throw his coronet in the ring in 1963.'[556] Douglas-Home also feared that, should the Conservatives split, 'the socialists would be "in" for long enough to do the country serious damage'.

'I felt that I could do something to ... appeal for the cooperation of the floating vote,' he added.[557]

The extent to which Harold Macmillan's preferences also influenced the outcome is still debated. While Butler was himself aware that his chances were slim, as David Dutton has remarked, 'it is hard to escape the conclusion that Macmillan was determined to avoid having Butler succeed him'.[558]

---

552 Ibid., p. 318.

553 Douglas-Home to Fraser, 30 December 1963 (M.48H/63, PREM 11/5006).

554 Reginald Maudling, *Memoirs*, London, Sidgwick & Jackson, 1978, p. 130.

555 Home, op. cit., pp. 182–4; Hennessy, op. cit., 2000, pp. 274, 280; K. Young, op. cit., pp. 164–6; Home to Fraser, December 1963 (M.48H/63, 30, PREM 11/5006).

556 Hennessy, op. cit., 2000, pp. 278, 280.

557 Douglas-Home to Fraser, 30 December 1963 (M.48H/63, PREM 11/5006).

558 Thorpe, op. cit., 1996, p. 273; David Dutton, *Douglas-Home*, London, Haus, 2006, p. 46.

The process by which soundings were taken and Douglas-Home 'emerged' ensured that the views of the Cabinet were not dominant over other sections of the party. Moreover, in addition to being asked for their first choice, ministers were asked if there was a candidate to whom they objected. They were also invited to give their opinion on Douglas-Home's candidature.[559] Douglas-Home disclaimed his titles on 23 October – following Tony Benn and the historian John Grigg to be the third person to renounce. With Douglas-Home in need of a seat in the Commons, future Defence Secretary George Younger withdrew his candidacy for the impending by-election in the safe seat of Kinross & Western Perthshire. The Prime Minister avoided the trapdoor, holding the seat comfortably against rivals who included Willie Rushton, co-founder of *Private Eye.*

Colleagues held Douglas-Home and his abilities in high regard. In the aftermath of the 1962 Nassau Conference, Macmillan described him to the Queen as 'steel painted as wood', while Eden also praised his 'firmness and discretion'.[560] Butler admired his calmness and ability to see simple solutions to problems. Oliver Wright, Douglas-Home's private secretary at the Foreign Office and No. 10, later described him as 'the nearest thing to a saint in politics as possible' and 'a superb Foreign Secretary', whose 'judgement was impeccable'.[561] Even Labour's Tony Benn believed Douglas-Home to be 'very competent and hardworking', and 'a much underestimated figure'.[562]

He was, however, far removed from senior ministerial experience of home affairs, and suffered from a BBC sketch that portrayed him as lacking knowledge in these matters.[563] Douglas-Home himself later admitted that, had he even considered that he might become Prime Minister, he 'would

559 Tim Bale, *The Conservatives since 1945: The Drivers of Party Change*, Oxford, Oxford University Press, 2012, p. 55.

560 Hennessy, op. cit., 2000, p. 278.

561 Interview with Wright, 18 September 1996 (DOHP 17, Churchill Archives Centre, Cambridge).

562 Quoted in John Lawton, *1963: Five Hundred Days: History as Melodrama*, London, Hodder & Stoughton, 1992, p. 307.

563 Thorpe, op. cit., 1996, p. 324.

have soaked myself more thoroughly in domestic issues, rather than specialising so completely in the foreign field'.[564] He had also been damaged by a September 1962 interview, during which he said: 'When I have to read economic documents, I have to have a box of matches and start moving them into position to simplify and illustrate the points to myself.'[565] He later reflected on the matchsticks comment as 'purely a chance remark … but it stuck, of course … Harold Wilson wasn't going to miss something like that'.[566]

The 'matchsticks' interview also illustrated how Douglas-Home was ill suited to the changing media environment of the 1960s. *Private Eye* was first published in 1961, while *That Was the Week That Was* debuted on the BBC in November 1962. At a time of increasing social upheaval and challenges to the establishment, Douglas-Home represented the 'grouse moor' image of the Conservative Party.[567] As John Ramsden put it: 'Macmillan might enjoy being photographed on the grouse moors, but Douglas-Home actually owned them.'[568] The contrast with Wilson in this regard was stark. In terms of communication, Douglas-Home preferred to write his own speeches.[569] By virtue of 'a peculiar personal quirk', he told Kenneth Harris of *The Observer*: 'I can't read a speech, a prepared brief, word for word … I can't get my tongue around other people's words and phrases.'[570] He therefore struggled to work with the speechwriters at the Conservative Research Department.[571] More seriously, he was uncomfortable on television. 'I fear that I could not conceal my distaste for the conception that the

---

564 Home, op. cit., p. 216.

565 *The Observer*, 16 September 1962.

566 'Lord Home of the Hirsel', *Premiership*, BBC Radio 3, 4 October 1989, quoted in Hennessy, op. cit., 2000, p. 276.

567 Ian Gilmour and Mark Garnett, *Whatever Happened to the Tories? The Conservative Party Since 1945*, London, Fourth Estate, 1997, p. 204.

568 John Ramsden, *The Winds of Change: Macmillan to Heath, 1957–75*, London, Longman, 1996, p. 209.

569 Home, op. cit., p. 203.

570 *The Observer*, 16 September 1962.

571 Ramsden, op. cit., 1996, p. 215.

political leader had also to be an actor on the screen,' he wrote in his memoirs, before recounting how a young woman applying his screen make-up had told him that he could not be made to look any better 'because you have a head like a skull'.[572]

Although Douglas-Home inherited a comfortable parliamentary majority, the climate was not a positive one for the Conservatives. The party had already been in power for twelve years, spanning three parliamentary terms and three previous leaders. Economic problems were mounting and Britain's application to join the EEC had been vetoed by French President Charles de Gaulle in January 1963. The Profumo affair remained in the public's memory. The Denning Report on the matter exonerated the security services, but its publication in September 1963, and the associated House of Commons adjournment debate in December, helped refresh memories of the original scandal.[573] Macmillan's resignation and the events in Blackpool had also left the party reeling. Both Enoch Powell and Iain Macleod refused to serve in Douglas-Home's government, and the absence of two young, dynamic figures undermined Douglas-Home from the outset. The St Marylebone by-election on 5 December saw Hailsham – now Quintin Hogg – return to the Commons, but again reawakened memories of October. Worse was to come just weeks later. While reviewing Randolph Churchill's book on the contest, Macleod, who had become editor of *The Spectator*, took the opportunity to give his own account. His reference to the 'magic circle' of Old Etonians and his insinuations of a conspiracy to make a fellow old boy premier were particularly damaging.[574] The article infuriated Douglas-Home. When electoral defeat came in October 1964, he could be heard 'blaming the defeat on Macleod in language those who were present had not heard him use before'.[575]

---

572 Home, op. cit., p. 203.

573 Hansard, HC, 16 December 1963, vol. 686, col. 853–983.

574 *The Spectator*, 17 January 1964.

575 Thorpe, op. cit., 2000, p. 344.

DOUGLAS-HOME'S TIME AS LEADER

Douglas-Home was clear from the outset that 'a Conservative government must govern well and must be seen to govern well'.[576] Economic problems lay on the horizon, however, damaging the Conservatives' reputation for economic competence. Chancellor Reginald Maudling had delivered the 1963 Budget in April and the 'dash for growth', and Douglas-Home had little option but to continue this path. The consequence was a widening gap between the value of British imports and exports. As this balance-of-payments deficit continued to grow, Douglas-Home was aware of the risks in seeking an International Monetary Fund loan, but he believed that the process should be open, and that Wilson might hesitate to attack given the risks to sterling.[577] An opinion poll commissioned in 1963 and carried out in 1964 also suggested that people believed the Conservatives to have lost their claim to competence, and that they were representing the rich and big business,[578] but the timing of the poll makes it difficult to attribute too much blame to Douglas-Home's leadership. In this context, Tim Bale suggests that the only economic option to improve Conservative fortunes may have been to use taxation to bring down the cost of land, and, in turn, housing. However, such a move would have left the government appearing cynical and opportunistic.[579]

The administration had a greater impact on the workings of government. Douglas-Home abolished the post of First Secretary of State and merged its functions into an enlarged Ministry of Trade, Industry and Regional Development. In April 1964, he created a new post of Secretary of State for Education and Science, and appointed Hogg to the office. He also streamlined government, reducing the number of Cabinet committees. Had the Conservatives been victorious in the election, Douglas-Home planned to charge Enoch

576 Quoted in *The Times*, 12 November 1963.

577 Home, op. cit., p. 213.

578 Bale, op. cit., p. 68.

579 Ibid., p. 101.

Powell with the task of further reorganisation of the civil service.[580] Finally, Douglas-Home presided over the strengthening of rules that allowed civil servants to informally meet with Labour ministers in advance of the election. The length of time since Labour last held office, combined with their radical plans for reorganisation of Whitehall, provided specific impetus for this.[581] The system governing these contacts became known as the Douglas-Home rules.

The main legislative measure to emerge from Douglas-Home's time as Prime Minister was the abolition of Resale Price Maintenance (RPM), the practice that allowed manufacturers to set retail prices for their goods. The eventual passage of the Resale Prices Act 1964 triggered 'a retail revolution' that permanently altered the nation's shopping habits.[582] However, it was unpopular with small shopkeepers, sections of the press and some members of the Cabinet.[583] The government's hand was forced to some extent by the progress of two private members' bills on the subject – one in favour of abolition; another proposing greater regulation. With a decision needed, president of the board of trade Edward Heath, keen to demonstrate his own modernising zeal, came out firmly in favour of the abolition. Indeed, a senior member of the Cabinet told Peter Hennessy that Heath had threatened resignation had prime ministerial support not been forthcoming.[584] The loss of Heath would have been disastrous for the government, especially with Powell and Macleod already outside of the Cabinet. Nevertheless, support was given willingly. Douglas-Home later said that 'I happened to think Ted Heath was right on that occasion so I backed him'.[585]

Historians have been divided on the wisdom of the abolition of RPM. David Dutton described it as 'unnecessarily divisive' and possibly responsible for

580 Peter Hennessy, *Whitehall*, London, Secker & Warburg, 1989, p. 174.

581 Peter Catterall, 'Handling the Transfer of Power: A Note on the 1964 Origins of the Douglas-Home rules', *Contemporary British History*, 11 (1997), 76–77.

582 Hennessy, op. cit., 2000, p. 280.

583 Ramsden, op. cit., p. 221.

584 Hennessy, op. cit., 2000, p. 281.

585 Quoted in 'Lord Home of the Hirsel', *Premiership*, BBC Radio 3, 4 October 1989, in Hennessy, ibid.

electoral defeat.[586] A similar view was later articulated by Douglas-Home himself, who also felt that RPM 'probably cost us seats at the general election'.[587] However, John Campbell has argued that lowering prices was popular with everyone apart from shopkeepers.[588] Moreover, as D. R. Thorpe has said, 'The main impact of the abolition of RPM was positive'. It showed that the government still had fresh ideas and was prepared to modernise.[589] David Butler and Anthony King found that the issue hardly featured at the election.[590]

While the prospect of the election hindered the government in foreign affairs, it was able to act decisively when necessary. Swift intervention in Cyprus in December 1963 helped to prevent a possible civil war between the Greek and Turkish communities on the island.[591] Douglas-Home also skilfully managed the 1964 Commonwealth prime ministers' conference at a time when Commonwealth tensions over Rhodesia's white-minority government were running high.[592] He was, however, unable to prevent a cooling of relations with the United States. On 22 November 1963, President John F. Kennedy was assassinated in Dallas, Texas. At the next Cabinet meeting, Butler reported the ambassador to Washington David Ormsby-Gore's warning that 'our forward plans must inevitably be based on the assumption that United States leadership would be less positive than hitherto'.[593] Douglas-Home and Kennedy's successor, Lyndon Johnson, did not establish the close relationship that had existed between their respective predecessors.[594] A deal between Leyland Motors and Fidel Castro's Cuba to supply

---

586 Dutton, op. cit., p. 71.

587 Home, quoted in 'The Unknown Premiership', *The Quality of Cabinet Government*, BBC Radio 3, 25 July 1985, in Hennessy, op. cit., 2000, p. 281.

588 John Campbell, *Edward Heath: A Biography*, London, Jonathan Cape, 1993, p. 157.

589 D. R. Thorpe, *Alec Douglas-Home*, p. 358.

590 D. E. Butler and Anthony King, *The British General Election of 1964*, London, Macmillan, 1965, p. 23.

591 Andrew Holt, *The Foreign Policy of the Douglas-Home Government: Britain, the United States and the End of Empire*, Basingstoke, Palgrave, 2014, pp. 126–8.

592 Ibid., pp. 78–80.

593 CM (63) 8, 6, 28 November 1963 (CAB 128/38, TNA).

594 Holt, op. cit., pp. 29–31.

buses was particularly controversial. With the Cuban Missile Crisis fresh in American minds, the Johnson administration sought to isolate Cuba. Britain, on the other hand, preferred to trade more freely, and the issue dominated the February 1964 summit meeting between the two men.[595] Johnson later became so incensed that he berated Foreign Secretary Rab Butler at a meeting in April 1964: 'He felt like asking our traders to ship the stuff to his own farm in Texas and send the bill to him. He was asking us as allies to choose between him and Castro.' Butler's account continued: 'He wanted to assure us that we were in danger of doing ourselves great harm by poisoning Anglo-American relations in this way and all apparently for a trivial sum of business.'[596]

Both foreign and domestic policy were influenced by the proximity of the general election. Douglas-Home's focus on the poll was clear from his first Cabinet as Prime Minister, when he declared that: 'Ministers should be alert to detect the emergence of new situations which might create embarrassment for the government.'[597] Upon his election as party leader, he was even more explicit: 'So from this moment on the fact that there is a general election ahead of us must never be out of our minds … because the one thing that matters is that this country should be saved from socialism and that a Conservative government should be returned.' (Though he later claimed: 'I was talking of course in a party organisational sense.')[598]

The first decision was when to call the poll. Aware of the worsening balance of payments situation, Chancellor Reginald Maudling favoured a May or June election.[599] The deficit was £73 million in the second quarter of 1964, rising sharply to £192 million by the third quarter. However, opinion polls gave little cause for optimism and Douglas-Home announced on 9 April his intention to seek a dissolution of Parliament before the autumn. Such

---

595 Ibid., pp. 31–5.

596 Butler to Douglas-Home, T.172/64, 29 April 1964 (PREM 11/4696, TNA).

597 CM (63) 1, 22 October 1963 (CAB 128/38, TNA).

598 Quoted in *The Times*, 12 November 1963; quoted in Young, *Douglas-Home*, p. 175.

599 Robert Blake, *The Conservative Party from Peel to Major*, London, Heinemann, 1997, p. 294.

a delay also allowed time for people to tire of Wilson's novelty value.[600] In February, Patrick Gordon Walker had told the Americans that Labour would win with a majority of forty to sixty were the election held in June, and by far more if the government waited until October.[601] This part of Douglas-Home's electoral strategy seemed to be vindicated as the polls narrowed over the summer. A national opinion poll showing a Conservative lead of 2.9 per cent was published on 30 September, but balance-of-payments figures appeared the same day.[602]

As Peter Barberis states: 'The milieu of 1964 was noticeably different from that of 1959. It placed a premium upon the politics of reform.'[603] This posed problems for the Conservatives and for Douglas-Home. Harold Macmillan had planned to focus the campaign on Europe and modernisation. However, de Gaulle's veto had removed the EEC from the agenda. Modernisation, on the other hand, did not appeal to party faithful and was seen as a stronger issue for Labour under Wilson.[604] Ultimately, the Conservatives' themes were similar to 1959, with a manifesto entitled *Prosperity with a Purpose*. Douglas-Home focused the election campaign on Britain's nuclear deterrent. While this was an issue on which he could speak with confidence and authority, it did not resonate with a public more concerned with domestic affairs. Even so, Douglas-Home's approach could have paid off had news of China's first successful nuclear test on 16 October broken sooner. [605]

The election highlighted the importance of television, and the appeal to youth featured more prominently than in previous campaigns.[606] Aware of his difficulties with the medium, Douglas-Home kept a low profile during

---

600 Thorpe, op. cit., p. 343.

601 Memorandum of Conversation, 18 February 1964, United Kingdom—Meetings with Walker, Country File, National Security File, Box 213, Lyndon Baines Johnson Presidential Library, Austin, Texas, United States.

602 Blake, op. cit., p. 296.

603 Peter Barberis, 'Introduction: The 1964 general election – the "Not Quite, But" and "But Only Just" Election', *Contemporary British History*, Vol. 21, 2007, p. 287.

604 Blake, op. cit., p. 295.

605 Holt, op. cit., pp. 147, 153–4.

606 Barberis, op. cit., p. 283.

the campaign and focused on speaking tours. Ultimately, however, this was to backfire as the Prime Minister struggled to deal with severe heckling at Birmingham's Bull Ring on 8 October. Robert Blake argues that party managers erred in not organising a final ticket-only event 'where he might have had a chance to remove this impression of ineffectiveness'.[607] Nevertheless, party chairman Lord Blakenham (John Hare) described the Birmingham heckling as the moment 'that support began to slide away from us'.[608] Butler's interview a week before the poll – in which he said that 'We're running neck and neck ... But things might start slipping in the last few days ... They won't slip towards us' – was also markedly unhelpful.[609]

In the event, the Conservatives came extremely close to victory. The final result left Douglas-Home's Conservatives with 304 seats (down from 365 in 1959), the Liberal Party with nine (up from six), and Labour with 317 (up from 258) – a majority of just four.[610] As few as 900 more votes, perfectly distributed, could have led to Conservative victory.[611] The Labour share of the vote was 44.1 per cent (an increase of only 0.3 per cent from October 1959). However, the Liberal vote rose from 5.9 to 11.2 per cent, while the Conservatives lost 6 per cent – the largest fall between elections since 1945. The effective swing of 3.5 per cent from Conservative to Labour was also greater than any post-war election.[612]

In the aftermath of this defeat, Douglas-Home helped make key contributions to party matters. Showing once again his belief in the value of party unity, he invited Enoch Powell and Iain Macleod to join his team. Seeking to promote new talent, Willie Whitelaw was made Chief Whip and in January 1965 Edward du Cann was appointed party chairman. He pursued his attempts to modernise the party. Douglas-Home and du Cann's predecessor,

607 Blake, op. cit., p. 296.

608 Home, op. cit., p. 215.

609 *Daily Express*, 9 October 1964.

610 See Butler and King, op. cit., pp. 301–36.

611 Ramsden, op. cit., p. 230.

612 Butler and King, op. cit., p. 294.

Lord Blakenham, had already made it clear that they wished the party to widen its search for new candidates.[613] Douglas-Home also tasked a committee headed by Lord Chelmer with devising proposals to address the recruitment and retention problems in the party's agency service. In terms of policy, Douglas-Home appointed Heath to chair policy committees,[614] and agreed to hold extra shadow Cabinet meetings dedicated to longer-term concerns.[615]

He also introduced new procedures for electing a party leader. While Douglas-Home still believed in the old system, the response to the events of his appointment, particularly the effects on party morale, convinced him that 'with all its disadvantages, it was necessary to adopt a system of election of a leader'.[616] The eventual solution involved up to three ballots of Conservative MPs. To emerge victorious on the first ballot, a candidate required 50 per cent of the vote and a lead of at least 15 per cent over their nearest challenger. An overall majority would suffice in the second ballot, while the third ballot would be held under the alternative vote system to ensure a winner. The rules remained in place until 1998, undergoing only slight modification in 1974 (following recommendations by a committee that Douglas-Home chaired) and 1991.

Douglas-Home's leadership was never particularly secure, however. His experience of government ensured that he was a competent Prime Minister, but leading the Conservative Party in opposition was a completely different challenge. While there was a feeling within the party that he had done well to get so close to victory, there was greater concern over his ability to be effective as Leader of the Opposition.[617] His struggles on television and difficulties in imposing himself on the House of Commons became even more problematic. Douglas-Home opposed the 'crude tactics'

---

613 Bale, op. cit., p. 103.

614 Campbell, op. cit., p. 172.

615 Bale, op. cit., p. 123.

616 Home, op. cit., p. 218.

617 Blake, op. cit., p. 297.

of opposition for its own sake,[618] and this attitude to opposition left him appearing insufficiently aggressive. For his part, Douglas-Home 'did not greatly relish the prospect of leading the Conservative opposition'.[619] The leader polled behind his party. He even did worse than Wilson when people were asked about sincerity.[620]

By-election results served to weaken Douglas-Home's position. Despite controversially losing his seat in a racially charged campaign in Smethwick, Patrick Gordon Walker was still made Foreign Secretary in Wilson's Cabinet. Gordon Walker's narrow defeat in the previously safe Labour seat of Leyton in a January 1965 by-election gave the impression that the Conservatives might indeed stand a chance at the next election, making the prize of the leadership more tempting. David Steel's victory at Roxburgh, Selkirk and Peebles in March inflicted greater damage on Douglas-Home personally. With the Conservatives unable to hold a previously safe seat in the Scottish borders under his leadership, questions were raised as to their prospects elsewhere.[621] Ironically, it was Conservative *gains* in May's local elections that partly precipitated the end of Douglas-Home's leadership. The results helped persuade Wilson against calling a general election in 1965. When this was announced, it left time for the new leadership process to take place. As unrest grew: 'My reaction was boredom with the whole business. I had been chosen as leader to fight the socialists, and I did not see why I should now be asked to battle with my own side.' After a decade of service in high office, 'I simply did not feel inclined to go into the arena for the doubtful satisfaction of confounding a number of those with whom I had campaigned on the same side.'[622]

He announced his decision to resign as leader to the 1922 Committee on 22 July 1965.

---

618 Home, op. cit., p. 217.

619 Ibid., p. 217.

620 Blake, op. cit., p. 298.

621 Thorpe, op. cit., p. 384–5.

622 Home, op. cit., p. 220.

ASSESSING DOUGLAS-HOME

Of twentieth-century premiers, only Andrew Bonar Law held office for less time than Douglas-Home. Excluding caretakers, he was also the shortest-serving post-war Leader of the Opposition. He therefore had only limited time to make his mark on the country, and on the Conservative Party. The most prevalent view of Douglas-Home's premiership is that espoused by Roy Jenkins, who described it as a 'suffix'.[623] Peter Hennessy agrees with this verdict, concluding that Douglas-Home 'could only be a punctuation mark between the two Harolds, given the length of his tenure'.[624] Similarly, Tim Bale has argued that 'Alec Douglas-Home, had, at least as Prime Minister, virtually no impact on change, inasmuch as there was any change in the year during which he did the top job'.[625] Douglas-Home said he did not simply want the government to 'bat out time', but the proximity of the election inevitably reduced his ability to effect domestic change.[626] He was, however, more progressive than his critics expected. He was seen to be on the right of the party because of his stance on communism and colonial matters, but early on in his administration he instructed his Cabinet that 'provided that we remain within the limits prescribed by a sense of economic responsibility, our policies should be, and should be seen to be, positive and constructive'.[627] The abolition of RPM was a modernising measure and showed his willingness to face down opposition within his own party. In foreign affairs, 'electoral considerations had a debilitating effect on policy', preventing proper action on certain questions and rendering other governments sceptical of making agreements with Britain.[628] Nevertheless his swift and decisive action over

---

623 Lord Jenkins, quoted in Hennessy, op. cit., 2000, p. 529.

624 Ibid., p. 532.

625 Bale, op. cit., p. 81.

626 Douglas-Home, quoted in Thorpe, op. cit., p. 325.

627 Note by Douglas-Home, CP (63) 20, 22 November 1963 (CAB 129/115, TNA).

628 John W. Young, 'International Factors and the 1964 Election', *Contemporary British History*, Vol. 21, 2007, p. 355.

Cyprus and careful management of the situation with Rhodesia highlighted his competence as a statesman.

Despite Douglas-Home's short time in office, Anthony Seldon rightly argues, that 'to dismiss him as a lightweight ... is seriously misleading'. Douglas-Home was 'charming and funny, straight and shrewd'; 'he stood out as a leader of probity'.[629] As Stuart Mitchell states: 'Home initiated very little in the way of policy ... contenting himself with lending support where necessary to ministerial initiatives', but, 'in truth, given the nature of his accession, Douglas-Home could do little else if he was to keep his Cabinet intact'.[630] Lacking an inner circle of advisors and spending his weekends with friends outside of politics wherever possible, some saw Douglas-Home as 'the most hands-off Prime Minister since Baldwin'.[631] This approach made him effective in terms of managing his team, however. He trusted his ministers to do their jobs and operated as 'a non-executive chairman rather than managing director'.[632] The experienced civil servant Sir Burke Trend privately rated Douglas-Home as the best of the premiers with whom he worked, especially as a chairman of Cabinet.[633] Douglas-Home was also 'unflappable'.[634] During the election campaign, the Prime Minister found himself alone in the Aberdeenshire home of Johnnie and Priscilla Tweedsmuir. With his bodyguard forced to stay elsewhere due to a lack of space, Douglas-Home answered the door to a group of left-wing Aberdeen University students. They duly informed the Prime Minister that they were there to kidnap him. With customary calmness, Douglas-Home diffused the situation by warning the would-be kidnappers that such an act would result in a Conservative landslide, playing for time and offering the students beer, which they accepted. The abduction

629 Hennessy, op. cit., 2000, p. 276; James Margach, quoted in Hennessy, ibid., p. 275.

630 Stuart Mitchell, 'Douglas-Home, the Conservative Party and the Threat of Rebellious Youth, 1963–64', *University of Sussex Journal of Contemporary History*, Vol. 4, 2002, p. 3.

631 Thorpe, op. cit., p. 376.

632 Jock Bruce-Gardyne and Nigel Lawson, *The Power Game: An Examination of Decision-Making in Government*, London, Macmillan, 1976, p. 167.

633 Hennessy, op. cit., 2000, p. 283; Thorpe, op. cit., p. 326.

634 Thorpe, ibid., p. 353.

was aborted, and no details of the episode released for fear of damaging the protection officer's career.[635]

Alec Douglas-Home did as good a job as Conservative leader as could have been expected of him. Had another candidate possessed a stronger claim to the position, it is unlikely that he would have sought it. Having done so, he had little time to change the strategy put in place by Macmillan. Given his previous statements on economics and perceived lack of knowledge of domestic matters, it made sense for Douglas-Home to focus on international issues. While the campaign may not have fully resonated with the public, Douglas-Home still came tantalisingly close to winning a fourth term in office for the Conservatives. His time as leader after the election was less happy. Michael Hill concluded that 'Douglas-Home can in many respects be seen as a failure as Leader of the Opposition,' and Labour minister Richard Crossman also thought him ineffective.[636] His reluctance to aggressively attack Labour and Harold Wilson and his struggles with the House of Commons and with television hindered him, as did his lack of enthusiasm for the role. Even so, he set in motion important reforms to the party organisation, began the process of policy renewal and introduced what became a long-standing system to elect a leader. Indeed, he left the party in a sufficiently healthy state that within six years the Conservatives were back in power, with Douglas-Home restored to the Foreign Office.

---

635 Hailsham diary, 9 January 1977, HLSM 1/1/11, Churcill Archive Centre, Cambridge.

636 Richard Crossman, *The Diaries of a Cabinet Minister, Vol. I: 1964–1966*, London, Holt, Rinehart & Winston, 1976, p. 118.

CHAPTER 17

EDWARD HEATH

MARK GARNETT

Heath's nearly ten years as Conservative leader encompassed four elections, a long and a brief stint as Leader of the Opposition, and four years as Prime Minister. Electoral success was largely elusive, while his wider political strategy as leader is, as a result, viewed in negative terms. His defeat to Harold Wilson in 1966 was widely anticipated, while his victory in 1970 was viewed by some, not least Heath himself, as a significant vindication of his leadership and political strategy. The election of February 1974 was a crushing blow, while the subsequent decisive election in October made his position untenable. Mark Garnett argues that the prevailing wisdom of personal failure is misguided. Ultimately, wider forces shaped both the failures of what was widely perceived as a disappointing tenure as leader and Prime Minister, as well as the successes. Disruptive and contingent events and crises beyond his control were critical. Yet throughout, the style and aims of his leadership were at once both overly optimistic in his power to shape his political landscape, and dismissive of plausible solutions that could have increased his electability and popularity.

• • •

Edward Heath was not the first Conservative to rise to the party leadership in defiance of social disadvantages; but he was certainly different from any of his predecessors in being born into a family that lacked either wealth or influential connections. His father, indeed, was a carpenter, and his mother had been a lady's maid. Winning a place at grammar school, then at

Balliol College, Oxford, undoubtedly owed much to the devoted encouragement of his mother. However, this would have been to no avail had Heath not enjoyed considerable intellectual talent and (in particular) dogged determination. At Oxford, he served as chairman of the Conservative Association and as president of the Oxford Union. While these positions obviously opened up the possibility of a successful political career, Heath was prepared to put such prospects at risk through vigorous public opposition to his own party's official policy of 'appeasement' towards Hitler's Germany. Subsequent wartime service in the Royal Artillery gave Heath the chance to show that his powers of organisation and leadership could stand the test of enemy fire. By the end of the war he had been promoted to lieutenant-colonel.

It is well known that Heath's experiences of Europe – as a tourist before the war, as well as in uniform – helped to create a lasting commitment to the cause of political cooperation. It is less often noted that Heath's active service in the European theatre of the Second World War made him unique among leaders of either of the two main parties – a quite remarkable fact, given the insatiable demands for service personnel of the appropriate age. On the Labour side, Wilson and Gaitskell were civil servants throughout the war, while James Callaghan served in the navy and Michael Foot was debarred from the services through ill health. The only Conservative leader who might have served in some capacity was Margaret Thatcher, who continued her studies at Oxford.

The other factor which made Heath's rise to the party leadership unusual was his protracted service in the Whips' Office – more than eight years, almost four of which he spent as Conservative Chief Whip. While Heath spent the majority of his long parliamentary career – twenty-seven out of fifty-one years – as a backbencher, he had to wait only twelve months between the 1950 general election, when he was first elected as MP for Bexley, and his first appointment to junior office. In that brief time he did make a notable maiden speech, which attacked Labour's negative approach to the Schumann Plan for European cooperation. But joining the Whips' Office prevented Heath from serving at least some of his apprenticeship as a junior minister dealing with fairly mundane departmental business. In 1960, Harold Macmillan promoted him to the Cabinet, but as Lord Privy Seal in charge of negotiating British membership of the EEC, Heath was still excluded from the normal cut and thrust of partisan conflict. His first 'orthodox' ministerial job was the presidency of the board of trade, which he accepted from Macmillan's successor Alec Douglas-Home in October 1963. By that time, Heath was in his forty-eighth year; his near-contemporary and bitter rival Harold Wilson had been appointed to the same job at the age of thirty-one.

This is not to say that Heath was disadvantaged against a skilful operator like Wilson because he was a 'slow starter' in political terms; rather, his rapid promotion after entering the Commons had diverted him onto a track which turned out to be a disadvantage. Heath did not need convincing that he was good at carrying out other people's orders – his experience in the Whips' Office merely confirmed what he had proved during the war. However, the fact that he and his fellow whips could keep the party on a relatively even keel amid the pitiless pelting of the Suez storm in 1956 seems to have given Heath too sanguine a view of the problems associated with party management. Certainly anyone who witnessed at close quarters Harold Macmillan's transformation from a hawkish supporter of Suez into the man who emerged as the best candidate to haul the Conservatives out of the ensuing wreckage could have been forgiven for thinking that the party's MPs were eminently malleable, if subjected to the appropriate encouragement. Having made this general assumption, Heath was likely to think that it was particularly applicable to the issue of European integration – after all, he had been made Chief Whip by Eden, who thought that serious negotiations with the original EEC countries would represent a betrayal of Britain's global role, yet just four years later he found himself trying to persuade de Gaulle et al. that the UK had suddenly been converted to a European destiny. The task of ministerial decision-makers, he seemed to conclude, was to lay down a policy-line and preferably to stick to it; even if the policy had to change, it was up to the whips to deliver the necessary votes, without expecting anyone higher up the political food chain to help them in this task. This would explain his inflexible stance when, as president of the board of trade, he drove through legislation to abolish RPM in the face of unmistakable symptoms of disquiet among Cabinet colleagues as well as backbenchers, and his lasting resentment against the Chief Whip of the time, Martin Redmayne, who argued in favour of concessions.[637]

Thus by the time he became a candidate for the leadership of his party, Heath had already decided that the emollient *persona* he had adopted as Chief Whip should be jettisoned in favour of 'the sneer of cold command' appropriate for Conservative Party leaders. The transformation was probably helped to some extent by a residual sense of social insecurity – someone of his background could aspire to be the faithful adjutant of a blue-blooded leader without undergoing any searching re-examination of the self. Apparently Heath had adapted easily to Oxford life, but the prospect of following in the footsteps of Churchill, Eden, Macmillan and Douglas-Home entailed psychological demands of a very different order. In 1969 Philip Toynbee, who had known him at Oxford, speculated 'that there is a tremendous effort being made to turn him into something which he wasn't originally'.[638] Toynbee was in no position to know that Heath was impervious to advice from image-makers, and that the 'tremendous effort' was entirely his own. With nothing beyond his abilities to recommend him, it was no coincidence that Heath should now regard activities (music and yachting) which would have been sources of relaxation for higher-born colleagues as alternative theatres in which he could prove his mettle. Second fiddle was no longer a role that held any attractions to the former Balliol organ scholar.

Possibly someone as resourceful as Heath could have turned out to be a successful Conservative leader despite the 'aloofness' for which he became notorious after defeating Reginald Maudling in the party's first leadership election of 1965. Unfortunately for him, this was not the only factor which worked against him. Sir Keith Joseph famously advised Margaret Thatcher

---

637 Edward Heath, *The Course of My Life: My Autobiography*, London, Hodder & Stoughton, 1998, p. 261.

638 Philip Toynbee in John Campbell, *Edward Heath: A Biography*, London, Jonathan Cape, 1993, p. 20.

to support Heath in the 1965 leadership election because 'he has a passion to get Britain right'.[639] Joseph's endorsement might have reflected a miscasting of Heath as an inflexible reformer, based on the latter's determination to abolish RPM. If so, this would only become a serious problem after 1970, when Heath showed that he was not the rigid economic liberal of Joseph's imaginings. In the short term, a more damaging mistake both for Heath and his party was made in 1965 by those MPs who saw him as the Conservative answer to Harold Wilson. The idea was that Heath would prove more adept than his Labour opponent in the use of Wilsonian weapons – tactical skill, debating dexterity, and mastery of the electronic media. Presumably such individuals assumed that a politician who was a stranger to the playing fields of Eton would be more than willing to take on Wilson according to the disagreeable new rules of modern politics, which Douglas-Home had proved unwilling to learn. In reality, Heath wanted to turn Wilson's supposed attractions against him; he felt genuine contempt for what he saw as his rival's gimmickry, and his tendency to put the superficial unity of his party ahead of the country's long-term interests.

Heath, in short, wanted to offer British voters an alternative between his own personal integrity and Wilson's crowd-pleasing antics. If, in the short-term, the crowd really did seem to prefer the 'all-licensed fool' to the tough-talking but candid advisor, Heath had no intention of giving up the task of persuading them to see reason. A few of Heath's supporters in 1965 – notably Willie Whitelaw, the Chief Whip he inherited from Douglas-Home – understood that their new leader saw himself as an *antidote* to Wilson, rather than just as an opponent. When, in their first parliamentary clashes, Wilson brushed Heath aside such observers were disappointed but not unduly surprised. By contrast, those who had voted for Heath in the expectation of morale-boosting battles at Prime Minister's questions began to wonder if they had made the right decision in choosing Heath rather than the languid Maudling.

---

639 Margaret Thatcher, *The Path to Power*, London, HarperCollins, 1995, p. 136.

For various reasons, then, even a run of dazzling successes was never going to make Heath into an overwhelmingly popular leader of his parliamentary party. As such, it was not reassuring that a sympathetic commentator, writing when Heath was Prime Minister and before his worst troubles began, felt that his 'most serious deficiency as party leader was an inability to communicate effectively beyond the party to the larger national audience'.[640] This was a direct result of Heath's refusal to compete with Wilson in what he regarded as a fraudulent contest for cheap popularity. Even without sharing Heath's contempt for Wilson it is possible to find something commendable in this general approach. However, the unvarnished record suggests that it did little good either for Heath or his party. He fought four elections as leader, and the Conservatives lost three of them. Having failed to retain the support of 'the larger national audience', in February 1975 he was forced to ask his party for a vote of confidence – and lost that contest, too.

WINNING ELECTORAL STRATEGY

Back in 1970 only Heath's implacable opponents could imagine that his period as leader would end so dismally. Heath was regarded as the architect of a Conservative victory that defied the message of most opinion polls and the expectations of astute media pundits. However, even without the benefit of hindsight it can be argued that the most surprising thing about the result of the 1970 general election was that it took so many people by surprise. Labour, after all, had endured the morale-sapping devaluation of the pound sterling in 1967, and two years later suffered another damaging reversal when its White Paper on industrial relations, *In Place of Strife*, was withdrawn under pressure from its union allies. Labour's foreign policy record was no better; having kept out of the Vietnam War due to Britain's

640 Robert Rhodes James, *Ambitions and Realities: British Politics, 1964–70*, London, Weidenfeld & Nicolson, 1972.

economic weakness, Wilson nevertheless offered moral support to the US in a conflict which was unpopular among many Labour supporters. Having proved unable to prevent racist Rhodesia's unilateral declaration of independence back in 1965, Wilson's dealings with that country continued to demonstrate British impotence in a fashion which caused dismay across the ideological spectrum. Withdrawal from bases east of Suez – another product of the need to contain public expenditure – might have been more cheering to Labour's anti-imperialist left had it not contradicted Wilson's previous pledges about the maintenance of overseas commitments.

In other respects – like the abandonment of the much-vaunted National Plan, its failure to take Britain into the EEC, and the outbreak of civil disorder in Northern Ireland – the record of the Wilson government was difficult to defend. Labour seemed to rest its positive appeal on evidence that the economic situation had stabilised after devaluation; but this final crutch of credibility suffered an untimely wobble when adverse balance of payments figures (which turned out to be misleading) were released during the election campaign.

In such circumstances, a 'winning electoral strategy' for the Conservatives seemed to write itself – just keep a relatively united front and present the voters with plausible reasons for regarding the party's frontbenchers as more competent than Wilson and his team. But while Heath certainly regarded himself and his team as far more competent than his Labour opponents, he did not want to gain office simply by default. Even before he won the party leadership, he had led a thorough review of party policy which resumed after an interruption in 1966, when Wilson called and predictably won an election whose sole purpose was to provide his party with a workable majority. What Heath required was a refreshed party platform, rather than a process of ideological renewal; and even if his outlook had been more radical he would have had good reason to avoid a significant swing to the right so soon after a similar move by US Republicans had led to Barry Goldwater's crushing defeat in the 1964 Presidential election. Thus Heath was able to brush aside the accusation by Angus Maude, a member of the party's front-bench team, that under his leadership the Conservatives were tending to 'talk like technocrats'.[641]

Unfortunately for the Conservatives, the policy review could not take place in isolation from events. Rhodesia, for example, split the party just as it divided Labour supporters. But the most notable 'event' was the Kenyan Asians crisis, which confronted Britain with some of the awkward consequences of the global role that was now relentlessly unravelling. In April 1968, the Conservative Defence spokesman Enoch Powell exploited the likely arrival in Britain of thousands of displaced Kenyan Asians by conjuring lurid visions of communal unrest. Heath responded decisively, but divisively, by sacking Powell from the shadow Cabinet. Powell had stood in the 1965 leadership election, attracting a miserable fifteen votes. His 1968 'Rivers of Blood' speech made him one of the best-loved (and most-hated) politicians in Britain; among his newly infatuated fans were a considerable number of Conservative supporters who now hated Heath.

In an era of increasingly personalised politics, the Powell problem was arguably more potent for Heath than all of Wilson's accumulated weaknesses on the score of 'governing competence'. As a result, during the 1970 general election campaign Heath's main weapon proved to be the 'negative campaigning' which he had hoped to eschew. In his personal confrontations with the Prime Minister, the need to keep his supporters united had confirmed Heath's own preference for portraying Wilson as not just maladroit but actively malevolent. This had inspired a mistaken tactical decision of his own, when he committed his party to oppose *In Place of Strife* when a more sober assessment of the situation indicated the offer of at least limited support for proposals which bore more than a passing resemblance to developing Conservative ideas on the crucial question of industrial relations.[642]

Overall, despite the meticulous preparation for power it is safest to conclude

---

641 Mark Garnett, 'Planning for Power', Stuart Ball and Anthony Seldon eds, *Recovering Power: The Conservatives in Opposition Since 1867*, Houndmills, Palgrave, 2005, pp. 200–201.

642 James Prior, *A Balance of Power*, London, Hamish Hamilton, 1986, p. 46; Ian Gilmour and Mark Garnett, *Whatever Happened to the Tories?*, London, Simon & Schuster, 1997, pp. 239–40.

that Heath's party did not win in 1970 because of any consciously devised 'election-winning strategy'; rather, like most changes of power in post-war Britain, this was an example of the incumbent government suffering misfortunes which convinced an adequate number of voters that a change was appropriate. However, Heath would have been even more robotic than his critics alleged if he had endorsed that view of the election. Quite naturally, he took the public's vote as a positive endorsement of his party's policies, and as a result he tended to exaggerate both their novelty and the extent to which the electorate had (at long last) warmed to his leadership. These might have been forgivable misjudgements on the human level, but, in conjunction with savagely unfavourable events, they turned out to be fatal for Heath.

POLITICAL ARGUMENT HEGEMONY

If the rhetoric of Heath's 1970 party conference speech is a reliable guide, he was aiming to establish a lasting hegemony over British political argument. He told the conference that 'we will have to embark on a change so radical, a revolution so quiet and yet so total that it will go far beyond the programme for a parliament'. In heralding a 'quiet revolution', Heath had borrowed a phrase which *The Spectator* magazine had used after his leadership election victory in 1965; as his best biographer has written, unlike most of his public utterances it 'seemed to give philosophical coherence to what his government was setting out to do'.[643] However, long after the euphoria of October 1970 had subsided it was used against him to considerable effect. There was some justice in this, because the speech was an unusual example of Heath laying himself open to the accusation once levelled at his recently deceased colleague Iain Macleod, and trying to be 'too clever by half'. He was hoping to placate the party's ideologues by promising a complete transformation of the country, while appeasing more traditional Conservatives by suggesting

643 Campbell, op. cit., p. 311.

that change would be virtually undetectable. As such, he risked alienating traditional Conservatives who would be alarmed if the effect of his reforms was noticeable after all, and frustrating neo-liberal ideologues if his proposed changes turned out to be incremental rather than radical.

A comparison with Harold Wilson's 'White Heat' speech of 1963 is instructive here. Admittedly, Wilson was speaking at his party's conference as opposition leader rather than as Prime Minister; but he had every reason to expect an election victory within a matter of months, and like Heath he spoke of an impending revolution. However, when predicting that a new Britain was going 'to be forged in the white heat of this revolution', he was referring to radical changes which were about to happen (or already happening) thanks to developments in science and technology, and whether politicians liked them or not. Wilson openly befriended such developments; and (unlike the benighted Tories) gave the impression of being ready to meet the inevitable challenges. In the same sentence, he clearly implied that impending changes were likely to discomfit his party's trade union allies: in the coming revolution there would be 'no place for restrictive practices or for outdated methods on either side of industry'. But, having laid down this unmistakable marker, Wilson used the rest of his speech to reassure his audience that he was on the side of ordinary workers against their class enemies, while closing with a reminder that while the Soviet Union might be taking impressive strides in science and technology, a Labour-led Britain could more than match them without compromising its democratic practices.

Thus while Wilson was inviting his audience inside and outside the conference hall to regard a future Labour government as a *mediator* of impending change which might otherwise be worrying, Heath's 'Quiet Revolution' conceit portrayed his government as the chief *instigator* of changes which Britain would have to undergo if it was to survive. This rhetorical strategy would have made sense if Heath had really been a radical, in ideological terms – if he had been, as pedlars of the 'Selsdon Man' myth never cease to claim, a worshipper at the altar of free-market economics who simply lacked the courage of his convictions. Yet Wilson had launched his attack on 'Selsdon

Man' at the beginning of the 1970 election year precisely because he knew that the suggestion of ideological excess would embarrass his pragmatic rival. Enoch Powell once jeered that 'If you showed [Heath] an idea he immediately became angry and went red in the face'; and although Powell was a very hostile witness, it is reasonable to suppose that his hostility arose at least in part from his recognition that Heath was anything but an ideological 'fellow traveller'.[644]

So one is entitled to ask why Heath chose to talk of a radical programme, in terms which suggested a desire to establish 'political argument hegemony' on a long-term basis. The answer is that Heath did indeed envisage radical and lasting change for Britain, but his vision was not one which can readily be associated with any ideological position, and was almost impossible for any aspiring politician to articulate in 1970. Since his wartime experiences – perhaps, dimly, even before then – he had accepted that the nineteenth-century definition of sovereignty in absolute terms was no longer applicable to Britain. After 1945 it was clear to him that if the country wanted to pursue its interests in the new, polarised post-war world, it should be ready to 'pool' its formal decision-making sovereignty with other European states. Joining the EEC would indeed represent a 'revolution' in the way Britain regarded its place in the world: as well as coming to see itself as primarily a European (and middle-ranking) power, it would have to abandon its attempt to use the supposedly 'special' relationship with the US as a fig-leaf to conceal its reduced status from British voters as well as the external audience. But the domestic impact would also be dramatic. Apart from destroying the Victorian illusion that parliament was able to take decisions without reference to developments in the wider world, competition on an equal basis with manufacturing powerhouses like West Germany would entail considerable challenges, as well as new opportunities if the country was ready to brace itself to the task. For Heath, membership of the EEC would have

---

644 John Campbell, 'Symposium on Conservative Party policymaking, 1965–70', *Contemporary Record*, 3(5), 1990, pp. 34–6

much the same effect that Wilson attributed to the 'scientific revolution' – for example, there would be 'no place for restrictive practices or for outdated methods on either side of industry'. But, of course, joining the EEC could only be the result of deliberate government action, whereas Wilson's scenario called upon the British state to take creative steps in response to *exogenous* developments.

If, as Heath expected, Britain could secure EEC membership on tolerable terms, and – as he assumed rather too readily – the benefits of membership would become clear to impartial observers after a period of transition, then the party which had led the country to its unavoidable destiny would deserve the lasting gratitude of the voting public. But Heath was not so intoxicated by his personal vision as to ignore opinion-poll evidence which showed that very few of his fellow Britons shared it. Again, Enoch Powell is a telling witness; he recalled that 'Ted didn't really think, I believe, that the House of Commons has a heart, let alone the British people'.[645] In short, he anticipated that most of the passion in the Europe debate would be generated by the opponents of EEC entry; so for the most part he directed his appeal to the head rather than the heart. His approach to parliamentary tactics before the impassioned and protracted debates of 1971, which ended in endorsement of British entry, provides eloquent testimony to his concerns, as well as revealing his loss of contact with the back-bench mood since his time as Chief Whip; it was left to his successor in the latter role, Francis Pym, to suggest that it would be safe to allow Conservative MPs a free vote, rather than alienating potential dissenters by imposing a three-line whip.

In any case, by temperament Heath was always disposed to build what he regarded as a rational case, rather than trying to engage the passions of his audience. It can be argued that this approach was based on an overestimate of the forward-looking capacity of fellow Britons who were still nursing their protracted Second World War hangover, and at any time

---

645 Philip Ziegler, *Edward Heath: The Authorised Biography*, London, HarperCollins, 2010.

would have prevented a party led by Heath from establishing 'political argument hegemony'. As it was, his dream of 'a revolution so quiet and yet so total that it will go far beyond the programme for a parliament' was brought to a cacophonous conclusion before the natural end of his government's first term.

GOVERNING COMPETENCE

In 1970, the Conservatives boasted that they had the best-prepared opposition front bench in history – the party laid claim to 'governing competence' before it had actually governed. It turned out, however, that Heath and his colleagues had been preparing themselves to govern a kind of utopia peopled by individuals of unimpeachable rationality, rather than the complex situation which confronted them after the election. The kindest verdict, expressed by Heath's faithful PPS Douglas Hurd, was that the government tried to do too much.[646] Even this, though, is a tacit admission that the government was incompetent, even if one accepts that it might have proved its competence if it had done a bit less. Examples of superfluous government actions include the reorganisation of local government, based on the proposals of the Labour-appointed Redcliffe–Maud commission which had been heavily criticised by Conservative activists. While some attempt to reform the trade unions could not have been avoided, the 1971 Industrial Relations Act depended on the full cooperation of the unions themselves if it was to solve a problem which even Labour had acknowledged. Only Heath and his ministers seemed surprised when, far from securing general compliance, loopholes in the legislation were disclosed which made it impossible even for well-disposed unions to work within the letter of the law; and Harold Wilson, remembering Tory tactics over *In Place of Strife*, repaid his opponent in the same coin. To some observers (overseas, as well as at home), the

646 Douglas Hurd, *An End to Promises: Sketch of a Government 1970–74*, London, Collins, 1979.

disorder arising from the Act suggested not just that the Conservatives were incompetent, but that Britain itself was becoming 'ungovernable'.

In the areas for which the government could prepare, therefore, the story was of measures which could have been shelved and unavoidable measures which were implemented badly. Above all, though, the Heath government gave the appearance of incompetence in its failure to master 'events'. Again, one can argue that the government was dealt an unfair hand in this respect. Even England's failure to qualify for the FIFA World Cup, thanks to a 1–1 draw with Poland at Wembley on 17 October 1973, seemed to make a mockery of the government's 1970 manifesto, which had been entitled *A Better Tomorrow*. On the same day that England's sporting pretensions were exposed by defensive mistakes, members of the Organisation of Petroleum Exporting Countries (OPEC) announced a restriction of oil supplies in an attempt to exert economic leverage against states which were supporting Israel in its successful counter-offensive during the Yom Kippur War. Ironically, true to its leader's strategy of distancing Britain from the 'special relationship', the Heath government had declared an arms embargo against both Israel and its Arab adversaries. But Britain, despite its close relationships within the Middle East and the existence of vast North Sea deposits, which would soon make it self-sufficient in oil, suffered more than most developed states from the OPEC policy.

In turn, the oil crisis greatly enhanced the bargaining position of the National Union of Mineworkers (NUM), which had already conducted a successful strike against the Heath government over pay and conditions and now announced an overtime ban. For Heath, the horrible coincidence of a fuel crisis and a rise in union militancy was compounded by a concerted move to reinvigorate a flagging economy, which had started with the Budget of March 1972. It was a small mercy for the Conservatives that the inevitable inflationary consequences were delayed until after Heath had left office; but the impression left by a three-day week, power cuts and the threat of petrol rationing would have been enough to destroy the reputation of any government, even if its previous record had been free from the slightest taint of incompetence.

ANOTHER ELECTION-WINNING STRATEGY[647]

For Heath, 'statecraft' meant winning an election in order to have the chance of demonstrating the 'governing competence' which, by his own reckoning, he and his front-bench colleagues possessed in abundance. Heath himself did not want to call the February 1974 election, which was sure to look like a trial of strength between the trade unions and the government; and his reservations were well founded. However, it is difficult to envisage that the verdict of the voters would have been more positive had he held on and postponed the election until May 1975, especially given the combined inflationary consequences of earlier decisions and global developments.

However, in their admirable edited study of the Heath government, Stuart Ball and Anthony Seldon appraise the record of the Heath government in a wider context. In those traumatic times, all Western governments tended to fail; one needs to look no further afield than the 1964–70 Wilson governments to realise that Heath and his ill-starred colleagues were hardly unique. Anthony Seldon thus concludes that, although Heath's government was obviously not a success, to dismiss it as a failure 'would be trite, and wrong'.[648]

This verdict can readily be endorsed when it is applied to commentators whose hostile judgements on the Heath government have been dictated by blatant ideological considerations. To the left at the time, symptoms of sympathy for Heath or his policies were regarded as the hallmarks of class treachery. The fact that many of these critics subsequently revised their view provides no sort of comfort or exoneration for the Heath government, which should have factored unremitting opposition from the left into its calculations from the moment its members took office. Heath's detractors on the

---

647 This chapter uses the statecraft framework developed by Jim Bulpitt in 1986, rather than the revised approach outlined in Chapter Two in which 'a winning electoral strategy' and 'another winning electoral strategy' are combined and the task of 'bending the rules of the game' is introduced. See: Jim Bulpitt, 'The Discipline of the New Democracy: Mrs Thatcher's Domestic Statecraft', Political Studies, 34(1), 19-39 and Toby S. James, *Elite Statecraft and Election Administration* (Basingstoke and New York, Palgrave, 2012), p. 81-5, which suggested a revised approach.

648 Anthony Seldon, 'The Heath Government in History', in Stuart Ball and Anthony Seldon eds, *The Heath Government: A Re-appraisal*, Harlow, Longman, 1996, pp. 18–19.

Thatcherite right, by contrast, have seen no reason to revise their viscerally hostile views.[649] Their personal vindictiveness towards Heath – a hapless, invertebrate leader who was also a bad loser despite his familiarity with the taste of defeat – originated in an unnecessary attempt to justify Margaret Thatcher's perfectly honourable leadership challenge of 1975. However, the vilification of Heath unwittingly endangers the more important Thatcherite argument, that his 'consensus' style of politics was doomed in any case. Heath's right-wing opponents would be better advised to extol Heath's virtues, since this would imply that even the most skilful of operators was unable to offer a viable alternative to Thatcherism. In any event, even a casual reading of Heath's subsequent attacks on Thatcherism will show that these were much like Churchill's jeremiads against Stanley Baldwin – personal pique certainly played a part, but their ultimate basis was a fundamental difference of *principle*.

While Ball and Seldon are right to caution against simplistic standards of 'success' and 'failure', the fact remains that the record of the Heath government was a crushing disappointment to people who wanted it to succeed – most notably, to most members of the government itself. After the disaster of February 1974 the dependency of Heath's strategy on a reputation for 'competence' was exposed by the party's sorry showing in opposition to Wilson's new minority administration. The only effective operator, seemingly, was Margaret Thatcher, who enjoyed the ideological certainties which Heath and his closest colleagues palpably lacked. Typically, between the elections of February and October 1974 Heath threw away the chance to build a potential election-winning strategy around the idea of a government of national unity, instinctively feeling that this was yet another example of the political 'gimmickry' which he had always deplored. Even so, in October the Conservatives performed well enough to deny Wilson the comfortable majority which he needed, offering Heath the chance to step aside in circumstances which

649 Martin Holmes, *Political Pressure and Economic Policy: British Government, 1970–74*, London, Butterworth, 1982.

could have ensured the succession of an ally rather than an enemy. Indeed, if Heath had been rational enough to understand his own best interest he should have accepted the inevitable and stood down after the February 1974 defeat; as it was, nothing so became his period of leadership as the manner of his refusal to end it voluntarily before Thatcher prised it from his grasp in February 1975.

CONCLUSION

Heath at least proved himself to be one of the greatest of ex-prime ministers by continuing as a very active member of the Commons, continually pricking what, with a degree of artistic licence, could be described as the Thatcherite 'conscience'. In 1987, though, just as his supplanter's star was about to fall, he suffered the last of his electoral defeats when he stood for the Chancellorship of Oxford University. At least this time his victorious rival, Roy Jenkins, was a friend and another exponent of 'consensus' politics. One suspects, however, that their relationship would not have been so amicable if they had been members of the same political party. By 1987 Jenkins had (belatedly) accepted that his style of politics was no longer suited to success on the national stage; for him the Chancellorship was an agreeable consolation prize. Jenkins duly deployed the full range of the social skills which had earned him a rather perplexing popularity in exalted circles. By contrast, while Heath took the contest seriously he campaigned as his authentic self, presenting a rational case to potential supporters while appearing irredeemably grumpy to the uncommitted.

Whether or not the UK remains within the EU, it is unlikely that Edward Heath will ever be given much credit for taking the country in. Since this was undoubtedly his government's greatest success, not even the most determined 'revisionist' could ever write favourably about Heath with a realistic hope of triggering a concerted drive to rehabilitate his reputation among academic historians, let alone the public at large. Yet there is no doubt that Douglas

Hurd had good reason to claim in 1979 – a particularly inopportune moment – that Heath 'was a most remarkable patriot and Prime Minister'.[650] The reference to patriotism is indisputable, whatever Europhobes might insinuate. As Prime Minister, Heath was certainly remarkable in his capacity to absorb the simultaneous impact of numerous crises and continue to work for 'rational' solutions to Britain's enveloping difficulties. In the end, the most apposite explanation for the Heath government's success is the one which the Thatcherites rejected: if someone with Heath's ability and energy succumbed in his attempts to stop the bleeding, the failure must be attributed to an over-ambitious style of government rather than to any individual. On this view, Heath's failure was an unusually instructive one; no fair observer could say that it was ignoble.

650 Hurd, op. cit.

CHAPTER 18

MARGARET THATCHER

JOHN CAMPBELL

The legacy of Margaret Thatcher's eleven-year tenure as Conservative leader is widely contested, but John Campbell paints a portrait of her leadership in which she fulfilled many of the benchmarks of successful statecraft. Her three successive victories – in 1979, 1983 and 1987 – are unrivalled in the history of the party. Aided by a shifting intellectual tide on the right, Thatcher successfully pursued a wave of free-market economic ideas that genuinely changed the political weather. Her ability to make these policies electorally viable, and indeed to embody them, was a key strength, he argues. The key caveat in Campbell's analysis is related to her management of the Conservative Party. She left a party in 1990 that was more divided and less harmonious than the one she inherited. Arguably, too, she had a similar effect on British society. The success in winning the economic battle of ideas was not matched in achieving the goals of her social policies. John Campbell's judgement of Thatcher's leadership and legacy, consequently, is of a mixed picture.

• • •

Measured simply by electoral success, Margaret Thatcher was clearly by far the most successful Conservative leader of the twentieth century. She won three consecutive general elections, the first (from opposition) comfortably, the second and third (as the incumbent Prime Minister) by three-figure majorities. No other leader comes close to matching this record. Baldwin led the Tory Party to overwhelmingly majorities in 1924, 1931 and 1935; but he had previously led it to an unnecessary defeat in 1923, and his later victories were in the special circumstances of a National Government when it would have been very difficult to lose. Macmillan won handsomely the only general election he fought as leader, in 1959, from a very unpromising position when he took over two years earlier; but a 100 per cent record based on one election does not compare with Mrs Thatcher's three victories out of three. The only other modern political leader to match that is Tony Blair; and he lies outside the scope of this book.

Measured, secondly, by the extent to which, as Prime Minister, she advanced the aims of the Conservative Party in government Mrs Thatcher must again be judged, overall, exceptionally successful – at least as she defined those aims. Part of her achievement as Tory leader was to radically redefine, or sharpen, the ideological stance of the party in a far more overtly capitalist direction; and in office she re-shaped the whole landscape of British politics in line with her free-market philosophy, to the extent that she forced the Labour Party to accept it as the new cross-party orthodoxy.

Nevertheless, there are some serious criticisms that can be made of Mrs Thatcher's leadership in the area of party management and particularly the legacy she left the Tory Party. But this is invariably the case with a leader as long-serving and dominating as Margaret Thatcher: it was the same with Gladstone and the Liberal Party in the nineteenth century, and with Blair and Labour in the late twentieth. The fact is that Mrs Thatcher was an exceptionally dominant leader who has to be judged on a different level from most of those others under discussion in this book. The questions to be considered are how she became so dominant and how she was able to be so successful.

She was extraordinarily lucky to become leader at all. Even a year before she seized the crown almost no one – either in the party or in the press – had identified her as a potential future leader: partly because she was a woman when the idea of a female leader was still unimaginable, but also because she was seen as a hardworking, capable but unremarkable middle-ranking Cabinet minister, a safe pair of hands but of little personality and limited electoral appeal. The opportunity to stand for the leadership in February

1975 came her way only because so many more senior and apparently better-qualified candidates fell by the wayside or ruled themselves out. First, if Edward Heath had shown the humility or self-awareness either to offer himself for re-election after losing the February 1974 general election or to resign following the second election that October, he would probably either have been re-elected or replaced by a colleague closer to his own way of thinking – probably Willie Whitelaw or perhaps Jim Prior. Second, the man who had been seen as the principal challenger to Heath for the past six years, Enoch Powell, was no longer a Conservative but had taken himself off to join the Ulster Unionists. Third, when Heath did reluctantly concede a leadership contest in 1975, the senior ex-minister who had laid down a clear ideological challenge by openly repudiating much of the legacy of Heath's premiership, Keith Joseph, ruled himself out after a disastrously misjudged speech which appeared to advocate eugenics; while another persistent critic of Heath's leadership, the chairman of the back-bench 1922 Committee Edward du Cann, also (after some hesitation) declined to stand. Mrs Thatcher would have been happy to back either Joseph or du Cann if they had stood; but when they did not she took up the challenge on the ground that 'someone has to represent our wing of the party'. She did not expect to win, and even then she would almost certainly not have done if Whitelaw or Prior had not been too constrained by loyalty to Heath to stand against him. On the first ballot she attracted a lot of votes from MPs who wanted Heath to go but did not seriously want her to succeed. But once she had defeated Heath, though Whitelaw, Prior, Francis Pym and Geoffrey Howe all piled into the race to try to stop her, it was too late. She had acquired 'momentum', and won a good deal of admiration for her courage, and she was elected – to general astonishment – on the second ballot.

So she was an outsider: the beneficiary of a 'peasants' revolt' of Tory back-benchers against an unpopular and failed leader. Only one or maybe two members of Heath's shadow Cabinet – Joseph and possibly Howe – voted for her; most of the rest were horrified and incredulous at what the party had done. At the same time, although she was an outsider in the unexpected way she snatched the leadership, and much was made of the fact that she was not only a woman but a grammar school girl from a relatively humble provincial background, she was also in many less appreciated ways an insider as well. She had after all been to Oxford, where she had been President of the Conservative Association, which gave her a lot of contacts useful for her later career. She had been an active Young Conservative (in Colchester) in her twenties, a candidate (at Dartford) in the 1950 and 1951 general elections (at the age of twenty-four and twenty-five) and – despite by then having two young children – an MP in 1959 at the age of not quite thirty-four; a junior minister under Macmillan and Douglas-Home and a shadow Cabinet and then Cabinet minister – Secretary of State for Education – under Heath. Few people had seen her potential because she had kept her strong right-wing convictions fairly well hidden while toeing the Heathite party line to advance her career; but she had worked her way diligently up the party ladder, she had a fair amount of ministerial experience and a strong belief in her own capability. When the accidents of politics – Heath's stubbornness and others' self-exclusion – put opportunity in her way she was ready for it and had the self-belief to seize it.

As leader, Mrs Thatcher remained for a long time – certainly for the four years when she was Leader of the Opposition and for her first three years in government – an object of appalled suspicion for much of the party establishment, who continued to believe that she was an accidental aberration who would not last. But the wider party largely took her to its heart, because ordinary Conservative members and Tory voters recognised her as one of themselves. Unlike so many previous leaders who took a somewhat lofty view of the rank and file – neither Macmillan nor Heath would have privately dissented from Arthur Balfour's view that he would no more take advice from the Tory conference than from his valet – she identified with them, and from the time she attended her first conference in 1948 positively loved the annual gathering of those she liked to call 'our people': she shared and articulated their instincts on matters like law and order, immigration, trade union reform and education. This was a huge source of strength to her when she found herself – as she often did – in a minority in her shadow Cabinet and later in Cabinet: she could always appeal over the heads of her 'wet' colleagues to the party faithful beyond Westminster.

Her electoral success was founded on two quite distinct bases. On the one hand she was lucky to become leader at a time when the intellectual tide – not just in Britain but around the world (literally from Chile to China) – was turning against socialism and corporatism towards a rediscovery of the free market and the greater dynamism of untrammelled capitalism. Friedrich Hayek and Milton Friedman had both won the Nobel Prize for Economics (in 1974 and 1976 respectively), and in Britain the once-derided views of the Institute of Economic Affairs were suddenly gaining acceptance among more thoughtful Tories, epitomised by Keith Joseph – not to mention some prominent former Labour supporters – as they struggled to absorb the painful lessons of the Heath and Wilson governments. Mrs Thatcher herself was not an intellectual and probably never fully understood the theoretical nuances of monetarism; she talked the common-sense language of thrift, sound money and 'housewife economics'. But the resurgence of free-market economics chimed with her instincts and helped give her the intellectual self-confidence to lead a counter-revolution against collectivism in all its forms. In this she was hugely assisted by the number of influential journalists like Samuel Brittan in the *Financial Times*, Peter Jay and William Rees-Mogg in *The Times*, T. E. Utley and others in the *Telegraph* who helped create a growing consensus among opinion-formers in support of her ideas.

At the same time, however – shrewdly advised by her media gurus Gordon Reece and Tim Bell – she also made a point of directing her appeal not so much to the highbrow broadsheet newspapers as to the middle-brow *Daily Mail* and *Daily Express* and most importantly to Rupert Murdoch's cheerfully low-brow *Sun,* which in the 1970s was rapidly overhauling the *Daily Mirror* as the bestselling mass-circulation daily. The crucial element in Mrs Thatcher's first electoral victory in 1979 was her capture of a large slice of the aspiring, patriotic, skilled working class – the so-called C1s – who had traditionally voted Labour but had been alienated by Labour's lurch to the far left and the unrepresentative militancy of the unions. *The Sun*'s enthusiastic adoption of Mrs Thatcher – now renamed 'Maggie' – did more than anything else to transform her image from the strait-laced Education Secretary of a few years earlier to the gutsy champion of the patriotic working class let down by socialism. Thus she managed to appeal simultaneously both to the intellectual elite – or at least a part of it – and to the wider public.

Nevertheless her electoral success should not be exaggerated. Though she won three consecutive general elections by clear majorities, she never won more than 44 per cent of the vote – well below Macmillan's 49 per cent in 1959, and only barely more than the 43.4 per cent Alec Douglas-Home won in losing in 1964. In winning a 144-seat landslide in 1983 she actually won fewer votes and a lower share of the poll (42.4 per cent) than in 1979 when her majority was only forty-three. (In 1987 her share of the poll crept up again to 43.4, yielding a return of nineteen fewer seats and a majority down to 102.) The reason of course was the divided opposition, with the SDP–Liberal alliance taking 25 per cent of the vote in 1983 (to Labour's 27 per cent, down from 37 per cent in 1979) and still 23 per cent in 1987 (to Labour's 32 per cent), which allowed her to rack up inflated majorities on a minority of the poll. To this extent Mrs Thatcher's overwhelming dominance of the 1980s was largely a product of the first-past-the-post electoral system. Her hard-nosed genius was to calculate, coolly and correctly, that she did not need a majority of the electorate: she could afford to ignore the sometimes violent opposition of a sizeable portion of the public – the trade unions, the unemployed and homeless, the liberal intelligentsia – so long as there were enough of 'our people', the prospering middle class, to keep voting her back in. In fact, 43 per cent was more than enough.

But of course politics is not solely a matter of figures. She did dominate the decade not just by the brute force of her parliamentary majorities but also by the power of her personality and the global momentum of the ideology she embodied. Here again she was lucky in her opponents. In 1979, as an untried Leader of the Opposition, she was lucky that the Prime Minister, the vastly more experienced, reassuring and popular Jim Callaghan, backed off calling the general election in the autumn of 1978 when he would probably have won, leaving his government exposed to the wave of public sector strikes – the so-called 'winter of discontent' – which destroyed its credibility and handed the Tories a victory which had looked improbable six months before.

In 1983 she was even luckier. The first two and a half years of her government were a desperate time of high unemployment, high inflation, riots in the cities, deep divisions in the Cabinet and scarcely concealed muttering against her leadership. With the newly formed SDP in alliance with the Liberals attracting extraordinary levels of support through 1981 she seemed destined to be a single-term Prime Minister; even when the economy showed signs of recovery and the Alliance's polls began to slip at the beginning of 1982 a three-way hung Parliament still seemed the most likely outcome of the next election. But then came the Falklands War – a potential national humiliation for which Mrs Thatcher bore some culpability but which she was able, by courage, nerve and luck, to turn into a national and personal triumph which transformed her reputation; from then on, against a divided opposition poorly led by the elderly, lovable but hopelessly un-prime ministerial Michael Foot on the one hand and the suddenly flabby and long-winded Roy Jenkins on the other, she was never going to lose.

In 1987, she still had the benefit of a divided opposition, and another unconvincing principal opponent in Neil Kinnock, who was beginning to lead the Labour Party back to sanity but looked to the country no more like a credible Prime Minister than Foot; neither Labour nor the Alliance – now led in uncomfortable tandem by the 'two Davids', Steel and Owen – offered a serious alternative government. Despite a completely unfounded wobble a few days before polling day there was again no way she was going to lose; and in the wake of that election, with the economy now apparently booming, it began to look as if she could be Prime Minister for ever. In fact within a couple of years everything began to go wrong: with the return of inflation, rifts with her senior colleagues over Europe, the unpopularity of the poll tax and a general sense that she had been in power too long, the government started to unravel until, unprecedentedly, the Tory Party – not the electorate – threw her out. Tory MPs, anxious to save their seats, judged that she had become an electoral liability and in 1990 installed the less divisive, almost unknown John Major to lead them into the next election. The substitution worked: in 1992 Major achieved a narrow majority of twenty-one with 42 per cent of the poll. In one sense the fact that she had to be so brutally replaced was an indictment of Mrs Thatcher's later leadership. On a longer view, however, it could be argued that her leadership established the Tory Party so successfully as the party of government that it was able to win a fourth successive general election, maintaining the winning habit even after her removal.

Electoral success is not everything. Once in government, parties exist to deliver policies that put their values into practice. By that criterion too, Mrs Thatcher was broadly speaking exceptionally successful. Over her two and a half terms in office totalling eleven years, from 1979 to 1990, her governments transformed the British economy. She curbed the power of the trade unions, creating a much more flexible labour market. She privatised most of the previously nationalised utilities – gas, electricity, water supply, telephones, airlines, oil and nuclear energy. She ended the whole paraphernalia of price controls, incomes policy, subsidies to 'lame duck' industries and a lot of other regulation, shifting the balance of the economy decisively from manufacturing to service industries. She cut income tax. She also ended exchange controls, allowing sterling to trade freely against other currencies. And she opened the financial markets of the City of London to foreign traders, sweeping away decades of restrictive practices in the so-called 'Big Bang'. By all these means she created a far more competitive, overtly capitalist, economy such as business leaders and free-market Conservatives had dreamed of – but imagined to be beyond the realm of practical possibility – for years.

In social policy she was less successful. By compelling local authorities to sell their council housing to sitting tenants she made a big advance towards fulfilling the longstanding Tory goal of a 'property-owning democracy' while incidentally creating a large new class of overwhelmingly Tory voters; but by not allowing them to spend the proceeds to build new social housing stored up a housing shortage for the future. She started a process of freeing schools from the control of local education authorities, while at the same time introducing a centrally dictated national curriculum and imposing tight funding conditions on the universities that effectively destroyed their independence. Altogether her social policy objectives were less clear than her economic ones and her policies produced mixed results. She raised prescription charges and introduced competitive tendering, the outsourcing of ancillary services and an internal market into the National Health Service, but stopped short of introducing a fully insurance-based service (as in her heart she would have liked), forced by public opinion to maintain that the principle of publicly funded free access was 'safe with us'. She cut benefits for the poor, yet was still unable to prevent the overall cost of the welfare state rising inexorably. She did her best to squeeze and undermine the BBC, but failed in her hope of funding it at least partly by advertising in place of the licence fee; she imposed a blind auction of commercial television franchises which had the effect of lowering standards, much to her own belated horror. From a Tory Party point of view this was not a wholly successful record of delivering Conservative social goals. The overall effect was to create a more divided, less equal society which conflicted sharply with traditional Conservative concern for 'one nation'. This was particularly marked in Scotland, where the unpopularity of Thatcherism fuelled the demand for devolution and stored up a long-term threat to the survival of the union.

In foreign policy her principal achievement was to underline Britain's role as America's most reliable ally in prosecuting – and at the very end of the decade winning – the Cold War. She formed a close personal alliance with President Ronald Reagan and initially played some part in encouraging him to see that Mikhail Gorbachev was a new kind of Soviet leader with whom the West could 'do business'. The breaching of the Berlin Wall and the collapse of the Soviet Union represented the ultimate victory for capitalism and defeat for communism in its heartland. Having always seen socialism as merely a paler British form of communism without the courage of its convictions she was able to paint the demise of the Soviet system as confirming and vindicating her defeat of 'socialism' at home. The triumph of Thatcherism at home and abroad was underlined by the way the Labour Party over the next decade jettisoned practically all traces of its socialist convictions in order to make itself eventually re-electable in 1997 and, once back in power, made no effort to reverse any of her achievements: rather it continued and extended them. Mrs Thatcher effectively abolished the old Labour Party by converting it to her ideas: this must be the ultimate success for a party leader.

She also – ironically – carried on what had been a distinctive Conservative policy since 1961 by taking Britain further into what became the EU. In the 1970s the Tories were predominantly the pro-European party which led Britain into the common market in 1972, with Labour predominantly against. On succeeding Ted Heath as leader in 1975 she inherited this pro-European stance; she supported (admittedly without enthusiasm) the 'Yes' campaign in the 1975 referendum which confirmed British membership of the Community; and in office – despite a bruising early row about the size of the British contribution to the European budget – she signed the Single European Act which committed Britain more inextricably to Europe by creating the single market in goods, services and the free movement of people. Only towards the end of her premiership did she turn suddenly and violently against any further integration. Her strident hostility to further integration was a principal reason for her still broadly pro-European senior colleagues throwing her out; yet within a few years, out of office, she had persuaded practically the whole Tory Party to swing behind her into ever more uncompromising 'Euroscepticism' – while Labour moved in the opposite direction to a broadly pro-European position: an extraordinary reversal of positions and a remarkable exertion of leadership by Lady Thatcher (as she now was) even after she had ceased to be leader. Indeed even from the grave she is still the inspiration behind the growing determination of the party to leave the EU altogether.

What, then, are the criticisms to be made of her leadership? It has to be said that she was not a good party manager. She was not really interested in that aspect of politics: she was not interested in placating her opponents. She was always a divisive leader who had seized the leadership by a daring coup against her predecessor with little or no support from the senior colleagues she inherited; and she never really united the party. As she grew in confidence and authority she gradually purged most of those inherited senior colleagues (the so-called 'wets' – Francis Pym, Jim Prior, Ian Gilmour and others), replacing them with others closer to her way of thinking (Nigel Lawson, Norman Tebbit, Cecil Parkinson etc.); but she also had to promote others from the 'wet' side of the party who tended to be the ablest candidates (Douglas Hurd, Ken Clarke, Chris Patten) so that by the end she was surrounded by a majority of younger colleagues who were loyal to her so long as she was electorally successful, but were not her natural supporters. Over her eleven years in Downing Street she suffered a very high level of resignations and other more or less involuntary departures. In particular she quarrelled with her two closest ministerial allies, her first two Chancellors who both played major roles in her success, Geoffrey Howe and Nigel Lawson; their unhappy resignations – Lawson in October 1989 and Howe in November 1990 – signalled the unravelling of her government and foreshadowed her own removal. With more sensitive management of colleagues she should have been able to carry on a good deal longer.

One measure of her party management is her sometimes curious choice of party chairmen. Her first chairman, Peter Thorneycroft, whom she appointed on first becoming leader in 1975, was an Old Etonian throwback to the Macmillan era and a sign of her initial lack of confidence in her own legitimacy. Thorneycroft saw her successfully elected in 1979 but was replaced in 1981 when he admitted to 'rising damp'. She then unexpectedly appointed Cecil Parkinson, one of her best appointments, who masterminded the 1983 election; but she then still more surprisingly appointed John Gummer, who made very little impact and was replaced in turn by Norman Tebbit, whose abrasive personality – not helped by his serious injuries in the Brighton bomb – and falling-out with Lord Young (her other favourite whom she appointed to second-guess him) made the 1987 election a bumpier ride than it should have been. After two years of Peter Brooke, another conciliatory patrician, her last chairman was Kenneth Baker, who was admirably loyal but unable to prevent her defenestration when the party lost confidence in her. In fact the key figure in maintaining the party's loyalty to her leadership, particularly in the early days when her position was still precarious, was Willie Whitelaw, who had been her principal rival in 1975 and was not instinctively in sympathy with her at all, but buckled down with military discipline and made it clear to potential rebels that he would not countenance any move against her. For nine years he was her bulwark; and many would date the beginning of her decline and fall from the moment he resigned from the government, after a mild heart attack, in January 1988.

Her other party appointments were equally hit and miss. Her successive chief whips had a relatively easy time, cushioned by her large majorities in 1983 and 1987; but as part of the hasty reshuffle in 1989 following Lawson's resignation when the parliamentary party was beginning to grow restive she made a serious mistake, from her own point of view, by appointing Tim Renton, who had never been a whip but was a close friend of Geoffrey Howe and definitely not a Thatcher loyalist. Perhaps it was intended as a conciliatory gesture, but Renton was not the chief whip she needed when her leadership was challenged by Michael Heseltine twelve months later. Likewise her choices for parliamentary private secretary were bizarre. Her first PPS in government, Ian Gow, was a brilliant appointment who was credited with keeping her in touch with her back benches in 1979–83; but after him she chose a succession of lightweights – all Old Etonians because she felt it unfair to appoint to an unpaid job anyone who did not have a private income – who allowed her to get progressively more out of touch until her last PPS, Peter Morrison, completely failed to anticipate the scale of the vote against her in November 1990. Again she contributed to her own downfall by deigning it beneath her dignity to go round the bars and tearooms to shore up her support. She left party management to others who were not well-chosen for the job.

Under Mrs Thatcher's leadership party membership declined, as did that of all political parties. More important than the headline membership figure, however, it can be argued that the Thatcher decade undermined the Tory Party in the country by weakening its traditional base in local government. Over eleven years in office her government conducted a sustained attack on the autonomy of local government, from rate-capping and the enforced sale of council houses in her first term, through the outsourcing of services through compulsory competitive tendering and the abolition of the Greater London Council and six other metropolitan councils in the second term, to letting schools opt out of local council control and the disastrous poll tax in the third; it was calculated that more than fifty separate Acts of Parliament in these years took power away from local government. As a matter of principle this trend contradicted the deep-rooted Conservative belief in the importance of local government as a counter to the centralising power of the state; while in practice the loss of worthwhile powers and functions meant that ever fewer able and public-spirited people came forward to serve in local government, so that activism at the grass roots of the party shrivelled – particularly in Scotland and the north. Thus when the triumphs of her general election victories passed away, Mrs Thatcher left her successors a much weakened – and ageing – power base concentrated disproportionately in southern England.

More obviously, she left behind her a divided party still haunted for the next two decades by bitter recrimination over the manner of her removal and by much of her political legacy – particularly over Europe, but also her reputation as a hard-faced leader lacking in compassion for the less fortunate in society: a reputation which her successors found it hard to shake off. John Major aspired to create a 'classless' country 'at ease with itself', and hoped to put Britain 'at the heart of Europe'; David Cameron had to insist that there *was* such a thing as society; and Theresa May famously warned in 2002 that the Conservatives were still seen as 'the nasty party'. Even as Mrs Thatcher had won the political argument and shifted the terrain of politics far to the right, forcing Labour to accept most of her policies in order to be electable again, she had become personally unpopular: a toxic association from which successive Tory leaders sought to distance themselves while Labour leaders tried to damn them with it. Ironically the very completeness of her smashing of 'Old Labour', which pulled Tony Blair's 'New Labour' to embrace a new post-Thatcherite consensus, pushed the Tory Party under William Hague, Iain Duncan Smith and Michael Howard further to the right as it struggled to find a new identity and *raison d'être*. Even when the Blair/Brown government ran out of steam after thirteen years, Cameron was unable to win an outright majority in 2010 largely because the Tories were still hobbled by the memory of the Iron Lady.

In conclusion, then: Margaret Thatcher was far and away the most successful Tory leader of the twentieth century in winning elections. She was a dynamic leader who led from the front by articulating clear policies which commanded enthusiastic support from sufficient of the electorate to win, while forcing grudging admiration and eventual acceptance even from those who initially opposed her. She was lucky in that she became leader at a time when a global counter-revolution against collectivism was taking hold all round the world; but she was the British expression of that counter-revolution and she seized her opportunity and rode her luck with remarkable single-mindedness and courage. She was exceptionally successful in pushing through a radical shake-up of the British economy, industry and finance in accordance with free-market ideas which created a much more competitive economy than she inherited; but less successful in her attempted reforms of the health service, education, housing and welfare, which combined with the creed of competitive individualism to create a more unequal and divided society. If the Tories before Mrs Thatcher had prided themselves on standing for 'one nation' – as they did, from Baldwin to Heath, though sometimes more in the breach than the observance – Thatcherism put a brutal end to that pretence. Mrs Thatcher changed the Tory Party, and the country, in her own image, but not necessarily for the better. Her success created serious problems for her successors.

CHAPTER 19

JOHN MAJOR

ANTHONY SELDON AND MARK DAVIES

John Major's seven years as leader from 1990 to 1997 were sandwiched between, at least in terms of successive electoral victories, the most successful of all Conservative and Labour leaders. Anthony Seldon and Mark Davies argue that, perhaps more so than any other Conservative leader, understanding this context is essential when assessing his leadership. On the one hand, he secured an unlikely victory in 1992 still unmatched in terms of the number of crosses next to Conservative candidates. On the other, the 1997 election was a crushing landslide so large that it would be ahistorical to blame Major solely for defeat. Seldon and Davies argue he made a good fist of an impossible task, holding considerable personal achievements on the economy and Europe. The sheer length of Conservative rule that preceded his time as leader dictated his political path and severely limited his opportunities, and meant managing an unruly party bereft of ideas with little incentive to be cohesive. However, his eventual inability to overcome these difficulties suggests he should be considered a very good – but not a great – Conservative leader.

• • •

Despite the particularly difficult circumstances in which John Major served as Prime Minister, his achievements were considerable. His government consolidated Thatcherism, produced a healthy economic record, provided strong and dignified leadership upon the international stage, and helped to bring peace to Northern Ireland. The incoming

Labour government in 1997 continued to pursue these, and other, aspects of his government's agenda. All of this was made possible by the spectacular victory – against all odds – in the 1992 general election, a victory for which Major was primarily responsible, and a victory that killed off Old Labour. The Conservative defeat in 1997 was due not to his failure to exhibit successful 'statecraft' but because of circumstances beyond his control, including the country's desire for change after eighteen years of Conservative rule. His government's enduring successes, achieved in the face of such adverse circumstances, make it possible to argue that Major was the most effective leader of any party since 1945.

JOHN MAJOR'S CHILDHOOD AND ITS POLITICAL INFLUENCE

Most prime ministers have either been born to wealthy and educated backgrounds, or showed early evidence of future distinction. John Major was bestowed with neither characteristic. His early years profoundly shaped his outlook on life. At the time of his birth, in 1943, his father was sixty-three – older than many children's grandfathers – and becoming increasingly blind due to a degenerative disease in both eyes. By the time that Major was twelve years old, his father was all but blind and bedridden. This had an obvious effect on the family's finances; they were forced to sell their home and move to cheap rented accommodation in Brixton in 1955, descending from a middle-class existence to a level of poverty and insecurity that their children had never known. Major vividly remembers 'waking up and seeing the water coming through the roof in the morning, and running down the light switch'.[651]

Following the move to Brixton, Major faced a three-hour round-trip to school each day, sometimes being bullied on the way. The family's reduced

651 Anthony Seldon, *Major – A Political Life*, London, Weidenfeld & Nicolson, 1997, p. 15.

circumstances highlighted his feelings of insecurity, and he was sensitive about coming to school in a cheaper and inferior uniform. Major explains that he did not succeed at school because 'if you had the sort of difficulties we faced at home at the time, you are alienated … I wasn't stupid at school, I just didn't work. I couldn't work'.[652] He left school at sixteen. His sensitivity about his lack of academic success haunted him throughout his political career.

Major's childhood may not have been unusual for any ordinary boy, but it was exceptional for a future Prime Minister. His first sixteen years saw scant evidence of the intellectual ability, independence of spirit, intense ambition, confidence and charm with people, which characterised his subsequent career. Nevertheless, some traits were already clearly established by the time of his sixteenth birthday. The feeling of being passed over, dismissed, is powerful within him, and owes much to these years. So, too, does the feeling of insecurity, which was to haunt him all his life. He was later to develop a brilliantly manicured exterior, but very few people claimed truly to understand him. A polished outer surface and exceptional drive, alongside a restless interior and a strong hunger for affirmation, are the keys to unlocking the Major enigma, combined with a deep sympathy for the less fortunate and marginalised members of society, a sympathy derived from his own personal experience of poverty and being an 'outsider'.

MAJOR'S PATH TO THE LEADERSHIP

Major entered Parliament in 1979. His assiduous hard work and pleasant manner soon brought him to the attention of the whips. Once he received his first job in 1983, as a whip, his attention to detail, accurate reading of people and congenial personality earned him wide recognition. As Social Security Minister from 1985, he revealed an outstanding ability to

---

652 Ibid., p 12.

master his brief in a department where detail is all, and he proved himself sensitive in dealing with individual cases of hardship as well as an effective parliamentary performer.

Now two patrons, and a fair smattering of luck, intervened to propel his rise. First, Nigel Lawson battled against Thatcher to secure him as Chief Secretary at the Treasury, a job tailor-made for his talents, where he gave the most complete ministerial performance of his political career. His next jump, his steepest, occurred when Mrs Thatcher, in a hurry, needed to find a new Foreign Secretary to succeed Geoffrey Howe. Major was, she thought, 'one of us': too young in Parliament to have associations with Ted Heath, and socially from the self-made stable she admired. Circumstance again ran in his favour when Lawson resigned as Chancellor in 1989 and when again there was no other obvious candidate available.

For Major's final leap, to No. 10, Howe's devastating resignation speech came at just the right moment. Major's excellent conference speech in the same month meant that his profile was at its height, and Thatcher's doubts about Major, for his lack of scepticism on Europe and his liberal domestic policy instincts, had yet to form. The three heavyweights from the Thatcher years – Howe, Lawson and Tebbit – had all ruled themselves out from standing. After Heseltine's first-ballot challenge, Thatcher was removed without fatal damage to Major's relations with her and he remained her anointed successor. The decks were now clear for Major to slink past Heseltine and Hurd in the second ballot, as the candidate of the right and the person best placed to unite the party.

THE DIFFICULT ENVIRONMENT OF MAJOR'S LEADERSHIP

Many of the harsher criticisms levelled against Major's performance as Prime Minister are intellectually limited because they have little regard for the circumstances under which Major served his premiership from 1990 to 1997. Great leaders throughout history have been made by great opportunities – war, economic depression, or a widespread shift in public mood that the leader can articulate. The historical opportunity for *any* leader who succeeded Mrs Thatcher in November 1990 was, in contrast, unusually restricting. The environment in which any historical figure acts needs to be considered under four headings: individuals, ideas, circumstances and interests.

Individuals: the lack of scope for assertive leadership in the 1990s

The scope for assertive leadership in the 1990s was less than in the 1980s. Not only was Major a collegiate leader, and such leaders do not make the weather, but he also faced far tougher Labour leaders than did Mrs Thatcher. She served opposite James Callaghan on his way out, Michael Foot, and a young Neil Kinnock; Major faced Kinnock in his prime, John Smith, and Tony Blair, the most effective Labour leader in opposition since Ramsay MacDonald. Unlike Mrs Thatcher, Major never found a senior figure such as Whitelaw to underpin his position. Neither did Major have, like Mrs Thatcher, a coterie of sympathetic interpreters of his policies and position in the media and intellectual life. Instead, he had the opposite, with obvious results.

No Conservative leader this century has had to contend with a predecessor so overtly questioning their premiership. Thatcher and Major were both at fault for their poisoned relationship. She was perhaps the more guilty, because she saw the damage she was doing, how divided was the party, and how small the majority after 1992, and above all because she had suffered herself from similar sniping from her predecessor Edward Heath. One of her closest friends concluded: 'She used all her political cunning to knife him and stab him and demoralise him and weaken him. Above all else she was thinking: "He is doing my job. How dare he?"'[653]

Although Major was served by some outstanding officials and very able ministers, the pool of political talent at his disposal after eleven years in office, and still more so after many Tories lost their seats in 1992, was restricted.

653 Ibid., p. 255.

The seventy former ministers on the back benches were often bitter and unbiddable. Those who knew they would not receive jobs – including many hardened Eurosceptics – saw little reason to be loyal to Major.

Ideas: the lack of fresh thinking on the right

The ideological background for Major in 1990 was similarly unpromising. Mrs Thatcher was able to adopt an intellectually coherent platform developed in universities and among thinkers dating back to Hayek's *Road to Serfdom* (1944) and before, and packaged for her in the 1970s and 1980s by friendly think tanks such as the Centre for Policy Studies. A coherent body of ideas was there for her to take off the peg. By the time Major became Prime Minister, the battle for ideas had been won, as had the Cold War, and the 1990s offered fewer certainties. Blair's adoption of much of the Thatcherite, and Majorite, agenda shows that in the 1990s fresh portmanteau ideas, certainly on the right, were not to be had.

Circumstances: recession, small majority, sleaze, skilled opposition leaders such as Blair, and polls predicting heavy defeat

Major served at a time when circumstances were especially difficult. Immediately upon becoming Prime Minister he was confronted by the Gulf crisis, deepening recession, the poll tax, and a party already deeply unpopular and divided over Europe. His in-tray also contained unexploded bombs such as arms trading with Iraq, the Pergau Dam, and the growth of shady lobbying companies. His first years were overshadowed by the recession and the consequent problems in the public finances. His later years suffered because of a dwindling parliamentary majority at the mercy of eccentric backbenchers, and the mischance of having to steer the Maastricht Treaty through in 1993 in very different circumstances from the acclaim that had greeted his original deal in 1991.

Sleaze, neither initiated nor encouraged by Major, and which was one of the defining issues of his premiership, proved a daunting subject to confront. Major responded by establishing Scott and Nolan, to the fury of his right, and then, when parliamentary pressures prevented him endorsing their reports to the full, he was castigated by the centre and left. The Hamilton affair, over which he had to battle with both an angry right and Hamilton's Tatton constituency, proved equally evasive of an early solution. Yet again, many more condemned Major over sleaze than came forward with practical and workable solutions. The irony remained: an honest man crippled by sleaze.

Where Heath had five years in opposition to plan, Mrs Thatcher four years and Blair three, Major had barely one month, after it seemed likely he would win in November 1990, to plan his policies and the personnel he wanted to serve him. Once in office, he again lacked the time to develop his ideas. For a cricketer, he was placed from the outset on the back foot, and only rarely did he have the chance to play forward.

In electoral terms, Major suffered from the emergence of New Labour, which stole the Tories' true secret weapon, not loyalty, but adaptability. In New Labour, Major faced the supreme 'flexi-party', willing to adopt almost any policy and position to appeal to centre-ground voters.

Interests: loss of support from the City, business, the press and the professions, and a lack of powerful incentives on the left for Major to slay

Tory hegemony this century has depended in significant part on the backing of the powerful interests in the country – the City, business and the press, as well as the professions. The last was alienated by Mrs Thatcher and never fully returned. Significant elements of the first three flew in the 1990s. In contrast, the interests that in electoral terms had handicapped Labour since the 1970s, the trade unions, were distanced from them. There were no powerful interests for Major to slay, or the equivalent to those whose vanquishing added so greatly to Mrs Thatcher's stature – a bloated state sector, inefficient nationalised industries, over-mighty trade unions. If Major's equivalent of the Falklands War was the Gulf War, which did not end in such conclusive fashion, the equivalent of the 1980s victory in the Cold War, where the popular forces of liberal democracy triumphed over corrupt statism, was Bosnia in the 1990s, without such clear moral absolutes.

The most difficult problem of all that Major faced was that, with polls and by-elections pointing continually to the likelihood of a heavy defeat, there was little incentive for his own parliamentary party to follow his lead when an alternative – any alternative – offered the prospect of a revival in fortunes.

Admittedly, Major did not play the hand he was dealt to best advantage. However, it would be shallow to judge a premier without balancing such factors as described above. In comparison to Major, Attlee and Thatcher both ruled in favourable circumstances. With regards to Tony Blair, almost all of the factors outlined above were favourable during his time in office. Yet what did Blair achieve?

THE 1992 AND 1997 GENERAL ELECTIONS

Major's achievement in securing a majority in the 1992 election was considerable. The election campaign had begun, as Michael White wrote, 'in the least favourable circumstances for a sitting government since Harold Wilson ended the last thirteen-year tenure in 1964'.[654] The country was in the middle of a recession, with the polls placing Labour 2 per cent ahead. Not since Clement Attlee in 1951 had a Prime Minister voluntarily called an election while his party was behind in the polls. Nevertheless, Major believed for virtually all of the campaign that he would win, driven by a belief in his own destiny. He enjoyed elections. The rough and tumble of debate appealed to him, and he drew energy from meeting voters. The Prime Minister standing on his soapbox was to become a regular feature of the campaign. He later explained:

> I don't like speaking to an audience on a platform … there is no contact, no humanity, no relationship. So I was looking to get on the soapbox all

654 *The Guardian*, 12 March 1992.

> the time. People kept saying, 'No, you mustn't do it, too dangerous, won't work, not prime ministerial.' Eventually ... I just did it.[655]

Major showed considerable bravery with his insistence on mixing with crowds, in contrast to Neil Kinnock — who was neither an IRA target, nor the subject of such venom on the streets. In Southampton, Major received his hardest direct hit from an egg, struck with such force in the face that he was nearly knocked over; for a few seconds he thought it might have been a bullet.

Major's public image was a significant factor in the eventual Conservative victory, in which they won 14,000,000 votes, a record that still stands. The Conservatives defeated Labour by 7.5 per cent, achieving 41.9 per cent of the popular vote, an achievement even more impressive when viewed with the benefit of hindsight; in the four elections since 1992, the Conservatives have averaged only 32.7 per cent. However, the parliamentary majority of only twenty-one was a poor reward for such a convincing victory. The electoral system operated against the Conservatives because of tactical voting; if the swing had been uniform across the country, they would have won a 71-seat majority. The history of the next five years would have been different had that been the case.

The huge defeat that the Conservatives suffered at the 1997 election happened because the country and the media were deeply bored with the Tories, and fed up with a party that seemed to have no common beliefs or loyalty to bind it together. The defeat was *not* caused because Major was not a Eurosceptic nor sufficiently Thatcherite. Politicians are fundamentally self-interested people. For most of the Conservative Party's history, self-interest has dictated loyalty; in the 1990s, with the polls continually showing a huge Labour advantage and the likelihood of a heavy Tory defeat, self-interest was better served by actions other than loyally following the party leader. Coupled with that, the Tories faced Tony Blair, the most creative leader in the Labour Party's history, who brilliantly exploited Tory divisions while stealing their natural voters.

---

655 Seldon, op. cit., p. 279.

MAJOR'S PRIME MINISTERIAL RECORD

Despite the particularly unfavourable circumstances in which Major served as Prime Minister, the achievements of his premiership were considerable. His government's agenda consolidated Thatcherism, succeeding in privatising coal and rail, as well as pursuing other radical policies such as the sale of the nuclear industry and traditional state organisations like HMSO. The Deregulation and Contracting Out Act 1994 produced a significant clear-out of regulations that had survived the 1980s. The government introduced welfare reforms which, for the first time since 1945, meant that welfare costs fell as a proportion of national income. The march of reform continued through institutions such as the Stock Exchange and the army, and through a mini-revolution in education.

The government produced a strong economic record. The Major years, after the recession of 1990–92, saw consistently low inflation and steady economic growth at 2–3 per cent which showed no sign of overheating or slackening. There were unsung improvements to public services through the Citizen's Charter, and a renaissance of culture and sport through National Lottery funding, which ultimately led to Britain's considerable gold medal success at the 2012 Olympics. In foreign policy, Major provided calm, proficient and dignified leadership throughout the Gulf War, which was the biggest British military campaign since Korea forty years earlier. He earned the respect and confidence of the armed services. He deserves the greatest credit among international leaders for the creation of safe havens for the Kurds, an initiative which saved thousands of lives from Saddam Hussein's reprisals. He was an equally steady and resolute leader over Bosnia.

Ejection from the ERM, more than any other single event, undermined the second Major government, destroying the reputation for economic competence that the Conservatives had developed under Thatcher. Yet it is important to remember that Labour, the Liberal Democrats, industry, the City, the TUC and most trade unions had supported entry into the ERM. Following the UK's departure from the ERM, stories appeared claiming that

Major had cracked and lost his nerve on that fateful day. There is no truth in any of these rumours: too many witnesses testify so. Throughout the key meetings and in all the decisions, he was almost inhumanely calm and self-possessed. Though obviously under heavy stress, he elicited opinions from everyone, asked the questions, summed up, and took the final decisions.

The Maastricht Treaty was to cause Major so much difficulty. The irony is that it was at first a personal triumph for him. He secured his twin objectives of ensuring Britain remained at the heart of European affairs while preserving freedom of action in those areas where the UK's sovereignty was deemed to be sacrosanct. Major's skills in holding Cabinet together were rarely better displayed than over the closing phases of the Maastricht Bill. David Hunt, who was at that time Secretary of State for Employment, recorded in his notes: 'When all this is looked back on within the party, we will see that it was his determination to drive that through that enabled us to survive.'[656]

Victory was achieved, but Major's reliance on a confidence motion to give the Maastricht Bill the last heave through Parliament exacted a price. The rebels had developed bonds of shared adversity, and the virtual party within a party was not to be disbanded as the leadership hoped. They resented the methods that had been used against them. They went on to form a hard core of plotters, posing the threat of a leadership challenge every autumn. However, could Major have acted differently? He had staked his leadership on the Maastricht Treaty, and that meant putting it through Parliament. Bar abandoning the treaty, he had little alternative but to act as he did. If he had won a Pyrrhic victory, it was perhaps the only victory on offer.

Major's consensual leadership style could be argued to have been exactly what was required for the times. Conservative unity on Europe, which fractured in the late 1980s, showed that Mrs Thatcher's style of leadership and negative stance on the EC was no longer tenable. Major had the difficult task of managing strong and complex trends of parliamentary and public opinion, which moved decisively in a Eurosceptic direction in the 1990s. Across

---

656 Ibid., p. 388.

a range of other policy issues, his undoctrinaire approach suited the tenor of the times. Instead of, like the right, wishing that the public sector would go away or, like much of the centre-left of his party, considering it sacrosanct, he took a case-by-case approach to reform. The same applies to privatisation: rail privatisation and the Private Finance Initiative involved innovative ways of mixing public and private sectors. Major's pragmatic and humane approach played a significant role in creating a lasting peace in Northern Ireland, which is a prime example where the accusation of Major lacking all principles or consistency falls apart. Failed leaders see little of their policy survive. This did not happen with Major, much of whose legacy was taken on board by the incoming Labour government in 1997.

MAJOR'S STYLE OF LEADERSHIP

Major belonged to no single school of Conservatism, had no mentors among past Tory leaders or theorists, and had no interest in redefining Toryism. He was by temperament and choice a conciliator, and had found Mrs Thatcher's style of 'macho leadership' distasteful. His chairmanship of Cabinet and Cabinet committees, in contrast, allowed ministers to express their views, and guided them to a conclusion in line with his intentions. Rather than have dissent in Cabinet, he preferred to delay decisions until he could reconcile differences. He presided over a regular and more public system of Cabinet committees, with less recourse to pressurising decisions in bilaterals than most of his predecessors. He did not have a 'kitchen Cabinet' of regular close aides and resorted to an *ad hoc* inner Cabinet only in the run-up to both general elections and during particularly difficult periods, such as late 1994. Major's consensual style extended, again in marked contrast to Mrs Thatcher, towards the civil service, with whom he enjoyed extremely good relations.

Major's qualities of emollience, pragmatism, wanting to hold all factions together, were attracting contempt from some quarters by the end of his premiership. However, the party as a whole in 1990 had wanted a change from Thatcher to a more collegiate, inclusive and unideological leader, and that is exactly what Major proved to be. Might a Hurd, a Heseltine or a Redwood premiership have proved much more successful? Would the much-vaunted 'strong leadership' have succeeded when the party was so fundamentally divided?

ASSESSING MAJOR'S LEADERSHIP

Major's was an important (albeit unruly) premiership at the end of the Conservative century, completing some parts of an earlier agenda while in some key respects helping to define a Conservatism for the twenty-first century. His weaknesses date back in part to his childhood insecurities. He did not happily assert himself nor like to be unpopular, and would sooner say 'yes' than 'no'. His track record on public spending in 1989–93, which led to the loss of the tax card, saw this vulnerability displayed at its most acute. His insecurity, coupled with his lack of grounding in Tory philosophy, made him often appear to be lacking in consistency. His lack of time to prepare for office, and disappearing parliamentary majority, prevented him from pushing ahead further with his deeply felt instincts, on constitutional reform, modernisation of his party, and reforms to help the underprivileged and dispossessed, towards whom he felt deep concern.

Much of his pleasure in being Prime Minister was taken away by the barrage of criticism, and the difficulty he found in making an appropriate response. His lack of deep personal security and positive self-image from childhood contributed to his inability to brush off the hostility. At Major's core was a vulnerability which no amount of success after his teens could ever remove, and which remained with him until the end of his premiership. The extent to which the barrage of criticism so obviously upset him emboldened those in the media who, scenting blood, wanted to go ever further in ridicule. Yet Major remained a dignified and polite premier, lacking arrogance in his dealings with people. He was perhaps the first Conservative premier to believe in race and sex equality, and in progress towards homosexual equality. He showed occasional political courage and a gambler's nerve, as in his defying his 'handlers' in the 1992 and 1997 general elections and in launching the 1995 leadership election.

Britain likes trashing its leaders when they are in power, and continues to do so after their fall. It is difficult for prime ministers to climb back up in public esteem. John Major stands out as a very rare holder of the office in the last century whose standing has risen after stepping away from power. In history, Major is not a towering figure, but nor is he a failure like Balfour or Eden, or a footnote in the Conservatives' evolution like Bonar Law or Douglas-Home. If circumstances had been different, Major might have been a Baldwin, presiding over a new deal between party and mass electorate. His place, nevertheless, in a league table, and when considering the opportunity open to a leader in 1990, would be in the second quartile from the top.

CHAPTER 20

WILLIAM HAGUE

JO-ANNE NADLER

The Conservative Party that William Hague inherited in 1997 was a shell-shocked parliamentary rump of 165 MPs. Upon his resignation, the day after the 2001 election and four years as opposition leader, the number of parliamentarians in Conservative ranks had crept up one higher, to 166. Thus, Hague became the first Conservative leader since Austen Chamberlain not to gain access to Downing Street. This reflected, Jo-Anne Nadler argues, strategic stagnation that meant Hague was unable to develop political arguments beyond the reactionary and defensive. Hindered by a governing Labour Party brimming with momentum and monopolising the elusive modernising agenda, Hague felt he had little choice but to revert to appeasement of his party and a reinforcement of a core, but outdated, culturally conservative message. Nadler points towards achievements in internal reform and success in active opposition to Britain's membership of the euro but, ultimately, a mixture of difficult context and a lack of intellectual and tactical bravado meant that Hague's leadership was a disappointment.

• • •

When William Hague announced his candidacy to lead the Conservative Party he had a near perfect CV. At the time of his birth in the early 1960s Britain was still emerging from the age of deference. It was then the Labour Party that could capture the zeitgeist by selecting a dynamic young Yorkshireman with whom to bask in the white heat of technology. The Conservative Party by contrast was still mired in the culture of the white smoke signal, allowing a cabal of party grandees to oversee the passing of the leader's role from aristocrat to patrician and so on.

Over the next three decades however, the Conservative Party, practical to its core, evolved a new tradition of middle-class, state-educated leaders; one had even been a woman, another had not gone to university. So by 1997 it was ready for Hague to be its youngest leader in two centuries. In the flat Yorkshire vowels of William Hague, son of a soft drinks manufacturer, comprehensive school attendee, and with a boyhood spent on the very terrain of the 1980s bloodiest industrial disputes, a party which urgently needed a fresh phase of modernisation to compete with the all-conquering brand of New Labour might have found the obvious answer. William Hague brought the real-world authenticity necessary to counter Labour claims that the Conservatives remained a party of privilege while also being able to reassure his own party with a long record of commitment and achievement. It had started with a precocious teenage conference speech under Maggie's gaze, was confirmed by a starred academic career at Oxford and been sealed by his seemingly effortless rise to John Major's Cabinet. In short as a candidate to lead his party in 1997 Hague had it all; he wasn't posh but he was very clever, he had ticked all the right boxes at university and in his career choice of management consultancy brought a professional approach to leadership, combined with killer debating skills, that indicated both a passionate Churchillian and an instinctive Thatcherite. So how in the space of only four years did a leadership that promised so much deliver so little, ending ignominiously for Hague himself with another landslide defeat, adding only a single seat to his party's all-time low parliamentary tally of 1997?

Those years from 1997 had their 'green shoots' five years previously when the Conservatives, against expectation, won a fourth successive general election victory, the first with John Major at the helm. For many Conservatives the election of 1992 was one that even without hindsight they would rather not have won. Within weeks of victory one Cabinet minister was debagged in the tabloid press for betraying his wife by consorting with a two-bit actress; another was exposed on the steps of the Treasury for betraying his country by consorting with a flawed economic plan. Falling into bed with partners other than their wives became the motif that blighted the self-titled 'back to basics' Conservatives as a party of hypercritical and hypocritical politicians epitomised by the fictional Alan B'Stard. Furthermore, falling out of the ERM eventually proved the economic stimulus required to bequeath New Labour a stable and growing economy but which, at the time, announced that the rot had set in and the Conservatives could no longer be trusted to run the economy.

Sexual and financial impropriety, ministerial incompetence and embittered splits over Europe set a course that sent the Conservatives limping into the general election campaign of 1997. And every cut and blow they had suffered after 1992 was contrasted by the growing confidence and popularity of the Labour Party. The untimely death of John Smith in 1994 had robbed Labour of a respected and decent leader but had hastened in a dynamic chemical reaction embodied in the triumvirate of Blair, Mandelson and Campbell, whose ruthlessness, savvy and instinctive grasp of the moment propelled them into Downing Street as heroes awaited by a desperate nation.

As the candidates declared for the Conservative leadership election of 1997 in the fallout of that rout by New Labour it was much to Hague's advantage that, while he had served in the Cabinet as Secretary of State for Wales, he remained a relative unknown, personally untainted by his party's recent failings. He quickly applied the political skills and judgement he had honed as a student operator par excellence and which had seen him conquer both hallowed apprenticeships of the Oxford University Conservative Association, and the Oxford Union. He proved ruthless, in pulling out of a deal to stand alongside the more experienced Michael Howard as his running mate; calculating, in assessing that the post-Portillo party would certainly elect him; and shrewd, in analysing and articulating where his party had failed and how it might address this under his leadership. And, aided by the dramatic last-minute chalk-and-cheese pact of Ken Clarke and John Redwood, William Hague, elected with a clear margin of twenty-two votes over these rivals, went from being the party's young pretender who had set his sights on this role twenty years previously to being its new leader.

The leadership campaign had allowed Hague to play to his strengths: oratory, pragmatism and indefatigability. The internal culture of the Conservative Party, which remained rooted in a pre-Blair age, was familiar to Hague, something he was well able to navigate, but the unforeseen events of the real world would prove far more challenging. During his short stint in Cabinet Hague's communication skills had shone. Unlike others on the right, as he was deemed by virtue of his teenage speeches and Euroscepticism, he had avoided vulgarising his message for popular effect. This intellectual grasp was evident throughout the drawn-out leadership campaign but the most obvious, most easily achievable aim outlined during the campaign was that of party reform and modernisation.

To suggest that Hague was only occupied with the issues of internal reform is to sell short the excellent, nuanced series of speeches which he made analysing the fate that had befallen his party. These were lectures rather than speeches and each indicated that he had recognised the complexity of the journey his party would have to take. One example was the reflection that Conservatives should be able to acknowledge a relationship between deprivation and crime, rather than immediately dismiss such an assertion as an indefensible 'cause and effect' argument. This was subtle stuff – suggesting that the policy rethink would be thorough. It proved too subtle and, in the face of 'events', impossible to apply despite a great deal of strategic policy work which was undertaken through the four years to 2001.

Making practical and tangible policy changes out of the analysis was always going to be tough. Far easier, and far more inclined to make the party feel it was getting on with something and making progress, was the call to internal reform. Creating a structure that would be 'fresh, open and clear' was as close to declaring a new Tory Party that Hague could get without using the word 'new', now monopolised by Labour. It was the first rung on a hoped-for ladder back to electoral success. That this was necessary was not in question, as the famed Conservative Party machine of the mid-1980s had long been in decline and was no match for the professionalised Labour operation. Hague himself demonstrated his commitment to this pledge by seeking confirmation of his own leadership victory, a decision to which only MPs had been privy, by holding a ballot of all party members – the result of which was announced at his first party conference as leader in 1997. Cynics would say this was simply a public relations exercise but for modernisers that was partly the point: finding ways to update the party's practices, and to show this being done, went some way to mirroring the very public and painful transformation that Labour's modernisers had successfully exemplified through the infamous 'Clause 4' moment.

Hague's own leadership election was thus the last to be decided wholly by his party's MPs. The extension of the franchise thereafter has given all party members a vote in the final ballot between the two candidates who have won through initial rounds decided by the MPs. It was a bold change yet, had he not made it, it would have left the party open to ridicule as an organisation that did not trust its own members despite a economic philosophy that expounded the wisdom of trusting the market. There is no evidence either that the move has energised the party base or encouraged new members to join. A less reported but important achievement of the reforms however has been, ironically, the increased security afforded to leaders in office. William Hague had sat in Cabinet throughout the years that John Major's leadership was blighted by constant speculation of stalking horse challenges. The Hague reforms appeared to give members more power but, by requiring a greater proportion of MPs to sign up to any leadership challenge, fewer opportunities to use that power are likely. Most Conservative supporters will consider that a reasonable balance. That the final say in any leadership election falls to the members may be democratic but whether it has been electorally helpful to the party is less obvious.

Taking party reform as a benchmark there is no doubt that a great deal was done by Hague, much of which was less headline-catching than changing the leadership selection, but was essential to establishing an organisation that can operate in a digital age. The main positive achievement was to unite the disparate sections of the party – voluntary, professional and elected – under one structure and leadership. This has allowed for a clearer chain of command

and for national membership lists, an essential tool for modern campaigning, and for establishing a wider financial contributory base. Hague's championing of party treasurer Michael Ashcroft was not without controversy but proved a shrewd decision for the party's finances went from dire in 1997 to sustainable in 2001, very much due to Michael, later Lord, Ashcroft's efforts.

Such 'below the line' reforms are not of great interest beyond the party's 'Egyptologists' despite being an essential part of rebuilding the machine. But, there was an associated debate about modernisation in which policy and image, partly informed by these internal matters, coincided. Labour had commandeered the cause of modernisation and that seemed to run through everything New Labour had done, so it was personified by its leaders, exemplified in its values and demonstrated in its policy platform. Hague's Conservative Party never achieved that harmonious balance. His capacity to make an impact with policy was limited both by external events and by his own image deficit. He talked about modernisation and to an extent achieved that in his reforms but his own style just did not meet the metropolitan tastes of his age. Early photo opportunities of Hague and new wife Ffion at the Notting Hill Carnival appeared inauthentic and inconsistent. For a man who championed the Countryside Alliance in its defence of fox-hunting and who sneered at the bogeyman 'liberal elite' a cloth cap and whippets would have been more appropriate than the baseball cap of another disastrous press release, revealing the poor judgement of his advisors but suggesting even worse; a party out of step with its country.

No incident better revealed this clash of cultures than the first and greatest unforeseen event that he encountered as leader. The death of Princess Diana rocked a nation and thereafter hindered Hague's capacity to reach out beyond his core vote. The way in which we reacted to this death dramatically challenged traditional assumptions about 'Britishness' and British behaviour. If the stuttering decline of John Major's government had seemed to mark the strange death of Conservative England, certainly the unprecedented public outpouring of grief for Diana marked even more the passing of small-'c' conservative England.

At that moment it was Tony Blair who spoke to the nation's mood. Spontaneous and affectionate, he personified our latest move away from conventional formality to a new informal and evolving set of social mores. Blair emoted for Britain. His were the values of 'cool Britannia' and 'dress-down Friday' and 'calling teachers by their first name' versus those of the 'old school tie', the 'stiff upper lip' and the 'Sunday roast' with which Hague, regardless of the accuracy of that perception, was associated. For Conservatives these new gods seemed suspiciously modish, attempts to reinvent rusting but renewable wheels. But, like it or not, established institutions including the Tory Party itself, the Church, royalty and even Marks & Spencer had been crumbling, largely due to liberalising reforms the Conservatives had themselves set in train. Society was increasingly diverse, choices increasingly numerous, and issues of identity and community increasingly complex. Post the high-water marks of socialism and capitalism consumerism had become the most observed 'ism' of the age and, taking its lead from the high street, New Labour has grasped the importance of packaging and presentation, of 'rebranding'. Hague's low-key tribute to Princess Diana revealed a man who quite reasonably did not want to claim the right to grieve publicly for a woman he barely knew. But his restraint seemed anachronistic, and worse, uncaring, recalling Nicholas Soames, then Defence Minister, and his pre-election criticisms of Diana's worthwhile crusade against landmines. And that brand was certainly out of favour. Outdated and hard-hearted – two characteristics that research proved were still indelibly and damagingly associated with Tories. According to popular perception Tony Blair, actually a public schoolboy, was 'blokeish' and appealing, whereas Hague, a comprehensive pupil, was assumed elitist and detached.

This one incident encapsulated the ways in which the political battleground had evolved. At the '97 election New Labour had shown, with devastating effect, that it understood, and had largely defined, this new territory. Labour had stopped fighting the battles they could no longer win and conceded the case for privatisation, low taxation, a sound economy and strong defences. They selected instead to fight culture wars (urban versus country, youth versus age, inclusive versus exclusive, broad-minded versus narrow-minded, Oasis versus opera) and to fill in the gaps that Thatcherism had not thought worth addressing. Equipped with the solid economy bequeathed by a Conservative government New Labour had appeared to offer the public a way to have it all – a 'third way' – that allowed us both to be acquisitive and compassionate.

This was a conundrum for the Conservatives – or at least for those who recognised how things had changed, as Hague while running for leadership indicated that he had. On the one hand, Labour had risen to power on the back of Tory economic policies, so where was the need for the Conservatives either to change or to apologise? On the other, Tories were clearly hated, so surely they must concede some public penitence and illustrate a changed agenda? With no immediate or obvious agreement on this dilemma, Hague decided to spend some time feeling for a resolution, hence the early energy spent on party reform.

The profound nature of the party's defeat had hit very deeply, producing something of a psychological trauma for many involved. The more that the party command came to grasp the depth of its problems the more this seemed to militate against making any significant decisions about direction. In practice William Hague took a sort of non-decision, choosing in the early months after defeat to keep the party's profile low, addressing only its immediate problems such as continued disagreements on their euro policy. Given the way the parliamentary party had torn itself apart over each painful step towards the closer integration of EU members the fact that Hague was able to halt that process of self-harm was a notable achievement. During his leadership campaign he had successfully developed a formula that placated both sides of the Tory euro debate. Essentially he deferred any absolute statement on British entry into the euro by ruling it out, not in principle, but over the course of the next two parliaments. The Conservatives would oppose any Labour moves to join the euro and themselves stand at the next election on that policy but would hold open, technically at least, the possibility of review should circumstances require.

It was a fix that proved a more compelling offer than the implausible union of Clarke and Redwood, so securing the leadership for Hague, but which sustained him also once he held office. After years of internecine warfare within his party Hague had at least united his remaining team. Unlike John Major, for whom Eurosceptics were a constant source of tension, Hague faced relatively little rebellion over Europe and what there was came from the euro enthusiasts, the best known of whom flirted openly with Blair in his 'big tent'.

The election rout of 1997 had bequeathed to Hague, simply through natural selection, a predominantly Eurosceptic parliamentary party. Coupled with that, his adept compromise over policy had certainly helped to ease those tensions that had previously threatened to rip the party apart. This presented William Hague with the tools to effect his most significant achievement as leader, and yet within that also lay one of the reasons he would be judged a failure in 2001. The dichotomy was thus; Hague correctly gauged that despite the flummery of New Labour many British people remained if not sceptical then certainly cautious about the European project and particularly of joining the euro. In campaigning to stay out of the euro Hague performed a national service in many ways at the expense of his own party because in so doing he summoned up again the whiff of the reactionary, the impression of bigotry, the smattering of chauvinism that had bedevilled Conservatism for a decade at least. In poll after poll the Conservative Party 'flatlined' after 1997, seldom claiming over 30 per cent support, and yet achieved a national victory in the European election results of 1999. For once Hague could claim success, but at what cost? The result seemed to vindicate a hardening of campaign rhetoric thereafter up to 2001. More worryingly, Europe became again the Conservatives' calling card, obscuring any policy work that had been developed on public services.

Public opinion polls consistently revealed too that the British people simply couldn't see William Hague as a leader. Surprisingly there were moments when Hague himself, however phlegmatic and resolute his character, underestimated the extent of the power he could command as leader. The transition to leadership had not been without effort but it had followed a faultless trajectory. The man had known only the love and security of a strong family and good friends alongside academic, professional and political success. This was not a leader whose ambition had been fuelled by childhood tragedy or an existential crisis. At thirty-six, he had never known bereavement, divorce or illness.

So Hague arrived as leader well-disposed to his fellow person and perhaps a little unseasoned and rather naïve. However brilliantly he had tackled the on-paper challenges of Insead business school and his job at McKinsey it hadn't prepared him for some of the personnel crises he would encounter as leader. If Bill Clinton had 'bimbo eruptions' William Hague could have been said to have 'big beast battles'. A betrayal by his own appointed leader in the House of Lords, Viscount Cranborne, was undermining. Here Hague, the young commoner, was pitched against an embodiment of inherited privilege, steeped in history. Cranborne had gone behind his leader's back to strike a deal on Lords reform with Tony Blair leaving Hague no option but to sack him. Although a decisive move, it had been forced on Hague and it damaged his credibility.

Far worse was his public endorsement of Lord Archer. Frequently teased by the press for taking judo sessions in Archer's private gym, Hague's approval of Archer extended to backing him as the Conservative candidate for the newly established elections for London Mayor. Any advantage the party might have gained from abandoning its objections to Blair's constitutional change for London was then lost in the public relations fiasco that followed Archer's exposé for perjury. The Conservative Party had surrounded his selection as its mayoral candidate with great fanfare, despite him having been a misadvised option throughout the process. Many people warned Hague that it was a risky choice. Even if Archer had not been proved a crook he had never been a serious politician and was hardly equipped to take on Labour in its metropolitan heartland. Hague should have realised this, he should not have backed him or allowed their friendship to cloud his judgement. It was an indication of inexperience, Hague's and his team, which for all of its emphasis on modernisation never came close to the effectiveness of its New Labour nemesis.

Throughout the first two years of Hague's leadership the noises which the party made about policy development appeared hesitant and indistinct. Relaunches and policy briefings came branded with well-intentioned catch phrases such as 'Compassionate Conservatism' to address the caring deficit and 'Kitchen Table Conservatism' to reflect voters' day-to-day priorities. Hague and his shadow team embarked on a national tour to listen to Britain. Clever advisors identified the urgent need for the party to be seen to understand and reflect the issues which voters determined as their priorities. These were education, health and transport rather than the Conservative favourites of Europe and defence, even if Tony Blair engaged the British forces in combat from the early days of his premiership. For these four years the economy had been largely neutralised as an issue. Conservatives could hardly mention it without reminding voters that they had overseen the drama of the exit from the ERM. Was this something the party should apologise for? Hague decided yes, much to the chagrin of some colleagues, but it was not enough to give the party a credible voice in opposing Chancellor Gordon Brown's early and reckless mismanagement of the economy. No one listened to Conservatives opposing New Labour's early raid on the pension funds or on the nation's gold reserves. The Conservatives themselves did not fully scrutinise Brown's badly constructed reforms of banking supervision, actually favouring extended independence to the central bank and missing the dangers that were lurking in the detail. This was not an oversight that made the party any more unpopular with the public at the time, but in assessing Hague's success as a leader this episode, for all the economic misery that it engendered, is worth remembering. New Labour's popularity when first in government, coupled with its powerful Commons majority, meant the business of opposition was tough, but on this matter it's as well for the Conservatives (and indeed for most of the media) that scant scrutiny has since been paid to their mutual ineffectiveness.

The return of Michael Portillo in a by-election in 1999 brought Hague a prominent and respected new colleague. He wisely promoted Portillo immediately but in the new shadow Chancellor Hague had ushered in a version, though less exaggerated, of the dysfunctional relationship between the actual

Chancellor and Prime Minister. Portillo was on a mission to modernise and was keen to make statement breaks with the toxic Tory past. He tore up the party's tax guarantee policy, on which many had hoped to fight the 2001 election, abandoned Conservative opposition to the minimum wage and approved further Bank of England independence. On such matters he had Hague's support but tension grew rapidly around the less tangible issues of tone and messaging. By this stage in the parliament the only successes that the Conservatives had scored appeared to come through reverting to their traditional values. It was being noted in the press, which alleged a 'lurch to the right'. Throughout 1999 there certainly had been a shift that confused and diffused the initial impression of an outreaching, broad-minded Conservatism that Hague had sought to articulate in his first months as leader.

What it seemed Hague had tried to do early on was address and correct many of the negative impressions about the Conservative Party. At some points this meant apologising, as he did about the ERM fiasco, to mark a public penance. At others it meant being seen to listen rather than to preach. In some cases it was about demythologising abstract testaments of the Tory faith, such as tax cuts, explaining why these can be benign rather than opportunist, how it can be possible to cut taxes and yet improve public services. And of course it meant addressing those areas, most notably the public services, which had concerned voters in a far more immediate way than the Tories' pre-election preoccupation with the threat to the Union and the nation. But delivered to select audiences during the prolonged New Labour honeymoon these arguments were never likely to register much with the general public now relieved of its recent constant diet of politics. That was not, however, sufficient reason to set aside the logic of their message. Given the real length of the Tory decline, from the poll tax through to 1997, it was always the case that 'rebranding' the Conservatives would be a long job, just as it had been for Labour. The route map, in so far as there was one, was in the model New Labour had developed. Although New Labour's pollster Philip Gould's insider account of this coup was required reading at Central Office in the early months of Hague's leadership, there were subsequently too many changes of direction for its central message, 'it's a long haul', to have made sufficient impact.

Hague was hardly the first politician, and certainly not the first Tory leader, to claim resolutely that he paid no attention to opinion poll results, but clearly after two and half years of his leadership the pressure was on for him to score some obvious successes. By switching his focus away from the long-term 'vision thing' to reacting more forcefully to the immediate concerns of any given day, Hague did raise his profile and, at certain points, the poll ratings of his party – most notably by allying himself with hauliers and motorists protesting at fuel price rises in autumn 2001. But his so-called 'lurch to the right' with its particular preoccupations of Section 28, Tony Martin and asylum issues raised the spectre of a very different kind of Hague leadership, not one with which Michael Portillo, who provocatively associated himself with the Liberal elite, could empathise. The latest brand of Conservatism penned by policy wonks in the party's HQ had borrowed from the practical lessons of the Canadian party, who had recovered from a malaise as deep as their British cousins on the back of a platform of 'common sense' policies. Such a platform was the perfect opportunity to present the party as the true representative of ordinary voters for whom New Labour's 'pizzazz' was no real response to practical, day-to-day problems. Somehow the best intentions of policy makers to present the Conservatives as offering pragmatic solutions morphed instead into a campaign against political correctness.

The pressure to score over the government militated against the required patient reassessment. In opposing Blair's proposals to remove Section 28 from the statute book, Hague had backed an anachronism and summoned up the spectre of the harshest cultural clashes of the Thatcher government. It was an own goal. But unlike all the careful rebranding it was noticed. Hague did make headlines, and reassured a particular right-wing tabloid audience, when he went back to his roots and campaigned on issues that chimed with his own earliest political stimuli. It proved an irresistible urge for him and his tabloid-trained media advisors. On law and order, Hague bristled with indignation at the shame of a lax criminal justice system, but in championing

Tony Martin, the Norfolk farmer who shot an intruder with an illegal firearm and was subsequently revealed to be paranoid, he was too quickly appealing to a cheap and easy sense of moral outrage. With a general election in sight the transition from figurative bandwagon to actual vehicle was seamless.

Finding the temptation to repeat the success of the European election result irresistible, the cool, rational tone of Hague's initial leadership outings was drowned out by sentiment, nostalgia and tourist-souvenir style patriotism of the Conservatives key election platform, the 'save the pound' campaign. Why discuss economics after all when waving a flag from the back of a flat-bed lorry makes a better photo opportunity? Of his generation Hague is the foremost public speaker, with his wounding performances at the despatch box the brightest and best moments of his leadership, but the town centre stand-up routine looked amateurish. It was simply naff. This attempt to appeal to emotion, rather than address coolly the substantial reasons for opposing euro entry, seemed likely also to play to a less benign strain of nationalism. Similarly, the Conservative Party's preoccupation with immigration and asylum issues was likely to play into the hands of its opponents, eager to reinforce old stereotypes of narrow Little Englanders. Perhaps Hague was brave and acted with foresight in raising issues that went on to bedevil both the Labour and coalition governments, but to give it higher priority than public services in the year running up to an election was, at that moment, self-defeating.

This miscalculation was most vividly encapsulated by the speech William Hague made to what would be the last meeting of his party before the 2001 election. The Conservatives' spring forum should have been the perfect springboard for the party's election campaign. Instead, a vision was offered of a Britain under threat of becoming a 'foreign land'. What subtlety there was in the original script was lost in the briefing and reporting of the speech which confirmed a 'dog whistle' appeal to the party's core vote. The proposal that a Britain which had joined the euro and lived under the yoke of a European super-state was effectively a foreign land was maybe not so controversial, but the inevitable conflation of the words with the rest of the party's rhetoric on immigration suggested an old-style reactionary. When Hague hesitated shortly afterwards, for human reasons perhaps, to condemn fully the racist statements of one of his retiring MPs the liberal elite, whether in the media, or even in the shadow Cabinet as allies of Michael Portillo, had their own prejudices about him and his leadership confirmed.

In the moment that William Hague resigned with such elegance and self-deprecation on the front drive of Conservative Central Office in the early hours of 8 June he instantly rewrote his own political obituaries. He had calculated months previously the numbers of new seats that would be necessary to save his leadership: fewer than twenty, far worse an outcome than was being considered, would mean immediate resignation. And so it proved to be irresistible in the face of only one new MP for the Tory benches. His self-critical resignation speech revealed the decision, while inevitable, had not been without deep regret and was not simply a mathematical construction. What it did not reveal was the fear that, had he fought to stay on, making the case for continuity over further disruption, the relationship between himself and Michael Portillo would have become unsustainable. One of them had had to go. Given how brutal the result, it was better that Hague usher in a leadership election than have one forced on him.

So poor was this election result for the Conservatives that no commentator or politician considered asking whether William Hague's core vote approach had at least prevented things getting any worse for the Conservatives. Might the party actually have lost seats in 2001 had it indeed stuck with the logic of the first two years of Hague's modernising approach? This seems extremely unlikely given that Hague's departure then ushered in the worst four years of the party's modern history, seeing it adopting two more leaders who tried to pick up from where Hague had left off in 2001. Only when David Cameron revived the modernising tone again after 2005 did things start to improve. Of course Cameron did not have to contend with the after-glow of the New Labour victory of 1997 but by identifying issues that voters prioritised as their key concerns he found a seam to mine which neither Iain Duncan Smith nor Michael Howard, any more than William Hague, managed to do.

William Hague's huge achievement for which his nation should always be grateful was to needle Tony Blair to such an extent that the Prime Minister, whose mandate allowed him to have taken Britain into the euro, found himself lacking the courage to do so. William Hague's flatbed lorry was vulgar but it was effective in rallying the anti-European sentiment that Blair hadn't dared take on, let alone to challenge at the expense of the counsel of his Chancellor, Gordon Brown. However, in so doing, William Hague did not in any way move the public's perception of his party. Perhaps it might have slipped further back and lost even more seats. But in politics momentum is vital and to have generated no momentum over four years was effectively to fall back. His departure, in many senses selfless, nonetheless inflicted an arguably worse succession on the party. His resignation announcement may have been refreshingly candid but in so being it revealed even more by default than was intended. Its focus on Hague's personality, and his own admission that people had not taken to him, indicated the real failure of the Tories to have made any impact with policies or ideas. True, there was no doubt that William Hague did not strike a natural chord with voters, but his persona would not have become the central issue if the party's message itself had been more coherent and attractive. In blaming his defeat on his personality, Hague was selling himself short but also disguising the more damaging truth: he had failed in 2001 not because he lacked charisma, but because he had lacked a consistent strategy.

CHAPTER 21

IAIN DUNCAN SMITH

TIMOTHY HEPPELL

Iain Duncan Smith's tenure of the Conservative leadership lasted just over two years – not long enough to face the electorate in a general election. Timothy Heppell argues that he was perhaps doomed from the start by a rise to the leadership that left him lacking majority support and vulnerable to internal dissent. That he did not do much to improve this situation was linked to his inability to sufficiently rouse either the party or the electorate. This was due to ineffective communication, his intellectually incoherent policy platform that only gestured towards moderation and modernisation, and failures of both short-term tactics and long-term strategy. As a result, Heppell concludes that Duncan Smith's leadership was a painful lesson in the importance of effective statecraft.

• • •

Iain Duncan Smith, often referred to by his initials IDS, served as Conservative Party leader between September 2001 and October 2003. His rise to the leadership was rapid and unexpected, and his exit was swift and brutal.[657] Considering IDS a decade after his eviction reveals that he experienced a strange career trajectory and that it was significantly different from that of his Conservative predecessors. He entered Parliament in 1992 and was quickly identified as a pure Thatcherite – economically liberal, socially

---

657 Tim Heppell, *Choosing the Tory Leader: Conservative Party Leadership Elections from Heath to Cameron*, London, I. B. Tauris, 2008, pp. 131–70.

conservative and Eurosceptic.[658] Although not a habitual rebel during the passage of the Treaty of European Union in 1992–93, he could by no sense be described as a loyalist.[659] In the aftermath of their electoral meltdown in May 1997 he acted as the campaign manager for John Redwood in his leadership challenge. Once Redwood was eliminated he switched his support to William Hague (rather than backing Kenneth Clarke as Redwood did).[660] His reward for backing Hague was promotion to the shadow Cabinet, where he served as shadow Social Security Secretary between 1997 and 1998, and then shadow Defence Secretary between 1998 and 2001.

His rise to the party leadership in September 2001, after the humiliating defeat that Hague suffered in the general election of that year, was a consequence of the fact that the Conservatives had changed their leadership selection and ejection rules in 1998. Using the so-called 'Hague rules', IDS would become the first leader to have a leadership mandate from party members. He defeated Clarke on a 'one member, one vote' (OMOV) ballot by 61 to 39 per cent.[661]

However, the sense that this provided him with a stronger mandate was undermined by two factors. First, the eliminative parliamentary ballots demonstrated that two-thirds of the Parliamentary Conservative Party (PCP) had not backed him (IDS had fifty-four backers to Clarke on fifty-nine, with Michael Portillo eliminated with fifty-three). Second, his mandate may have flowed from the membership, but any decision to evict was in the hands of the PCP alone. The new confidence motion for evicting an incumbent meant that triggering his removal was theoretically straightforward. Critics needed the support of only twenty-five Conservative MPs to activate a confidence motion; they did not need an alternative candidate; and IDS needed

658 Tim Heppell, 'The Ideological Composition of the Parliamentary Conservative Party 1992 to 1997', *British Journal of Politics and International Relations*, 4(2), 2002, p. 315.

659 Keith Alderman and Neil Carter, 'The Conservative Party Leadership Election of 2001', *Parliamentary Affairs*, 55(3), 2002, p. 573.

660 Hywel Wiliams, *Guilty Men: Conservative Decline and Fall 1992–1997*, London, Aurum, 1998, p. 226.

661 Bale, op. cit., p. 144.

eighty-four votes (a majority of the 166-strong PCP) in the confidence motion, when only fifty-four had originally wanted him. In October 2003, just over two years after being elected by the members, IDS was ejected by his fellow Conservative parliamentarians with ninety expressing no confidence in him and seventy-five supporting him. Such was their lack of faith in his abilities that they removed him before facing the electorate in a general election rather than after. However, given the limitations that IDS would showcase between 2001 and 2003 the question is not why he was axed, but why the executioner took so long.[662]

DID IDS FACE DIFFICULT CIRCUMSTANCES?

The Leader of the Opposition needs to demonstrate that they are a Prime Minister in waiting, and the primary problem for IDS was that too few believed that he could become Prime Minister. The second part of this chapter will analyse how and why this impression was created. However, before considering his performance it is important to outline the constraints that undermined him.

IDS acquired the leadership and then operated during the age of New Labour dominance.[663] New Labour established a reputation for governing competence as they delivered prolonged economic growth, falling unemployment and low inflation rates.[664] The additional tax revenues that were the by-product of a booming economy enabled them to invest in public services without increasing income tax. Critically in an age of prosperity the Conservatives struggled to respond to New Labour framing electoral competition as a choice between cuts under the Conservatives or growth and investment under New Labour.[665]

---

662 Ibid., p. 193.

663 Tom Bentley, 'British Politics after Tony Blair', *British Politics*, 2(2), 2007, pp. 111–17.

664 Andrew Gamble, 'New Labour and Political Change', *Parliamentary Affairs*, 63(4), 2010, p. 648.

665 Bale, op. cit., p. 5.

Demonstrating governing competence helped to solidify the reputation of Tony Blair as a highly effective political leader. Blair was the personification of New Labour. This was reflective of the shift away from positional class-based politics and towards valence politics, where identification flowed as much through demonstrating leadership competence. For New Labour electoral strategy was about inspiring trust within the electorate in the leadership abilities of Blair.[666] The perception that Blair was a strong and assertive political leader contributed to the handsome parliamentary majorities that New Labour secured in 1997 (179) and 2001 (167). Indeed, it could be argued that IDS inherited the leadership of the party in the aftermath of their worst electoral performance ever. The Conservative return of 8,500,000 votes was actually 1,250,000 fewer than in 1997. The slight increase in their vote share (up from 30.7 to 31.7 per cent) was a reflection of a low turnout (59.4 per cent as opposed to 71.3 per cent in 1997), and a larger turnout would probably have resulted in an even heavier defeat.[667]

Not only did IDS have the parliamentary arithmetic and the economic cycles working against him, but he also faced an unfavourable media climate. New Labour had secured the backing of the majority of the British press. Six out of ten papers backed New Labour in 1997, and remained broadly supportive by the time of IDS. The most notable conversion had been by *The Sun*, and thus IDS was not able to benefit from the aggressive anti-Labour propaganda that had, for example, been a defining feature of the 1992 general election.[668]

It was not just the economic, parliamentary, leadership and media context that was working against him. IDS suffered from the circumstances through which he had become leader of the party. As was identified in the introduction to this chapter, IDS was the first leader selected via the new

---

666 Alan Finlayson, 'Elements of the Blairite Image of Leadership', *Parliamentary Affairs*, 55(3), 2002, pp. 586–99.

667 David Butler and Dennis Kavanagh, *The British General Election of 2001*, Basingstoke, Palgrave, 2001, pp. 251–64.

668 Raymond Kuhn, 'Media Management', in Anthony Seldon ed., *Blair's Britain 1997–2007*, Cambridge, Cambridge University Press, 2007, pp. 129–31.

hybrid system known as the Hague rules. The system operated in two stages. Stage one was the eliminative parliamentary ballots, through which the two leading candidates went forward to stage two: an OMOV ballot of Conservative members. Given the overwhelmingly Thatcherite inclinations of the PCP, it could be argued that a credible pure Thatcherite candidate (i.e. economic liberal, socially conservative Eurosceptic) should have secured a substantial final ballot lead, but IDS secured only fifty-four votes behind Clarke on fifty-nine.[669] It has been argued that IDS secured his passage through to the membership ballot because he was *not* Portillo – i.e. socially conservative MPs feared the social liberalism of Portillo and thus voted IDS to block off Portillo. It has also been suggested that he won the membership ballot because he was *not* Clarke – i.e. the broadly Eurosceptic membership feared the divisiveness of selecting the most Europhilic Conservative as their leader.[670]

A conundrum would exist with regard to his mandate to lead. He had the backing of 60.7 per cent of the party membership who voted – (i.e. 155,933 votes for him as compared to 100,864 for Clarke on 39.3).[671] This was a stronger mandate than those received by any newly elected leader since the onset of democratisation: Heath, 49.3 per cent in 1965; Thatcher 47.1 per cent in 1975; Major 49.7 per cent in 1990; or Hague 56.1 per cent – all of which were PCP ballots, not membership ballots.[672] IDS could also feel that his mandate was stronger because it came from the membership; a claim that no previous leader could make. However, his PCP support base was weaker than all of his predecessors in the democratised era, partly due to the new eliminative electoral procedures being used. In the final ballot he received only fifty-four supporters (or 32.5 per cent of the PCP). Critically, however, the decision on whether to remove him rested in the hands

---

669 Heppell, op. cit., 2008, p. 158.

670 Richard Hayton, 'Iain Duncan Smith, 2001–03', in Tim Heppell ed., *Leaders of the Opposition: From Churchill to Cameron*, Basingstoke, Palgrave, 2012, p. 198.

671 Heppell, op. cit., 2008, p. 147.

672 Ibid. p. 149.

of the PCP and not the membership.[673] Holding a disputed mandate to lead, his security as leader rested on his ability to demonstrate leadership competence.[674]

HOW SHOULD WE JUDGE IDS AS A PARTY LEADER?

The main problem for IDS was that he lacked political credibility. Initially his poor reputation stemmed from two factors. First, he was not respected by some of his colleagues on an intellectual level. Second, not only did some colleagues feel that he was 'not very bright' but they also doubted him for being 'not very loyal'.[675] Those who had worked in the Whips' Office in the Major government, and who had dealt with IDS the abstainer or rebel, 'were convinced that [he] neither should *nor* could lead the party'.[676]

These doubts were then compounded by his poor communication skills once he was leader.[677] In Parliament, his performances against Blair at Prime Minister's questions were lamentable. His interventions were characterised by embarrassing pauses and coughs and his inability to at least match Blair, let alone outsmart or outpoint him, undermined morale among the PCP.[678] These communicative limitations were also evident in television interviews. Here he simply failed to present his message 'convincingly'.

His advisors attempted to portray him as an antidote to the presentational slickness of Blair and New Labour. This led to the rhetorical presentation of IDS as the 'quiet man' at the 2002 annual conference. However, it made no

673 Hayton, op. cit., p. 198.

674 Richard Hayton and Timothy Heppell, 'The Quiet Man of British Politics: The Rise, Fall and Significance of Iain Duncan Smith', *Parliamentary Affairs*, 63(3), 2010, p. 450.

675 Bale, op. cit., p. 139.

676 Ibid. pp. 138–9.

677 Hayton, op. cit., p. 199.

678 Simon Walters, *Tory Wars: Conservatives in Crisis*, London, Politicos, 2001, p. 225.

impact upon opinion polling rating of the party.[679] Although he was widely mocked for the 'quiet man' speech, IDS decided to return to it and adapt it at the 2003 annual conference. In a 'toe-curling' speech he announced that 'the quiet man is here to stay, and he is turning up the volume'.[680]

These limitations meant that the policy agenda that IDS would attempt to develop was either ignored or criticised by an unsympathetic press. However, despite being perceived to be a pure Thatcherite IDS initially tried to reorient Conservatism and apply it to its post-Thatcherite environment. He recognised the need to address the perception that the Conservatives were seen as narrow, selfish and elitist, and which led Theresa May in 2002 to admit that the Conservatives were seen as the 'nasty party'.[681]

To address these image problems IDS initially wanted to downgrade the emphasis on traditional Thatcherite themes such as Europe, immigration and taxation. Indeed, it can be argued that IDS brought greater clarity to their position on Europe. He feared that the Conservatives undermined themselves by their focus on Europe. This was not a priority for the electorate and it was the issue that solidified perceptions of Conservative divisions. Moreover, IDS felt that the European approach that he had inherited from Hague was intellectually incoherent. The 2001 general election campaign had been dominated by the importance of saving the pound, but the official party position was to rule out membership of the single currency for the lifetime of the next parliament. IDS felt that this lacked credibility. He would move to a harder but quieter position.[682] The single currency option was ruled out permanently and by doing so the debate subsided (temporarily as it turned out as, post-IDS, the battle between Europhiles and Eurosceptics morphed into a battle between soft Eurosceptics and hard Eurosceptics). That this was possible in the 2001–03 period was partly aided by the smaller number

679 Andrew Denham and Kieron O'Hara, *Democratising Conservative Leadership Selection: From Grey Suits to Grass Roots*, Manchester, Manchester University Press, 2008.

680 Hayton, op. cit., p. 200.

681 Bale, op. cit., p. 162–5.

682 Ibid., pp. 146–7

of Europhiles within the PCP by the 2001 parliament (only eight identified Europhiles as opposed to 149 Eurosceptics and nine agnostic or neutral).[683]

This rhetorical downgrading of traditional Thatcherite themes was intended to give the Conservatives the space to focus on tackling poverty and emphasising their commitment to improving public services.[684] These policy developments under IDS would be encapsulated by two documents – *Leadership with a Purpose: A Better Society* (2002) and *A Fair Deal for Everyone* (2003). In *Leadership with a Purpose,* IDS identified the five priorities that would guide his new administration: schools, crime prevention, health care, child poverty and insecurity in old age. IDS appeared to have taken a clear strategic line. Their critique of New Labour should be based on delivery of public services and this should be the new narrative for Conservatism.[685] *A Fair Deal for Everyone* reinforced much of the above but placed an added emphasis on inner city deprivation.[686]

However, the new approach was problematic in two ways. First, a gap existing between the inclusive rhetoric of helping the vulnerable and prioritising public services delivery over cuts in taxation, and the solutions that were being advocated. The rhetoric that no one would be 'left behind' was designed to reassure those who questioned the Conservatives' motives and feared that they were 'nasty', 'extreme' and 'strange' – this was the rhetoric designed for 'brand decontamination'.[687] However, the very same people who feared the Conservatives' motives were then being presented with policy solutions that appeared to solidify and continue Thatcherism. The more detailed policy solutions on health and education, but also with regard to care for the elderly, 'seemed directed at wooing affluent voters by subsidising them

683 Tim Heppell and Michael Hill, 'The Voting Motivations of Conservative Parliamentarians in the Conservative Party Leadership Election of 2001', *Politics*, 30(1), 2010, p. 46.

684 Hayton and Heppell, op. cit., p. 430.

685 Andrew Taylor, 'Economic Statecraft', in Kevin Hickson ed., *The Political Thought of the Conservative Party since 1945*, Basingstoke, Palgrave, 2005, pp. 149–51.

686 Bale, op. cit., p. 179.

687 Ibid., pp. 158, 165.

to go private or doing away with means-testing'.[688] The rhetoric may have been designed to broaden their appeal, but behind the rhetoric appeared to be a commitment to 'roll back the state' and reward 'those who sought independence from it'.[689]

Second, if the message was slightly confusing it was also inconsistent. Having spent the initial period of his leadership tenure committed to matching Labour spending on education and health, this was abandoned in late 2002. The commitment to match spending meant that their critique of the New Labour government would be that a Conservative government would spend the same amount, but more effectively. Abandoning that commitment handed political ammunition to New Labour. How could the Conservatives claim to care about the vulnerable and improve public services by spending less?[690]

The inconsistency in terms of policy formulation has to be viewed within the context of the difficulties in terms of party management that IDS faced. Ironically he managed the European issue reasonably effectively (as discussed above). What exposed him were divisions on morality.

In the era of Conservative opposition the economic divide between dries and wets, that had dominated the Thatcher era, had been effectively won by the dries – in the 2001 PCP there were 121 dries and thirty-four wets (and nine neutral).[691] The European divide between the Europhiles and the Eurosceptics that had disfigured the Major era had been won by the Eurosceptics by the era of IDS (before morphing into the soft and hard Eurosceptic factions over the Cameron era).[692] The most divisive issue within post-Thatcherite Conservatism was the moral, sexual and social policy divide – between traditionalist social conservatives (132 in the 2001 PCP) and modernising social liberals (twenty-five in the 2001 PCP, with nine neutral).[693] On this divide,

688 Ibid., p. 165.

689 Ibid.

690 Ibid., p. 159.

691 Heppell and Hill, op. cit., pp. 36–51.

692 Hayton and Heppell, op. cit., p. 432.

693 Heppell and Hill, op. cit., p. 46.

IDS got himself in a terrible tangle. Despite being by instinct a traditionalist, he had been trying to make 'change' an emblem of leadership and his reorientation of the policy agenda. This meant that traditionalists become wary of his emphasis on change, but modernisers doubted the sincerity of his efforts and the extent to which he would countenance change.[694]

A parliamentary division on the adoption of children by homosexual unmarried couples (November 2002) would showcase IDS as a maladroit party manager.[695] An effective party manager would have identified two issues. First, it was inevitable that the New Labour government would prevail given their parliamentary majority. Second, as this was a conscience issue, parliamentary tradition suggested that permitting a free vote would be acceptable and would draw only limited attention to Conservative divisions on this issue. Defying logic and precedent, IDS imposed a three-line whip instructing the PCP to vote against the legislation. In the ensuing parliamentary division, eight Conservatives voted with the government (including Clarke and Portillo) and a further thirty-five abstained.[696] Having drawn attention to their divisions that could have been minimised by a free vote, IDS then compounded his original mistake by holding a hastily arranged press conference. Attempting to demonstrate strength, but showcasing weakness, IDS announced that: 'For a few, last night's vote was not about adoption but an attempt to challenge my mandate to lead the party … the party had to "unite or die".'[697]

This was a self-induced crisis.[698] It represented a failure of short-term tactics, but it also raised questions about his longer-term strategic thinking. He had spent a considerable amount of time trying to emphasise how the party needed to change. Early on in his leadership tenure he stated that the party would have to go through the 'necessary and sometimes painful process of

694 Hayton, op. cit., p. 205.

695 Ibid., p. 204.

696 Philip Cowley and Mark Stuart, 'Still Causing Trouble: The Conservative Parliamentary Party', *Political Quarterly*, 75(4), 2004, pp. 356–61.

697 Philip Norton, 'The Conservative Party: The Politics of Panic', in *Britain at the Polls*, John Bartle and Anthony King eds, Washington, CQ Press, 2005, p. 39.

698 Snowdon, op. cit., p. 109.

modernisation' and yet he had now 'sided with the traditionalists on such an iconic issue'.[699]

IDS is also open to criticism in terms of his people management skills, both in terms of relations within the shadow Cabinet and within Conservative Central Office. Many of the most credible and high-profile Conservatives – notably Clarke and Portillo – were unwilling to serve within his shadow Cabinet.[700] Credible figures within the Clarke campaign team – Ian Taylor, Andrew Tyrie, John Maples, and David Curry – were not offered positions. Key players within the IDS campaign team were, however, offered positions including Bernard Jenkin (Defence) and John Whittingdale (Trade and Industry). The perception that the new shadow Cabinet 'drew disproportionately from the right'[701] seemed a plausible claim given the above and the appointments of Liam Fox (shadow Health Minister), Eric Forth (shadow Leader of the House), Michael Howard (shadow Chancellor) and David Davis (Conservative Party chair). The appointment of the notorious Eurosceptic rebel, Bill Cash, as shadow Attorney General, prompted one disaffected moderate to note that IDS had 'handed over control of the asylum to the lunatics'.[702]

Inside a year, however, Davis would be demoted. An increasingly insecure IDS decided to marginalise the ambitious Davis (switched to local government spokesperson) as he feared Davis still retained leadership aspirations. That the reshuffle was conducted while Davis was on holiday prompted 'media hysteria' and gave an impression of cowardice. Davis was not the only senior Conservative to make IDS feel insecure. He was also anxious about Portillo. This would put him on a collision course with three key players in Conservative Central Office: party chief executive Mark MacGregor, director of field operations Stephen Gilbert, and head of the Conservative Research Department Rick Nye. Assuming they were all aligned to the Portillo modernising

699 Bale, op. cit., p. 167.

700 Ibid. p. 145.

701 Hayton, op. cit., p. 206.

702 Bale, op. cit., p. 145.

faction, IDS removed them from their positions.[703] IDS then proposed that Barry Legg, a Thatcherite Eurosceptic ally in the 1992–97 parliament, should assume the position of chief executive. IDS made this decision without consulting the seventeen-member party board, which was technically responsible for making the appointment. However, after initially assuming the role of chief executive, Legg was forced out when the party board refused to ratify his appointment. Michael Spicer, chair of the 1922 Committee, would later reveal that IDS was 'almost in tears' and had threatened to resign unless the party board endorsed Legg.[704] During this chaotic period, IDS saw his credibility eroded further over the removal of Gilbert, who was 'reinstated following protests from the board'.[705]

Therefore, it is clear that his ability to provide effective leadership was undermined by his own insecurities and his poor judgement.[706] These factors contributed to inconsistencies and contradictions in terms of the marrying up of political rhetoric and policy solutions. They contributed to both poor short-term tactics and long-term strategy. They also contributed to his difficulties in terms of managing the parliamentary party, the shadow Cabinet and Central Office.[707]

WAS IDS A SUCCESSFUL LEADER?

The barometer for success for a leader who acquires the leadership in opposition is to propel them back into office. So against this definition he has to be defined as a failure. However, Hague (2001) and Howard (2005) were allowed to lead the party into general election campaigns. Rather than wait for the inevitable electoral rejection that would flow from IDS leading them into

703 Hayton, op. cit., p. 207.

704 Michael Spicer, 'Tears of Rage Over Leadership Battle', *Sunday Telegraph*, 1 April 2012.

705 Snowdon, op. cit., p. 110.

706 Ibid., p. 107.

707 Bale, op. cit., p. 134–93.

a general election, the PCP chose to forcibly eject him. It was not defeat itself that caused his removal, it was *fear* of defeat and the *scale* of that defeat.

His removal was made possible because of his failings in terms of his poor public communication, the failure of his policy reappraisal to gain traction and his limited skills as a party manager, as discussed earlier in the chapter. However, the scale of limitations are evident from the additional triggers that contributed to the willingness of his colleagues to initiate a confidence motion against him.

First, throughout his time as leader there was little comfort from the opinion polls, either for the party as a whole or for him individually. For the majority of his tenure the Conservatives trailed Labour (often by double digits), and they would be unable to exploit Blair's evolving unpopularity as the Iraqi crisis unfolded. It was the Liberal Democrats who saw their opinion polling ratings increase by opposing intervention, whereas IDS had backed the government.[708] Academics responded to the rise in support for the Liberal Democrats by speculating about a possible realignment of British party politics. Now it was not just pessimistic Tories who were examining the prospect of the Liberal Democrats replacing the Conservatives as the most credible party of opposition.[709] However, IDS had personal ratings even more dire than the overall ratings of the party. What was also of concern was that they were getting worse as the electorate saw more of him. In June 2002, MORI reported that his net satisfaction rating was minus nine (twenty-four satisfied, thirty-three dissatisfied, forty-three don't know), but, by February 2003, MORI were reporting it was minus thirty-seven (twenty-one satisfied, forty-seven dissatisfied, thirty-two don't know).

Second, as the electorate viewed him as a failure so this would have financial implications for the party. Donations to the Conservatives remained at low levels as those disgruntled with IDS either stopped making donations

708 David Broughton, 'Doomed to Defeat? Electoral Support and the Conservative Party', *Political Quarterly*, 75(4), 2005, pp. 350–55.

709 Paul Webb, 'Parties and Party System: Prospects for Realignment', *Parliamentary Affairs*, 56(2), 2003, pp. 283–96.

or made smaller donations.[710] Few donors made their reservations public until October 2003. Then the millionaire spread betting tycoon, Stuart Wheeler, implied that he would no longer offer financial backing until the party changed leader. Given that Wheeler had donated £5 million to the party during Hague's leadership tenure this was a significant rebuff. Nor was the language ambiguous. Wheeler announced that IDS was 'weak' and 'terribly bad at communicating'.[711] Conservative MPs who were prevaricating over whether to initiate a confidence motion against IDS now had a strong 'financial inducement'.[712] When Howard replaced IDS Wheeler donated £500,000 to the party coffers.[713]

Third, in addition to the electoral perception that he was a failure, and that of key Conservative donors, IDS was now facing the realisation that the Conservative Whips' Office had 'effectively closed down'.[714] By late 2003 the Chief Whip, David Maclean, had come to view one of his tasks as 'regime change'.[715] To facilitate change Maclean was interviewed on television (highly unusual for a Chief Whip) and informed the party of the need to 'lance the boil'.[716] It was a highly manipulative intervention. On face value his interview was an attempt to impose discipline. In reality it was an open invitation to his critics to launch their attack.[717]

Fourth, undermined by poor polling data, and with donors and the Whips' Office removing their backing and defining IDS as a failure, IDS clung to his belief that his mandate from the membership might scare the PCP away from initiating a confidence motion. However, by late 2003 a YouGov poll of Conservative members revealed that (a) a majority of them now believed

710 Justin Fisher, 'Money Matters: The Financing of the Conservative Party', *Political Quarterly*, 75(4), 2004, pp. 406–7.

711 Bale, op. cit., p. 190.

712 Heppell, op. cit., p. 164.

713 Fisher,, op. cit., pp. 406–9.

714 Hayton and Heppell, op. cit., p. 435.

715 Michael Crick, *In Search of Michael Howard*, London, Simon & Schuster, 2005, pp. 422–4.

716 Bale, op. cit., p. 187.

717 Ibid., p. 187.

that they had made a mistake in electing IDS and (b) almost half felt that it was time for him to be replaced.[718]

By October 2003 enough key players within the party now believed that IDS needed to be removed. In the ensuing confidence motion IDS secured the support of seventy-five Conservative MPs (an increase of twenty-one from the fifty-four that voted for him the final parliamentary ballot of 2001) but that amounted to only 45.5 per cent of the PCP. The remaining ninety Conservative MPs (54.5 per cent) voted for his removal. The fear of a long drawn-out succession process when IDS stood down was avoided. Howard was the only candidate who stood for the vacancy. Membership involvement was not required as the Conservatives constructed a modernised version of the old magic circle.[719]

CONCLUSION

Like Hague before him, IDS found himself an ex-leader before he hit the age of fifty, and after only eleven years in Parliament (Hague was forty years old and had been in Parliament twelve years). Most of his predecessors, prior to Hague, were still to acquire the leadership at around the same age and time in Parliament. However, regardless of the limitations that IDS was to demonstrate during his two-year tenure as leader, one has to admire his resilience. After the humiliation of rejection in October 2003 he co-founded the Centre for Social Justice (CSJ) in 2004, and revived his front-bench career when the Conservatives entered office in May 2010, serving as Secretary of State for Work and Pensions. However, whatever he achieves as a Cabinet minister he will be remembered as the worst leader of the Conservative Party since 1945.

His strongest critics would, however, acknowledge that he faced hugely

718 Ibid., p. 186.

719 Norton, op. cit., p. 40.

constraining circumstances. A booming economy gave him few political opportunities to exploit. He faced a massive parliamentary majority, which contributed to low morale within the PCP and doubts about whether they could realistically win at the next general election given the size of the swing required. He was unfortunate to be opposed by one of the more effective prime ministers of the post-war era, and had to do so with a level of press support that few of his Conservative predecessors would have wanted.

In addition to citing difficult circumstances, those who wish to resuscitate his reputation could speak of the significance of IDS in terms of policy development and strategic repositioning. This interpretation would focus in on how it was IDS who took the difficult initial steps in terms of brand decontamination. Although at times lacking in clarity and also not always sustained, IDS made a contribution by transcending the traditional Conservative emphasis on the politics of economy (notably tax) and identity (usually Europe and immigration). He set the parameters for future policy development on the public services and social justice that would be developed in the Cameron opposition era. Cameron extended the process of brand decontamination by adding other areas (environmentalism, feminisation, international aid) and he was able to sustain this process of policy development and strategic repositioning due to three factors. First, Cameron faced a weaker New Labour government undermined by the transition from Blair to Gordon Brown, and then the Brown administration was engulfed by the financial crisis. Second, Cameron was a better political commentator and thus more credible than IDS, but he was also a more astute political operator who managed the party more effectively. Third, due to the first two factors Cameron was able to make an impact in terms of the opinion polls, and thus sustain his brand of modernisation in a way that IDS was not.[720]

However, arguing that IDS was facing difficult circumstances, and that some continuities can be identified between his 2001–02 approach and that of Cameron post-2005, cannot detract from the ineptitude that characterised his

720 Hayton and Heppell, op. cit., pp. 425–55.

leadership. He was devoid of the necessary political skills to be an effective Leader of the Opposition, let alone Prime Minister. He was a weak political communicator and a poor party manager. These limitations undermined both his credibility and his attempts at changing the policy agenda of the party. Anxious and insecure, he lacked either short-term tactical acumen or long-term strategic thinking. His approach to leading the party was erratic. At times he could be consensual and attempt to bridge the divide between socially conservative traditionalists and the socially liberal modernisers, but he could also be dictatorial on issues that were damaging to himself and the party (for example, on the same-sex adoption legislation and in terms of appointments within Central Office).[721]

Many of these limitations became more pronounced because the party continued to flatline in the opinion polls. The crisis of identity that Conservatism continued to face in the post-Thatcher era[722] became personalised around the inadequacies of IDS. The institutional apparatus of the party gradually withdrew its support. Doubts intensified within the shadow Cabinet and within the PCP. Support from Central Office and eventually the Whips' Office ebbed away. When donors withdrew their support it was inevitable, especially as the backing of Conservative members was now questionable, that IDS would be removed via the new confidence motion procedure.[723]

The period between 2001 and 2003 was a painful experience for the Conservatives and especially for IDS. His election on a disputed mandate, characterised by limited support from the PCP, raised questions about the appropriateness of the Hague rules (although an attempt to reform them initiated by Howard in 2005 was rejected). If this was a lesson that the Conservatives did not learn, then their subsequent selection of Cameron in 2005 demonstrated that two lessons had been learned. First, intellect and loyalty

---

721 Hayton, op. cit., p. 208.

722 Richard Hayton, *Reconstructing Conservatism? The Conservative Party in Opposition 1997–2010*, Manchester, Manchester University Press, 2012.

723 Heppell, op. cit., pp. 155–70.

do matter. IDS was perceived to lack the intellect to lead the party. He was also undermined by his back-bench career as a rebel (or abstainer). A leader who was previously a back-bench rebel looks like a hypocrite when as leader they demand loyalty is owed to them. Second, image and communication skills cannot be ignored in the modern political age. Party leadership is about communication and persuasion. Selecting an uncharismatic self-proclaimed 'quiet man' was a strange decision in an era of valence politics when perceptions of leadership image dominate.

CHAPTER 22

MICHAEL HOWARD

TIM BALE

Given the electoral arithmetic Michael Howard inherited and bequeathed, we might conclude that he made a good fist of a difficult hand as leader of the Conservatives between 2003 and 2005. Tim Bale's conclusions are more nuanced, and he outlines Howard's mixed record of leadership. Successes in party management and a return to some sort of electoral progress were matched by little change in the party's offering and over-arching strategy – if anything, ambitions of widening the scope and appeal of the party's message were swiftly abandoned. If existing division and incoherence meant the principal aim of Howard's two years at the helm was to begin the process of rejuvenation and renewal primarily through cohesion and conciliation, he was partially successful. The Conservatives were largely united under Howard, and the 2005 election saw the party with thirty-two more MPs than they had previously, and Labour's majority reduced to sixty-six, though the party's vote share crept up by less than 1 per cent. Overall, though, an inability or unwillingness to address weaknesses in electoral and political strategy remained.

• • •

Michael Howard is quite a contradiction. Rarely is anything written about him without reference to the remark by Ann Widdecombe, who worked under him when he was Home Secretary between 1993 and 1997, that there was 'something of the night' about her former boss – a remark which helped sink his chances of becoming Tory leader some six years before the job eventually dropped into his lap when he was elected unopposed to replace Iain Duncan Smith. And yet anyone who has met Lord Howard will testify to the fact that, on the right day anyway, he has a twinkle in his eye and a wicked sense of humour to match: it was he, after all, who told an interviewer in 2006 that, damaging or not, Widdecombe's words had at least saved him 'from the thankless task of becoming leader of the party in 1997'.

The contradiction extends to his own record. Howard, after all, is a party leader who fought just one election, which he lost heavily, and who was only in the job just two years, the last six months of which he was basically in a caretaker position. And yet his ranking in the tables produced by Charles Clarke for this volume is relatively high: seventh out of seventeen in terms of seats won, and ninth in terms of vote share. Clearly such tables tend to favour leaders who fight elections from opposition and therefore avoid paying the penalty paid by virtually all incumbents. And clearly, given the drubbing the Tories received at the hands of New Labour in 1997 and 2001, it may not be too much of an exaggeration to say that, in 2005, as the shine began to come off Tony Blair in the wake of the Iraq War, the only way was up. Surely, however, there is something in the old adage that the numbers don't lie?

WINNING ELECTORAL STRATEGY

When it comes to the requirement that a leader formulate a winning electoral strategy, there is at first glance very little to say about Michael Howard. By definition, since the Conservatives lost the 2005 general election, he was unable to do this, and even his 'success' in the European and local elections that were held a year before then has to be heavily qualified. Indeed, the way he fought them may actually have been counterproductive in both the short and the medium to long term, since it set in stone a populist approach from which he was subsequently unable and, indeed, unwilling to break free – and one which ultimately may have helped the United Kingdom Independence Party (UKIP) more than it did the Tories.

Most opposition parties use European Parliament elections as a way of testing their attack lines and kicking the government on domestic issues. But not the Tories under Michael Howard. Understandably convinced that he could not simply ignore the revival of the EU Constitutional Treaty, Howard launched a petition for a referendum on the Treaty only to see his fox shot when Blair, prioritising, as usual, long-term electoral success over short-term political embarrassment, executed a screeching U-turn and agreed to hold a referendum. Howard (though only in private) then considered upping the ante by calling for a referendum on a fundamental renegotiation of the UK's membership of the EU – until, that is, he was talked out of it by, among others, David Cameron, then one of the Tories' rising stars, on the grounds that it would only serve to legitimise UKIP, which was already hoping to improve on the 7 per cent it had taken in the 1999 European elections.

Despite this, Howard continued to believe that the Conservatives were best advised to try to outperform their dismal opinion poll ratings by fighting on European issues, presumably in the hope that, in so doing, they would mobilise their supporters to get out and vote while Labour's stayed sullenly at home. Indeed, he ensured that the party's programme, which promised to keep Britain out of 'a country called Europe', was even more sceptical than before, promising to hold a referendum on any future treaty agreed by the EU that would transfer significant powers from Britain to Brussels. The consequences were predictable enough: with a couple of weeks to go, polls suggested UKIP was set to take nearly 20 per cent of the vote in June. The Conservative Research Department responded by sending candidates a misjudged fourteen-page briefing paper on UKIP (leaked to the media) which belittled the party as a home for Little Englanders and for 'cranks and political gadflies'. Worse, perhaps suffering from the fatigue brought on by his travelling 8,000 miles around the country on the campaign trail, Howard chose, as polling day approached, to pray in aid Margaret Thatcher, reminding voters how she had been able to say no to Brussels without leaving the EU. Labour, not for the first or last time, could hardly believe its luck. They were determined to convince the country that

Howard, as well as being an opportunist, was a Thatcherite dinosaur. Now here he was doing their work for them.

The local elections held on the same day in June 2004 as those for the European Parliament looked reasonably good for the Conservatives – but only on the face of it. Extrapolating nationally, the party won 37 per cent of the vote to the Blair government's miserable 26 per cent – a figure so low that Labour was beaten into third place by the Lib Dems. However, there was little genuine cause for celebration, especially when one compares the result with, say, the local elections of 2000, when Hague had won a notional 38 per cent to Labour's 29 per cent, only to lose the following year's general election by a landslide. In the Europeans, Labour did appallingly badly, taking just 22.6 per cent of the vote nationally – its lowest share since 1918. The Lib Dems were also disappointed by their 14.9 per cent. But the Tory result – 26.7 per cent of the vote – was 9 per cent down on its performance under William Hague in 1999 and the worst the party had obtained at a national election since 1832. It was rendered all the more wounding by the fact that UKIP had won 16.1 per cent and by post-election polls which revealed that 45 per cent of UKIP voters had supported the Conservatives in 2001 (as opposed to 20 per cent who had supported Labour).

The rational response to this, perhaps, would have been to re-think the strategy for the general election, and to stop staking out positions which effectively signalled that the Conservative Party was still obsessed with Europe and immigration and, when it could tear itself away from those subjects, wanted to extend the Thatcher revolution from the economy into key public services like health and education. Instead, Michael Howard decided to double-down on that approach. The Tories' line on health and education would be 'the right to choose' backed up by state assistance to allow patients and pupils to move into the private sector – a line immediately and effectively caricatured by Blair as 'the right to charge'.

Rather than stopping to re-think, however, Howard moved straight on to the next stage – called (in a straight lift from the Sainsbury's ad campaign) 'good government costs less'. When it became apparent that voters were similarly unconvinced by his logic, however, Howard, rather than changing direction, decided simply to ease up on policy for a while and focus instead on trying to project, though media appearances on daytime television and radio, his more human side – immigrant parents, a lovely wife and family and a passion for Liverpool Football Club. Any hopes that sitting on sofas or being cast away to a mythical desert island might blunt Labour's portrayal of him as the Thatcherite 'Mr Poll Tax' and consummate opportunist, however, were swiftly dashed. In the lead-up to the release of the Butler Report and in the wake of a couple of third-place finishes in by-elections, Howard confessed that, had he known at the time what he later learned about the weakness of the case for the existence of WMD in Iraq, he would not have voted for war. This allowed an otherwise beleaguered Tony Blair to turn the tables: 'The public respect politicians who were for the war, or against the war,' he told the Commons, 'but not politicians who were for and against the war in the same newspaper article.'

It was brutal but effective – so much so that Nick Robinson, then ITN's political editor, wrote in *The Times* that he 'felt impelled to leap from my ring-side seat to jump into the ring and stop the fight'. Rather than retiring hurt, however, Howard proceeded, like William Hague before him, to hit the button marked populism, promising to 'stand up for the silent, law-abiding majority, who play by the rules and pay their dues'. The latter were also promised at various points during that summer of 2004 an end to the 'asylum shambles' and 'the compensation culture' created by the Human Rights Act, and (just in case the Conservatives had missed anyone with a grievance) help for those objecting to, among other things, wind farms, speed cameras, and mobile phone masts. And as polls began to suggest that the Tories were not merely becalmed but were doing worse under his leadership than they had been at the same point the year before under IDS, Howard promised that 'Whenever there is a conflict between political correctness and common sense, I stand firmly on the side of common sense.' It really was déjà vu all over again.

Little wonder, then, that Gregor Mackay, former press secretary to William Hague, thought it all sounded terribly familiar: 'They're going to make the same mistake we did in 2001,' he predicted in the *Telegraph* in October 2004. 'They start off fishing in the sea for votes and they end up poking around in a puddle outside their front door.' Howard's decision to hire Australian political strategist, Lynton Crosby, to run the party's election campaign in the autumn of 2004 virtually guaranteed that this would be the case. This was not so much because immigration and asylum was all Crosby knew how to do, or because he thought he could win with some sort of 'core vote strategy', but because he (not unreasonably and not uniquely) believed parties were best off focusing on the issues on which they enjoyed a lead rather than on fighting on whatever their opponent had long since turned into their territory – especially if those issues were 'wedge issues' that had the potential to divide that opponent's supporters.

POLITICAL ARGUMENT HEGEMONY

It may or may not be true that, as the Conservative Party assured readers of its policy statement, *The Right Approach*, in 1976 that 'the facts of life invariably do turn out to be Tory'. But precious few voters seemed to agree with the assertion when Michael Howard was leader – at least when it came to the economy and public services. On health and education, anyway, the country seemed much more persuaded by Labour's line that you can't get something for nothing and that, by helping to engineer and ensure economic growth, and then taking a fair share of the dividend in taxation, government could and should improve 'schools 'n' hospitals', both of which had clearly been massively underfunded over eighteen years of Conservative government. Tax cuts, it was generally agreed, would be nice but not if it meant cuts to services – something which Gordon Brown seemed to have convinced most people would inevitably follow as night follows day were the Tories to return to Downing Street.

On Europe, on immigration and asylum and 'law and order', it was a slightly different matter. Given the generally Eurosceptic and overwhelmingly restrictive and authoritarian tenor of British public opinion, Howard should have been on much firmer and fertile territory on such issues. Even here, however, things were shakier than one might have imagined. In marked contrast to what would happen once the numbers of EU citizens settling in the UK ballooned in the years after 2004, neither Europe nor immigration – at that stage anyway – was seen as sufficiently important to allow it to trump Labour's lead on 'bread and butter' issues. Law and order was admittedly more of a concern. But it was also an issue the ownership of which Blair was determined not to cede to the Tories. That meant that Howard, if he wanted to retain his party's edge, was forced to adopt increasingly hysterical, tabloid-driven stances, his support for the right of householders to use force against intruders and campaigns against the illegal occupation of land by travellers being two (painfully) obvious examples. Obsessing over such things imposed a significant opportunity cost: it made the Tories appear inward-looking and it meant they wasted a lot of time that could have been more profitably spent talking about the issues that voters really did want to talk about. Just as problematically, rather than a subtle toot on the dog-whistle it was more like a blast on the foghorn which, however well it might have gone down with the now legendary 'white van man', signalled to those well-heeled, well-educated, middle-class AB voters whom the Conservatives desperately needed to lure back to their electoral coalition that it was still 'the nasty party'.

In fact, such concerns had clearly spread into the electorate more generally, as was confirmed by Michael Ashcroft's post-election polling, which showed that support for a summary of the party's immigration policy dropped from a net 55 per cent to 43 per cent when respondents were informed that it was being proposed by the Conservatives.[724] Just as damagingly, for Howard at least, was the fact that, even if they could relate to his increasingly tough line, many voters were cynical about his motives for pursuing it. In the Commons in January, just after the Tories had announced that a Conservative government would effectively withdraw from the 1951 UN Convention on Refugees,

724 Michael Ashcroft, *Smell the Coffee*, London, Politico's, 2005, pp. 51–2.

Blair had once again played a blinder. 'I am not accusing you of being a racist,' he assured the Leader of the Opposition. 'You are not a racist; you are just a shameless opportunist.' The first opinion poll to be published thereafter suggested that this was a line which resonated with the public, with only 36 per cent of respondents agreeing that Howard 'genuinely believes immigration should be limited', while 58 per cent believed he was focusing on the issue because he 'desperately wants to win votes for his party'.

Howard's response to his failure to establish – or as some in his party might have seen it, re-establish – the Tory world view as common wisdom was to heed the advice of Cameron (and back-room boy Steve Hilton) that he should instead focus on convincing people that he was a realistic, practical leader who would not promise the earth but instead offer them a modest and therefore credible 'timetable for action'. This would be outlined for each area by each shadow spokesman and then confirmed in a deliberately short pre-manifesto which would project a Conservative government as one that would do what it said on the tin. This would not only allow Howard to show he was listening but dovetailed with his belief that politics should above all be about tangible delivery.

The choice of this approach was not only a symptom of Howard's inability to win political argument hegemony. It also reflected the fact that those working alongside him realised that, on balance, it was probably better to have their leader try to sell something he was comfortable with rather than run the risk of being seen as inauthentic. While this approach had the advantage of helping to turn what Howard increasingly saw as the necessity of not promising too much on tax into something approaching a virtue, it also risked, as co-chairman Maurice Saatchi argued, appearing small-minded rather than inspiring. Just as seriously, it also relied on the policies selected to radiate the sense of a party that, in Cameron's words, was 'credible, decent, tolerant, sensible, moderate', rather than plunging it even further into the clear blue water of which, at least in his opinion, there was already 'enough ... to drown in'. Yet the right-wing populist policies that had been inherited from Hague and IDS, as well as the initiatives developed since – policies crystallised in the so-called 'ten words to remember' (school discipline, more police, cleaner hospitals, lower taxes, controlled immigration) – were simply incapable of doing that.

GOVERNING COMPETENCE

To those who were keen for the party to go ahead with this approach, there was another argument in its favour. Not only was it well suited to the age of 'valence' rather than 'position' politics, wherein a party's ability to manage the country efficiently mattered more to voters than its ideology, it also played to what they saw, anyway, as Howard's personal strengths, namely that he was, to coin a phrase, 'a grown up', with 'grip', 'gravitas' and governmental experience. Whether this was such a good idea, and whether he was quite as efficient and as effective as they seemed to think, however, was surely a moot point. It was also an important one: projecting governing competence is hard enough anyway in opposition – and if the leader of that opposition fails to give the impression that he is in command and knows what he is doing, voters may be more prepared than they should be to give the incumbent government the benefit of the doubt.

When Howard had first taken over, *The Sun*'s reliably right-wing columnist Richard Littlejohn had helpfully reminded readers that, at the Home Office, Howard 'cut crime, banged up villains, tackled illegal immigration and put noses out of joint'. Choosing a politician, he had suggested, was like hiring a lawyer: 'Do you want someone everybody likes, or a ruthless bastard who takes no prisoners?' But that, of course, was only one side of the coin. Even leaving aside Widdecombe's infamous jibe, there were other, less positive aspects of Howard's time as Home Secretary that voters could be unhelpfully reminded of, not least high-profile prisoner escapes and his notorious refusal to answer Jeremy Paxman's question about them during an interview on *Newsnight* – an encounter that 'went viral' before YouTube was even invented. And even if Labour chose not to make too much of that particular incident, there was enough it could do simply with the fact that Howard had been a first-rank member of a government (a regime, almost) that had come to be seen as uncaring, unsuccessful and unpopular.

In the second poll published after Howard first took over as leader, Populus revealed that two-thirds of respondents thought that Howard's role in the Major government made it 'very important for the Tories to show that they [had] really changed' since then. Labour was determined to do everything in its power to suggest that they hadn't. Indeed, it used the European elections in June 2004 as a chance to road-test its attack on Howard as a throwback associated with the extremes of the '80s and the economic failures of the early '90s, in particular the poll tax and 'three million unemployed'. It launched its campaign with a poster picturing Howard, Thatcher, Major, Hague and Duncan Smith with the slogan 'Britain is working. Don't let the Tories wreck it again.' And Labour's first television broadcast of the campaign featured footage of poll tax riots, house repossessions and Howard in his various ministerial roles, accompanied not by a voiceover but by Simply Red's version of the soul classic 'If You Don't Know Me by Now' – a technique that Labour repeated at the general election a year later, albeit with a change of soundtrack to Barbara Streisand's 'The Way We Were'.

But that was then. What about Howard's performance in opposition? Did that project governing competence? Not always. By no means all of Howard's appointments were poor ones: putting Guy Black in charge of the party's press operation, for example, was generally regarded as a good move. Getting young guns like David Cameron and George Osborne to assist him in his preparation for PMQs was probably a good idea, too, even if it did nothing to dampen the mounting resentment among senior MPs (some of whom were prepared to express it publicly) of what came to be called 'the Notting Hill Set' of young, socially liberal MPs, Central Office staffers and aspiring candidates who some old hands suspected of plotting to take control of the party after the election. Some of Howard's other personnel decisions, however, proved rather less inspired. Short of stars (Hague, Clarke and Portillo declined to serve), he tried to make a virtue of necessity by reducing the size of the shadow Cabinet in order to try and make it more of a meaningful directorate, composed of just twelve members. But replacing Theresa May with both veteran ad man Maurice Saatchi and former shadow Health Secretary Liam Fox proved a bit of a disaster. Both were thoroughgoing Thatcherites but it did not seem to help them cut through the inevitable demarcation disputes that splitting the role involved. It was also difficult to see how Tim Yeo, supposedly in charge of both health and education, was going to be able to answer for the Tories on such huge (and hugely important) subjects. Moreover, it allowed Labour to argue that the Tories cared so little about two such vital public services that they believed just one man could run them both.

It was, however, Howard's two biggest appointments who turned out to be the biggest *dis*appointments. David Davis was not an impressive shadow Home Secretary – possibly because he was too busy planning his post-election leadership bid. And Oliver Letwin, even if one ignores the bad publicity generated by his reluctance to give up his six-figure salary from a merchant bank, did no better as shadow Chancellor. He was unable to establish and hold a line on tax cuts and was incapable of reassuring the public that the Tories were going to be able to make huge savings in public spending without hurting public services – especially when another of Howard's appointments, the über-Thatcherite, John Redwood, appeared to confirm that his plans for reductions were just the beginning of something much bigger and (Labour alleged) more insidious.

Howard's own performance could also be erratic. True, he was occasionally capable of besting the Prime Minister in the Commons: everyone remembers his retort to Blair in early December 2003 that 'This grammar school boy is not going to take any lessons from a public schoolboy on the importance of children from less privileged backgrounds gaining access to university.' But in reality it was one of the exceptions that proved the rule. Indeed, he often came badly unstuck – either because he was no more able than Hague and Duncan Smith to see a bandwagon without jumping on it or because, once committed to a cause or course of action, he was too determined to see it through.

A case in point was the heavy investment Howard made in the Hutton Report criticising Blair, even suggesting before its release that the Prime

Minister might have to go. But when Howard and Cameron (who had been tasked with tracking the inquiry) came to see the finished product, and realised it was going to favour the government and not the BBC, they chose to soldier on rather than admit defeat, allowing Blair to wipe the floor with his opposite number in the Commons: 'Yesterday [the day Labour's top-up fees legislation squeaked through without Tory support] was a test of policy,' crowed Blair, 'and he failed it. Today is a test for his character and he failed that too. What he should understand is being nasty is not the same as being effective, and opportunism is not the same as leadership.' Things were not quite so bad when the Conservatives' plans to use state funding to help the public move into the private sector in health and education came under serious public scrutiny – but they were not much better: 'The fact is,' Blair told Howard at PMQs, 'that where your policies are coherent they are reactionary and divisive. Where they aren't reactionary and divisive they are utterly incoherent.'

PARTY MANAGEMENT

Sadly for Howard, Blair's comments on his policies could just as easily have been applied to his picks for party chairmen – although not necessarily to his party management more generally. The awkward division of the post between Fox and Saatchi became even less clear after the appointment of Lynton Crosby. The Australian was not very impressed by what he had found on his arrival and made little secret of the fact. Saatchi was dismissed as 'twenty years out of date', while the voter-identification system ('voter vault') that Fox managed to get from the US Republicans was nowhere near as impressive as the hype surrounding it. Moreover, Crosby, whose speciality was motivating his staff and zeroing in on swing voters in marginal, but winnable constituencies, was, not surprisingly, unimpressed with the idea that the party spread its limited resources over the 167 seats that Saatchi had, rather laughably, claimed at one stage to be targeting. The leaking to the media of his criticisms led to Saatchi and Fox demanding, and getting, an apology and then circulating an email (also leaked) to all at Central Office (now renamed Conservative Campaign Headquarters or CCHQ) to publicise, rather pathetically perhaps, the fact Crosby had said sorry.

Meanwhile, concern that all was not well at CCHQ was only made worse by the dire state of the party's finances. It had been unable to negotiate the quick sale of (nor find a tenant for) Smith Square before it moved in (at huge expense) to its refurbished offices in Victoria Street – a location it would eventually abandon for a more permanent base at Millbank in any case. Although the party could probably count on donors stumping up to help it fight an election, it was clear that it was also going to have to dip into both its substantial overdraft and whatever reserves it could muster. It was also clear that much of the money pledged would come in the form of loans, some of which might eventually be converted into donations but a proportion of which would have to be repaid in the long term. Meanwhile, it was obvious that something was not quite right when one of those who had given the party considerable amounts of money, former treasurer Michael Ashcroft, had so little confidence in its target-seats strategy that he had decided to set up his own parallel system of funding. Indeed, he even opted to commission his own opinion research in the belief that CCHQ (not for the first time) was going with polling and focus groups that told the leadership what it wanted, rather than what it needed, to hear.

Howard also had to cope with the fact that there were some sections of the party that made even hard-core Thatcherites look like metropolitan liberals – and not just at Westminster. In early September 2004, he had to intervene personally to prevent the constituency association in Falmouth from deselecting its candidate, a gay barrister, who had run into trouble by supporting action against some of its members (later dismissed and disqualified) for promoting UKIP – a stand which had seen both him and his family subjected to some pretty vicious homophobic abuse. On the upside Howard's intervention proved that he took the need to stamp out discrimination seriously. On the downside, however, the fact that he had to get involved at all (and the sheer nastiness of some of the stuff quoted by the media) indicated that the party had a long way to go in this respect. It also had a long way to go to improve the representation of women at Westminster, too – but this was something to which Howard paid virtually no attention.

Ignoring the issue was not, however, something he could do when a month or so out from the 2005 election, the media got hold of an illicit tape recording of right-wing MP Howard Flight seemingly confirming the existence of a secret Tory plan to cut spending that would be put into place once the public had been fooled into voting in a party that, fundamentally, had never really changed. Within a couple of hours of his being confronted with what had happened, Howard forced Flight to issue an apology. The next day he went even further, withdrawing the whip and declaring he would no longer be a candidate. Given how difficult John Major had found it to prevent constituency parties from re-selecting MPs who were clearly causing the party massive embarrassment, it was testament to Howard's personal authority that Flight's local association accepted his fate. However, the reaction in the parliamentary party to Howard's 'nuclear response' was one of alarm. Even those who saw the advantage in having a leader who could now be portrayed as ruthless and brutally honest, wondered if he might not have overdone it. Given the extent of these concerns it was, once again, a testament to the discipline that Howard (and his Chief Whip David Maclean) had instilled at Westminster that almost nobody in the parliamentary party was prepared to be quoted by journalists on the issue, either on or off the record. For all his faults, Howard steadied a ship that, during the last few months of his predecessor's leadership, had been listing badly. It may have sailed on to defeat under his captaincy but at least it never looked remotely like capsizing.

BENDING THE RULES OF THE GAME

Since Michael Howard never became Prime Minister, we cannot know what he might have done to the country's constitution. We should note, however, that he was certainly prepared to try to change the Conservative

Party's. Following the election, Howard immediately announced that he would step down. But he would remain in place until a specially convened Constitutional College would vote later on in the year on returning the sole right to elect the leader to the party's MPs. In the event, support for what amounted to a return to the old days fell short of the required margin of victory and so the party stayed stuck with the system set up by William Hague. However, by insisting on the long drawn-out consultation and vote on the new system, Howard effectively delayed the leadership contest and in so doing helped to ensure that his own preferred candidate, David Cameron, had time to emerge as a credible alternative to the man who might otherwise have won hands-down, David Davis. Whether, of course, that was a good thing depends ultimately on whether one believes that, in doing so, Howard saved the Conservative Party from a fate worse than death or whether, instead, one believes that he denied the top job to a man who might have been much better suited to seeing off UKIP than the liberal Old Etonian who ended up getting it.

CONCLUSION

Polls taken during and after the 2005 general election showed that the Conservative campaign was judged by voters to be the worst of those mounted by the three main parties and that Labour improved its position relative to the Conservatives on almost every issue. The gap between Howard and Blair also widened – to the disadvantage of the Tory leader. That said, Labour won its historic third consecutive majority on a much reduced share of the vote and with a majority down to double rather than triple figures, having held on to only around seven out of ten of its 2001 voters and losing the rest mainly to abstention or the Lib Dems. The Conservatives held on to nine out of ten of their voters from 2001 and the UKIP threat failed to materialise. However, they gained just thirty-two extra seats on a share of the vote that increased by less than one percentage point compared to 2001.

There were still only 198 Tories entitled to sit in the Commons – fewer than the 209 MPs who sat on the Labour benches after the *annus horribilis*, which that party experienced in 1983.

It didn't have to be like that. Within the limits imposed by his own reputation and the colleagues he needed to reward and keep on board, Michael Howard could have done pretty much what he wanted with the Tory Party when he took over in November 2003. He chose to tackle what he saw as the party's most urgent problem – the public's impression of it as a divided and rudderless outfit that could not lay a glove even on a Prime Minister widely regarded as slippery. But he either left policy much as he found it or else extended and emphasised its rightward, authoritarian thrust, forgetting all about the 'compassionate' conservatism on which his predecessor had occasionally focused and the modernisation he himself had fleetingly hinted at in a speech he made at the Saatchi gallery when he first became leader.

In so doing, Michael Howard arguably did the Tories considerable damage, although he also did them a favour or two. He failed to move the party out of the ideological and institutional rut in which it had been stuck since the early 1990s, meaning it had almost as far to go after 2005 as it had after 1997 and 2001. On the other hand, he at least helped prevent it slipping into third place behind the Lib Dems. He was also able to hand over the leadership to a group of younger politicians who appeared to understand that the Conservative Party cannot win a majority on a platform built solely on populist promises on immigration, law and order, and Europe, and on taking up where Margaret Thatcher left off.

CHAPTER 23

DAVID CAMERON

MATTHEW D'ANCONA

David Cameron's time as leader of the Conservative party is not over, and Matthew d'Ancona's portrait of Cameron ends as his second term as Prime Minister has just begun. Yet his time as leader from December 2005 means he has been at the helm for almost a decade, long enough to make an informed measurement of his ability as a party leader. His period in opposition, and a strategy of notable if short-lived modernisation, was electorally successful enough in 2010 to form a coalition government with the Liberal Democrats, but not to govern alone. D'Ancona judges Cameron's management of the coalition as masterly, his shepherding of his party through it less so. This was due to particularly difficult circumstances that arose from inter-party government and the emergence of UKIP. His second election as leader and a slim Conservative majority, in circumstances where an outright victory was both difficult and unexpected, mean Cameron has a credible claim to be a successful exponent of political statecraft.

• • •

On 16 April 2015, I interviewed David Cameron for *The Guardian* in the leader's private office (the 'power pod') on the Conservative battle bus. As we drove out of Leeds, the conversation on board – among senior Conservative aides, broadcasters, reporters – had turned to the fizzing complexity of the race, and the multiple permutations and combinations that would arise if (as was almost universally expected) the general election on 7 May spawned another hung parliament.

The Conservative leader was not persuaded by the assumptions underpinning the gossip – assumptions that were hardening into political orthodoxy. 'People keep saying the two-party system has broken down,' Cameron mused:

> Well, actually, hold on one second – I'm not sure about that. Because there's such a big binary choice in this election that part of my argument is going to be – if you want to avoid the calamity of Ed Miliband plus the SNP, you need to give the Conservatives a majority. You know what you'll get with me.[725]

The voters did indeed know what they would get, and, with epic disregard for the opinion polls' consistent prophecy of a Labour victory or hung parliament, rewarded Cameron with a Commons majority of twelve – the first time since December 1996 that a Conservative Prime Minister could claim single-party control of the lower house.

The 2015 election result was not as statistically spectacular as, say, Labour's victories in 1945 and 1997, or Margaret Thatcher's destruction of Michael Foot in 1983. Cameron's majority was perilously slender and left him structurally vulnerable to rebellion by the back-bench right; particularly, though not exclusively, over Europe. It was tempting to compare him to John Major between 1992 and 1997, at the mercy of his own mutinous MPs who were militantly opposed to the EU Maastricht Treaty and (in many cases) missed the firm hand of the Iron Lady.

Unlike Major, however, Cameron had already announced his intention to stand down before the 2020 general election. He believed that the implicit

---

725 Interview with the author; this, and many other conversations, informed a *Guardian* Long Read on Cameron, Tuesday 5 May 2015, and a BBC *Newsnight* film on the Prime Minister's prospects that was broadcast on 6 May. For a lengthier analysis of Cameron's performance during his first term (and earlier), see: Matthew d'Ancona, *In It Together: The Inside Story of the Coalition Government*, London, Penguin, 2014; Anthony Seldon and Mike Finn eds, *The Coalition Effect 2010–2015*, Cambridge, Cambridge University Press, 2015; Robert Hazell and Ben Yong eds, *The Politics of Coalition: How the Conservative–Liberal Democrat Government Works*, Oxford, Hart Publishing, 2012; Francis Elliott and James Hanning, *Cameron: Practically a Conservative*, London, Fourth Estate, 2012; Matt Beech and Simon Lee eds, *The Conservative–Liberal Coalition: Examining the Cameron-Clegg Government*, London, Palgrave, 2015.

corollary of the Fixed-Term Parliaments Act was statesmanlike restraint by Prime Ministers: they should accept, he argued, a two-term limit. At no point did Cameron propose a legislative equivalent of the 22nd Amendment to the US Constitution ('No person shall be elected to the office of the President more than twice'). But, in practice, this was precisely what he meant.

Inevitably, the knowledge that he would not be contesting the 2020 election inspired some to disdain him as a lame duck. Invariably the optimist, Cameron did not see matters thus: he believed that he had seized control of his destiny and could choreograph his exit from the top job.

To understand the leadership of David Cameron – or to begin to do so – one must first take stock of its broader context, which is to say the specific circumstances in which it began and the shifting backdrop against which it has unfolded. To understand what he had achieved (and the respects in which he had failed) by 2015, one must go back to 2005 and, in particular, the party chairmanship of Francis Maude.[726]

Had the leadership election that followed Michael Howard's resignation been held quickly, it is all but certain that David Davis would have won. Davis had – or so it seemed – the contest sewn up, with more than sixty MPs signed up officially or privately as backers. But Howard had become persuaded of two things.

First, the outgoing leader – defeated by Blair – had gradually reached the conclusion that the young modernisers had analysed the Tory Party's problems more accurately than he had initially thought. The 2005 result demonstrated, in Howard's view, that winning the policy argument was not enough. A party had to be trusted, and its motives respected. So there would have to be radical change. But Howard – second – did not think that he or, for that matter, Davis were capable of carrying out this transformative work.

---

726 Much of this section is based on a paper delivered at a conference on Tory leaders at Queen Mary University, London, on 5 December 2014. There are surprisingly few essential accounts of this important period in Tory evolution. Two conspicuous exceptions are Tim Bale, *The Conservative Party: From Thatcher to Cameron*, London, Polity Press, 2011, and Peter Snowdon, *Back from the Brink: The Extraordinary Fall and Rise of the Conservative Party*, London, HarperPress, 2010. For superb insights into the Cameron years in general (and not only the 2015 election campaign), see Nick Robinson, *Election Notebook: The inside story of the battle over Britain's future and my personal battle to report it*, London, Bantam Press, 2015.

That burden would fall on the shoulders of either George Osborne (whom Howard urged to stand in the race to succeed him) or Cameron (his former special advisor at the Home Office). For one of them to prevail in the leadership contest would take time, a probationary period of several months in which they could show the party what they were capable of and what they would do if handed the reins.

Hence, the long timetable of the race: launched in May, with the initial parliamentary rounds held in October and the final run-off completed only in December. Osborne politely resisted Howard's encouragement to run: as a former political secretary to William Hague, he knew all about the perils of becoming leader too early. Even Cameron who was almost five years older than Osborne was not sure, initially, whether the time was right. There were moments during the contest when he and Osborne seriously considered drawing stumps, ready to fight and win another day. But they stayed the course, with unexpected and spectacular success.

Overseeing it all with a beady eye was Maude, notionally neutral as party chairman but well-established as a patron of the modernisers, whose 'killer slide' was projected at the party conference in Blackpool. The slide showed something compelling and chilling about the Tory Party and its policy. Maude revealed that 60 per cent of the public backed the Conservative position on immigration, before being told that it was the party's policy. But once the voters learned that it was a Tory idea public support *halved*. This was a devastating message and one that cut through faction, ideology and caucus affiliation: the Tory Party was so unpopular that it contaminated the very policies it espoused. The surest way to kill an idea was to say that the Conservatives supported it.

Cameron's victory rested upon that simple proposition and the rare moment of unity that it occasioned – a recognition that the party needed a new face, literally and metaphorically. The problem went much deeper than image or public relations. It was not a cosmetic pathology. When the senior Tory strategist Steve Hilton encouraged his boss to quote Gandhi's maxim 'Be the Change', he was not simply annexing its trendy spirituality. He was expressing the heart of the matter. At the Blackpool conference, which became an unofficial leadership hustings, Cameron's performance captured that message in masterly political choreography.

Early Cameronism focused zealously upon the need to change. It was Trotskyite in its fervour and remorseless energy. The party was steered – at least officially – towards an evangelical position on environmentalism and international development. Cameron made the NHS the core of his and therefore the party's politics. Ties were out, the 'Big Society' was in. Unfunded tax cuts were also ruled out, to the dismay of enthusiasts of the Laffer curve.

An 'A list' of candidates was drawn up to ensure that the parliamentary face of the party – again, in theory – looked like the country it aspired to govern: it was Cameron's express intention that Tories would not all be white middle-aged men, and that his colleagues in the Commons should include many more women and people from ethnic minorities. The pace was deliberately relentless, the zeal a part of the message. Hilton wanted voters to see a party in a tearing hurry, impatient to change itself and, by extension, to make Britain fit for the twenty-first century.[727]

Not since Sir Alec Douglas-Home's wife lambasted the shiny 'bright new party' that Ted Heath aspired to create when he became leader in 1965 had modernity been so central to the party's public activities. When Cameron said to Blair that 'you were the future once', he was turning New Labour's guns on itself – exploiting the core Blairite idea that novelty and success are closely related, perhaps even co-terminous.

What was Cameron up to? Too much, I think, has been made of his background as a PR man and Hilton's origins at Saatchi.[728] Their ambitions were emphatically not confined to photo ops, branding and symbols – though there was plenty of all three.

More than Hague, IDS or Howard, Cameron grasped – not immediately

727 For an authentic account of Cameron's thinking in this period, see Dylan Jones, *Cameron on Cameron: Conversations with Dylan Jones*, London, Fourth Estate, 2010.

728 Cameron was director of corporate affairs at Carlton from July 1994 to February 2001: a sabbatical from politics separating his years as a Cabinet special advisor and his parliamentary career.

but certainly by 2005 – that the political prospects of the Conservative Party had changed fundamentally. It was not simply memories of sleaze or Black Wednesday that was driving the general election defeats. It was a host of factors conspiring against the Tories ever again winning a Commons majority as they had in 1992.

First, the old paternalism–deference equation was gone for good. This was old news, of course. What was new was the popular suspicion that the Tories still believed they were born to rule, that the country is simply better off when the Conservatives are in charge. Cameron did believe the second proposition, as did most Tories of his background and class. But he had learned the hard way that this was emphatically not the default position of the British electorate.

Second, the party no longer had an obvious dragon to slay – other than Brussels. Thatcher had faced inflation, the trade unions and international communism, and seen off Galtieri too. In 2005, the bestiary was bare. 'Banging on about Europe' caused more problems than it solved, publicising the party's most toxic divisions and making it seem like the political wing of a single-issue group rather than a national movement.

It was also no longer enough to be the party of effective action – 'cruel but competent', to borrow Maurice Saatchi's phrase, was no longer enough. As Michael Gove was to put it in an appreciation of Margaret Thatcher after her death in April 2013: 'time has underlined how crucial it is to ensure that we also applaud the values of care, nurture and solidarity that protect the vulnerable at time of change'. His point – and Cameron's – was not to disown the Thatcher era but to remind his fellow Tories that the culture and texture of everyday life had changed profoundly since her fall in 1990. There was no future in karaoke Thatcherism, the second-rate impersonation of a former leader.

But early Cameronism was not simply defined by what it was not. It also represented the first reasonably coherent attempt by a Tory leader since the Blair landslide to respond to the new post-Cold War age of globalisation, climate change, the digital revolution and the fraught relationship between fundamentalist and open modes of thought.

Correctly, Cameron detected a historic opportunity: a potential match between the unprecedented plurality of the modern world and the Conservative embrace of heterogeneity in preference to uniformity. What he called the 'Big Society' was really no different to Burke's 'little platoons' armed with iPads. He grasped that gay marriage was an essentially conservative idea, extending a social institution to embrace same-sex commitment as well as its heterosexual form. In greenery – at least at first – he saw a way to express community and protect the British landscape that he adored. He also believed that a reckoning lay ahead on the proper limits of the state and of public spending, and he wanted the Conservative Party to take the lead, especially in public service reform and big change to the welfare system. But he knew that the public would never give his party 'permission' to address such issues until it believed that Tories had trustworthy motives.

Too many voters still regarded the party as a harsh, pitiless clique, afflicted, to borrow a phrase of E. M. Forster, by 'an undeveloped heart'. In essence, his initial campaign was defined by a single objective: to do something about both the heart and the public's assessment of it.

In one particular respect, Cameron was not suited to the task he had set himself. The principal characteristic that is required of a party moderniser is persistence. The early energy of Cameron's 'detoxification' strategy was remarkable. But that urgency did not endure. Cameron was a pragmatist by temperament, supple in negotiations, and confident rather than confrontational. He disliked being hemmed in, preferring strategic versatility to the implacable obstinacy that is required of the true moderniser.

When he left office in 2007, Tony Blair was *still* trying to change Labour with the same zeal he had displayed in 1994. But Cameron did not pursue his own modernisation programme with comparable fervour. When the A list of candidates did not work, it was quietly dropped. Though ministers insisted otherwise, greenery was vulnerable at the first whiff of economic trouble – dismissed, in fact, as 'green crap' before the 2013 Autumn Statement in an effort to head off a fuel tax rebellion.

Tellingly, there was no modernising phalanx on the parliamentary benches. Cameron conspicuously failed to build up a coterie of true believers, which raised the question: was he ever one himself? His courage over gay marriage suggests that he was. The fact that his first big speech after the 2015 election concerned 'one-nation' social reform strengthened the case. But the self-styled 'heir to Blair' was no such thing when it came to the long haul of party modernisation; it was his intermittent concern, but never his passion.

To understand his oscillating strategy – his uneven emphasis upon party reform – it is essential to grasp the impact upon British politics *tout court* of the collapse of Lehman Bros on 15 September 2008 (the eve of the Tory conference). It was already clear that the party's public spending programme required major surgery; that whoever became the Prime Minister would have to deal with the escalating deficit. The stakes at this point in time were vertiginously high and – even though he had squandered his best chance by deciding against a snap election in 2007 – Gordon Brown looked threateningly capable as a globe-trotting financial magus.

Now it was clear that the deficit would be the principal economic challenge facing the next government. As Cameron and Osborne rightly concentrated upon the unpopular decisions they would have to take in office, they wrongly turned away from the modernising strategy they had deployed before the financial crisis. It was, they suggested, time to put aside childish things, and, figuratively, to wear ties again. This was true, as far as it went: the work of economic repair would take many years and supplant social reform as Cameron's top priority. But the error was to retreat to the party's campaigning comfort zone of governing competence, and to suspend the all-important work on motive.

Now that Tory ministers would be making cuts, it was *more important than ever* that their values be trusted by the voters. Nobody minds why a government is spending extra cash on the NHS, or on schools or roads, unless the expenditure is brazen gerrymandering. But voters mind very much when the same government proposes swingeing cuts for some departments, ring-fencing for others, and salami-slicing for others still. They need reassurance that the cuts are being made without relish and reflect sound ethical priorities. So consumed was Cameron to appear grave and serious that he forgot, almost overnight, much of what he had learned about emotional intelligence generally and the public's deep distrust of his party specifically.

The phrase 'in this together' blandly echoed the idea of a community in adversity. But the message began to lose its depth and heft. It is no accident that the 2010 campaign was, as Cameron privately admitted, such a mess. It signally lacked the clarity and energy of early Cameronism. It relied far too much upon Labour's mistakes, Brown's exhaustion and the public's weariness with the party that had governed for thirteen years. Years afterwards, memory of this campaign could still infuriate Cameron.

Second, and with almost tragic inevitability, the issue of Europe returned with a vengeance to haunt and distract the Tory leader. Cameron knew that the right would never forgive him for – as they saw it – welching on his 'cast-iron' promise to hold a referendum on the Lisbon Treaty. He grasped that the European Union Act of 2011, though it promised a referendum on any significant future transfer of sovereignty to Brussels, would not satisfy the hard core. He even expected a rump of irreconcilables to reject his Bloomberg speech of January 2013 pledging an in/out referendum by the end of 2017.

What he did not reckon with was the coalescing of hard-line Eurosceptic opinion into a serious breakaway rebellion – nor for that rebellion to serve as a proxy for a whole host of reactionary cultural positions, some of them distinctly unpleasant. Posturing as a campaign for constitutional change – the repatriation of British sovereignty from Brussels – the UK Independence Party was, in fact, a much broader resistance movement.[729] The familiar issue of Britain's membership of the EU provided a flag of convenience, but the party's principal impulse was really a recoil from migration, social diversity and modern pluralism in all its forms. In this respect, it was the polar opposite of early Cameronism, raising a clenched fist rather than an open hand to global modernity.

As such, UKIP was doomed to ultimate failure, pitched as it was against

729 See Robert Ford and Matthew Goodwin, *Revolt on the Right: Explaining Support for the Radical Right in Britain*, Abingdon, Routledge, 2014.

planet-wide change. As the 2015 election proved, furthermore, it had yet to discover a way of turning its national share of the vote (12.6 per cent) into parliamentary seats (only one, retained by Douglas Carswell, a Tory defector). UKIP had not broken through in the Commons, as its leader, Nigel Farage, had hoped that it would. But the movement still fizzed and hissed its way through the political landscape like lava.

Cameron defended his strategy against UKIP with reference to the 2015 results. He had refused to let Farage define the terms of trade, and (manifestly) thwarted UKIP's objective to destroy his leadership. The counter-argument was that Cameron had merely postponed the moment of decisive confrontation, first by ignoring and then by appeasing Farage's party. UKIP was an institutional contradiction: a movement standing athwart history while exploiting all the political tricks of hyper-modernity. No political group better understood the web's love of the shrill, the digital amplification of anger. It was a party demanding 'change' while resisting it in almost every corner of the social fabric.

Undoubtedly, Cameron out-manoeuvred Farage in 2015, refusing to engage with him in a series of television debates, following the advice of his election strategist, Lynton Crosby, to remain ruthlessly focused upon the economy and his superiority to Miliband as a national leader. But a reckoning with UKIP still lay ahead for the Conservative Party. Throughout 2014, Farage's most successful year to date, there was fatuous talk on the Tory side of reuniting the 'Conservative family' – which is to say, being just reactionary enough on immigration and cultural matters to keep UKIP happy. But that was to misunderstand the primary directive of the party – which was to be unappeasable. This was its very *raison d'être*, its defining characteristic: it objected, it opposed, it resisted. UKIP had not broken through in 2015, but it had not broken up, either. Sooner it later it would have to be taken on directly by a Conservative leader: a task as forbidding as it was unavoidable.

Any audit of Cameron's leadership between 2005 and 2015 must keep constant sight of the circumstances in which he took the decisions that he did. An era of austerity and a coalition in office: either would be a formidable pressure upon any Tory leader, but their conjunction was exceptionally demanding. Cameron proved to be a masterly manager of the coalition, which, remarkably, faced collapse only once (in August 2012, when the Lib Dems withdrew support from the new parliamentary boundaries in retaliation for the backbench Tory sabotage of Lords reform).

Yet there was always an intrinsic tension between the demands of coalition and the demands of party. Most obviously, Cameron had less patronage to dispense because so many government posts had to go to the Lib Dems. There was a general (if illogical) prejudice in the Tory Party and press in May 2010 that Cameron should have tried minority government. He made an undoubted error early in the life of the coalition by seeking full voting rights at the 1922 Committee for Conservative ministers.

In retrospect, Cameron's leadership was probably never in genuine peril between 2010 and 2015. But his relationship with the parliamentary party was never warm, and the normal ties of loyalty were frayed both by the fact of coalition and the perception that he took little notice of his own MPs, preferring the counsel of a kitchen Cabinet of friends. In the first ten months of the new government, a quarter of Tory MPs voted against the government on at least one occasion.[730] More than 130 voted against gay marriage; 100 against Lords reform; and thirty against Cameron's planned action in Syria – a significant rebellion on an issue of security and foreign policy.

Had the Scottish referendum resulted in the end of the Union, there would have been immense pressure upon him to resign. As late as October 2014, an unnamed Cabinet minister was warning that the loss of Rochester and Strood in the by-election following Mark Reckless's defection to UKIP would trigger a vote of confidence in Cameron. The by-election was indeed lost (Reckless retained the seat, but as the UKIP candidate).[731] Yet the threatened confidence vote, the mechanism that had ended Duncan Smith's leadership, never came to pass. However distasteful the coalition was to most Tories, it

730 See Philip Norton, 'The coalition and the Conservatives', in Seldon and Finn, op. cit., p. 477.

731 He lost it to the Conservative candidate Kelly Tolhurst in the 2015 general election.

was doing too many things of which they approved – fiscal restraint, welfare reform, a long-awaited 'classroom revolution' – for Cameron's defenestration to make any sort of political sense.

There was undoubtedly a diffidence to Cameron that puzzled pundits, pollsters and politicians alike. His lack of visible fervour and his reputation as the 'chillaxing' Prime Minister was sometimes confused with detachment or arrogance. He was well aware of this problem of perception. Yet, time and again, he confounded those who assumed that he was detached and unfocused. What looked like diffidence was often the calm of self-assurance and the instinct not to compound moments of tension with political theatricality. It was an instinct he shared with Barack 'No Drama' Obama.

To a greater extent than is often acknowledged, Cameron's campaign to rescue his party was successful. True, membership was falling, from 253,600 eligible to vote in the 2005 leadership contest, to 149,800 in September 2014. But that was a problem common to most mass political movements, rather than a uniquely Conservative erosion.[732] There were indeed many frustrations and abrasions between centre and shires. Lord Feldman, a university friend of Cameron, was alleged to have called Tory activists 'swivel-eyed loons' (a charge he strongly denied). But as co-chairman of the party between 2010 and 2015, and sole occupant of the post thereafter, Feldman was also a highly effective fund-raiser, clearing party debt while he secured new donations. According to the electoral commission's figures, the party raised £15,404,569 between 1 January and 31 March 2015, well ahead of Labour's £9,334,757.

The Tories gained ninety-seven seats in the 2010 election, more than at any other general election since the 1931 landslide; still not enough for a majority, but the basis for a coalition with the Lib Dems. This unlikely governing pact was read the last rites by many pundits before the ink was dry – and yet

732 Less than 1 per cent of the UK electorate was a member of the Conservative, Labour or Liberal Democrat parties in 2015, compared to 3.8 per cent in 1983. See House of Commons Library Research Briefing: Richard Keen, *Membership of UK political parties,* SN/SG/5125.

survived until what became the designated day of parliamentary dissolution (30 March 2015).

The Cameron–Clegg partnership had no modern precedent, and, if nothing else, its durability added an option to the constitutional menu. But it achieved much more. Though Osborne missed his original fiscal targets, he and Cameron made fiscal conservatism all but orthodox and ensured that the apparently dry and abstract task of deficit reduction became a kitchen table issue with popular resonance. They forced discussion of spending priorities, and the painful recognition that one person's ring-fence is another's 25 per cent departmental cut (as the so-called 'National Union of Ministers' – those who headed unprotected departments – discovered the hard way).

In December 2014, Cameron marked nine years as Conservative leader: longer than Macmillan, Major, and the aggregated trio of Hague, Duncan Smith and Howard, and closing in on Heath's ten-year tenure. That said, he had never wanted to go 'on and on' in office. In an interview with me in 2013, he insisted that, if re-elected, he would serve a second 'full term' – and that he would not step down after two years as Blair had done in 2007.[733] During the 2015 election campaign, however, he told the BBC's James Landale that, if re-elected, he would not seek a third term. As it turned out, the two disclosures were not inconsistent: Cameron wanted to pursue a fully Conservative agenda, unrestrained by the compromises and postponements of coalition, for as much of the parliament as he could. But, as we have seen, he also believed that 21st-century prime ministers should observe a two-term limit. So he would step down in time to allow a successor to be chosen; but not, as some speculated, after a year or two. He had work to do, unexpectedly free of the Lib Dem veto. In private, he was surprised that so many in the Westminster elite had to have this spelt out to them.

The Union with Scotland survived the referendum called by Cameron – again, a bold measure, criticised by many Tories as an unnecessary risk,

733 'I will be the one, and the Conservatives will be the party, offering genuine change ... Do you want to hand the keys back to the people who crashed the car?', *Sunday Telegraph*, 6 January 2013.

which will be more kindly judged by history than it was by his contemporaries. At the time of writing, he still faced a series of daunting challenges, especially in the prospective EU referendum. After May 2015, he no longer had the excuse of coalition to explain setbacks and delay. After a decade of modernisation and then coalition, his party craved a period of neat Conservatism, undiluted and true blue. But ideological purity is rarely as easy to maintain in practice as its adherents believe.

In 2013, I wrote of Cameron that he was 'a cluster of paradoxes: a pragmatist at the helm of a radical government; a foreign policy realist demanding intervention; the ultimate Tory insider insisting that his mission was to spread privilege; a tribalist who had formed a coalition.'[734]

In the 2015 election he became the party leader who, after five years lagging behind in the polls, clinging on to power only with the politically costly help of the Lib Dems, defied expectation by winning an outright Commons majority. This alone ensured that he would be remembered as a good Conservative leader. He had set himself a range of tasks – to clear the deficit, to transform welfare, to reform secondary schools, to save the Union by constitutional change, and to resolve the European question – of a scale that might lift him to the ranks of the great. Only posterity would make that verdict. But in the summer of 2015 those ready to bet against him were fast dwindling in number.

734 D'Ancona, op. cit., p. 360.

PART III

LEADERSHIP PERSPECTIVES

CHAPTER 24

MICHAEL HOWARD ON LEADERSHIP, THE CONSERVATIVE PARTY AND STATECRAFT THEORY

MICHAEL HOWARD, TOBY S. JAMES AND CHARLES CLARKE[735]

This chapter is an edited transcript of an interview with Michael Howard to gain his views about how leaders should be judged, the challenges they face and whether the statecraft approach is a useful framework for assessing them. Michael Howard argues that evaluating leaders purely on electoral performance or the statecraft approach is too narrow. An assessment should also consider their record in office, in the event that they become the Prime Minister. The personal characteristics of leaders can also be important, he suggests, although it is the public's perception of the leader's personality that can shape their success.

• • •

REFLECTIONS ON THE ROAD TO BECOMING LEADER

TOBY JAMES: Thinking back to when you first decided to set out in politics, what was it that you wanted to try to achieve at that time?

---

735 This interview took place in the House of Lords, London, on Tuesday 12 May 2015.

MICHAEL HOWARD: What I wanted to do was what virtually everybody who goes into politics wants to do, which is to make a difference and make your community a better place. I think what I've just said applies to people who go into local politics as well as national politics; they want to make their town or county a better place, and we want to make our country a better place. Some people want to make the world a better place. We want to further the lot of our fellow citizens; we want to make a difference.

I think that's the reason everybody I know who has gone into politics from different parties has. We may have differences in how to achieve that objective or even precisely how you define that objective but that is the motive. It is the only valid motive, but I think it applies to almost everyone I know.

TOBY JAMES: Were there particular changes that you wanted to make in Britain?

MICHAEL HOWARD: Well, I suppose, from the time I started to think about politics, I always rejected socialism. It seemed to me that it was basically misguided and that the right way forward was to encourage the individual rather than to seek collective answers to the challenges that every community faces. So that instinctively made me a Conservative. But did I have very specific objectives when I came to get interested in politics? Not really.

TOBY JAMES: Did you always have aspirations to go on to become Conservative Party leader?

MICHAEL HOWARD: When I started out?

TOBY JAMES: Yes.

MICHAEL HOWARD: No, absolutely not at all. I wanted to become a Member of Parliament. I thought, and still think, that it's a great honour to be able to serve one's citizens in that way. Beyond that, to be honest, I was a practising lawyer for over twenty years and I thought that if I ended up as Attorney General, I would be very fortunate. But that never happened.

TOBY JAMES: Could you describe a little bit more the circumstances by which you became leader? What made you decide to make that jump?

MICHAEL HOWARD: Well, I had been Home Secretary for four years, so it would have been strange if I hadn't stood for the leadership in 1997. One of the best things that happened to me was that I wasn't successful in that leadership election. Then I served as shadow Foreign Secretary for two years and, after that, I went to the back benches, really in order to see whether I enjoyed that sufficiently or found it sufficiently worthwhile to stand for Parliament again in 2001.

I found that I did quite enjoy life on the back benches, so I decided to stand again. Then, to my surprise, Iain Duncan Smith asked me to become shadow Chancellor. I wasn't really anticipating any return to the front bench at all. You know what happened after that, with the unravelling of the leadership of Iain Duncan Smith, and everybody then said: 'You've got to stand and you've got to do it.'

REFLECTIONS ON HOW WE SHOULD ASSESS PARTY LEADERS

TOBY JAMES: By what criteria do you think we should assess the main party leaders in Britain?

MICHAEL HOWARD: Yes, I must confess that I have some difficulty with the criteria you have adopted because I think that looking at election performances is a bit too mechanical. It doesn't really give full weight to what you call context [in Chapter 2] and what I would call events. It's a bit more valid – considerably more valid – in terms of leaders of the opposition, because you become Leader of the Opposition to win an election, and so your performance in the election is absolutely a fair way of judging your performance overall. It is a lot less valid when it comes to judging the performance of prime ministers though, because you should really judge the performances of prime ministers on the record of their performance in government. Did the economy grow while they were Prime Minister? That is not the only objective, but it is not bad shorthand for other objectives. So, I think to concentrate solely on their electoral performance is not really a proper measure of the effectiveness of the Prime Minister. Even as Leader of the Opposition, there are problems in using electoral performances.

TOBY JAMES: So, what are the other things that we should take into account then? Obviously whether leaders win elections, but what else?

MICHAEL HOWARD: In terms of prime ministers, I think that you really ought to take into account their record.

Take Tony Blair. I think, on your basis, Tony Blair clearly and rightly comes out as one of the most successful Labour prime ministers. His electoral form was outstanding and nobody can deny him that.

His record as Prime Minister is much more mixed, to put it as neutrally as I can. I don't think he was a particularly good Prime Minister. Even if you leave out Iraq, on the domestic front he squandered the most wonderful opportunity an incoming British Prime Minister has ever had. There was a huge appetite for reform, but he was very half-hearted. He did make some reforms, and they were, on the whole, quite good reforms, but I think he could have gone much, much further. He could have put in reforms that really could have been transformative for the country, but he didn't do that when he had the opportunity to do so.

So, when it comes to prime ministers, just to look at their electoral performance – although it is a highly relevant factor, and Charles is quite right in saying every Prime Minister has in mind re-election – I think only tells part of the story.

REFLECTIONS ON STATECRAFT THEORY AND HIS OWN LEADERSHIP

TOBY JAMES: The theory we are using in the book – the statecraft theory – suggests that leaders have to achieve five tasks. The first of those, perhaps self-evidently, is to devise a successful winning electoral strategy. What would you say are the main challenges party leaders face in terms of developing a successful strategy?

MICHAEL HOWARD: The main challenge is you don't know, when you're setting out to devise your strategy, what is going to be a winning strategy. You can't tell.

Nowadays, there are very sophisticated polling techniques available. Everybody has their own view on whether it is a good thing or a bad thing. When you're close to an election, however, they can be of very considerable help in guiding you to what would be a winning strategy. But, by that time, it is often too late. The decisions that you have taken earlier on, by the time you have got to the election, narrow your options very considerably.

If you go, say, four years back – or, in my case, eighteen months back, as I only had eighteen months between the time I was elected leader and the election – you might do things differently. Even eighteen months from the election, to know exactly what people are going to be thinking – and what is going to influence their votes eighteen months ahead – is a big task. I mean you can learn from previous mistakes and you can try to put them right, but that only takes you somewhere along the road.

TOBY JAMES: Do you think that winning the election drives everything party leaders are trying to do in their five years, eighteen months or whatever the length of their tenure is? Are leaders constantly having to make sacrifices, when they are thinking about the policies that they are going to introduce, to make sure that they have winning that forthcoming election in their mind?

MICHAEL HOWARD: Not if you're Prime Minister. If you're Prime Minister you have to govern the country and do the things you think are right for the country.

Actually, I think this is probably a mistaken view in many ways, from the point of view of winning elections. My own view, and I'm rather old-fashioned about these things, is that, even as Leader of the Opposition, you've got to put forward the policies you think are right for the country. Now, they may not win you the next election – so there is a tension there.

CHARLES CLARKE: For what it's worth, I don't think that is an old-fashioned view at all; I think it is entirely correct. The challenge in opposition is do you simply oppose everything the government is doing, or do you contrast what the government is doing with what you would do if you were in government at that point?

MICHAEL HOWARD: Oh, you would do the second. There's no question. You don't oppose everything the government does.

CHARLES CLARKE: Some do. The Miliband opposition did that. I agree with you strongly that the second option is the right one.

MICHAEL HOWARD: You've got to take the second option and you've got to do what you think is right, but that's not necessarily going to win you the election.

I will give you an example. I did something that I don't think has ever been done before – or since. I wanted to reduce spending, but I didn't want to be open to the charge of destroying the health service or anything of that kind, so I commissioned and published a very detailed set of proposals as to where we would find the money I'd said we would save. I know that some of the people who were involved in that exercise, who later went on to occupy positions of great influence, certainly, in retrospect (and possibly even at the time), thought that that was a great mistake. It probably cost us some seats where our opponents were able to identify some of the things we were going to do that would have a disproportionate impact on that particular area. To some extent, it was successful in blunting the predictable attacks from the Labour Party on the health service – when they made those attacks, some would say to them: 'That is not true; the Conservatives have indicated where they are going to make these cuts.' However, it certainly didn't have the positive impact I had hoped it would.

CHARLES CLARKE: Do you recall how long before the election you published this?

MICHAEL HOWARD: A few months before.

CHARLES CLARKE: We, as you know, had a massive controversy about the shadow Budget in 1992. It was designed to do exactly the same – showing that we did have responsible economic policy. Neil Kinnock said in his interview with us that, had it not been published in the election campaign, had it been published six months before, it may have worked better.

MICHAEL HOWARD: It didn't go into the detail that our exercise did.

CHARLES CLARKE: It didn't do the detail of your spending exercise, but it did do the detail of tax rates and those kinds of things.

MICHAEL HOWARD: That's right. Well, I know we did publish it a few months in advance. It was very detailed and I commissioned it as soon as I became leader. It was an extraordinary exercise, but it didn't really have the impact I had hoped.

TOBY JAMES: The second component of the statecraft framework is establishing a reputation for competence, especially on the issue of the economy, which tends to be foremost in the voters' minds. What are the key challenges leaders face in trying to achieve a reputation for competence?

MICHAEL HOWARD: Well, that varies completely according to the circumstances. The problem I had was that, at the time of the 2005 election, the general perception was that the economy was in great shape. We said Gordon Brown was borrowing too much, and a large chunk of the savings I was going to make was explicitly going to be devoted to reducing government borrowing. With the benefit of hindsight, I can say 'I told you so', but, at the time, everybody thought that unemployment was low, interest rates were low, mortgage rates were low. All that had been the case since before 1997, since the time we emerged from the Exchange Rate Mechanism. Everybody thought that Labour deserved the credit for that. So it wasn't so much in our case establishing a reputation for economic competence; it was the difficulty of challenging the government's record of economic competence, which, at that time, was extremely well established in voters' minds.

If you contrast that with the problem Ed Miliband faced when Labour's reputation for economic competence was trashed by the 2008 crash (in the same way our reputation for economic competence had been destroyed by the ERM): he had the task of re-establishing a reputation for economic competence, which he lamentably failed to achieve.

TOBY JAMES: Is the economy the key issue that shapes whether leaders are successful in winning elections?

MICHAEL HOWARD: It varies, it is not always all about the economy, because if you go back to 1997, the economy by then was in great shape. The recovery was well under way and everything was going very well. That was the foundation for what happened for the next however many years until 2008.

TOBY JAMES: But people's perceptions of economic competence?

MICHAEL HOWARD: The visuals of our emergence from the ERM and Norman Lamont standing on the threshold of the Treasury were so entrenched in people's minds that what was actually happening in the economy didn't cut through. These are all examples, in my opinion, of what you call context [in Chapter 2] and I call events, and why they are so fundamentally important.

TOBY JAMES: The third one is about managing the party, the parliamentary party and the broader party. What are the key challenges leaders face?

MICHAEL HOWARD: Yes, and I would claim that was probably my greatest success, because the Tory Party had been riven with bickering, dissent, back-biting and division from before 1997, really. Obviously the John Major years were characterised by that behaviour, and it continued under William Hague and under Iain Duncan Smith.

I was able to restore a very considerable degree of discipline to the Conservative Party, and there were really no arguments or dissent during the eighteen months before the election. Of course, after that – when I said I was going, and during the leadership election – things were different. But in the eighteen months leading up to the election, I did lead a disciplined, coherent party that was free of all the things that had been such a mess before.

CHARLES CLARKE: I think you've generally got credit for that. People respect both that fact and the fact that you have created a coherent leadership election system for the future.

MICHAEL HOWARD: After the election, I was under a lot of pressure once I said I would go to go quickly. A huge amount of pressure. My main thought when I was elected – I was the fourth leader of the Conservative Party in six years – was: I don't want people in eighteen months' time to say if only we hadn't done it in such a rush, we might have chosen someone different. I wanted to give the party no excuse for attacking whoever they chose as leader. So I was determined to give them a long run at it so they could look at everyone carefully. That was my main consideration.

CHARLES CLARKE: And you succeeded.

MICHAEL HOWARD: Yes.

TOBY JAMES: Were there any thoughts in your own mind that you would not resign after the election? Is there a 'golden rule' that leaders have to resign after the election?

MICHAEL HOWARD: No, I had given it a lot of thought. All the people around me tried to persuade me in the hours after the election to change my mind. But I had decided that, if I had managed to destroy the overall majority, then I would stay; but if there was an overall majority, then I would go. I worked out that I would have been sixty-eight or sixty-nine by the time of the next election, and a younger leader would have had a much better chance.

We weren't far from that. Although we were sixty seats behind, it would only have taken 14,500 or so votes in the key constituencies to switch to us to deprive Tony Blair of his majority.

TOBY JAMES: The fourth component was about winning the battle of ideas on key policy issues. How do you think you did on that?

MICHAEL HOWARD: Well, clearly we didn't win the election, so I can't pretend that we won the battle of ideas. I thought that when we honed down our message – the pledges on things that people obviously cared about: schools, hospitals, law and order, and immigration – that we would win people over.

There is a big argument about whether you talk about the vision or you talk about practical things. My view, which was probably wrong, but… My view was that people had had enough of politicians fighting about their vision. They really wanted someone who was going to make a practical difference to the things that mattered to them in their daily lives. That was my thinking. We devised specific policies such as cleaner hospitals and better discipline in schools (which I think is still an issue). I thought that if I could persuade people I really had ideas about the things that really mattered to them in their daily lives, it would persuade them. Well, it didn't. Whether it did persuade them or not, whether they didn't want to risk what they thought was a splendid economy… It is very hard, I think, for an opposition to win when people think the economy is in great shape.

TOBY JAMES: I guess one of the main challenges in trying to make those arguments is that the media doesn't always look at the policy details.

MICHAEL HOWARD: Enoch Powell once said: 'A politician who complains about the media is like a fisherman who complains about the sea.'

TOBY JAMES: The last component is about managing the constitution and the party's and leader's interests.

MICHAEL HOWARD: I don't think that really cropped up at all. I mean I did champion English votes for English laws. That was, I think, the only constitutional issue that I got involved with.

I did have one regret. There was a theme in my mind that unified the policies I was putting forward, and that was fairness. I thought that all the things I was putting forward were fair – fair to working people. English votes for English laws were fair to the English voters, and I never properly articulated them as a theme, and perhaps I could have.

TOBY JAMES: Would you say that the challenges of leading are different for each of the parties?

MICHAEL HOWARD: Yes, of course, because each party has to confront those challenges in the light of its history and its record. The history of those parties is very different and starts off at very different standpoints, yes.

The Labour Party's challenge is to convince people that it is, to put it in shorthand, not just about the least well off in society. We all care about the least well off in society; we have different views on how they can best be helped. But if you just talk about the least well off in society, or you convey the impression that that is all you're really interested in, then that is not going to cut the mustard. The Conservatives, by contrast, have to confront the image of being selfish and out only to help the rich.

Now, neither of those caricatures is true; it is certainly not true that the Labour Party is only concerned with the least well off in society, although it sounded a lot like that in the 2015 general election. It is certainly not true that the Conservative Party is out to help the rich and the selfish, but those are the caricatures that the leaders of each party have to try to counter.

REFLECTIONS ON THE IMPORTANCE OF THE LEADER'S PERSONALITY

CHARLES CLARKE: That is the list of the five criteria. You have noted the importance of context and events. But do you think there are any that aren't included that really should be, if one is trying to assess the quality of leadership? Is there anything missing from the model that you felt was important when you were there and trying to conduct your job as leader of the Conservative Party?

MICHAEL HOWARD: Well, I have already made my point about the difference between how you assess the importance of prime ministers and opposition.

CHARLES CLARKE: Yes, that is an important point.

MICHAEL HOWARD: One obvious missing factor – but it is entirely subjective – is the personality of the leader. That is a huge factor in determining the outcome of elections and I was found wanting in that regard.

CHARLES CLARKE: I actually think there is a lot in this and have thought about it in the past without being able to nail it down. There are some people who walk into a room and everybody looks, and there are other people who kind of float around in the corner and nobody notices, and so on. I think you're right about personality, but it is hard to be clear. What do you think are the components? Do you have a concept of what you mean by personality or charisma or articulacy?

MICHAEL HOWARD: It is, I suppose, charisma, and so many things go into it. At the end of the day, it is entirely subjective. Appearance, voice…

CHARLES CLARKE: Robin Cook once said that he wasn't running for the leadership of the Labour Party in 1994 because he didn't look the part. He felt he looked like a pixie or something, which I always thought was nonsense. Are you sympathetic to his line of thinking?

MICHAEL HOWARD: I think it is a factor. I don't think it is *the* factor. Robin Cook was a remarkable man and he might have overcome that.

CHARLES CLARKE: I agree. Personality. I think Michael has got a very good point here; my problem is concluding anything sensible about it.

MICHAEL HOWARD: You can't, because it is how the voters see someone.

TOBY JAMES: And does personality also matter in terms of many of the other statecraft tasks, such as managing the party?

MICHAEL HOWARD: Well, yes. One of the elements that goes into personality is the ability to convey a sense of authority. That is critical; you have to be able to convey a sense of authority. Authority, after all, is almost the essence of leadership.

CHARLES CLARKE: I think that relates very much to intellectual self-confidence, and indeed confidence generally. I think the more you feel confident in what you're saying, the more you feel you're going in the right direction with people.

MICHAEL HOWARD: Funnily enough, I'm not quite so sure about that, because I think Ed Miliband was very confident in what he believed. I think he really was, but that is not enough. If what you're confident in is so blatantly wrong, then you are not going to do business.

CHARLES CLARKE: No, I agree with you.

TOBY JAMES: Final question: in the round, how would you evaluate yourself in your time as leader?

MICHAEL HOWARD: That is the question I am not going to answer. I will leave that to others.

CHAPTER 25

WILLIAM HAGUE ON LEADERSHIP, THE CONSERVATIVE PARTY AND STATECRAFT THEORY

WILLIAM HAGUE, TOBY S. JAMES AND CHARLES CLARKE[736]

This chapter is an edited transcript of an interview with William Hague on how leaders should be judged, the challenges they face and whether the statecraft approach is a useful way of assessing them. Although William Hague contends that the statecraft model provides a viable framework, he also suggests that building strong institutional capacity within your party and demonstrating an ability to manage foreign affairs effectively are important tasks leaders need to pay attention to in order to achieve statecraft. His own time as leader took place in a very difficult context, and he considers his tenure unsuccessful in terms of developing a winning electoral strategy and demonstrating a reputation for governing competence. He argues, however, that he was much more successful in terms of party management. More broadly, he makes the point that achieving many of the statecraft goals can be very difficult in opposition, particularly when a party has only recently lost power.

• • •

736 This interview took place in the Blue Boar Hotel, London, on Wednesday 3 June 2015.

ON THE ROAD TO BECOMING LEADER

TOBY JAMES: What first motivated you to set out in politics?

WILLIAM HAGUE: Well, as with most politicians, a mixture of personal ambition and national factors. Some of us are drawn to politics because we are that sort of person. If you're interested in everything going on in public life and enjoy being the centre of attention to some extent yourself, you're drawn to these things.

But in the 1970s, in particular, there was a sense of crisis, of national drift, of big decisions having to be made about Europe and the size of the state. There was quite a significant difference between the Labour and Conservative parties on these issues, so I was easily drawn into that political debate. There were, in fact, a lot of young people joining political youth movements at that time, so I was part of that really.

TOBY JAMES: Were there key people who inspired you to get involved in politics?

WILLIAM HAGUE: Margaret Thatcher! She became leader of the Conservative Party when I was fourteen years old. The Young Conservatives and Federation of Conservative Students[737] were gaining in strength at the time – partly because of her. But what was also important to me was that I was growing up in South Yorkshire, from a Conservative point of view, with a small business background, which was the family I was brought up in. The context was one of widespread nationalised industries, large local authorities, considerable state housing and Britain being the so-called 'sick man of Europe'. You really felt change was necessary and along came this leader who said, 'We can make change!' and was convincing. So that was an added draw into politics.

737 The Young Conservatives became known as Conservative Future in 1998. Meanwhile, the Federation of Conservative Students was dissolved in 1986 and became known as the Conservative Collegiate Forum. They merged with Conservative Future in 1998.

I then went off to the 1977 Conservative Party conference, famously, and decided I should urge her on. I didn't realise that, at that point, she didn't need any urging on whatsoever! But I urged her on anyway.

CHARLES CLARKE: It was an extraordinary thing for you to get such national prominence so early in your political life. You are very unusual in that respect. Did it have an impact either on you or your future political career?

WILLIAM HAGUE: Well, it happened very innocently. Really, I didn't know anybody. I turned up at the party conference only knowing the two kind ladies from Rotherham who drove me there. I just literally put in a speaker's slip to speak. I was able to write on the slip that I'd won the Yorkshire Television public speaking competition at the age of sixteen and that perhaps helped me to be picked – but, at a few minutes' notice. They didn't know who I was otherwise. The party conferences were less prepared then than they are now in any of the main parties. It just happened of its own accord. I gave a speech nobody else had ever seen. I had written it in bed the night before and it became a media sensation.

Thanks to my mother, it didn't permanently affect my life. I was offered newspaper columns, for what seemed considerable sums of money to a schoolboy. But my mother was very clear: 'No, you're not going anywhere, you're going back to your A levels; get back to normal now.' That was very good advice, she did me a lot of good with that really.

I don't think it's been a particular advantage or disadvantage. It could easily have been a disadvantage. It can create a certain amount of jealousy or premature notoriety when you're a student or a young candidate. I did end up, at the age of seventeen, in *Private Eye*'s list of 'who never to invite to a Christmas party', because I was already a political has-been. But I enjoyed all that; it confirmed my wish to go into politics.

I was involved with student politics, but I was always conscious you had to have some other career as well. So I also went to do an MBA and worked as a management consultant at McKinsey & Company to develop myself a bit in the business world, and make sure I could always earn a living some other way – which, at times in the last few decades, I've been grateful for.

TOBY JAMES: Did you have aspirations back in 1977 to become party leader some day?

WILLIAM HAGUE: Oh, undoubtedly, yes! I think the *Daily Mail* asked me at the time whether I'd be Prime Minister one day. I tactfully said, 'Perhaps.' For a sixteen-year-old to give a more confident answer than that would have been *too* much. So yes, I certainly envisaged I was going into politics to become an MP, and who knew what would happen after that? It wasn't any more specific than that, I don't think.

TOBY JAMES: And did that stay with you after the age of sixteen? Once you became elected as an MP, you wanted to become the leader some day?

WILLIAM HAGUE: Yes, that always was my ambition, but I didn't know it would come up as quickly as it did. I couldn't have anticipated that, after I got into the Cabinet in my mid-thirties, my party would be so devastated at the 1997 general election and a lot of its potential leaders would be removed, which is one of the things that opened the way for me.

REFLECTIONS ON HOW TO ASSESS PARTY LEADERS

TOBY JAMES: You eventually became leader. By what criteria should contemporary party leaders of the main three political parties be evaluated?

WILLIAM HAGUE: I think your criteria [in Chapter 2] provide a pretty good framework. So I don't want to reinvent the wheel, which you have already invented. These are clearly very important and central points that you have. There are a couple of additional points, however. One, which can easily get overlooked, is building long-term capacity and institutional strength in your party, so that when you leave, everything you worked for isn't lost. It's surprising how many very, very successful political leaders don't provide the platform for their successors that they would have wanted for themselves. And they're then furious about the performance of those who succeed them. We can think of examples in both main parties in recent decades – even with the most successful leaders of both parties – in terms of longevity and government, and that's a wider issue.

This matters a lot to me because, in my situation, I had to think more in terms of the party's institution in the longer term than the short term, a lot of the time. It was a long shot to get the Conservative Party back into power a few years after it had lost in 1997. So there had to be some long-term building, and this meant rewriting its constitution. I don't claim to have done all that perfectly or successfully, but the longer-term institution-building is important.

Institutional capacity in local government is also really important. Active and numerous councillors with a ward-level organisation are important for fighting campaigns. Facing a long-term challenge, I gave a lot of attention to party recruitment in local government. I spent, what would have been for most leaders in those circumstances, an excessive amount of time on local government. But the Conservative Party had gone down to being third in the number of councillors in the UK. The *Conservative Party* was *third.* I think by the end of that parliament we were back to being the biggest party in local government.

Now, strength in local government happens almost of its own accord in opposition, but not *entirely* of its own accord. You need to put some time in. I spent a lot of time going around the country saying that we had to put in a full slate of council candidates and put a national effort behind local campaigns.

The other lapse of your framework is in terms of governing. There are aspects of governing that are part of establishing a reputation of confidence or a winning electoral strategy that need greater emphasis. Particularly in foreign affairs. The party leader has to be able to conduct the affairs of the nation at the top level, and success or failure in that can make a big difference to everything else. Even though foreign affairs are rarely prominent in general elections, some of the things we most remember Margaret Thatcher and Tony Blair for, favourably and unfavourably, are in foreign affairs. The ability to conduct the affairs of states at a global level is crucial. A political party leader who isn't regarded by the electorate as likely to be able to do that is at a big disadvantage in becoming Prime Minister.

So, I would add those points. They're not inconsistent with your framework, but I would accentuate them.

TOBY JAMES: The statecraft criteria really assess leaders in terms of whether they win elections or move their party in their directions. Is that a fair test of leaders?

WILLIAM HAGUE: Well, overall, I think yes – subject to the additional points that I've just been making on the previous question. I do think, overall, flexibly interpreted, it's a fair framework.

DEVELOPING A WINNING ELECTORAL STRATEGY

TOBY JAMES: So, taking each of the components in turn, the first is developing a winning electoral strategy. What do you say are the main challenges leaders face in trying to achieve that goal?

WILLIAM HAGUE: Well, where to begin on that? The first challenge is to be clear about what it is; what strategy you're pursuing. Some leadership elections produce a clear answer to that: it's the candidate who sets out a particular political strategy. Of course, they then develop it in more detail. When Margaret Thatcher was elected Conservative leader, it was clear which direction she was going in. There were many more compromises along the way than people know, or often remember, but there was a direction nevertheless that was different from Ted Heath's. The party chose a direction as well as a leader.

When Tony Blair was elected, his party also chose a direction as well as a leader. There are other elections where they chose a leader but not a direction. And this happens very commonly in the immediate aftermath of an election defeat, when the party isn't yet ready for a new direction. And I would say it's true of the Labour Party in the 2010 parliament, and it's true of my party when I was elected in 1997. They were choosing me partly because of a direction on Europe they wanted to take. None of us could yet define exactly the rest of the political directions we were going to go in.

So, that's the first requirement of a winning electoral strategy. The strategy was part of the leadership election and it isn't always.

The second, of course, is making sure the party has a sufficient consensus about the strategy and that it *will* follow the leader.

The third is that, when those two things are satisfied, the electoral strategy is commanding enough centre ground or common ground with the electorate. Unless all those three things apply, you don't have a winning strategy.

TOBY JAMES: To what extent do you think developing a winning electoral strategy occupies the entirety of a leader's mind? Do they always have their mind on the forthcoming general election?

WILLIAM HAGUE: Well, if they're the Leader of the Opposition then it's their *raison d'être*. You are doing that job in order to win the election and get another job – the job of Prime Minister. So you are always thinking about that.

But you can be distracted enormously by trying to achieve one of your other criteria: managing your own party. You can, particularly in a defeated party, or even in government if you have a small majority, spend a lot of time being preoccupied with managing those difficult things rather than forming a winning electoral strategy.

That can suck away a lot of time and energy. Certainly in my case, because it was a pretty turbulent party. Sometimes in opposition, a leader can only show to the country that he or she can govern by governing their own party.

So the party management task is part of how you demonstrate that successfully or unsuccessfully to the country.

TOBY JAMES: How do you think you've fared in terms of developing a winning electoral strategy in the context of the times?

WILLIAM HAGUE: Well, not successfully at the general election level, which is the main one. Funnily enough, I did have a winning electoral strategy for the European elections and local elections, although those are not so difficult to win in opposition.

At the general election level we failed because, for most of the country, it didn't seem as if we had a complete, coherent, alternative vision for the country. That's largely because we felt so hemmed-in on so many different subjects. Labour's pre-eminence in the public mind on matters like health and education was so overwhelming; it was very difficult to establish an alternative agenda that gained any traction.

We did have an alternative agenda: we developed the idea of free schools that's now coming into action. But it was barely noticed and we didn't do enough to present a whole philosophy around that. So we didn't succeed, clearly, in having a winning electoral strategy.

TOBY JAMES: Were there things, in hindsight, that you could have done differently? Or was it that the context was just so difficult?

WILLIAM HAGUE: We could have been more consistent. I think one of the temptations in office is, when something doesn't work, to try something else. You don't get much of a hearing if you're in opposition and not expected to win the election. In fact, trying one thing after another also doesn't work. It is better to plug away at something, which you may take years to get known for, rather than try different approaches. So, if I had it to do again – which I never will have to do again, thankfully – that's what I'd do.

CHARLES CLARKE: You're young enough.

WILLIAM HAGUE: Young enough, but not daft enough!

If I were to do it again, I'd give more attention to not just the party reforms and the party manifesto, but the ideas. Of course, it's something that's hard to anticipate, having just lost office after eighteen years of government, what can then be developed consistently through the following four years. That proved difficult to do in our circumstances and we weren't strict enough about doing it.

TOBY JAMES: After the 2001 election, did you consider trying to stay on as leader?

WILLIAM HAGUE: Well, I pre-empted that by announcing my resignation immediately. I got all that clear in my mind beforehand. Under the right circumstances, I would have been very willing to carry on. But I think if you are in my position, or Neil Kinnock's position in the 1980s, people understand that it would likely take two terms to get back into government.

You've only got those two terms, however, you can't lose in opposition for more than two terms. To carry on into a second term, you therefore need to have got roughly halfway without laying down the exact number of seats. There wasn't a target. You just know halfway when you see it, in whatever combination of votes and seats it occurs, depending on the quirks of the system on election day. In 1987, Neil Kinnock could make a case for having got halfway: there was a swing back to Labour, and you could imagine Labour winning the next election. It didn't happen but it was perfectly credible. We didn't get to that point in 2001, so I don't think there would have been any point, therefore, in carrying on.

There was a huge debate, not among my advisors, who all understood me well enough to know that was that and probably agreed with it, but among shadow Cabinet colleagues who gathered the morning after the election. Many said: 'You can't leave us now; we need you – at least for the time being.' Now, that could have been decisive, but, from my own point of view, it seemed like a complete waste of time.

CHARLES CLARKE: Is it worth staying on for a few months to help the party transition? For example, Ed Miliband didn't in 2015 and Neil Kinnock did in 1992.

WILLIAM HAGUE: Yes, it is. I strongly belonged to the Callaghan, Major, Hague way of doing it. Not what Ed Miliband did, because I think you do have an obligation to the party, and you still have quite a bit of authority in that context to try to stabilise the party, to represent it in Parliament, and to react to any national or international crisis. The country needs a Leader of the Opposition. It's important again for the long-term health of a party that the leader doesn't just walk out that minute. I served, after we lost the election in early June, until the middle of September. I served an extra day because of 9/11; we suspended the counting of votes for my successor when the Twin Towers were attacked. So I did more than three months in that situation, which I rather enjoyed, knowing I was standing down. You welcome the new Members of Parliament who have just got in, and do all of that. It's slightly different in the Labour Party, though, because there's a constitutional deputy leader position.

CHARLES CLARKE: Do you have any reflections on image? The phrase 'detoxifying the brand' is often used after a party suffers a major defeat. For example, Labour used a red rose rather than the red flags under Neil Kinnock to signify change; Tony Blair used 'New Labour' as opposed to 'Labour'; and, David Cameron was famous for 'hugging a hoodie' and driving a sledge of huskies. In your case, you tried with the Notting Hill Carnival and wore a baseball cap to try to change the image, not just of yourself but of your party. I think that you were less than successful and I never quite understood why that was the case. Did you have any reflections on that?

WILLIAM HAGUE: Well, yes, I do think perhaps our efforts to change the image at that time were almost too soon. We went straight into that and thus were open to criticism. Perhaps they were clumsy efforts in themselves, or perhaps they were subject to more ridicule than parties who'd been in opposition for a few years.

When the image has been successfully changed, as in the cases that you are pointing to, Charles, the party will have had quite a number of years in opposition. But if you try immediately to do that, you're up against the ridicule of: 'Oh, they've lost completely, and *now* they are claiming to be different.' And, actually, time has to elapse, particularly for your own party to accept it.

It's often only after they've lost a second time that they do see the need for a change of image and a new strategic direction. So I think we rushed into that a bit too quickly and perhaps clumsily. That was the right direction but the wrong time, and not brilliantly executed.

And that shows you can be the right leader at the wrong time, and that's better than the other way round. But, of course, you have to roll the dice now and again in politics. Politics is full of people who waited for the perfect moment to be leader, then the chance never came along again. You just don't know what will happen a few years ahead.

GOVERNING COMPETENCE

TOBY JAMES: The second aspect of the framework is about establishing a reputation for competence on the key issues of the day, which invariably is the economy. What were the key challenges that you see party leaders in general facing and that you faced?

WILLIAM HAGUE: Well, if you are in opposition, you only get the chance to do this if the government is doing something wrong, if people think the economy is going wrong. Otherwise, you don't have any chance to prove this, except by avoiding commitments that are a disadvantage when it comes to the election.

We did have a direction, which was lower spending and lower taxes – true to the Conservative Party direction. But, since Britain was going through a period of sustained economic expansion at the time, there wasn't a lot of room in the world for a focus on the economic policies of the Conservative Party.

It's a very, very important area. The other problem is that the public's perception of a party's credibility takes a long time to change. The Conservative Party, when I was leader, had experienced a massive blow to its reputation for economic competence five years earlier. It took a great blow in 2007–08 to Labour's reputation for that to be turned around again. So this does depend a lot on events and on the record of who's in government. When that record goes wrong, the opposition has the chance to take over the reputation for economic competence. But without those circumstances, you are up against formidable obstacles. It's when those opportunities arise, or if you are in government, that this is the absolute thing the leader has to focus on more than anything else, perhaps.

TOBY JAMES: Is it always the economy and the perceptions of economic competence that decide leaders' fortunes, do you think?

WILLIAM HAGUE: Well, it is the largest factor. You can preside over a successful economy and lose, as we did in 1997, but such was the blow of 1992 that people didn't attribute the economic success that followed to the Conservative government. They actually thought the country was succeeding in spite of the government. But in all normal circumstances, it's a vitally decisive factor, and certainly, I think, it has been in the general election we've just had [2015].

TOBY JAMES: When you were developing your own electoral strategy for 2001, you must have faced a dilemma. On one hand, the economy is a key issue that would decide the election, so it would have been logical to focus on that. On the other, Labour had established their reputation, so there was a case for focusing on other issues.

WILLIAM HAGUE: There was, and we developed our thinking about trying to explain the moral case for lower taxation, and how spending was getting too high, and taxation of pension funds would mean long-term damage. But I didn't find there was much hearing for that, except for a minority of the country. So we did develop a pretty clear alternative economic agenda, as I say. Many of our proposals from then, twenty years later, are actually being done today. For example, abolishing tax on savings at the basic rate – an idea that popped up again in the last Budget – was part of our proposals to reward savers. But there was no groundswell for that at the time.

PARTY MANAGEMENT

TOBY JAMES: You've touched a little on managing your own party already, but this is one of the key statecraft tasks set out in Chapter 2. What are the key challenges that party leaders in general – and you, in particular – faced in that area?

WILLIAM HAGUE: Well, this varies enormously from one leader to another, but it's a big part of the leader's job. This is the area I gave a lot of attention to, because the Conservative Party was very divided in 1997. I remember in the leadership hustings, when I told the Conservative MPs that there would have to be a single shadow Cabinet line on whether or not to join the euro, there were gasps around the room. Is it possible to have a single line? Can anybody imagine us having a single line?

Now, we did manage to do that. The policy was to not join the euro in that parliament or the next. There was one resignation along the way, but, actually, I did take the less Eurosceptic element of the Conservative Party along with me in the anti-euro policy in the end.

That was a big challenge, especially when you've just left government, because we'd lost half the party, but not necessarily the right half. You're managing 'big names', who were substantial figures in previous governments, but you need to move on from them. I gave a lot of time and attention to reshuffles, to changing the personnel of the party. While I didn't succeed in a lot of things, I did succeed in that parliament. I almost completely renewed the personnel of the shadow Cabinet over the course of the four years. That was done without a coup, rebellion or a counter-reaction. The 'old faces', for want of a better term, were retired. You have to be quite ruthless and calculating, and think a year ahead every time, so that every reshuffle contains, for those who look very hard, the clues for the next reshuffle.

CHARLES CLARKE: It was often joked that you had a stronger shadow Cabinet on the back benches than the front benches. Can you just talk about the reasons why you took this approach? Why not have some of the 'big beasts' from former Thatcher/Major governments in the opposition shadow Cabinet?

WILLIAM HAGUE: Well, it was clearly a long-term project to rebuild the Conservative Party. I think it goes back to the discussion about changing one's image. I think if parties lose very heavily, they can't just present the same people again at the next election. They're too closely identified with the policies associated with that defeat. The Labour Party suffered from this with Ed Balls in the 2015 election. So it was necessary.

I started off, in order to create unity and manage the party, with a whole range of people: Peter Lilley, Stephen Dorrell, Brian Mawhinney, and many others, were all in the key positions in the shadow Cabinet. But, over time, a mixture of their own wish to leave after a year or two and my desire to move some of them on meant that, within two or three years, I'd changed all of that and I'd brought in new peers, too. I brought in Theresa May and Andrew Lansley in that first parliament into the shadow Cabinet. It was vital for long-term renewal to do that.

The other thing on managing the party is the challenge of managing your predecessors. This varies greatly from one leader to another because, again, it gets easier the longer a party has been in opposition. But, if you've just gone into opposition, then you have a lot of former prime ministers around. Ed Miliband had that experience. I'm not saying it was a negative one, in his case, but there were two big former prime ministers to manage. In my case, there were three. Three, who, if mixed together on any occasion, created the political equivalent of a nuclear explosion. Do not underestimate the management of running a party conference where Ted Heath and Margaret Thatcher decide to come on the same day. Both have to be accommodated on a platform and are loose in the building giving comments about things. I used to think that Tony Blair doesn't have any former leaders – the last Prime Minister was Jim Callaghan, who wasn't as troublesome. Don't underestimate it. Former leaders can be quite distracting for the contemporary leader.

CHARLES CLARKE: I wonder if Tony saw to that by putting a former leader's daughter in his Cabinet.

WILLIAM HAGUE: Well, that was a good move, but there was no such move available to me.

CHARLES CLARKE: Mark Thatcher?

I was very interested in your discussion about unity around the euro decision. Of course, everybody thinks divided parties are losers. I was nonetheless struck by the force with which you put the point that you *had* to be united on the euro. Why did you feel that unity was so central on this euro question when you came in? Was it because of the issue itself, or the desire to demonstrate strength in the opposition party?

WILLIAM HAGUE: It was because in my two years in the Cabinet – I had been in the Cabinet just two years before the election defeat – it had become debilitating in the Conservative Party.

CHARLES CLARKE: The issue about Europe, in particular?

WILLIAM HAGUE: Yes, the issue about how we approached the euro created factions within the Cabinet. It created long, difficult Cabinet meetings that exhibited the divisions within the party. And that then fed down into the entire party. So, if you recall in the 1997 election, we had a whole spate of arguments about which candidates were going to express John Major's line on the euro and which ones were definitely against joining the euro anyway. Of course, there were dozens, including in the Cabinet, who were against joining the euro. This then came down to textual analysis of every election address and front pages of newspapers. All these rebels... So it became a destructive thing in the party and far greater than the importance of the issue when ranked alongside many other issues. It was really a cancer in the party. Therefore, if a new leader couldn't deal with that decisively, that was the test of a new leader. To establish your authority you had to deal with that, but also you didn't want to fight another election with that same chaos.

WINNING THE BATTLE OF IDEAS

TOBY JAMES: The fourth statecraft task is about winning the battle of ideas on key policy areas, particularly within the parliamentary parties, on both sides of the House of Commons. Is that an area you felt you succeeded in?

WILLIAM HAGUE: Well, we didn't succeed. We started on that, but no, we didn't succeed.

Again, there's a partial excuse, if you like, which was the overwhelming, very prolonged honeymoon of the Labour government at the time. We tried to tackle this with various think-piece speeches and we engaged in the battle of ideas, particularly about taxation and education and the future of Europe. But we never remotely got into the position where we were in, what you call, 'political argument hegemony'. We were on the reverse end of that. We were not in a position to do it, I think, in the first period in opposition. Maybe we didn't make a sufficiently coherent, sustained and across-the-board effort at it. So I agree it is an important criterion, but not one we succeeded in doing in 2001.

TOBY JAMES: What about the euro? Obviously Britain never joined the euro; it was on the agenda at the time and it was something that you argued against.

WILLIAM HAGUE: Certainly we did win the argument about that in the country, and that affected what was happening, because a referendum would have been necessary to join the euro. So that made it harder for a Labour government to put it forward and win. But that, in the view of most voters, was not one of the top issues that they were worried about in the election. On the whole, they didn't worry too much about those issues in elections, which is a terrible position for an opposition to be in.

CONSTITUTIONAL MANAGEMENT

TOBY JAMES: The fifth statecraft task is about constitution…

WILLIAM HAGUE: Yes. Now, here, you're talking about the UK constitution, and you're right to have it in there, because it's about changes to the electoral system or the House of Lords or devolution, and balancing the composition of the United Kingdom.

It can be of vast political importance. How successful were we at this? Well, we weren't really in a position to *manage* it, but we had to reconcile ourselves to it – the biggest change being structural change. The referendums in Scotland and Wales, and in London on having a Mayor of London – those were very important constitutional changes.

With the Conservative Party having been dead set against devolution, I then had to turn that around to accepting the democratic outcome of the referendums, and campaigning to win seats in the Scottish Parliament and the Welsh Assembly. We decided to create our own party structure in Scotland that mirrored the new settlement in Scotland, with a more independent party that elects its own leader in the Scottish Parliament.

So we took the decision after the referendum to embrace devolution, which I think has been vindicated fifteen years on. The Conservative Party has a very credible leader in Scotland, who was a distinctive Scottish leader. We took the decision that permitted that to happen, with benefits that are long term, hopefully. I also removed our opposition to the creation of the office of the Mayor of London, and continued to not keep opposing things that involved decentralisation. That was a bit tricky in the party, and now we are standing on our head, but perhaps it was time to do that. I think we did it successfully.

TOBY JAMES: At the time, electoral system reform was, in some ways, on the agenda. That could have had a significant impact on the Conservative Party.

WILLIAM HAGUE: Well, there was the Jenkins Commission. We didn't have much of a role in managing that from opposition. We never really thought there was any chance of that, we thought Paddy Ashdown was being strung along by Tony Blair, and perhaps we were right. We just couldn't see how electoral reform could be introduced by a Labour Party with 420 Members of Parliament. Electoral system reform was a proposal predicated on a narrow Labour victory, since it could realign the left and create that centre-left majority. But there was such a centre-left majority in the election anyway, all that became academic. So that wasn't something for the Conservative Party to manage; we were managing all these other things.

PERSONALITY

CHARLES CLARKE: You're probably the only party leader ever to have been trained as a management consultant at McKinsey. Do you think that training helped you in being a leader? Should we require all party leaders to go through some McKinsey-type training to deal with the issues they have to address?

It's not an entirely serious question but it's not entirely flippant either. Some party leaders – throughout the history of Labour, at least – would absolutely, completely excoriate the idea of management being a skill you had to have, or that you could be trained in anyway.

WILLIAM HAGUE: Well, broadly, the answer is no. Being a management consultant, I found it very useful to me in running government departments. Particularly in my first job as junior minister – Minister of Pensions – there were reams of data, figures and complex calculations. 'This is what I'm trained to do,' I thought! In having a sense of how you motivate and lead a large government department, that management training can be useful. Less so in politics, because these are not people you employ in a party. You order them to do something and they do the opposite. It is a very different situation.

I did re-organise the party, and I created a new constitution with Archie Norman, who was a friend of mine from the McKinsey days. In a sense, we brought a bit of management consultancy to the party. But this wouldn't have helped with the decisive factors that you identify in your framework.

TOBY JAMES: Are there other skills or personality traits or characteristics that you think party leaders need in order to succeed?

WILLIAM HAGUE: Obviously communications skills are essential; you can't get very far without good all-round communication skills.

The managerial skill in the sense of, not so much the consultancy analysis, but the ability to take time and trouble over people, is very important. This is one of the reasons why, once I stood down as leader of the party, I was very clear I'd never do it again. People will say to you when you're the leader: 'If only you spent half an hour having a whisky or a cup of tea with so-and-so, they would be much happier.' But you've worked eighteen hours by then, that day, and you're preparing a speech for the morning, and so I often said: 'No, this is a grown person who doesn't need to be upset about something. They can jolly well look after themselves.'

There's a constant need, if you're a party leader, to give people a bit of your time, because that's what they crave. Whoever they are, a whole mixture: MPs, ministers, shadow ministers, activists, trade union leaders (if you are in the Labour Party), journalists, donors – you can go on for ever. You have to have the patience to do that, and some of us, after a few years of doing it, decide that's actually not our biggest skill, or it's not how we're going to spend our time. It was one of the reasons that I thought if I came back into politics after being leader, I'd happily be Foreign Secretary, negotiating something substantial with a foreign leader. But I am not going to be cheering up the latest MP who is disappointed that they haven't become Chancellor of the Exchequer in the past few weeks.

Extraordinary stamina's also required. Relentless energy. If you falter at all, the whole system falters around you and it's very obvious. You lose your authority very quickly, so tremendous daily stamina is required, in terms of personal attributes.

CHARLES CLARKE: Would you put it as building a personal support team in government and your private office?

WILLIAM HAGUE: Yes, that's a good point.

CHARLES CLARKE: What types of people are needed to be part of that team? When you were Leader of the Opposition, did you feel you relied on those people in various degrees?

WILLIAM HAGUE: Very good point, I should have mentioned that. That's very important and it's important they complement your skills, that they fill in the gaps. For instance, if you're not going to spend that half an hour having a whisky with someone, one of your team is doing it. In my case, Sebastian Coe, my great friend and chief of staff, very often did it. He was chief of staff not in the sense of sitting in the office running things – we had somebody else who did that – but he was the chief of staff who would go and see that person and say: 'William really does care about you, and you tell me what you want me to pass on to him.' You do need that somebody who everybody knows has your ear, who can double your reach and can be solving little problems and unhappinesses. Not all leaders have that, which is quite a gap.

I had an exceptional group of people, which sustained me because they were so good-humoured and such a good team. It helped me get through a very difficult period of immense criticism and regular setbacks. Quite often, articles were written about how dreadful my advisors must have been because things were not going well enough. But Seb Coe went on to organise one of the best Olympic Games in the history of the world. George Osborne has gone on to become a successful and highly regarded Chancellor of the Exchequer. Tina Stowell is now Baroness Stowell and capable Leader of the House of Lords. And Danny Finkelstein is an acclaimed writer. Those were my four closest advisors, so clearly anything that went wrong was my fault actually, because I had these brilliant people working for me. But they did make a difference; it would have been much more difficult to even get through those four years in opposition without that group of people.

I've sat on the inside of No. 10 for the last five years, and it's not always appreciated outside that David Cameron's long-term chief of staff and his deputy (Ed Llewellyn and Catherine Fall), who have been with him all the time for ten years, provide stability and an hourly solving of problems that otherwise would drain the Prime Minister's time and energy. He has complete confidence in them and they can always do what Seb Coe used to do with me.

BIBLIOGRAPHY

ACADEMIC ARTICLES

Stuart Ball,

'The Conservative Party and the formation of the National Government: August 1931', Historical Journal, 29(1), March 1986.

'The legacy of coalition: fear and loathing in Conservative politics, 1922–1931', *Contemporary British History*, 25(1), 2011.

'The politics of appeasement: the fall of the Duchess of Atholl and the Kinross & West Perth by-election, December 1938', *Scottish Historical Review*, Vol. 69, 1990.

Peter Barberis, 'Introduction: The 1964 General Election – the "Not Quite, But" and "But Only Just" Election', *Contemporary British History*, Vol. 21, 2007.

Jim Buller and Toby S. James,

'Statecraft and the Assessment of National Political Leaders: The Case of New Labour and Tony Blair', *The British Journal of Politics & International Relations*, 14(4), 2012.

'Integrating Structural Context into the Assessment of Political Leadership: Realism, 978184954 Gordon Brown and the Great Financial Crisis', *Parliamentary Affairs*, 68(1), January 2015.

John Campbell, Symposium on 'Conservative Party policy making, 1965–70', *Contemporary Record*, 3(3), 1990.

Peter Catterall, 'Handling the Transfer of Power: A Note on the 1964 Origins of the Douglas-Home Rules', *Contemporary British History*, Vol. 11, 1997.

Robert Cecil,

'Conservative Reaction', *Quarterly Review*, Vol. 115; 270–1, 1860.

'Democracy on Its Trial', *Quarterly Review* Vol. 110, 1861.

'The Confederate Struggle and Recognition', *Quarterly Review*, Vol. 112; 535–70, 1862.

'The House of Commons', *Quarterly Review*, Vol. 116, 1864.

'The Past and Future of Conservative Policy', *Quarterly Review*, Vol. 127, 1869.

Huw Clapton, 'How not to run a Political Campaign: the Failure of the Unionist Free Traders 1903–06', *Parliamentary History*, 30(2), 2011.

N. J. Crowson. 'Conservative Parliamentary dissent over foreign policy during the premiership of Neville Chamberlain: myth or reality?', *Parliamentary History*, 14(3), 1995.

G. N. Curzon, 'Two Demagogues: A Parallel and a Moral', *The New Review*, 12(71), 1895.

Peter Davis, 'The Liberal Unionist Party and the Irish Policy of Lord Salisbury's Government, 1886–1892', *Historical Journal*, 18(1), 1975.

David Dutton, 'Power Brokers or just "Glamour Boys"? The Eden Group, September 1939–May 1940', *English Historical Review*, Vol. 118, 2003.

David Eastwood, 'Peel and the Tory Party Reconsidered', *History Today*, 42(3), 1992.

Norman Gash,

'Peel and the Party System, 1830–1850', *Transactions of the Royal Historical Society, 5th series*, Vol. 1, 1951.

'The Organization of the Conservative Party, 1832–46, Part I: The Parliamentary Organization', *Parliamentary History*, Vol. 1, 1982.

'The Organization of the Conservative Party, 1832–1846, Part II: The Electoral Organization', *Parliamentary History*, Vol. 2, 1983.

Richard Gaunt, 'A Power behind the Throne? Sir Robert Peel, Prince Albert and the Making of the Modern Monarchy', *Conservative History Journal*, 11(2), 2014.

Neil T. Gavin and David Sanders, 'The Economy and Voting', *Parliamentary Affairs*, 50(4), 1997.

Angus Hawkins, '"Parliamentary Government" and Victorian Political Parties, c.1830–1880', *English Historical Review*, Vol. 104, 1989.

Andrew Holt, 'Lord Home and Anglo-American Relations, 1961–1963', *Diplomacy and Statecraft*, Vol. 16, 2005.

Edwin Jaggard, 'The 1841 British General Election: A Reconsideration', *Australian Journal of Politics and History*, Vol. 30, 1984.

Toby S. James, 'Electoral Administration and Voter Turnout: Towards an International Public Policy Continuum', *Representation*, 45(4), 2010.

Kevin Jefferys, 'May 1940: the downfall of Neville Chamberlain', *Parliamentary History*, 10(2), 1991.

Richard S. Katz and Peter Mair, 'Changing Models of Party Organisation and Party Democracy', *Party Politics*, 1(1), 1995.

Elie Kedourie, 'Tory Ideologue: Salisbury as a Conservative Intellectual', *Encounter*, Vol. 225, 1972.

Betty Kemp, 'The General Election of 1841', *History*, Vol. 37, 1952.

J. F. A. Mason, 'Lord Salisbury and the *Saturday Review*', *Bulletin of the Institute of Historical Research*, 24(1), 1961.

Stuart Mitchell, 'Douglas-Home, the Conservative Party and the Threat of Rebellious Youth, 1963–64', *University of Sussex Journal of Contemporary History*, 4(3), 2002.

I. D. C. Newbould, 'Sir Robert Peel and the Conservative Party, 1832–1841: A Study in failure?', *English Historical Review*, Vol. 98, 1983.

Pippa Norris, 'The Apathetic Landslide: The 2001 British General Election', *Parliamentary Affairs*, October 2001, 54(4).

Thomas Otte, '"Avenge England's Honour": By-elections, Parliament and Foreign and Imperial Policy in 1898', *English Historical Review*, 121(491), 2006.

Roland Quinault, 'Lord Randolph Churchill and Tory Democracy, 1880–1885', *Historical Journal*, 22(1), 1979.

J. S. Rasmussen, 'Party discipline in wartime: the downfall of the Chamberlain Government', *Journal of Politics*, Vol. 32, 1970.

Paul Readman, 'The Conservative Party, Patriotism and British Politics', *Journal of British Studies*, 11(1), 2001.

Jane Ridley, 'The Unionist Opposition and the House of Lords, 1906–1910', Parliamentary History, 11(2), 1992.

The Royal Holloway Group PR3710, 'British MPs on British PMs: Parliamentary Evaluations of Prime Ministerial Success', *Politics*, 35(2), June 2015.

James Sack, 'The *Quarterly Review* and the Baptism of the "Conservative Party": A Conundrum Resolved', *Victorian Periodicals Review*, 24(4), 1991.

Lord Salisbury,

'The Programme of the Radicals', *Quarterly Review*, Vol. 135, 1873.

'The Value of Redistribution: A Note on Electoral Statistics', *National Review*, Vol. 10, 1884.

David Sanders, Harold Clarke, Marianne Stewart and Paul Whiteley, 'The Economy and Voting', *Parliamentary Affairs,* October 2001, 54(4).

Nick Smart, 'Four days in May: the Norway debates and the downfall of Neville Chamberlain', *Parliamentary History*, 17(2), 1998.

Alastair Smith, 'Election Timing in Majoritarian Parliaments', *British Journal of Political Science*, 33(3), July 2003.

David Thackeray, 'Rethinking the Edwardian Crisis of Conservatism', *Historical Journal*, 54(1), 2011.

Kevin Theakston and Mark Gill,

'The Post-War Premiership League', *Political Quarterly*, 82(1), January–March 2011.

'Ranking Twentieth-Century British Prime Ministers', *British Journal of Politics and International Relations*, Vol. 8, 2006.

Larry Witherell, 'Sir Henry Page Croft and Conservative Backbench Campaigns for Empire, 1903–1932', *Parliamentary History*, 25(3), 2006.

John W. Young, 'International Factors and the 1964 Election', *Contemporary British History*, Vol. 21, 2007.

BOOKS

R. J. Q. Adams,

Bonar Law, London, John Murray, 1999.

Balfour: the Last Grandee, London, John Murray, 2007.

Paul Addison, *The Road to 1945: British Politics and the Second World War*, London, Cape, 1975.

Julian Amery, *The Life of Joseph Chamberlain, Vol. 4*, London: Macmillan, 1951.

L. S. Amery,

My Political Life, Vol. 1, London: Hutchinson, 1953.

My Political Life, Vol. 3 London: Hutchinson, 1955.

Matthew d'Ancona, *In It Together: The Inside Story of the Coalition Government*, London, Penguin, 2014.

Lord Avon, *The Reckoning*, London, Houghton Mifflin, 1965.

Walter Bagehot and Norman St John-Stevas, *Bagehot's Historical Essays*, London, Dobson, 1971.

Stanley Baldwin, *On England, and Other Addresses*, London, P. Allan, 1926.

Tim Bale, *The Conservatives since 1945: The Drivers of Party Change*, Oxford, Oxford University Press, 2012.

Stuart Ball,

Baldwin and the Conservative Party: the Crisis of 1929–1931, New Haven, Yale University Press, 1988.

Portrait of a Party, Oxford, Oxford University Press, 2013.

Parliament and Politics in the Age of Churchill and Attlee: the Headlam Diaries 1935–1951, Cambridge, Cambridge University Press, 1999.

Stuart Ball and Anthony Seldon eds,

The Conservative Century: The Conservative Party since 1900, Oxford, Oxford University Press, 1994.

The Heath Government: A Re-appraisal, Harlow, Essex, Longman, 1996.

Recovering Power: The Conservatives in Opposition Since 1867, Houndmills, Palgrave, 2005.

Thomas Barman, *Diplomatic Correspondent*, London, Hamish Hamilton, 1968.

John Barnes and David Nicholson eds,

The Leo Amery Diaries Volume 1: 1896–1929, London, Hutchinson 1980.

The Empire at Bay – The Leo Amery Diaries, Volume 2: 1929–1945, London, Hutchinson, 1988.

Arthur Baumann, *The Last Victorians*, London, Benn, 1924.

J. V. Beckett, *The Aristocracy in England, 1660–1914*, Oxford, Blackwell, 1986.

Matt Beech and Lee Simon eds, *The Conservative-Liberal Coalition: Examining the Cameron-Clegg Government*, London, Palgrave, 2015.

Michael Bentley, *Salisbury's World: Conservative Environments in Late-Victorian Britain*, Cambridge, Cambridge University Press, 2001.

Jeremy Black ed., *The Tory World. Deep History and the Tory Theme in British Foreign Policy, 1679–2014*, Farnham and Burlington, Ashgate, 2015.

Robert Blake,

The Unknown Prime Minister, London, Odhams, 1955.

Disraeli, New York, St Martin's Press, 1967 .

The Conservative Party from Peel to Thatcher, London, Fontana, 1985.

The Conservative Party from Peel to Major, London, Heinemann, 1997.

Violet Bonham Carter, *Winston Churchill As I Knew Him*, London, Eyre and Spottiswoode, 1965.

John Boyd-Carpenter, *Way of Life*, London, Sidgwick & Jackson, 1980.

Michael Brock, *The Great Reform Act*, London, Hutchinson, 1973.

Laurence Brockliss and David Eastwood eds, *A Union of Multiple Identities. The British Isles, c.1750–c.1850*, Manchester, Manchester University Press, 1997.

Lord Broughton and Lady Dorchester, *Recollections of a Long Life by Lord Broughton, Vol. 6*, London, J. Murray, 1909.

Jock Bruce-Gardyne and Nigel Lawson, *The Power Game: An Examination of Decision-Making in Government*, London, Macmillan, 1976.

George Buckle ed., *The Letters of Queen Victoria, Second Series, Vol. 1*, London, J. Murray, 1926.

Jim Buller, *National Statecraft and European Integration*, London, Cassell, 2000.

David Butler, *The British General Election of 1955*, London, Macmillan, 1955.

David Butler and Anthony King, *The British General Election of 1964*, London, Macmillan, 1965.

David Butler and Donald Stokes, *Political Change in Britain*, London, Macmillan, 1974.

David Butler and Gareth Butler eds, *Twentieth Century British Political Facts 1900–2000*, Basingstoke, Macmillan, 2000.

David Butler and Anne Sloman eds, *British Political Facts 1900–1979*, London, Macmillan, 1980.

Fulvio Cammarano, *Strategie del conservatismo britannico nella crisi del liberalismo: "National Party of Common Sense" (1885–1892)*, Bari, Lacaita, 1990.

John Campbell, *Edward Heath: A Biography*, London, Jonathan Cape, 1993.

Edward Cardwell and Philip Stanhope eds, *Memoirs of Sir Robert Peel,* two volumes [1856–7], New York, Kraus Publishers, 1969.

Peter Catterall ed., *The Macmillan Diaries 1950–57*, London, Macmillan, 2003.

Gwendolen Cecil, *The Life of Robert, Marquis of Salisbury, Vol. 1*, London, Hodder & Stoughton, 1921.

Austen Chamberlain,

Down the Years, London, Cassell, 1935.

Politics from Inside, London, Cassell, 1936.

John Charmley,

Lord Lloyd and the Decline of the British Empire, London, Weidenfeld & Nicolson, 1987.

Churchill: The End of Glory, London, Hodder & Stoughton, 1993.

Churchill's Grand Alliance, London, Hodder & Stoughton, 1996.

A History of Conservative Politics since 1830, Basingstoke, Palgrave, 2008.

E. A. Chilston, *Chief Whip: The Political Life and Times of Aretas Akers-Douglas, 1st Viscount Chilston*, London, Routledge and Kegan Paul, 1961.

Winston Churchill,

Great Contemporaries, London, Butterworth, 1937.

The Gathering Storm, London, Cassell, 1948.

The Hinge of Fate, London, Cassell, 1951.

Alan Clark, *The Tories: Conservatives and the Nation State 1922–1997*, London, Weidenfeld & Nicolson, 1988.

Harold D. Clarke, David Sanders, Marianne C. Stewart and Paul Whiteley,

Political Choice in Britain, Oxford and New York, Oxford University Press, 2004.

Performance, Politics and the British Voter, Cambridge, Cambridge University Press, 2009.

Peter Clarke, *A Question of Leadership: Gladstone to Thatcher*, London, Hamish Hamilton, 1991.

P. W. Clayden, *England under the Coalition: The Political History of Great Britain and Ireland from the General Election of 1885 to May 1892*, London, T. F. Unwin, 1892.

Franz Coetzee, *For Party or Country: Nationalism and the Dilemmas of Popular Conservatism in Edwardian England*, New York, Oxford University Press, 1990.

John Colville, *The Fringes of Power*, London, W. W. Norton, 1985.

Chris Cook, *The Age of Alignment. Electoral Politics in Britain 1922–29*, London, Macmillan 1975.

A. B. Cooke ed., *The Conservative Party: Seven Historical Studies, 1680 to the 1990s*, London, Conservative Political Centre, 1997.

Maurice Cowling,

The Impact of Labour 1920–1924, Cambridge, Cambridge University Press 1971.

The Impact of Hitler: British Politics and British Policies 1933–1940, Cambridge, Cambridge University Press, 1975.

Conservative Essays, London, Cassell, 1978.

Gary Cox, *Making Votes Count: Strategic Coordination in the World's Electoral Systems*, Cambridge, Cambridge University Press, 1997.

Richard Crossman, *The Diaries of a Cabinet Minister, Vol. I: 1964–1966*, London, Holt, Rinehart & Winston, 1976.

N. J. Crowson, *The Longman Companion to the Conservative Party since 1830*, Harlow, Pearson Education, 2001.

Iain Dale ed., *Volume One. Conservative Party General Election Manifestos 1900–1997*, Abingdon, Routledge, 2013.

Martin Daunton, *Trusting Leviathan: The Politics of Taxation in Britain, 1799–1914*, Cambridge, Cambridge University Press, 2001.

Richard Davis, *A Political History of the House of Lords, 1811–1846: from the Regency to Corn Law Repeal*, Stanford, 2008.

John Dickie, *The Uncommon Commoner: A Study of Sir Alec Douglas-Home*, London, Pall Mall Press, 1964.

Benjamin Disraeli,

The Revolutionary Epick, London, E. Moxon, 1834.

Coningsby: Or, The New Generation Vol. II, London, Dunne, 1844.

Sybil: Or, The Two Nations Book IV, London, H. Colborn, 1845.

Lord George Bentinck: A Political Biography, London, A. Constable, 1905.

Blanche Dugdale, *Arthur James Balfour*, London, Hutchinson, 1936.

David Dutton,

Austen Chamberlain: Gentleman in Politics, Bolton, Ross Anderson, 1985.

'His Majesty's Loyal Opposition': the Unionist Party in Opposition, 1905–1915, Liverpool, Liverpool University Press, 1992.

Neville Chamberlain, London, Arnold, 2001.

Douglas-Home, London, Haus, 2006.

Anthony Eden, *Freedom and Order, selected speeches 1939–1946*, London, Faber and Faber, 1947.

Max Egremont, *Balfour*, London, Phoenix, 1998.

Francis Elliot and James Hanning, *Cameron: Practically a Conservative*, London, Fourth Estate, 2012.

Keith Feiling, *The Life of Neville Chamberlain*, London, Macmillan, 1946.

Nigel Fisher, *Harold Macmillan*, London, Weidenfeld & Nicolson, 1982.

Robert Ford and Matthew Goodwin, *Revolt on the Right*, Abingdon, Routledge, 2014.

Martin Francis and Ina Zweiniger-Bargielowska eds, *The Conservatives and British Society 1880–1990*, Cardiff, Cardiff University Press, 1996.

Geoffrey Fry, *The Politics of Crisis: An Interpretation of British Politics 1931–1945*, Basingstoke, Houndmills, 2001.

Anna Gambles, *Protection and Politics: Conservative Economic Discourse, 1815–1852*, Woodbridge, Boydell & Brewer, 1999.

John Gardiner, *The Victorians: An Age in Retrospect*, London, Hambledon, 2006.

Norman Gash,

Mr. Secretary Peel: the Life of Sir Robert Peel to 1830, London, Faber, 1961.

Lord Liverpool, London, Weidenfeld & Nicolson, 1984.

Sir Robert Peel, revised edition, Harlow, Longman, 1986.

Norman Gash et al. eds, *The Conservatives: A History from their Origins to 1965*, London, Allen & Unwin, 1977.

Richard Gaunt,

Sir Robert Peel. The Life and Legacy, London and New York, I. B. Tauris, 2010.

Peel in Caricature. The 'Political Sketches' of John Doyle ('HB'), Tamworth, The Peel Society, 2014.

Martin Gilbert,

Winston S. Churchill, Volume IV, Companion Part III, London, Heinemann, 1977.

Winston S. Churchill Volume VIII, Boston, Houghton Mifflin, 1988.

Ian Gilmour and Mark Garnett, *Whatever Happened to the Tories? The Conservative Party Since 1945*, London, Fourth Estate, 1997.

Alfred Gollin, *Balfour's Burden: Arthur Balfour and Imperial Preference*, London, Anthony Blond, 1965.

E. H. H. Green,

The Crisis of Conservatism, 1880–1914, London, Routledge & Kegan Paul, 1995.

Ideologies of Conservatism: Conservative Political Ideas in the Twentieth Century, Oxford, Oxford University Press, 2002.

Frederick Hamer ed., *The Personal Papers of Lord Rendel*, London, Benn, 1931.

Robin Harcourt Williams ed., *The Salisbury-Balfour Correspondence, 1869–1892*, Hertfordshire, Hertfordshire Record Society, 1988.

John Harvey ed., *The War Diaries of Oliver Harvey*, London, Collins, 1978.

Angus Hawkins,

The Forgotten Prime Minister, The 14th Earl of Derby, Ascent, 1799–1851, Oxford, Oxford University Press, 2007.

The Forgotten Prime Minister, The 14th Earl of Derby: Achievement, 1851–1869, Oxford, Oxford University Press, 2008.

Robert Hazell and Ben Yong eds, *The Politics of Coalition: How the Conservative-Liberal Democrat Government Works*, Oxford, Hart Publishing,

Edward Heath, *The Course of My Life*, London, Hodder & Stoughton, 1998.

Peter Hennessy,

Whitehall, London, Secker & Warburg, 1989.

Muddling Through, London, Indigo, 1997.

The Prime Minister: *the Office and its Holders since 1945*, London, Penguin, 2000.

Tim Heppell, *Choosing a Tory Leader*, London, I. B. Tauris, 2007.

Tim Heppell and Nigel Fletcher ed., *Leaders of the Opposition: From Churchill to Cameron*, Basingstoke, Palgrave, 2012.

Boyd Hilton, *A Mad, Bad and Dangerous People? England, 1783–1846*, Oxford, Oxford University Press, 2006.

Martin Holmes, *Political Pressure and Economic Policy: British Government, 1970–4*, London, Butterworth, 1982.

Andrew Holt, *The Foreign Policy of the Douglas-Home Government: Britain, the United States and the End of Empire*, Basingstoke, Palgrave, 2014.

Lord Home, *The Way the Wind Blows: An Autobiography*, London, Collins, 1976.

Robert Horton, *Reform in 1839 and Reform in 1831*, London, John Murray, 1839.

F. D. How, *The Marquis of Salisbury*, London, Isbister, 1902.

Anthony Howard, *Rab*, London, Jonathan Cape, 1987.

C. H. D. Howard ed., *Joseph Chamberlain: A Political Memoir, 1880–1892*, London, Batchworth Press, 1953.

Douglas Hurd, *An End to Promises: Sketch of a Government 1970–74*, London, Collins, 1979.

Michael Hurst, *Joseph Chamberlain and Liberal Reunion: The Round Table Conference 1887*, London, Routledge, 1967.

John Hutcheson, *Leopold Maxse and the National Review, 1893–1914*, London, Garland, 1989.

H. M. Hyde, *Neville Chamberlain*, London, Weidenfeld & Nicolson, 1976.

Ronald Inglehart, *Culture Shift in Advanced Industrial Society*, Princeton NJ, Princeton University Press, 1990.

Toby S. James, *Elite Statecraft and Election Administration: Bending the Rules of the Game*, Basingstoke, Palgrave, 2012.

Andrew Jones, *The Politics of Reform 1884*, Cambridge, Cambridge University Press, 1972.

Dylan Jones, *Cameron on Cameron: Conversations with Dylan Jones*, London, Fourth Estate, 2010.

Thomas Jones,

A Diary with Letters 1931–1950, London, Oxford University Press, 1954.

Whitehall Diary Volume 1, 1916–1925, London, Oxford University Press, 1969.

Denis Judd, *Radical Joe: A Life of Joseph Chamberlain*, Cardiff, University of Wales Press, 1993.

Peter Jupp, *The Governing of Britain, 1688–1848: The Executive, Parliament and the People*, London, Routledge, 2006.

John Kendle, *Walter Long, Ireland and the Union, 1905–1920*, Dublin, Glendale, 1992.

A. L. Kennedy, *Salisbury, 1830–1903: Portrait of a Statesman*, London, J. Murray, 1954.

Paul Kennedy, *The Rise of the Anglo-German Antagonism, 1860–1914*, London, Allen & Unwin, 1982.

Nigel Keohane, *The Party of Patriotism: the Conservative Party and the First World War*, Farnham, Ashgate, 2010.

Donal Kerr, *Peel, Priests and Politics, Sir Robert Peel's Administration and the Roman Catholic Church in Ireland, 1841–1846*, Oxford, Oxford University Press, 1982.

John Maynard Keynes, *The Writings of John Maynard Keynes. Volume X, Essays in Biography*, London, Macmillan, 1972.

Anthony King, *Britain at the Polls 1992*, Chatham NJ, Chatham House, 1993.

Anthony King and Robert Wybrow eds, *British Political Opinion 1937–2000: The Gallup Polls*, London, Politico's, 2001.

John Lawton, *1963: Five Hundred Days: History as Melodrama*, London, Hodder & Stoughton, 1992.

W. C. Lubenow, *Parliamentary Politics and the Home Rule Crisis: The British House of Commons in 1886*, Oxford, Clarendon Press, 1988.

Frank McDonough, *The Conservative Party and Anglo-German Relations, 1905–1914*, London, Palgrave, 2007.

James MacGregor Burns, *Leadership*, New York, Harper & Row, 1978.

J. P. Mackintosh ed., *British Prime Ministers in the Twentieth Century: Volume 1*, London, Weidenfeld & Nicolson, 1977.

Iain McLean, *Rational Choice and British Politics. An Analysis of Rhetoric and Manipulation from Peel to Blair*, Oxford, Oxford University Press, 2001.

Iain Macleod, *Neville Chamberlain*, London, F. Muller, 1961.

Harold Macmillan,

Riding the Storm, London, Macmillan, 1971.

The Past Masters, London, Macmillan, 1975.

Peter Marsh,

The Discipline of Popular Government: Lord Salisbury's Domestic Statecraft, 1881–1902, Aldershot, Gregg Revivals, 1993.

Joseph Chamberlain, Entrepreneur in Politics, Yale, Yale University Press, 1994.

The Chamberlain Litany, London, Heinemann, 2010.

H. C. G. Matthew and Ruddock Mackay, *Oxford Dictionary of National Biography*, Oxford, Oxford University Press, 2004.

Keith Middlemas and John Barnes, *Baldwin: A Biography,* London, Weidenfeld & Nicolson, 1969.

William Monypenny and George Buckle, *The Life of Benjamin Disraeli, Earl of Beaconsfield*, *Vol. 3*, London, 1910.

Kenneth Morgan,

The People's Peace, Oxford, Oxford University Press, 1992.

Consensus and Disunity. The Lloyd George Coalition Government 1918–1922, Oxford, Oxford University Press, 1995.

John Morley, *The Life of William Ewart Gladstone*, *Vol.* 2, London, Macmillan, 1903.

Nigel Nicolson ed.,

Harold Nicolson: Diaries and Letters 1930–1939, London, Collins, 1966.

Harold Nicolson: Diaries and Letters 1939–1945, London, Collins, 1967.

Alan O'Day ed., *The Edwardian Age: Conflict and Stability, 1900–14*, London, Macmillan, 1979.

Thomas Otte,

'Black Michael': Sir Michael Hicks Beach and the Problems of Late Victorian Conservatism, Tunbridge Wells, Conservative History Group, 2006.

The Makers of British Foreign Policy: From Pitt to Thatcher, Basingstoke and New York, Palgrave, 2002.

Thomas Otte and Paul Readman eds, *By-elections in British Politics, 1832–1914*, Woodbridge, Boydell & Brewer, 2013.

David Owen, *In Sickness and in Power*, London, Methuen & Co., 2008.

Michel Parand, et al. ed., *Letters of Benjamin Disraeli,* nine volumes, Toronto, University of Toronto Press, 1982.

George Peel, *The Private Letters of Sir Robert Peel*, London, John Murray, 1920.

Robert Peel, *Speeches delivered in the House of Commons by the late Rt Hon. Sir Robert Peel,* four volumes [1853], New York, Kraus Publishers, 1972.

Charles Petrie, *The Chamberlain Tradition*, London, Lovat Dickson, 1938.

Charles Petrie and Alistair Cooke, *The Carlton Club 1832–2007*, London, The Carlton Club, 2007.

Michael Pinto-Duschinsky, *The Political Thought of Lord Salisbury, 1854–1868*, London, Constable, 1967.

Bernard Porter, *Britannia's Burden*, London, Edward Arnold, 1994.

Mark Pottle ed., *Daring to Hope* [Violet Bonham Carter], London, Weidenfeld & Nicolson, 2000.

James Prior, *A Balance of Power*, London, Hamish Hamilton, 1986.

Martin Pugh,

Electoral Reform in Peace and War, 1906–1918, London, Routledge, 1978.

The Tories and the People, 1880–1935, Oxford, Blackwell, 1985.

Thomas Quinn, *Electing and Ejecting Party Leaders in Britain*, Basingstoke, Palgrave, 2012.

Colin Rallings and Michael Thrasher,

British Electoral Facts, London, Total Politics, 2009.

British Electoral Facts 1832–2012, London, Biteback, 2012.

John Ramsden,

The Age of Balfour and Baldwin 1902–1940, London, Longman, 1978.

The Making of Conservative Party Policy: The Conservative Research Department since 1929, London, Longman, 1980.

The Winds of Change: Macmillan to Heath, 1957–75, London, Longman, 1996.

An Appetite for Power. A History of the Conservative Party, London, HarperCollins, 1998.

Man of the Century, London, HarperCollins, 2002.

Real Old Tory Politics: the Political Diaries of Robert Sanders, Lord Bayford, 1910–35, London, Historian's Press, 1984.

Donald Read, *Peel and the Victorians*, Oxford, Basil Blackwell, 1987.

Robert Rhodes James,

Memoirs of a Conservative, J. C. C. Davidson's Memoirs and Papers, 1910–1937, London, Weidenfeld & Nicolson, 1969.

Churchill: a study in failure, London, Weidenfeld & Nicolson, 1970.

Ambitions and Realities: British Politics, 1964–70, London, Weidenfeld & Nicolson, 1972.

Chips: The Diaries of Sir Henry Channon, London, Weidenfeld & Nicolson, 1967.

Janet Robb, *The Primrose League, 1883–1906*, New York, Columbia University Press, 1968.

Keith Robbins ed., *The Blackwell Biographical Dictionary of British Political Life in the Twentieth Century*, Oxford, Blackwell, 1990.

Andrew Roberts, *Salisbury: Victorian Titan*, London, Phoenix, 2000.

Nick Robinson, *Election Notebook: The Inside Story of the Battle over Britain's Future and My Personal Battle to Report It*, London, Bantam Press, 2015.

Robert Robson ed., *Ideas and Institutions of Victorian Britain: Essays in Honour of George Kitson Clarke*, London, Bell, 1967.

Stephen Roskill, *Hankey: Man of Secrets Volume II, 1918–1931*, London, Collins, 1972.

Peter Rowland, *The Last Liberal Governments, Vol. 1*, London, Macmillan, 1968.

G. W. E. Russell ed., *Letters of Matthew Arnold, 1848–1888*, London, Macmillan, 1904.

Marquess Salisbury, *Essays by the Late Marquess of Salisbury, KG: Biographical*, London, J. Murray, 1905.

Philip Salmon, *Electoral Reform at Work. Local Politics and National Parties, 1832–1841*, Woodbridge, Boydell and Brewer, 2002.

Robert Saunders, *Democracy and the Vote in British Politics, 1848–1867: The Making of the Second Reform Act*, Farnham, Ashgate, 2011.

Anthony Seldon,

Churchill's Indian Summer, London, Hodder & Stoughton, 1981.

How Tory Governments Fall. The Tory Party in Power since 1783, London, Fontana Press, 1996.

Anthony Seldon and Mike Finn eds, *The Coalition Effect 2010–2015*, Cambridge, Cambridge University Press, 2015.

Robert Self,

Neville Chamberlain, Aldershot, Ashgate, 2006.

The Austen Chamberlain Diary Letters, Volume 5, Cambridge, Cambridge University Press, 1995.

The Neville Chamberlain Diary Letters: Volume 2, The Reform Years 1921–1927, Aldershot, Ashgate, 2000.

The Neville Chamberlain Diary Letters: Volume 4, The Downing Street Years 1933–1940, Aldershot, Ashgate, 2005.

Richard Shannon, *The Age of Salisbury, 1881–1902: Unionism and Empire*, London, Longman, 1996.

Robert Skidelsky ed., *Thatcherism*, Oxford, Blackwell, 1988.

Nick Smart,

The Diaries and Letters of Robert Bernays 1932–1939, Lewiston, E. Mellen Press, 1996.

The National Government 1931–1940, Basingtoke, Macmillan, 1999.

Neville Chamberlain, Abingdon, Routledge, 2009.

Jeremy Smith, *The Tories and Ireland, Conservative Party politics and the home rule crisis, 1910–1914*, Dublin, Irish Academic Press, 2000.

Paul Smith

Disraeli: A Brief Life, Cambridge, Cambridge University Press, 1996.

Lord Salisbury on Politics: A Selection from His Articles in the Quarterly Review, 1860–1885, London, Cambridge University Press, 1972.

The English Constitution, Cambridge, Cambridge University Press, 2001.

Peter Snowdon, *Back from the Brink: The Extraordinary Fall and Rise of the Conservative Party*, London, HarperPress, 2010.

Donald Southgate, *The Conservative Leadership, 1832–1932*, London, Macmillan, 1974.

Gareth Stedman Jones, *Languages of Class: Studies in English Working Class History, 1832–1982*, Cambridge, Cambridge University Press, 1983.

E. D. Steele, *Lord Salisbury: A Political Biography*, London, UCL Press, 1999.

Graham Stewart, *Burying Caesar: Churchill, Chamberlain and the Battle for the Tory Party*, London, Weidenfeld & Nicolson, 1999.

John Street, Mass Media Politics and Democracy, Basingstoke, Palgrave, 2001.

John Swift, *Labour in Crisis: Clement Attlee and the Labour Party in Opposition 1931–1940*, Basingstoke, Palgrave, 2001.

A. J. P. Taylor, *English History 1914–1945*, Harmondsworth, Penguin, 1975.

A. J. P. Taylor and Chris Wrigley ed., *Warfare, Diplomacy and Politics*, London, H. Hamilton, 1986.

Andrew Taylor, *Bonar Law*, London, Haus, 2006.

Robert Taylor, *Lord Salisbury*, London, Allen Lane, 1975.

Margaret Thatcher, *The Path to Power*, London, HarperCollins, 1995.

Neville Thompson, *The Anti-Appeasers: Conservative Opposition to Appeasement in the 1930s*, Oxford, Clarendon Press, 1971.

D. R. Thorpe,

The Uncrowned Prime Ministers, London, Darkhorse, 1980.

Alec Douglas-Home, London, Sinclair-Stevenson, 1996.

Eden, London, Chatto & Windus, 2003.

Supermac, London, Chatto & Windus, 2010.

John Vincent,

Disraeli, Oxford, Oxford University Press, 1990.

Disraeli, Derby and the Conservative Party: The Political Journals of Lord Stanley, 1849–1869, Sussex, Harvester Press, 1978.

The Crawford Papers: The Journal of David Lindsay, 27th Earl of Crawford and 10th Earl of Balcarres, 1871–1940, Manchester, Manchester University Press, 1984.

Corinna Wagner, Joanne Parker and Nick Groom eds, *The Oxford Handbook of Medieval Victorianism*, Oxford, Oxford University Press, 2015.

David Walsh, *Making Angels in Marble: The Conservatives, the Early Industrial Working Class and Attempts at Political Incorporation*, London, Breviary Stuff Publications, 2012.

Rhodri Williams, *Defending the Empire*, London, Yale University Press, 1991.

Philip Williamson,

National Crisis and National Government. British Politics, the Economy and Empire 1926–1932, Cambridge, Cambridge University Press, 1992.

Stanley Baldwin: Conservative Leadership and National Values, Cambridge, Cambridge University Press, 1999.

The Modernisation of Conservative Politics: The Diaries and Letters of William Bridgeman 1904–1935, London, The Historians Press, 1988.

Philip Williamson and Edward Baldwin, *Baldwin Papers: A Conservative Statesman 1908–1947*, Cambridge, Cambridge University Press, 2004.

Harold Wilson, *Purpose in Politics*, London, Weidenfeld & Nicolson, 1964.

C. M. Woolgar ed., *Wellington Studies V*, Southampton, The Hartley Institute, 2013.

Kenneth Young, *Sir Alec Douglas-Home*, London, Dent, 1970.

Philip Ziegler, *Edward Heath: The Authorised Biography*, London, HarperCollins, 2010.

MISCELLANEOUS

Alistair Cooke and A. P. W. Malcolmson eds, *The Ashbourne Papers, 1869–1913*, Belfast, H. M. Stationary Office, 2007.

D. R. Fisher, 'The Opposition to Sir Robert Peel in the Conservative Party, 1841–1846', PhD thesis, University of Cambridge, 1970.

INDEX

abdication crisis (1936) 209–10
Aberdeen, Earl of 67
Adams, R. J. Q. 151
Adamson, William 12
Addison, Christopher 12
Addison, Paul 238
Agadir Crisis 150
Albert, Prince 68
Amery, Leo 139, 144, 168, 169, 172, 181, 182
Anderson, Sir John 241
Anti-Corn Law League 70
appeasement policy 219–20, 224, 253
Archer, Jeffrey 356–7
Ashbourne, Lord 146
Ashcroft, Michael 352, 387, 393
Ashdown, Paddy 444
Asquith, H. H. 159
At the End of the Day (Macmillan) 279
Atholl, Duchess of 219
Attlee, Clement
  governing competence 50
  on Lord Salisbury 111–12
  during National Government 217
  in wartime coalition 240
  and 1945 general election 241
  foreign policy views 246–7
  and 1950 general election 247–8
  and 1951 general election 263–4

Bagehot, Walter 88, 89, 158, 279
Baker, Kenneth 329
Balcarres, Lord 141
Baldwin, Stanley 252
  overview of 7, 195–6
  and 1931 general election 11–12, 15
  and 1935 general election 12
  performance in general elections 33, 37–8, 39, 40, 41, 42, 43, 44, 45, 46, 47, 48, 49, 50, 51, 319–20
  loses leadership 33
  becomes leader of Conservative Party 34, 133–4, 199
  prime ministerial ranking 54, 55
  and Andrew Bonar Law 156, 171, 176
  early life and career 196–9
  opposition to coalition with Liberal Party 197–9
  during Labour Party's first government 200–202
  view of Conservatism 201–2
  and general strike 203–4
  after 1929 general election 204–7
  in National Government 207–9
  during abdication crisis 209–10
Balfour, Arthur 181
  overview of 7
  performance in general elections 33, 38, 39, 40, 41, 42, 43, 44, 45, 47, 48, 49, 53, 135–6
  loses leadership 33, 182
  and 1906 general election 53
  prime ministerial ranking 54, 55, 56
  under Lord Salisbury 128
  early life and career 134
  description of 134–5
  governing competence 136–8
  electoral strategy 138–42
  and Nonconformists 139–40
  political style of 140–41
  battle of ideas 148–50
  constitutional change 150–52
  assessment as leader 152–4
  under Andrew Bonar Law 166
Ball, Joseph 223

Barberis, Peter 293
Barman, Thomas 257
battle of ideas
  as factor in statecraft 25–6
  Margaret Thatcher 25–6, 320, 323, 324–5
  Arthur Balfour 148–50
  Andrew Bonar Law 167–70
  Edward Heath 309–13
  John Major 338
  William Hague 350, 357–60, 442–3
  Iain Duncan Smith 369–71
  Michael Howard 386–9, 422–3
  David Cameron 401–4
Beaverbrook, Lord 206, 208, 224, 241, 242
Bell, Tim 323
Benn, Anthony Wedgwood 275–6, 286
Benn, William Wedgwood 12
Bentinck, George 70, 81, 82, 99
Bevan, Aneurin 227, 263
Bevin, Ernest 240, 246–7
Birch, Nigel 274
Birkenhead, Lord 166
Bismarck, Otto von 106
Black, Guy 390
'Black Wednesday' 22
Blair, Tony 9, 16, 436, 441
  performance in general elections 49, 416
  as Leader of Opposition 337, 338, 339, 349
  and 1997 general election 341
  and death of Princess Diana 352
  governing competence 365–6
  and Iraq War 382, 385
  attacks Michael Howard 385, 387–8, 391–2
  electoral strategy 416, 433
Blake, Robert 294
Boer War 128, 130, 136, 149
Bogdanor, Vernon 275
Bonar Law, Andrew
  overview of 7, 155–6
  performance in general elections 32–3, 38, 39, 40, 41, 42, 43, 44, 45, 47, 48, 49, 50–51, 52–3, 161–3
  loses leadership 33, 35
  prime ministerial ranking 54, 55, 56
  early life and career 156–8
  Stanley Baldwin on 156
  becomes leader of Conservative Party 157–8, 184, 192
  in coalition with Liberal Party 158–61, 166–7, 198–9, 213
  and 1922 general election 163–5, 168, 192
  party management 165–7
  battle of ideas 167–70
  governing competence 170–72
  style as prime minister 172–3
  assessment as leader 174–6
Bonham Carter, Violet 259, 262
Boothby, Robert 252, 278
Bracken, Brendan 241
Bray, Stephen 55
Bridgeman, William 252
Bright, John 108
Britain Since 1918 (Marquand) 275
Brittan, Samuel 323
Brooke, Peter 329
Brown, Gordon 49, 357, 362, 386, 404, 405, 420
Bull, William 145–6
Burns, James MacGregor 15
Butler, Rab
  possible leader of Conservative Party 34, 269, 275, 284
  and Stanley Baldwin 196
  under Winston Churchill 240, 243, 247, 248
  and 1955 general election 261
  under Anthony Eden 265
  and 1945 general election 269
  under Alec Douglas-Home 286, 291, 292

Callaghan, James 49, 302, 324–5, 441
Cameron, David 395, 436, 447
  overview of 10
  and constitutional change 27
  performance in general elections 33, 37, 39, 41, 43, 44, 45, 46, 48, 49–50, 51
  becomes leader of Conservative Party 34, 399–401
  and 2010 general election 51, 405, 408
  and 2015 general election 51, 397–8, 409–10
  prime ministerial ranking 54, 55

under Michael Howard 383, 390
battle of ideas 401–4
governing competence 404–5
and European Union 405–6
as coalition Prime Minister 406–9
Campbell, Alistair 349
Campbell, John 291
Cann, Edward du 294, 321
Carlton Club 65, 161, 191
Carlyle, Thomas 96
Carr, Robert 264
Carson, Sir Edward 184
Carswell, Douglas 406
Cash, Bill 373
Centre for Policy Studies 338
Centre for Social Justice 377
Chamberlain, Austen 213, 252
overview of 7, 177–8
and general elections 32, 33, 35
loses leadership 33, 190–92
under Arthur Balfour 143, 149
possible challenge for leadership 157–8, 182–5
and coalition with Liberal Party 161, 198
under Andrew Bonar Law 166, 172, 185–6
relationship with father 179–82
as leader of Liberal Unionists 182
as leader of Conservative Party 186–93
party management 187–9, 190–91
Chamberlain, Beatrice 185
Chamberlain, Hilda 180, 188
Chamberlain, Ida 185, 188
Chamberlain, Joseph 118, 127–8, 129, 134, 140, 142–3, 149, 178, 179–82, 212–13
Chamberlain, Neville 178, 187–8
overview of 7, 211–12
and general elections 33, 35
loses leadership 33, 228–34, 239, 240
prime ministerial ranking 54, 55, 56
on Andrew Bonar Law 165, 169–70
under Stanley Baldwin 206, 208, 210
early life and career 212–15
as leader of Conservative Party 214–28
appeasement policy 219–20
assessment as leader 234–6
and Alec Douglas-Home 283
Chanak Crisis 164
Chandos, Marquess of 61, 67
Channon, 'Chips' 178
Charitable Bequests Act (1844) 68
Chelmer, Lord 295
Chesterton, G. K. 270
Church of England
and Lord Derby 77, 78
and Lord Salisbury 116–17
Churchill, Randolph 89, 90, 122, 130, 284
Churchill, Winston
overview of 7–8
and 1951 general election 20, 52
performance in general elections 32, 33, 37, 39, 40, 41, 42, 43, 44, 45, 46, 48, 49, 50, 51, 238, 248–9
loses leadership 33
and 1945 general election 52, 241–4
and 1950 general election 52, 247–8
prime ministerial ranking 54, 55
under Arthur Balfour 144
on Andrew Bonar Law 165
on Joseph Chamberlain 178
on Stanley Baldwin 196
under Stanley Baldwin 205, 206, 208, 239
under Neville Chamberlain 219, 232, 239
becomes Prime Minister 233–4, 239–40
statecraft of 237–8, 248
early life and career 238–9
as wartime leader 239–40
stays as leader after 1945 244–6
anti-communism of 245, 246–7
and 1951 general election 248
and Alec Douglas-Home 283
Citizen's Charter 342
Clarendon, Lord 83
Clarke, Ken 34, 329, 349, 364, 367, 372
Clegg, Nick 27
Clinton, Bill 22
Cobden, Richard 70, 108
Coe, Sebastian 446–7
Committee of Imperial Defence 150
Common Market
attempted entries blocked 273, 288, 303
Edward Heath's support for membership 311–13

Congress of Berlin 106
Conservative Party
reaction to Great Reform Act 6, 62, 64
performance in general elections 11–12, 13, 31–56
and electoral system 19–21, 27–8
media support for 20–21, 323–4
under Margaret Thatcher 23, 320, 322–3, 328–32
and party management 24–5
creation of leadership role 32
becomes 'Conservative' 62
under Robert Peel 64–5, 72–3
under Lord Derby 81–2, 85–7, 90, 91
under Benjamin Disraeli 101–4, 107–9
under Lord Salisbury 113–14, 115–16
under Arthur Balfour 141–7, 152
under Andrew Bonar Law 159, 165–7, 174–5
under Austen Chamberlain 187–9, 190–91
under Neville Chamberlain 223–4
under Winston Churchill 23, 240
under Alec Douglas-Home 294–6
under William Hague 350–52, 358–9
under Iain Duncan Smith 371–4
constitutional change
as factor in statecraft 26–9
Arthur Balfour 150–52
Margaret Thatcher 326–8
Michael Howard 394–5, 423–4
William Hague 443–4
Cook, Robin 425
Cooper, Duff 209, 218
Corn Laws 6, 25, 66, 67–8, 70, 80–81, 82–3, 90, 98, 100, 101–2, 191
Cranborne, Lord 356
Cripps, Sir Stafford 227
Croker, J. W. 82
Crosby, Lynton 386, 392–3, 406
Cross, Richard 104
Crossman, Richard 299
Curry, David 373
Curzon, Lord
leadership bid 34, 199
and Arthur Balfour 146
Daily Express 206, 224, 323
Daily Herald 224
Daily Mail 206, 224, 283, 323, 430
Daily Mirror 224, 247
Daily Telegraph 224
Davidson, J. C. C. 168, 186, 204, 206
Davis, David 34, 373, 391, 395, 399–400
Defence of Philosophical Doubt, A (Balfour) 148
Derby, Lord
overview of 6, 75–6
performance in general elections 33, 38, 39, 40, 41, 42, 43, 44, 45, 47, 48, 49, 50, 52, 107
loses leadership 33, 87–8
prime ministerial ranking 54, 56
early life and career 76–81
'Knowsley Creed' 77–8
becomes leader of Conservative Party 81
as leader of Conservative Party 81–91
and 1847 general election 82
dislike of campaigning 88–9
assessment of leadership 88–91
Disraeli on 94
Derby Dilly 63, 77
Deregulation and Contracting Out Act (1994) 342
devolution 28, 407, 443–4
Diana, Princess of Wales 352–3
Dickson, Sir William 265
Disraeli, Benjamin
overview of 6, 93–5
and constitutional change 27, 102–4
performance in general elections 33, 38, 39, 40, 41, 42, 43, 44, 45, 47, 48, 50–51, 107
loses leadership 33
prime ministerial ranking 54, 55
in Carlton Club 65
under Robert Peel 69, 70, 81, 82, 98
under Lord Derby 82, 85, 86–7, 90, 98–104
as celebrity 89
early life and career 95–104
early political views 95–7
and Reform Acts (1867–68) 102–4

and party management 103
as leader of Conservative Party 104–6
and 1874 general election 104, 107
and 1880 general election 106, 107
assessment of leadership 107–9
Douglas-Home, Alec
overview of 8, 281–2
becomes leader of Conservative Party 32, 34, 274–5, 284–7
performance in general elections 33, 37, 40, 42, 43, 44, 45, 46, 48, 49, 53
loses leadership 33, 296
prime ministerial ranking 54, 55, 56
early life and career 282–4
as leader of Conservative Party 288–96
and 1964 general election 292–4
party management 294–6
assessment as leader 297–9
kidnap attempt 298–9
and Edward Heath 303
and Margaret Thatcher 322
Duncan Smith, Iain
overview of 9–10
and general elections 32, 33, 35–6
loses leadership 33, 374–7
becomes leader of Conservative Party 34, 364–7
early life and career 363–4
as leader of Conservative Party 368–74
'quiet man' speech 368
battle of ideas 369–71
party management 371–4
assessment of leadership 374–9
and Michael Howard 415
Dutton, David 285, 290

Eden, Anthony 209
overview of 8, 251–2
performance in general elections 33, 37, 39, 41, 43, 44, 45, 46, 48, 52, 252
loses leadership 33, 261
becomes leader of Conservative Party 34, 259
prime ministerial ranking 54, 55, 56
under Neville Chamberlain 216–18, 253–4
under Winston Churchill 240, 248, 255–9
and 1945 general election 242–3, 244, 269
and 1955 general election 252, 259–61
early life and career 252–9
in National Government 252–4
as leader of Conservative Party 261–6
and Alec Douglas-Home 283, 286
Edward VIII, King 209–10
Eisenhower, Dwight D. 269
electoral strategy
as factor in statecraft 18, 19–21
in general elections 50
Arthur Balfour 138–42
Edward Heath 306–9, 315–17
Michael Howard 382–6, 415–16
Tony Blair 416, 433
William Hague 432–7
Margaret Thatcher 432
Elliot, Walter 218
English Constitution, The (Bagehot) 88
Erskine Mather affair 84
European Exchange Rate Mechanism (ERM) 22, 342, 357, 358, 420
European Union (EU)
and constitutional change 28
and Margaret Thatcher 328, 331
and John Major 338
and William Hague 354–5
and Iain Duncan Smith 369, 371
and Michael Howard 383
and David Cameron 405–6

Factory Acts
1833 64
1937 222
Fair Deal for Everyone 370
Falklands War 325
Fall, Catherine 447
Farage, Nigel 406
Feldman, Lord 408
Finkelstein, Danny 447
Fisher, Geoffrey 269
Fisher, 'Jackie' 137
Fitzwilliam, Earl 83
Fixed-Term Parliaments Act (2011) 21, 399
Flight, Howard 394
Foot, Michael 49, 302, 325

Forth, Eric 373
Fox, Liam 373, 391, 392–3
Franks, Sir Oliver 275
Friedman, Milton 323

Gaitskell, Hugh 302
Gash, Norman 71, 90
Gaulle, Charles de 273, 303
general elections
  Conservative Party performance in 11–12, 13, 31–56
  1835 32, 62–3
  1837 65
  1841 64, 66–7, 72, 76
  1847 50, 82, 101
  1852 101
  1865 50, 252
  1868 88–9, 107
  1874 76, 104, 107, 134
  1880 50, 106, 107, 115
  1885 112
  1886 112, 118
  1892 112, 125
  1895 112, 126
  1900 112, 129, 135, 136
  1906 50, 53, 135, 138, 139
  1910 136, 139, 161
  1918 50, 51, 52–3, 161–2
  1922 52, 161–2, 163–5, 168, 192
  1923 50, 214, 239
  1924 202
  1929 204, 239
  1931 11–12, 15, 199, 282
  1935 12, 226
  1945 52, 241–4, 257, 269
  1950 52, 247–8, 269, 282
  1951 20, 52, 248, 258, 263–4, 269
  1955 252, 259–61
  1959 50, 270–71
  1964 292–4
  1970 21, 306–9
  1974 20, 50, 315–17
  1979 324–5
  1983 50, 324, 325
  1987 324, 325
  1992 22, 53, 334, 340–41
  1997 22–3, 334, 341, 354, 366, 442
  2001 12–13, 16,360–61, 366, 369
  2005 394, 395–6, 420
  2010 51, 405, 408
  2015 51, 397–8, 409–10
general strike (1926) 203–4
George VI, King 210
Gilbert, Martin 244
Gilbert, Stephen 373
Gilmour, Ian 329
Gladstone, Herbert 139
Gladstone, William 67, 79, 83, 88, 100, 104, 105, 108, 115, 118, 121, 146
Globe, The 89
Goderich, Lord 76
Goschen, George Joachim 122
Goulburn, Henry 67, 79
Gould, Philip 359
Gove, Michael 402
governing competence
  John Major 22
  as factor in statecraft 22–3
  and general elections 50
  Arthur Balfour 136–8
  Andrew Bonar Law 170–72
  Edward Heath 313–14
  Tony Blair 365–6
  Michael Howard 389–92, 419–21
  David Cameron 404–5
  William Hague 437–9
Gow, Ian 330
Graham, James 63, 67, 79
Graham, William 12
Granby, Lord 82, 99
Great Reform Act (1832) 6, 27, 49, 51, 61–2, 64, 71–2, 76, 101
Green, E. H. H. 148
Grey, Lord 76, 77, 83
Grigg, John 286
Grimond, Jo 283–4
Guardian, The 397
Gummer, John 329

Hacking, Douglas 223–4
Hague, Ffion 352
Hague, William 177

overview of 9
and 2001 general election 12–13, 16
as leader of Conservative Party 16, 351–61
performance in general elections 33, 37, 39, 41, 43, 44, 45, 46, 48, 52
loses leadership 33, 361, 364, 435–6
becomes leader of Conservative Party 34, 347–51, 354–5, 364
early life and career 348, 428–30
battle of ideas 350, 357–60, 442–3
party management 350–52, 358–9, 439–42
and death of Princess Diana 352–3
and Viscount Cranborne 356
and Jeffrey Archer 356–7
assessment of leadership 361–2
on party leadership 430–32, 436–7, 444–7
electoral strategy 432–7
governing competence 437–9
constitutional change 443–4
Hailsham, Lord 232, 262, 274, 284, 288, 289
Halifax, Lord 218, 254, 256
Hamilton, Neil 338
Hardy, Thomas 268
Hare, John 294, 295
Harris, Kenneth 287
Hartington, Lord 88, 118, 119, 122
Hayek, Friedrich 323, 338
Headlam, Cuthbert 256
Headlam, Maurice 216
Heath, Edward 247, 441
overview of 8–9
performance in general elections 32–3, 37, 39, 40, 41, 42, 43, 44, 45, 46, 48, 50, 52, 306
loses leadership 33, 316, 320–22
prime ministerial ranking 54, 55
on Anthony Eden 254
under Alec Douglas-Home 290, 295
early life and career 301–3
becomes leader of Conservative Party 303–6
electoral strategy 306–9, 315–17
and 1970 general election 306–9
battle of ideas 309–13
'quiet' revolution' speech 309–10
support for Common Market 33–13
governing competence 313–14
and 1974 general elections 315–16
assessment of leadership 315–18
and Margaret Thatcher 322
Heathcoat-Amory, Derick 272
Heffer, Simon 12–13
Hennessy, Peter 261–2, 290
Herries, John 82, 99
Heseltine, Michael 34, 330, 336
Hill, Michael 299
Hilton, Steve 388, 400, 401
Hitler, Adolf 229, 230
Hoare, Sir Samuel 217, 254
Hogg, Quintin *see* Hailsham, Lord
Hore-Belisha, Leslie 230–31
Horne, Robert 166
Horsman, Edward 83
Housing Act (1919) 170
Howard, Michael 349
overview of 9
performance in general elections 33, 37, 39, 41, 43, 44, 45, 46, 48, 52
loses leadership 33, 395
under Iain Duncan Smith 373
and Ann Widdecombe 381–2, 389
electoral strategy 382–6
battle of ideas 386–9, 422–3
governing competence 389–92, 419–21
party management 392–4, 421–2
and 2005 general election 394, 395–6
constitutional change 394–5, 423–4
support for David Cameron 399–400
early life and career 413–15
as leader of Conservative Party 415, 417–24
on statecraft theory 417–24
on party leadership 42–6
Howe, Geoffrey 321, 329, 330, 336
Hunt, David 343
Hurd, Douglas 329, 336
Hutton Report 391–2

In Place of Strife 306, 308
Inskip, Sir Thomas 218
Iraq War 382, 385, 391–2
Ireland
and Robert Peel 68, 69, 70, 71, 80

and Lord Derby 76–7, 80
and Liberal Party 84, 117–21
and Arthur Balfour 137–8
and Andrew Bonar Law 166–7
Irish Coercion Bill (1886) 118
'Iron Curtain' speech (1946) 245, 246

Jay, Peter 323
Jenkin, Bernard 373
Jenkins, Roy 297, 317, 325
Jenkins Commission 444
Johnson, Lyndon 291–2
Jones, T. 169
Joseph, Keith 304–5, 321, 323

Keeler, Christine 274
Kennedy, John F. 271, 276, 291
Keynes, John Maynard 176, 268
Kilmuir, Lord 275
Kinnock, Neil 325, 340–41, 435, 436
Kipling, Rudyard 196, 268
'Knowsley Creed' 77–8

Labour Party
and electoral system 20
rise of 138–9, 160–61, 162, 186, 187, 198
first government 200–202
second government 204–7, 214
during National Government 217, 225–6, 227
and 1955 general election 260
after 1951 general election 263
leadership of Harold Wilson 273–4
and 1964 general election 294
and 1970 general election 306–7
and New Labour 339, 349, 353–4, 359, 366
Lamont, Norman 420
Lansdowne, Lord 146, 151
Lawson, Nigel 329, 330, 336
Leadership with a Purpose: A Better Society 370
Legg, Barry 373–4
Letwin, Oliver 391
Liberal Democrats
rise of 375, 395, 396
in coalition 406–9
Liberal Party
and Lord Derby 83–4
and Ireland 84, 117–21
under William Gladstone 104, 105, 115
Progressive Alliance with Labour Party 139
and Arthur Balfour 149–50
in coalition with Conservative Party 158–61, 166–7, 189–91, 197–9, 213
and 1918 general election 162
decline of 186, 227
in National Government 220
Orpington by-election 273
and 1964 general election 294
alliance with SDP 324, 325
Liberal Unionists 84, 119, 121–2, 125, 126–30, 182–3, 212–13
Littlejohn, Richard 389
Liverpool, 2nd Earl of 60, 94
Llewellyn, Ed 447
Lloyd, George 144
Lloyd, Selwyn 265, 272–3, 274
Lloyd George, David 7, 52
1909 Budget 145
proposes National Government with Balfour 147
in coalition with Conservative Party 158–61, 166–7, 189–91, 197, 198
on Andrew Bonar Law 176
Austen Chamberlain on 185
resignation of 192
Long, Walter 143, 157–8, 183, 184
Lothian, Lord 256
Low, David 241
Lowe, Robert 83

Maastricht Treaty 338, 343
MacDonald, Ramsay 12, 15, 139, 202, 207
MacDonnell, Antony 138
McGregor, Mark 373
Mackay, Gregor 385–6
Maclean, David 376, 394
Macleod, Iain 247, 272, 288, 290, 294, 309
Macmillan, Dorothy 268
Macmillan, Harold 209, 252

overview of 8, 267–8
performance in general elections 33, 37, 39, 41, 43, 44, 45, 46, 48, 50, 52, 320
loses leadership 33, 274–5, 284
prime ministerial ranking 54, 55–6
on Austen Chamberlain 181, 183
and 1945 general election 243, 269
and Anthony Eden 257, 265
and 1955 general election 261
becomes leader of Conservative Party 262, 269–70
early life and career 268–70
as leader of Conservative Party 270–79
and 1959 general election 270–71
foreign policy 271–2
assessment of leadership 275–9
and Alec Douglas-Home 283, 284, 285–6
and Edward Heath 303
and Margaret Thatcher 322
Macmillan, Maurice 268
Major, John 35
overview of 9, 333–4
governing competence 22
and 1992 general election 22, 53, 334, 340–41
and 1997 general election 22–3, 334, 341
performance in general elections 33, 37, 40, 41, 42, 43, 44, 45, 46, 48, 49, 53, 340–41
loses leadership 33
becomes leader of Conservative Party 34, 336
prime ministerial ranking 54, 55, 56
early life and career 334–6
as leader of Conservative Party 336–40, 341–4
Margaret's Thatcher's reaction to 337
battle of ideas 338
sleaze problems 338–9
as Prime Minister 341–4
leadership style 343–4
assessment of leadership 345–6
Mandleson, Peter 349
Maples, John 373
Margesson, David 216, 219–20, 231
Marquand, David 275
Marsh, Peter 187–8
Martin, Tony 359–60
Maude, Angus 307–8
Maude, Francis 400
Maudling, Reginald 274, 275, 284, 289, 292, 304, 305
Maxse, Leo 145
May, Theresa 369, 391
Middle Way, The (Macmillan) 268, 277
Middleton, Richard 'The Skipper' 115
Miliband, Ed 49–50, 406, 420, 426, 436, 441
Monnet, Jean 271
Morley, John 121
Morrison, Herbert 240
Morrison, John 275
Morrison, Peter 330
Morrison, William 'Shakes' 218
Muggeridge, Malcolm 275
Munich Agreement 218, 219, 220, 222, 232

National Government 12, 15, 207–9, 214–28, 239, 252–4
National Incomes Commission 273
National Liberal Party 217
National Review 145
Naval Defence Act (1889) 124
Newbould, Ian 71
Newdegate, Charles 86
News Chronicle 224
Newsnight 389–90
Night of the Long Knives 273, 274
Nye, Rick 373

Oastler, Richard 69
O'Connell, Daniel 63, 68
Ormsby-Gore, David 291
Orpington by-election (1962) 273, 274
Orsini affair 85
Osborne, George 390, 400, 404, 409, 447
Owen, David 264, 325

Palmerston, Lord 79, 83, 94
Parkinson, Cecil 329
Parnell, Charles 118
party leaders
importance of 14

assessment difficulties 14–16
Benjamin Disraeli on 94, 96–7
Michael Howard on 424–6
William Hague on 430–32, 436–7, 444–7
party management
Margaret Thatcher 23, 320, 322–3, 328–32
as factor in statecraft 23–5
and general elections 50
Benjamin Disraeli 103
Arthur Balfour 141–7
Andrew Bonar Law 165–7
Austen Chamberlain 187–9, 190–91
Winston Churchill 237–8, 248
Alec Douglas-Home 294–6
William Hague 350–52, 358–9, 439–2
Iain Duncan Smith 371–4
Michael Howard 392–4, 421–2
Patten, Chris 329
Paxman, Jeremy 389
Peel, Robert
overview of 6
performance in general elections 32, 33, 38, 39, 41, 43, 44, 45, 47, 48, 49, 50, 51, 107
loses leadership 33, 70–71, 81
prime ministerial ranking 54, 55
early life and career 60
becomes leader 60
and Great Reform Act 61–2
in opposition 62–5
as Prime Minister 63, 67–71
and 1841 general election 66–7, 72
assessment of leadership 71–3
and Lord Derby 79
Disraeli on 94
Place, Francis 61
political argument hegemony *see* battle of ideas
Ponsonby, Lord 83
Poole, Lord 262
Poor Laws 64, 69
Portillo, Michael 34, 358, 361, 367, 372, 373
Powell, Enoch 247, 288, 289, 290, 294, 308, 311, 312, 321
Prescott, John 16
prime ministerial rankings 54–6
Primrose League 114, 115
Prior, Jim 321, 329
Private Eye 287, 429
Profumo scandal 274, 288
Prosperity with a Purpose (1964 manifesto) 293
Pym, Francis 312, 329

Quarterly Review 62, 82

Ramsden, John 141, 287
Reckless, Mark 407
Redmayne, Martin 304
Redwood, John 349, 364, 391
Reece, Gordon 323
Rees-Mogg, William 323
Reform Acts
1832 6, 27, 49, 51, 61–2, 64, 71–2, 76, 101
1859 85
1867 76, 83–4, 85–6, 87–8, 102–4, 107, 108
Reform Club 65
Renton, Tim 330
Representation of the People Act (1918) 162
Resale Price Maintenance (RPM) 290–91, 304, 305
Revolutionary Epick, The (Disraeli) 95–6, 107
Richmond, Duke of 63
Right Approach, The 386
Ripon, Lord 63, 67
'Rivers of Blood' speech 308
Road to Serfdom (Hayek) 338
Robinson, Nick 385
Roman Catholic Relief Act (1829) 61
Rothermere, Lord 206, 224
Rushton, Willie 286
Russell, Lord John 79, 83

Saatchi, Maurice 388, 391, 392, 402
Safety First campaign 205
Salisbury, Lord 88
overview of 6, 111–12
performance in general elections 32–3, 38, 39, 40, 41, 42, 43, 44, 47, 48, 49, 50, 51, 107, 112
loses leadership 33, 129–30, 133–4
prime ministerial ranking 54, 55

political views of 112–17
and Ireland 117–21
statecraft of 121–3
foreign affairs 123–5
and 1892 general election 125
and 1895 general election 126
in coalition with Liberal Unionists 126–30
assessment of leadership 130–31
Samuel, Sir Herbert 15
Sanders, Jack 137, 146
Sandys, Duncan 254
SDP 324, 325
Seldon, Anthony 282, 298
'Selsdon Man' 310–11
Simon, Sir John 217, 241, 254
Simpson, Wallis 209
Smith, John 349
Snow, C. P. 278–9
Somerset, Granville 65
Special Areas Act (1934) 221
Spectator, The 134, 309
Spicer, Michael 373–4
Stamfordham, Lord 205
Stanley, Lord 63, 67, 102
Stanley, Oliver 218, 231, 252
statecraft
description of 17–18
and winning electoral strategy 18, 19–21
and governing competence 22–3
and party management 23–5
and battle of ideas 25–6
and constitutional change 26–9
Michael Howard on 417–24
Steel, David 296, 325
Stowell, Tina 447
Sybil, or the Two Nations (Disraeli) 69
Suez crisis (1956) 261–2, 269, 303
Sun, The 323–4, 366, 389

Taff Vale judgement 138–9
'Tamworth Manifesto' 32, 62–3
Tancred (Disraeli) 96
Taylor, A. J. P. 157
Taylor, Ian 373
Tebbit, Norman 329
That Was the Week That Was 287
Thatcher, Margaret 302, 402, 428, 441
overview of 9
as party leader 14
and party management 23, 320, 322–3, 328–32
and battle of ideas 25–6, 320, 323, 324–5
performance in general elections 32–3, 37, 39, 40, 41, 42, 43, 44, 45, 46, 48, 49, 50, 51, 319–20, 324–6
loses leadership 33, 325–6, 329–30, 336
prime ministerial ranking 54, 55
supports Edward Heath's leadership bid 304–5
becomes leader of Conservative Party 316, 320–22
early life and career 322
and 1979 general election 324–5
and 1983 general election 324, 325
and 1987 general election 324, 325
constitutional change 326–8
position on European Union 328, 331
legacy of 331–2
reaction to John Major's leadership 338
electoral strategy 432
Thomas, J. P. L. 256
Thorneycroft, Peter 272, 329
Thorpe, D. R. 291
Thorpe, Jeremy 273
Times, The 12, 66, 79, 83, 138, 171, 197, 224, 385
Topping, Robert 223
Toynbee, Philip 304
Treaty of London 84
Trend, Sir Burke 298
Tyrie, Andrew 373

United Empire Party 206
United Kingdom Independence Party (UKIP) 382, 383, 393, 395, 405–6
Utley, T. E. 323

Victoria, Queen 68, 70

Walker, Patrick Gordon 292, 293, 296
Walter, John 66
Wellington, Lord

performance in general elections 38
and Robert Peel 60, 65, 67
and Great Reform Act 61
and Corn Laws 70
Wetherell, Sir Charles 61
Wheeler, Stuart 375–6
Whigs
and Robert Peel 64, 65
and 1841 general election 66
and Lord Derby 76–7, 83
and Lord Salisbury 119
White, Michael 340
Whitelaw, Willie 294, 305, 321, 330
Whittingdale, John 373
Widdecombe, Ann 381–2, 389
William IV, King 60, 63
Wilmot-Horton, Sir Robert 62
Wilson, Harold 8
and 1970 general election 21
and governing competence 22
performance in general elections 49
and Alec Douglas-Home 289
decides against 1965 general election 296
and Edward Heath 302, 303, 305–6, 310–11
and 1970 general election 307
'White Heat' speech 310
and 1974 general elections 316–17
winning electoral strategy *see* electoral strategy
Woolton, Lord 241, 247
Wright, Oliver 286
Wyndham, George 137–8, 146

Yeo, Tim 391
Yorkshire Post 224
Young England 69
Younger, George 190–91, 286

Zinoviev letter 202